THE

SHAH NAMEH

THE

SHAH NAMEH

OF

THE PERSIAN POET

FIRDAUSI

TRANSLATED AND ABRIDGED IN PROSE AND VERSE

JAMES ATKINSON, ESQ.

EDITED BY

REV. J. A. ATKINSON, M. A.

GYAN

Published by

Gyan Publishing House
5, Ansari Road
Daryaganj, New Delhi-110002
Phone: 011-47034999, 9811692060
E-mail: books@gyanbooks.com

Distribution Network
gyanbooks.com
India, USA, Canada, UK, Australia, France

ISBN : 978-81-212-9164-4 (PB)
First Published, 1892

2nd Impression 2023

Printed at: Gyan Press, Delhi.

THE SHAH NAMEH
Translator: JAMES ATKINSON, Editor: REV J. A. ATKINSON

SIR JOHN LUBBOCK'S HUNDRED BOOKS

18

THE SHÁH NÁMEH

SIR JOHN LUBBOCK'S HUNDRED BOOKS
18

THE
SHÁH NÁMEH
OF
THE PERSIAN POET
FIRDAUSI.

TRANSLATED AND ABRIDGED IN PROSE AND VERSE,

BY
JAMES ATKINSON, ESQ.,
OF THE HONOURABLE EAST-INDIA COMPANY'S BENGAL MEDICAL SERVICE

EDITED BY
REV. J. A. ATKINSON, M.A.,
RECTOR OF LONGSIGHT; HON. CANON OF MANCHESTER.

LONDON
GEORGE ROUTLEDGE AND SONS, LIMITED
BROADWAY, LUDGATE HILL
GLASGOW, MANCHESTER, AND NEW YORK
1892

INTRODUCTION

BY

THE RIGHT HON. SIR JOHN LUBBOCK, BART., M.P., F.R.S., D.C.L., LL.D.

In the year 1886 I gave an address on "Books and Reading" at the Working Men's College, which in the following year was printed as one of the chapters in my "Pleasures of Life."

In it I mentioned about one hundred names, and the list has been frequently referred to since as my list of "the hundred best books." That, however, is not quite a correct statement. If I were really to make a list of what are in my judgment the hundred greatest books, it would contain several—Newton's "Principia," for instance—which I did not include, and it would exclude several—the "Koran," for instance—which I inserted in deference to the judgment of others. Again, I excluded living authors, from some of whom—Ruskin and Tennyson, Huxley and Tyndall, for instance, to mention no others—I have myself derived the keenest enjoyment; and especially I expressly stated that I did not select the books on my own authority, but as being those most frequently mentioned with approval by those writers who have referred directly or indirectly to the pleasure of reading, rather than as suggestions of my own.

I have no doubt that on reading the list, many names of books which might well be added would occur to almost any one. Indeed, various criticisms on the list have appeared, and many books have been mentioned which it is said ought to have been included. On the other hand no corresponding omissions have been suggested. I have referred to several of the criticisms, and find that, while 300 or 400 names have been proposed for addition, only half a dozen are suggested for omission. Moreover, it is remarkable that not one of the additional books suggested appears in all the lists, or even in half of them, and only about half a dozen in more than one.

But while, perhaps, no two persons would entirely concur as to all the books to be included in such a list, I believe no one would deny that those suggested are not only good, but among the best.

I am, however, ready, and indeed glad, to consider any suggestions, and very willing to make any changes which can be shown to be improvements. I have indeed made two changes in the list as it originally appeared, having inserted Kalidasa's "Sakoontala, or The Ring," and Schiller's "William Tell"; omitting Lucretius, which is perhaps rather too difficult, and Miss Austen, as English novelists were somewhat over-represented.

Another objection made has been that the books mentioned are known to every one, at any rate by name; that they are as household words. Every one, it has been said, knows about Herodotus and Homer, Shakespeare and Milton. There is, no doubt, some truth in this. But even Lord Iddesleigh, as Mr. Lang has pointed out in his "Life," had never read Marcus Aurelius, and I may add that he afterwards thanked me warmly for having suggested the "Meditations" to him.* If, then, even Lord Iddesleigh, "probably one of the last of English statesmen who knew the literature of Greece and Rome widely and well," had not read Marcus Aurelius, we may well suppose that others also may be in the same position. It is also a curious commentary on what was no doubt an unusually wide knowledge of classical literature that Mr. Lang should ascribe—and probably quite correctly—Lord Iddesleigh's never having had his attention called to one of the most beautiful and improving books in classical, or indeed in any other literature, to the fact that the emperor wrote in "crabbed and corrupt Greek."

Again, a popular writer in a recent work has observed that "why any one should select the best hundred, more than the best eleven, or the best thirty books, it is hard to conjecture." But this remark entirely misses the point. Eleven books, or even thirty, would be very few; but no doubt I might just as well have given 90, or 110. Indeed, if our arithmetical notation had been duodecimal instead of decimal, I should no doubt have made up the number to 120. I only chose 100 as being a round number.

Another objection has been that every one should be left to choose for himself. And so he must. No list can be more than a suggestion. But a great literary authority can hardly perhaps realize the difficulty of selection. An ordinary person turned into a library and sarcastically told to choose for himself, has to do so almost at haphazard. He may perhaps light upon a book with an attractive title, and after wasting on it much valuable time and patience, find that, instead of either pleasure or profit, he has weakened, or perhaps lost, his love of reading.

Messrs. George Routledge and Sons have conceived the idea of publishing the books contained in my list in a handy and cheap form, selecting themselves the editions which they prefer; and I believe that in doing so they will confer a benefit on many who have not funds or space to collect a large library.

JOHN LUBBOCK.

HIGH ELMS,
DOWN, KENT,
30 *March*, 1891.

* I have since had many other letters to the same effect.

TO

THE RIGHT HONOURABLE

THE EARL OF MUNSTER,

DISTINGUISHED FOR HIS ZEAL AND EXERTIONS

IN PROMOTING

A MORE GENERAL DIFFUSION

OF

ORIENTAL LITERATURE

THIS

Abridgment of the Sháh Námeh

IS

MOST RESPECTFULLY INSCRIBED

BY

THE AUTHOR.

TRANSLATOR'S PREFACE.

THE work here submitted to the public, presents for the first time in the English language an abridgment of the heroic poem of the great poet of Persia. It is now about five-and-twenty years since I first contemplated an abstract of the Sháh Námeh, in prose and verse; and it was in the course of reading for that purpose that the episode containing the story of Sohráb, which I published with the original text in Calcutta in 1814, struck me as peculiarly meriting, from its highly chivalrous spirit and pathetic denouement, a more full translation than could be given to the whole poem. But it was not till 1829 that the sea-voyage from India gave me an opportunity of making such progress in the present undertaking, as to enable me to bring it to a speedy conclusion, and prepare it for the press. The general reader will now have the means of forming his own estimate of a production so celebrated, and so often referred to under the flattering designation of the Iliad of the East. He will at any rate see through an unpretending but intelligible medium, of what materials it is composed.

The Sháh Námeh is indeed a history in rhyme. It comprises the annals and achievements of the ancient kings of Persia, from Kaiúmers down to the invasion and conquest of that empire by the Saracens, in 636, an estimated period of more than 3,600 years !* It was finished early in the eleventh century, gathered from the tales and legends for ages traditionally known throughout the country, and in accordance with that origin, it abounds in adventures of the most wild and romantic description, in prodigious efforts of strength and valour, and there are heroines to be met with in the Persian bard as intrepid and beautiful as ever vanquished heart or wielded sword in western poetry. It is, in fact, considered one of the finest productions of the kind which Oriental, or rather, perhaps, Mahommedan nations can boast; and though the general character of Persian composition is well known to be excess of ornament and inflation of style, the language of Firdausí is comparatively simple, and possesses a greater portion of the energy and grace of our own poets than has been commonly admitted. His verse is exquisitely smooth and flowing, and never interrupted by inverted and harsh forms of construction. He is perhaps the sweetest as well as the most sublime poet of Persia. In epic grandeur he is above all, and he is besides one of the easiest to be understood.

The author of the Sháh Námeh has usually been called the Homer of the East, but it certainly could not be from any consideration of placing the Greek and Persian together in the same scale of excellence. Each may be more properly looked upon as the best of his own country. Sir William Jones, in his essay on the Poetry of the Eastern Nations, does "not pretend to assert that the poet of Persia is equal to that of Greece; but there is certainly," he observes, "a very great resemblance between the works of those extraordinary men; both drew their images from nature herself, without catching

* Kaiúmers is understood to be the Adam of the fire-worshippers, and the grandson of Nú, or Noah, of the Mahommedans.

them only from reflection, and painting, in the manner of the modern poets, the likeness of a likeness; and both possessed, in an eminent degree, the rich and creative invention, which is the very soul of poetry." There is another resemblance, which is, however, unconnected with their comparative merits; but it is one which has chiefly, I think, given occasion to the Persian being called the Homer of the East; the heroic poems of Firdausí are held exactly in the same estimation with reference to the works of other poets of Persia, as those of Homer are in the West. Like Homer, too, he describes a rude age, when personal strength and ferocious courage were chiefly valued, and when the tumultuous passions of the mind had not been softened and harmonized by civilization, or brought under the control of reason and reflection. Firdausí is also as much the father of Persian poetry as Homer is of the Greek; but it would be little less than sacrilege to draw a critical comparison between the Sháh Námeh and the Iliad!

It has been observed by Dr. Hurd, in his letters on Chivalry and Romance, that "there is a remarkable correspondence between the manners of the old heroic times, as painted by their great romancer Homer, and those which are represented to us in the modern books of knight-errantry." The correspondence is, however, infinitely more striking between the manners described by Firdausí and those of the age of European chivalry. It is well known that the Moors carried into Spain the fictions and romances of Arabia and Persia, and most of our best tales are supposed to be derived from the same source. It has already been said that Firdausí wrote in the beginning of the eleventh century, but it was not till the twelfth that romances of chivalry began to amuse and delight the western world. Although the *Roman de la Rose* was the first considerable work of the kind in verse, the poem which gave life and character to all succeeding tales of chivalry was the *Orlando Innamorato* of Boyardo, afterwards improved and paraphrased by Berni. To this production we are indebted for the *Orlando Furioso* of Ariosto ; and in a similar relation to each other stand the Bastan-Námeh, of which we shall presently speak, and the Sháh Námeh of Firdausí.

In the series of romantic adventures which constitute the Sháh Námeh, the principal hero is Rustem. He is born during the reign of Minúchihr, and it is not till some centuries afterwards, whilst Gushtásp is sovereign of Persia, that he perishes by treachery, to avenge the death of Isfendiyár, involuntarily slain by the champion. The career of this prodigy of strength, and piety, and valour, must thus have been of more than antediluvian duration, unless indeed it could be imagined that Rustem was adopted by the champion of every successive reign as a name or title of distinction ; but that is impossible, for his brother Zúára dies with him : he is always the son of Zál, who indeed survives him, and the grandson of Sám, and there can be no doubt of his being the same individual throughout, the same everlasting conqueror.* So well has Firdausí preserved the indomitable spirit of this heroic character, that, even in his last moments, he slays the wretch who had betrayed him.

Rustem has been generally called the Persian Hercules, and in bravery and power the two heroes present many points of resemblance. Sir William Ouseley, in his valuable travels, has drawn an ingenious parallel between them, especially with regard to the labours of these celebrated champions. The

* But the Sháh Námeh cannot be said to have any pretensions to true history, and chronology is equally disregarded in the poetical imagination of Firdausí; for, according to him, Jemshíd had reigned seven hundred years before he was inspired with the impious ambition which occasioned his downfall, and the despotism of the usurper Zohák is stated to have lasted one thousand years!

labours of Rustem were however only seven, whilst those of Hercules were twelve. It is not, I believe, understood that the series of exploits performed by the Persian hero are at all figurative, like those of the Grecian god; for according to the theory of Dupuis, Hercules is considered as no other than the sun, and his twelve labours are regarded as a representation of the annual course of that luminary through the signs of the Zodiac. In the Sháh Námeh, Isfendiyár has also his seven labours as well as Rustem, and both consist in the overthrow of devouring monsters, and the destruction of talismans and works of enchantment. Rustem, however, performs his exploits alone, mounted on his famous horse Rakush, whilst Isfendiyár is accompanied and assisted by a numerous party of horsemen. All nations, indeed, have had their unconquerable knights and destructive dragons. We had our St. George, and other countries can no doubt boast of cavaliers equally valiant, and of monsters equally pestiferous and horrible.

Of Abul Kásim Firdausí, the author of this celebrated work, little is satisfactorily known. He was born at Tús, a city of Khorassán, about the year 950. But in Daulet Shah's account of the Persian poets, his proper name is said to have been Hassan, and that of his father Ishak Sheríf Shah, who worked as a gardener on the domain of the governor of Tús. The following circumstances, respecting the origin of the poem and the life of the poet, are chiefly derived from the preface to the copy of the Sháh Námeh which was collated in the year of the Hejira 829, about 400 years ago, by order of Bayisunghur Bahádor Khán. It appears from that preface that Yezdjird, the last king of the Sassanian race, took considerable pains in collecting all the chronicles, histories and traditions, connected with Persia and the sovereigns of that country, from the time of Kaiúmers to the accession of the Khosráus, which, by his direction, were digested and brought into one view, and formed the book known by the name of Syur-al-Múluk, or the Bastan-Námeh. When the followers of Mahommed overturned the Persian monarchy, this work was found in the plundered library of Yezdjird. The preface above alluded to minutely traces its progress through different hands in Arabia, Ethiopia, and Hindústan. The chronicle was afterwards continued to the time of Yezdjird. In the tenth century, one of the Kings of the Samánian dynasty directed Dukíkí to versify that extensive work, but the poet only lived to finish a thousand distiches, having been assassinated by his own slave. Nothing further was done till the reign of Sultán Mahmúd Sabuktugín, in the beginning of the eleventh century. That illustrious conqueror, whose restless ambition extended his dominion from the Tigris to the Ganges, and from the mountains of Tartary to the Indian Ocean, with the intention of augmenting the glories of his reign projected a history of the kings of Persia, and ordered the literary characters of his court conjointly to prepare one from all accessible records. While they were engaged upon this laborious undertaking, a romantic accident, which it is unnecessary to describe, furnished the Sultan with a copy of the Bastan-Námeh, the existence of which was till then unknown to him. From this work Mahmúd selected seven Stories or Romances, which he delivered to seven poets to be composed in verse, that he might be able to ascertain the merits of each competitor. The poet Unsarí, to whom the story of Rustem and Sohráb was given, gained the palm, and he was accordingly engaged to arrange the whole history in verse.

Firdausí was at this time at Tús, his native city, where he cultivated his poetical talents with assiduity and success. He had heard of the attempt of Dukíkí to versify the history of the kings of Persia, and of the determination of the reigning king, Mahmúd, to patronize an undertaking which promised to add lustre to the age in which he lived. Having fortunately succeeded in procuring a copy of the Bastan-Námeh, he pursued his studies with unremitting zeal, and soon produced that part of the poem in which the battles of Zohák and Feridún are described. The performance was universally read and admired, and it was not long before his fame reached the ears of the Sultan, who immediately invited him to his court.

Another notice of his life states, that he and his brother Mahsúd were originally husbandmen, occupied in the labours of the field at Tús, and that it was the persecution of a malicious enemy which drove the poet from his native place. Firdausí told his brother that he was unable to endure the insults that were continually heaped upon him, and proposed that they should depart together to another country; but Mahsúd, not disposed to abandon his home, objected to this scheme. Firdausí however was determined to remain no longer at Tús, and immediately set out unfriended and alone on his way to Ghizní.

When our author had reached the vicinity of the capital, he happened to pass near a garden where Unsarí, Usjudí, and Furrokí were sitting drinking wine. These celebrated poets observed a stranger approach, and one of them said: "If that fellow comes hither he will spoil our pleasure, let us therefore get rid of him at once by scolding him away." But the others disapproved of this harsh mode of proceeding, and thought it would be better, and more consistent with their condition and character, to overcome him by some stroke of learning or waggery. When Firdausí drew near, mutual salutations having passed between them, they thus familiarly addressed him: "Here we are, engaged in making extemporaneous verses, and whoever is able to follow them up with promptitude and effect, shall be admitted as an approved companion to our social board." Firdausí was willing and ready to submit to this test, and Unsarí thus commenced upon an apostrophe to a beautiful woman:

> The light of the moon to thy splendour is weak

Usjudí rejoined:

> The rose is eclipsed by the bloom of thy cheek.

Then Furrokí:

> Thy eye-lashes dart through the folds of the joshun.*

It was now Firdausí's turn; and he said without a moment's pause, but with admirable felicity:

> Like the javelin of Gíw in the battle with Poshun.

The poets were astonished at the readiness of the stranger; and being totally ignorant of the story of Gíw and Poshun, inquired of him from whence it was derived, when Firdausí related to them the onslaught or encounter as described in the Bastan-Námeh. Upon which they treated him with the greatest kindness and respect, and were so pleased with the power and genius he displayed on other subjects, that they recommended him to the patronage of Shah Mahmúd; an instance of disinterestedness, if true, highly honourable to the rival poets.

It is also related that the Sultan, when Firdausí was first introduced to him, requested the poet to compose some verses

* Joshun armour

in his presence; upon which, Firdausí instantly pronounced the following:

> The cradled infant, whose sweet lips are yet.
> Balmy with milk from its own mother's breast,
> Lisps first the name of Mahmúd.

This rare compliment delighted the king, and confirmed his high opinion of the extraordinary merits of the poet.

When Firdausí arrived at Ghizni, the success of Unsarí, in giving a poetical dress to the romance of Rustem and Sohráb, was the subject of general observation and praise. Animated by this proof of literary taste at court, he commenced upon the story of the battles of Isfendiyár and Rustem; and having completed it, he embraced the earliest opportunity of getting that poem presented to the Sultan, who had already seen abundant evidence of the transcendent talents of the author. Mahmúd regarded the production with admiration and delight. He without hesitating a moment appointed him to complete the Sháh Námeh, and ordered his chief minister* to pay him a thousand miskals for every thousand distichs, and at the same time honoured him with the surname of Firdausí, because that he had diffused over his court the delights of paradise.† Unsarí himself liberally acknowledged the superiority of Firdausí's genius, and relinquished the undertaking without apparent regret.

The minister, in compliance with the injunctions of Mahmúd, offered to pay the sums as the work went on; but Firdausí unfortunately preferred waiting till he had completed his engagement, and receiving the whole at once, as he had long indulged the hope of being able to do something of importance for the benefit of his native city.

It appears that Firdausí, in his new situation, did not act

* Ahmed Mymundí.

† Firdaus signifies paradise.

with becoming discretion. He had composed verses in honour of the minister whose office it was to supply him with whatever he might require, but did nothing to conciliate the good graces of Aiyar, one of the principal favourites of Mahmúd. In consequence of this omission, Aiyar sought every opportunity to injure Firdausí and ruin his interests with the king. Several passages in his poems were extracted and invidiously commented upon, as containing sentiments contrary to the principles of the true faith! It was alleged that they proved him to be a hypocritical philosopher, and a schismatic. The king was highly indignant on hearing that the poet was guilty of cherishing impious doctrines; upon which occasion Firdausí solicited an audience, and throwing himself at the feet of Mahmúd, protested against the malignant calumny which had been brought against him; but Mahmúd replied that all the people of Tús were of the same character, all heretics alike! The situation of the poet under royal displeasure had thus become critical, and he remained at Ghizni, though still prosecuting his labours, in a state of great anxiety and alarm. But in spite of all that artifice and malignity could frame, the poet rose in the esteem of the public. Admiration followed him in the progress of the work, and presents were showered upon him from every quarter. The poems were at length completed. The composition of sixty thousand couplets* ap-

* In a dissertation called *Yamini*, it is said that the ancient poet Rudiki, who flourished half a century before Firdausí, had written one million and three hundred verses; an Oriental Lope de Vega!

The copies of the Sháh Námeh now generally met with, vary in extent many thousand couplets—few of them containing the original number. This inequality has been thus accounted for; the katibs, or copyers, engaged upon so immense a work, are apt to expedite the accomplishment of their task by omissions in different parts, whilst, on the other hand, many of them have not only interpolated passages but whole episodes. The curious in composition and style have long been amused in conjecturing what is genuine, and what is added or doubtful, but to very little purpose, some of the questioned stories being fully equal to the best parts of the poem.

pears to have cost him the labour of thirty years. The Sultan was fully sensible of the value and excellence of that splendid monument of genius and talents, and proud of being the patroniser of a work which promised to perpetuate his name, he ordered an elephant-load of gold to be given to the author. But the malignity of the favourite was unappeased, and he was still bent upon the degradation and ruin of the poet. Contriving to establish his own success with the king, instead of the elephant-load of gold, he managed to get sent to him 60,000 silver dirhems! Firdausí was in the public bath at the time; and when he found that the bags contained only silver, he was so enraged at the insult offered to him, that on the spot he gave 20,000 to the keeper of the bath, 20,000 to the seller of refreshments, and 20,000 to the slave who brought them. "The Sultan shall know," said he, "that I did not bestow the labour of thirty years on a work, to be rewarded with dirhems!" When this circumstance came to the knowledge of the king, he was exceedingly exasperated at the conduct of his favourite, who had, however, artifice and ingenuity enough to exculpate himself, and to cast all the blame upon the poet. Firdausí was charged with disrespectful and insulting behaviour to his sovereign; and Mahmúd, thus stimulated to resentment, and no longer questioning the veracity of the favourite, passed an order that the next morning he should be trampled to death under the feet of an elephant! The unfortunate poet was thrown into the greatest consternation when he heard of the will of the Sultan. He immediately hurried to the presence, and again falling at the feet of the king, begged for mercy, pronouncing at the same time an elegant eulogium on the glories of his reign, and the innate generosity of his heart. The king, touched by his agitation, and still respecting the brilliancy of his talents, at length condescended to revoke the order.

But the wound was deep, and not to be endured without a murmur. He immediately obtained from the librarian of Mahmúd the copy of the Sháh Námeh which he had presented to the king, and wrote in it his satire on the Sultan with all the bitterness of reproach which insulted merit could devise, and instantly fled from the court. He passed some time at Mázinderán (Hyrcania), and afterwards took refuge at Bagdád, where he was in high favour with the Kalif al Káder Billah, in whose praise he added a thousand couplets to the Sháh Námeh, and for which he received a robe of honour and 60,000 dínars. He also wrote a poem called Joseph during his stay in that city.

Another account says, that after abandoning his own country, Firdausí remained for some time in the house of Abú el Máali, a dealer in books at Herát. Mahmúd had, after his escape, sent persons in search of him in every direction; and as they made known the purpose of their mission in every town they came to, our poet in great sorrow returned to Tús; but afraid of not being safe there, he took leave of his relations and friends and obtained a place of refuge in Rustemdar. The governor received him with kindness, and offered him one hundred and sixty miskals * of gold if he would cancel from the Sháh Námeh the satire composed by him against Mahmúd. Firdausí, adds this account, agreed to the proposal, cancelled the verses, and then returned to Tús, where he lived obscurely to an old age.

It is further said that Mahmúd at length became acquainted with the falsehood and treachery of the vizír, whose cruel persecution of the unoffending poet had involved the character and reputation of his court in disgrace. His indignation appeared to be extreme, and the favourite was banished for ever from his

* A miskal is about a drachm and a half in weight.

presence. Anxious to make all the reparation in his power for the injustice he had been guilty of, whether purposely or otherwise, he immediately dispatched a present of 60,000 dínars and a robe of state with many apologies for what had happened. But Firdausí did not live to be gratified by this consoling acknowledgment. He had returned to his friends at Tús, where he died before the present from the king arrived. His family, however, scrupulously devoted it to the benevolent purposes which the poet had originally intended, *viz.* the erection of public buildings, and the general improvement of his native city.

This latter circumstance is somewhat differently related in Daulet Shah's biography. Mahmúd, it is said, in one of his twelve expeditions to India, hearing his minister repeat a passage from the Sháh Námeh happily descriptive of his situation at the time, was strongly reminded of Firdausí; and recollecting with regret the injustice he had done the poet, inquired what had become of him. The minister replied that he was now very old and infirm, and living obscurely at Tús. The Sultan instantly ordered a present, worthy of the poet and of himself, to be forwarded to him; but at the moment the persons in charge of this present entered the gate of Tús, the body of Firdausí was being conveyed through the same gate to be buried. When the funeral ceremony was over, however, the amount was carried to his surviving sister: but she refused to receive it, saying, "What have I to do now with the wealth of kings?"

This brief biographical notice is the sum of all that is known of the great Firdausí. The poet seems to have lived to a considerable age. When he wrote the satire against Mahmúd, according to his own account, he was more than seventy.

When charity demands a bounteous dole,
Close is thy hand, contracted as thy soul;
Now seventy years have marked my long career,
Nay more, but age has no protection here!

Probably about ten years elapsed during his sojourn at Mázinderán and Bagdád, after he quitted the court of Ghizni, so that he must have been at least eighty when he died. It appears from several parts of the satire, that a period of thirty years was employed in the composition of the Sháh Námeh, from which it must be inferred that he had been engaged upon that work long before the accession of Mahmúd to the throne, for that monarch survived Firdausí ten years, and the period of his reign was only thirty-one. Although there be nothing in the preceding memoir to indicate that the poet had commenced versifying the Bastan Námeh nine years before the reign of Mahmúd, the circumstance can hardly be questioned. All oriental biography is so vague, metaphorical, and undetermined, that there is always great difficulty in arriving at the simplest fact, yet it is not at all probable that the round number of thirty years was falsely assumed by the poet.

Notwithstanding the turn which is given, by the preface just mentioned, to the cause of Firdausí's disappointment, in referring it solely to the rancour of the minister, the conduct of Mahmúd appears to have been, in the highest degree, inconsiderate and cruel. He must have well known that dirhems had been sent instead of the elephant-load of gold, and it was unworthy of the conqueror of the world to suffer himself to be flattered and cajoled into petty resentment against the man who had immortalized the exploits of so many ancient heroes, and who, in the opening verses of the poem, had done such honour to his name. The present of 60,000 dínars which he afterwards sent to him seems at any rate to shew (upon the presumption of his having been purposely unjust) that he felt some stings of conscience, and that he wished to recover from the disgrace which attached to him, as a patron of literature, from so dishonourable a transaction.

A more favourable construction, however, may be entertained from the facts adduced. The order for an elephant-load of gold to be presented to the poet, whatever might be meant by that imposing term, appears to have arisen from a spontaneous impulse of generosity. Mahmúd may have been afterwards the dupe of the minister, and his last atoning act of liberality would seem to favour that conclusion; but no dependence can be placed on the humour of an Asiatic despot. Yet it might be presumed that the sovereign who had the justice and magnanimity to punish with death an offender whom he would not see till after execution, suspecting him to be his own son,* would hardly treat a poor poet so disgracefully. However this may have been, the satire of Firdausí, written at the moment of provocation, and with strongly exasperated feelings, appears to have had the power of stamping with obloquy in this respect the character of Mahmúd, and of giving negative effect to the adulation which he had lavishly bestowed upon the same individual at the commencement of his poem. Thus singularly enough the work begins with an extravagant eulogy, and ends with the most scornful vituperation of his patron.

The tomb of Firdausí is in the city of Tús, and much frequented by pilgrims. It is said of Shaik Abul Kasim Korkani that he refused to offer up the customary prayer for Firdausí, because he had written so much in praise of the fire-worshippers. But upon the following night he dreamt that he saw Firdausí

* The story is told by Gibbon in his Decline and Fall of the Roman Empire.

in Paradise raised to a high degree of glory, when he asked him how he had merited that distinction, and the poet replied, "On account of the passages in which I have celebrated the greatness and the unity of God."

In delivering this abridgment to the public, I have been anxious to make it as comprehensive and interesting to the general reader, as the extent of the labour I had prescribed to myself, and my own ability would allow. But it necessarily contains merely the substance of the Sháh Námeh, though in many parts in considerable detail; and I have therefore deemed it important, with the view of showing more fully Firdausí's powers as a poet, to add a revised edition of my translation of Sohrab. Thus whilst the abridgment exhibits the scope and character of the poem, this favourite episode will at once display the force and spirit with which Firdausí's outlines are traced and his colouring supplied.

But I must not conclude without remarking, that Firdausí's great work continues to be held in the highest estimation throughout Persia, and favourite passages from the various adventures are still treasured up and quoted on all fitting occasions. So popular is our old romancer, that the copies of the Sháh Námeh are innumerable, and some of them are not only admirable specimens of fine ornamental writing, but they are generally enriched with coloured drawings of exquisite finish, illustrative of the most prominent events of the work. One of the copies which I used in the execution of the present abridgment was of this kind, splendidly illuminated and sprinkled with gold, and cost upwards of one hundred guineas. In India even, that is Hindustan and the southern regions of the East, wherever the Persian language is understood and cultivated, the Sháh Námeh is also highly prized; but it is perhaps most known by a very clever epitome of it, written in the same language, by Shumshír Khán in the year 1063 of the Mahommedan era. The original work has outlived eight centuries with undiminished lustre, in countries, too, where copies can only be multiplied at a great expense, verifying the prophecy of the poet, who predicted the immortality of his verse with as much confidence as Ovid when he wrote his celebrated peroration—

> Jamque opus exegi; quod nec Jovis ira, nec ignis,
> Nec poterit ferrum, nec edax abolere vetustas.

LONDON, *May* 1, 1832.

CONTENTS.

The system of Sir William Jones in the printing of Oriental words has been kept in view in the following work, *viz.* The letter *a* represents the short vowel as in *bat*, *á* with an accent the broad sound of *a* in *hall*, *i* as in *lily*, *í* with an accent as in *police*, *u* as in *bull*, *ú* with an accent as in *rude*, *ó* with an accent as *o* in *pole*, the diphthong *ai* as in *aisle*, *au* as in the German word *kraut* or *ou* in *house*.

THE SHÁH NÁMEH.

KAIÚMERS.

ACCORDING to the traditions of former ages, recorded in the Bastan-námeh, the first person who established a code of laws and exercised the functions of a monarch in Persia, was Kaiúmers. It is said that he dwelt among the mountains, and that his garments were made of the skins of beasts.

His reign was thirty years, and o'er the earth
He spread the blessings of paternal sway;
Wild animals, obsequious to his will,
Assembled round his throne, and did him homage.
He had a son named Saiámuk, a youth
Of lovely form and countenance, in war
Brave and accomplished, and the dear delight
Of his fond father, who adored the boy,
And only dreaded to be parted from him.
So is it ever with the world—the parent
Still doating on his offspring. Kaiúmers
Had not a foe, save one, a hideous Demon,*

* The first encounter in the Sháh Námeh is between the son of Kaiúmers and a demon. There does not seem to exist among the Persians any very well defined notion respecting these demons, diws, or dives. They are, however, generally represented in human shape, with horns, long ears, and sometimes with a tail, as Lord Monboddo says, "depending from their gable ends," yet possessed of superior power and intelligence. They are also enchanters, and sorcerers. The most renowned were those of Mazinderán, whom Rustem overthrew. They were always considered superior to common human beings, and always the most effective allies, and the most formidable foes. They were often of caliban-aspect, giants; and though they had the faculty of vanishing whenever they chose, we frequently see them dispatched and slain in battle, in the common way, by sword or battle-axe. They are sometimes like spirits of the storm, wild and destructive, and sometimes they are of less consequence, and occupied in inferior duties. Jemshíd had many

Who viewed his power with envy, and aspired
To work his ruin. He, too, had a son,
Fierce as a wolf, whose days were dark and bitter,
Because the favouring heavens in kinder mood
Smiled on the monarch and his gallant heir.
—When Saiámuk first heard the Demon's aim
Was to o'erthrow his father and himself,
Surprise and indignation filled his heart,
And speedily a martial force he raised,
To punish the invader. Proudly garbed
In leopard's skin, he hastened to the war;
But when the combatants, with eager mien,
Impatient met upon the battle-field,
And both together tried their utmost strength,
Down from his enemy's dragon-grasp soon fell
The luckless son of royal Kaiúmers,
Vanquished and lifeless. Sad, unhappy fate!

Disheartened by this disastrous event, the army immediately retreated, and returned to Kaiúmers, who wept bitterly for the loss of his son, and continued a long time inconsolable. But after a year had elapsed a mysterious voice addressed him, saying:—"Be patient, and despair not,—thou hast only to send another army against the Demons, and the triumph and the victory will be thine.

Drive from the earth that Demon horrible,
And sorrow will be rooted from thy heart."

Saiámuk left a son whose name was Húsheng, whom the king loved much more even than his father.

Húsheng his name. There seemed in him combined,
Knowledge and goodness eminent. To him
Was given his father's dignity and station.
And the old man, his grandsire, scarcely deigned
To look upon another, his affection
For him was so unbounded.

Kaiúmers having appointed Húsheng the leader of the army,

in his service. The demons taught Tahúmers the use of letters, after he had conquered them, and had acquired the appellation of Diw-búnd, or the chainer of demons. Diw, or demon, means also a god, or personage of a higher class in the scale of earthly beings.

the young hero set out with an immense body of troops to engage the Demon and his son. It is said that at that time every species of animal, wild and tame, was obedient to his command.

> The savage beasts, and those of gentler kind,
> Alike reposed before him, and appeared
> To do him homage.

The wolf, the tiger, the lion, the panther, and even the fowls of the air, assembled in aid of him, and he, by the blessing of God, slew the Demon and his offspring with his own hand. After which the army of Kaiúmers, and the devouring animals that accompanied him in his march, defeated and tore to pieces the scattered legions of the enemy. Upon the death of Kaiúmers Húsheng ascended the throne of Persia.

HÚSHENG.

It is recorded that Húsheng was the first who brought out fire from stone, and from that circumstance he founded the religion of the Fire-worshippers, calling the flame which was produced, the Light of the Divinity.* The accidental discovery of this element is thus described :—

> Passing, one day, towards the mountain's side,
> Attended by his train, surprised he saw
> Something in aspect terrible—its eyes
> Fountains of blood; its dreadful mouth sent forth

---

* Firdausí speaks here of Húsheng, the second king of the Peshdadian dynasty, having founded the religion of the fire-worshippers, but from that time the faith seems to have slept till the appearance of Zerdusht, in the reign of Gushtásp, many centuries afterwards, when Isfendiyár propagated it at the point of the sword.

Volumes of smoke that darkened all the air.
Fixing his gaze upon that hideous form,
He seized a stone, and with prodigious force
Hurling it, chanced to strike a jutting rock,
Whence sparks arose, and presently a fire
O'erspread the plain, in which the monster perished.
—Thus Húsheng found the element which shed
Light through the world. The monarch prostrate bowed,
Praising the great Creator, for the good
Bestowed on man, and, pious, then he said,
"This is the Light from Heaven, sent down from God;
If ye be wise, adore and worship it!"

It is also related that, in the evening of the day on which the luminous flash appeared to him from the stone, he lighted an immense fire, and, having made a royal entertainment, he called it the Festival of Siddeh. By him the art of the blacksmith was discovered, and he taught river and streamlet to supply the towns, and irrigate the fields for the purposes of cultivation. And he also brought into use the fur of the sable, and the squirrel, and the ermine. Before his time mankind had nothing for food but fruit, and the leaves of trees and the skins of animals for clothing. He introduced, and taught his people, the method of making bread, and the art of cookery.

Then ate they their own bread, for it was good,
And they were grateful to their benefactor;
Mild laws were framed—the very land rejoiced,
Smiling with cultivation; all the world
Remembering Húsheng's virtues.

The period of his government is said to have lasted forty years, and he was succeeded by his son, Tahúmers.

TAHÚMERS.

This sovereign was also called Diw-bund, or the Binder of Demons. He assembled together all the wise men in his dominions, to consider and deliberate upon whatever might be of utility and advantage to the people of God. In his days wool was spun and woven, and garments and carpets manufactured, and various animals, such as panthers, falcons, hawks, and syagoshes, were tamed, and taught to assist in the sports of the field. Tahúmers had also a vizír, renowned for his wisdom and understanding. Having one day charmed a Demon into his power by philters and magic, he conveyed him to Tahúmers; upon which, the brethren and allies of the prisoner, feeling ashamed and degraded by the insult, collected an army, and went to war against the king. Tahúmers was equally in wrath when he heard of these hostile proceedings, and having also gathered together an army on his part, presented himself before the enemy. The name of the leader of the Demons was Ghú. On one side the force consisted of fire, and smoke, and Demons; on the other, brave and magnanimous warriors. Tahúmers lifted his mace, as soon as he was opposed to the enemy, and giving Ghú a blow on the head, killed him on the spot. The other Demons being taken prisoners, he ordered them to be destroyed; but they petitioned for mercy, promising, if their lives were spared, that they would teach him a wonderful art. Tahúmers assented, and they immediately brought their books, and pens and ink, and instructed him how to read and write.

> They taught him letters, and his eager mind
> With learning was illumined. The world was blest
> With quiet and repose, Peris and Demons
> Submitting to his will.

The reign of Tahúmers lasted thirty years and after him the monarchy descended to Jemshíd, his son.

JEMSHÍD.

Jemshíd was eminently distinguished for learning and wisdom. It is said that coats of mail, cuirasses, and swords, and various kinds of armour, were invented and manufactured in his time, and also that garments of silk were made and worn by his people.

Helmets and swords, with curious art they made,
Guided by Jemshid's skill; and silks and linen
And robes of fur and ermine. Desert lands
Were cultivated; and wherever stream
Or rivulet wandered, and the soil was good,
He fixed the habitations of his people;
And there they ploughed and reaped: for in that age
All laboured; none in sloth and idleness
Were suffered to remain, since indolence
Too often vanquishes the best, and turns
To nought the noblest, firmest resolution.

Jemshíd afterwards commanded his Demons to construct a splendid palace, and he directed his people how to make the foundations strong.

He taught the unholy Demon-train to mingle
Water and clay, with which, formed into bricks,
The walls were built, and then high turrets, towers,
And balconies, and roofs to keep out rain
And cold, and sunshine. Every art was known
To Jemshid, without equal in the world.

He also made vessels for the sea and the river, and erected a magnificent throne, embellished with pearls and precious stones; and having seated himself upon it, commanded his Demons to raise him up in the air, that he might be able to transport himself in a moment wherever he chose. He named the first day of the year *Nú-rúz*, and on every *Nú-rúz* he made a royal feast, so that under his hospitable roof, mortals, and Genii, and Demons, and Peris, were delighted and happy, every one being equally regaled with wine and music. His government is said to have continued in existence seven hundred years, and during that period, it is added, none of his subjects suffered death, or were afflicted with disease.

> Man seemed immortal, sickness was unknown,
> And life rolled on in happiness and joy.

After the lapse of seven hundred years, however, inordinate ambition inflamed the heart of Jemshíd, and, having assembled all the illustrious personages and learned men in his dominions before him, he said to them :—"Tell me if there exists, or ever existed, in all the world, a king of such magnificence and power as I am?" They unanimously replied :—"Thou art alone, the mightiest, the most victorious : there is no equal to thee!" The just God beheld this foolish pride and vanity with displeasure, and, as a punishment, cast him from the government of an empire into a state of utter degradation and misery.

> All looked upon the throne, and heard and saw
> Nothing but Jemshíd, he alone was king,
> Absorbing every thought ; and in their praise,
> And adoration of that mortal man,
> Forgot the worship of the great Creator.
> Then proudly thus he to his nobles spoke,
> Intoxicated with their loud applause,
> "I am unequalled, for to me the earth
> Owes all its science, never did exist
> A sovereignty like mine, beneficent
> And glorious, driving from the populous land
> Disease and want. Domestic joy and rest
> Proceed from me, all that is good and great
> Waits my behest ; the universal voice
> Declares the splendour of my government,
> Beyond whatever human heart conceived,
> And me the only monarch of the world."
> —Soon as these words had parted from his lips,
> Words impious, and insulting to high heaven,
> His earthly grandeur faded,—then all tongues
> Grew clamorous and bold. The day of Jemshíd
> Passed into gloom, his brightness all obscured.
> What said the Moralist? "When thou wert a king
> Thy subjects were obedient, but whoever
> Proudly neglects the worship of his God,
> Brings desolation on his house and home."
> —And when he marked the insolence of his people,
> He knew the wrath of Heaven had been provoked,
> And terror overcame him.

MIRTÁS-TÁZÍ, AND HIS SON ZOHÁK.

The old historians relate that Mirtás was the name of a king of the Arabs; and that he had a thousand animals which gave milk, and the milk of these animals he always distributed in charity among the poor. God was pleased with his goodness, and accordingly increased his favour upon him.

> Goats, sheep, and camels, yielded up their store
> Of balmy milk, with which the generous king
> Nourished the indigent and helpless poor.

Mirtás had a son called Zohák, who possessed ten thousand Arab horses, or Tazís, upon which account he was surnamed Biwurasp; biwur meaning ten thousand, and asp a horse. One day Iblís, the Evil Spirit, appeared to Zohák in the disguise of a good and virtuous man, and conversed with him in the most agreeable manner.

> Pleased with his eloquence, the youth
> Suspected not the speaker's truth;
> But praised the sweet impassioned strain,
> And asked him to discourse again.

Iblís replied, that he was master of still sweeter converse, but he could not address it to him, unless he first entered into a solemn compact, and engaged never on any pretence to divulge his secret.

> Zohák in perfect innocence of heart
> Assented to the oath, and bound himself
> Never to tell the secret; all he wished
> Was still to hear the good man's honey words.

But as soon as the oath was taken, Iblís said to him: "Thy father has become old and worthless, and thou art young, and wise, and valiant. Let him no longer stand in thy way, but kill him; the robes of sovereignty are ready, and better adapted for thee."

The youth in agony of mind,
Heard what the stranger now designed;
Could crime like this be understood!
The shedding of a parent's blood!
Iblís would no excuses hear—
The oath was sworn—his death was near.
"For if thou think'st to pass it by,
The peril's thine, and thou must die!"

Zohák was terrified and subdued by this warning, and asked Iblís in what manner he proposed to sacrifice his father. Iblís replied, that he would dig a pit on the path-way which led to Mirtás-Tází's house of prayer. Accordingly he secretly made a deep well upon the spot most convenient for the purpose, and covered it over with grass. At night, as the king was going, as usual, to the house of prayer, he fell into the pit, and his legs and arms being broken by the fall, he shortly expired. O righteous Heaven! that father too, whose tenderness would not suffer even the winds to blow upon his son too roughly,—and that son, by the temptation of Iblís, to bring such a father to a miserable end!

Thus urged to crime, through cruel treachery,
Zohák usurped his pious father's throne.

When Iblís found that he had got Zohák completely in his power, he told him that, if he followed his counsel and advice implicitly, he would become the greatest monarch of the age, the sovereign of the seven climes, signifying the whole world. Zohák agreed to every thing, and Iblís continued to bestow upon him the most devoted attention and flattery for the purpose of moulding him entirely to his will. To such an extreme degree had his authority attained, that he became the sole director even in the royal kitchen, and prepared for Zohák the most delicious and savoury food imaginable; for in those days bread and fruit only were the usual articles of food. Iblís himself was the original inventor of the cooking art. Zohák was delighted with the dishes, made from every variety of bird and four-footed animal. Every day something new and rare was brought to his table, and every day Iblís increased in favour. But an egg was to him the most delicate of all! "What can there be superior to this?" said he. "To-morrow," replied Iblís, "thou shalt have something better, and of a far superior kind."

> Next day he brought delicious fare, and dressed
> In manner exquisite to please the eye,
> As well as taste; partridge and pheasant rich,
> A banquet for a prince. Zohák beheld
> Delighted the repast, and eagerly
> Relished its flavour; then in gratitude,
> And admiration of the matchless art
> Which thus had ministered to his appetite,
> He cried:—"For this, whatever thou desirest,
> And I can give, is thine." Iblís was glad,
> And, little anxious, had but one request—
> One unimportant wish—it was to kiss
> The monarch's naked shoulder—a mere whim.
> And promptly did Zohák comply, for he
> Was unsuspicious still, and stripped himself,
> Ready to gratify that simple wish.
> Iblís then kissed the part with fiendish glee,
> And vanished in an instant.
> From the touch
> Sprang two black serpents! Then a tumult rose
> Among the people, searching for Iblís
> Through all the palace, but they sought in vain.
> To young and old it was a marvellous thing;
> The serpents writhed about as seeking food,
> And learned men to see the wonder came,
> And sage magicians tried to charm away
> That dreadful evil, but no cure was found.

Some time afterwards Iblís returned to Zohák, but in the shape of a physician, and told him that it was according to his own horoscope that he suffered in this manner—it was, in short, his destiny—and that the serpents would continue connected with him throughout his life, involving him in perpetual misery. Zohák sunk into despair, upon the assurance of there being no remedy for him, but Iblís again roused him by saying, that if the serpents were fed daily with human brains, which would probably kill them, his life might be prolonged, and made easy.

If life has any charm for thee,
The brain of man their food must be!

With the adoption of this deceitful stratagem, Iblís was highly pleased, and congratulated himself upon the success of his wicked exertions, thinking that in this manner a great portion of the human race would be destroyed He was not aware that his craft and cunning had no influence in the house of God; and that the descendants of Adam are continually increasing.

When the people of Irán and Túrán heard that Zohák kept near him two devouring serpents, alarm and terror spread everywhere, and so universal was the dread produced by this intelligence, that the nobles of Persia were induced to abandon their allegiance to Jemshíd, and, turning through fear to Zohák, confederated with the Arab troops against their own country. Jemshíd continued for some time to resist their efforts, but was at last defeated, and became a wanderer on the face of the earth.

To him existence was a burthen now,
The world a desert—for Zohák had gained
The imperial crown, and from all acts and deeds
Of royal import, razed out the very name
Of Jemshíd hateful in the tyrant's eyes.

THE STORY OF JEMSHÍD RESUMED.

The Persian government having fallen into the hands of the usurper, he sent his spies in every direction for the purpose of getting possession of Jemshíd wherever he might be found, but their labour was not crowned with success. The unfortunate wanderer, after experiencing numberless misfortunes, at length took refuge in Zábulistán.

> Flying from place to place, through wilderness,
> Wide plain, and mountain, veiled from human eye,
> Hungry and worn out with fatigue and sorrow,
> He came to Zábul.

The king of Zábulistán, whose name was Gúreng, had a daughter of extreme beauty. She was also remarkable for her mental endowments, and was familiar with warlike exercises.

> So graceful in her movements, and so sweet,
> Her very look plucked from the breast of age
> The root of sorrow,—her wine-sipping lips,
> And mouth like sugar, cheeks all dimpled o'er
> With smiles, and glowing as the summer rose—
> Won every heart.

This damsel, possessed of these beauties and charms, was accustomed to dress herself in the warlike habiliments of a man, and to combat with heroes. She was then only fifteen years of age, but so accomplished in valour, judgment, and discretion, that Minúchihr, who had in that year commenced hostile operations against her father, was compelled to relinquish his pretensions, and submit to the gallantry which she displayed on that occasion. Her father's realm was saved by her magnanimity. Many kings were her suitors, but Gúreng would not give his consent to her marriage with any of them. He only agreed that she should marry the sovereign whom she might spontaneously love.

> It must be love, and love alone,*
> That binds thee to another's throne;
> In this my father has no voice,
> Thine the election, thine the choice.

---

* Love at first sight, and of the most enthusiastic kind, is the passion described in all Persian poems, as if a whole life of love were condensed into one moment. It is all wild and rapturous. It has nothing of a rational cast. A casual glance from an unknown beauty often affords the subject of a poem. The poets whom Dr. Johnson has denominated metaphysical, such

The daughter of Gúreng had a Kábul woman for her nurse, who was deeply skilled in all sorts of magic and sorcery.

The old enchantress well could say,
What would befall on distant day;
And by her art omnipotent,
Could from the watery element
Draw fire, and with her magic breath,
Seal up a dragon's eyes in death.
Could from the flint-stone conjure dew;
The moon and seven stars she knew;
And of all things invisible
To human sight, this crone could tell.

---

as Donne, Jonson, and Cowley, bear a strong resemblance to the Persians on the subject of love.

Now, sure, within this twelvemonth past,
I've loved at least some twenty years or more;
Th' account of love runs much more fast,
Than that with which our life does score:
So, though my life be short, yet I may prove,
The Great Methusalem of love!!!
"LOVE AND LIFE." COWLEY.

The odes of Hafiz also, with all their spirit and richness of expression, abound in conceit and extravagant metaphor. There is, however, something very beautiful in the passage which may be paraphrased thus:

Zephyr thro' thy locks is straying,
Stealing fragrance, charms displaying;
Should it pass where Hafiz lies,
From his conscious dust would rise,
Flowrets of a thousand dyes!

Sir W. Jones, in quoting this distich, seems to have neglected the peculiar turn of the thought, and has translated the second line, *a hundred thousand flowers will spring from the earth that* HIDES *his corse!* But the passage implies that even the ashes of the Poet will still retain enough of sensibility to be affected by the presence, or by any token, of his beloved. Cowley has a similar notion, but he pursues and amplifies it till it becomes ridiculous.

'Tis well, 'tis well with them, say I,
Whose short-lived passions with themselves can die;
Whatever parts of me remain,
Those parts will still the love of thee retain;
My affection no more perish can,
Than the first matter that compounds a man!
Hereafter, if one dust of me,
Mix'd with another's substance be;
'Twill leaven that whole lump with love of thee!
Let nature if she please, disperse
My atoms over all the universe;
At the last they easily shall
Themselves know, and together call;
For thy love, like a mark, is stampt on all! ALL-OVER LOVE.

This Kábul sorceress had long before intimated to the damsel that, conformably with her destiny, which had been distinctly ascertained from the motions of the heavenly bodies, she would, after a certain time, be married to king Jemshíd, and bear him a beautiful son. The damsel was overjoyed at these tidings, and her father received them with equal pleasure, refusing in consequence the solicitations of every other suitor. Now according to the prophecy, Jemshíd arrived at the city of Zábul * in the spring season, when the roses were in bloom; and it so happened that the garden of king Gúreng was in the way, and also that his daughter was amusing herself at the time in the garden. Jemshíd proceeded in that direction, but the keepers of the garden would not allow him to pass, and therefore, fatigued and dispirited, he sat down by the garden-door under the shade of a tree. Whilst he was sitting there a slave-girl chanced to come out of the garden, and, observing him, was surprised at his melancholy and forlorn condition. She said to him involuntarily: "Who art thou?" and Jemshíd raising up his eyes, replied:—"I was once possessed of wealth and lived in great affluence, but I am now abandoned by fortune, and have come from a distant country. Would to heaven I could be blessed with a few cups of wine, my fatigue and affliction might then be relieved." The girl smiled, and returned hastily to the princess, and told her that a young man, wearied with travelling, was sitting at the garden gate, whose countenance was more lovely even than that of her mistress, and who requested to have a few cups of wine. When the damsel heard such high praise of the stranger's features she

* Zábul, or Zábulistán, the name of a province, bordering on Hindústan, which some place in the number of those now composing the country of Sind. It abounds in rivers, forests, lakes, and mountains. It was also called Rustemdar. The ancient Persians considered Zábulistán and Sístán, or Segestán, as one principality, where Rustem usually resided with his family, and which they held in appanage from the Kings of Persia. Segestan is the Drangiana of the Greeks. It was formerly the residence of many Persian Kings. One of its cities, Ghizni, produced the celebrated Mahmúd, the patron of Firdausí.

was exceedingly pleased, and said: "He asks only for wine, but I will give him both wine and music, and a beautiful mistress beside."

This saying, she repaired towards the gate,
In motion graceful as the waving cypress,
Attended by her hand-maid; seeing him,
She thought he was a warrior of Irán
With spreading shoulders, and his loins well bound.
His visage pale as the pomegranate flower,
He looked like light in darkness. Warm emotions
Rose in her heart, and softly thus she spoke:
"Grief-broken stranger, rest thee underneath
These shady bowers; if wine can make thee glad,
Enter this pleasant place, and drink thy fill."

Whilst the damsel was still speaking and inviting Jemshíd into the garden, he looked at her thoughtfully, and hesitated; and she said to him: "Why do you hesitate? I am permitted by my father to do what I please, and my heart is my own.

"Stranger, my father is the monarch mild
Of Zábulistán, and I his only child;
On me is all his fond affection shown;
My wish is his, on me he doats alone."

Jemshíd had before heard of the character and renown of this extraordinary damsel, yet he was not disposed to comply with her entreaty; but contemplating again her lovely face, his heart became enamoured, when she took him by the hand and led him along the beautiful walks.

With dignity and elegance she passed—
As moves the mountain partridge through the meads;
Her tresses richly falling to her feet,
And filling with perfume the softened breeze.

In their promenade they arrived at the basin of a fountain, near which they seated themselves upon royal carpets, and the damsel having placed Jemshíd in such a manner that they might face each other, she called for music and wine.

But first the rose-cheeked handmaids gathered round,
And washed obsequiously the stranger's feet;
Then on the margin of the silvery lake
Attentive sate.

The youth, after this, readily took the wine and refreshments which were ordered by the princess.

Three cups he drank with eager zest,*
Three cups of ruby wine;
Which banished sorrow from his breast,
For memory left no sign
Of past affliction; not a trace
Remained upon his heart, or smiling face.

Whilst he was drinking the princess observed his peculiar action and elegance of manner, and instantly said in her heart: "This must be a king!" She then offered him some more food, as he had come a long journey, and from a distant land, but he only asked for more wine. "Is your fondness for wine so great?" said she. And he replied: "With wine I have no enemy; yet, without it I can be resigned and contented.

* It is not unusual for Firdausí to say "they were all intoxicated!" Homer's heroes are more celebrated for eating than drinking, and the bravest always had the largest share! The ancient as well as the modern Persians, it appears, were passionately devoted to wine. Some lines which I have paraphrased from the Sakí-nameh of Hafiz, will show their adoration of it, defended by their notions of the uncertainty of life:

Saki! ere our life decline,
Bring the ruby-tinted wine;
Sorrow on my bosom preys,
Wine alone delights my days!
Bring it, let its sweets impart
Rapture to my fainting heart;
Sakí! fill the bumper high—
Why should man unhappy sigh?
Mark the glittering bubbles swim,
Round the goblet's smiling brim;
Now they burst, the charm is gone!
Fretful life will soon be done;
Jemshid's regal sway is o'er,
Kai-kobád is now no more.
Fill the goblet, all must sever,
Drink the liquid gem for ever!
Thou shalt still, in bowers divine,
Quaff the soul-expanding wine!

Whilst drinking wine I never see
The frowning face of my enemy;
Drink freely of the grape, and nought
Can give the soul one mournful thought;
Wine is a bride of witching power,
And wisdom is her marriage dower;
Wine can the purest joy impart,
Wine inspires the saddest heart;
Wine gives cowards valour's rage,
Wine gives youth to tottering age;
Wine gives vigour to the weak,
And crimson to the pallid cheek;
And dries up sorrow, as the sun
Absorbs the dew it shines upon."

From the voice and eloquence of the speaker she now conjectured that this certainly must be king Jemshíd, and she felt satisfied that her notions would soon be realized. At this moment she recollected that there was a picture of Jemshíd in her father's gallery, and thought of sending for it to compare the features; but again she considered that the person before her was certainly and truly Jemshíd, and that the picture would be unnecessary on the occasion.

It is said that two ring-doves, a male and female, happened to alight on the garden wall near the fountain where they were sitting, and began billing and cooing in amorous play, so that seeing them together in such soft intercourse, blushes overspread the cheeks of the princess, who immediately called for her bow and arrows. When they were brought she said to Jemshíd, "Point out which of them I shall hit, and I will bring it to the ground. Jemshíd replied: "Where a man is, a woman's aid is not required—give me the bow, and mark my skill;

However brave a woman may appear,
Whatever strength of arm she may possess,
She is but half a man!"

Upon this observation being made, the damsel turned her head aside ashamed, and gave him the bow. Her heart was full of love. Jemshíd took the bow, and selecting a feathered arrow out of her hand, said:—"Nor for a wager. If I hit the female, shall the lady whom I most admire in this company be mine?" The damsel assented. Jemshíd drew the string, and the arrow struck the female dove so skilfully as to transfix both the wings, and pin them together. The male ring-dove flew away, but moved by natural affection it soon returned, and settled on the same spot as before. The bow was said to be so strong that there was not a warrior in the whole kingdom who could even draw the string; and when the damsel witnessed the dexterity of the stranger, and the ease with which he used the weapon, she thought within her heart, "There can be no necessity for the picture; I am certain that this can be no other than the king Jemshíd, the son of Tahúmers, called the Binder of Demons." Then she took the bow from the hand of Jemshíd, and observed: "The male bird has returned to its former place, if *my* aim be successful shall the man whom I choose in this company be my husband?" Jemshíd instantly understood her meaning. At that moment the Kábul nurse appeared, and the young princess communicated to her all that had occurred. The nurse leisurely examined Jemshíd from head to foot with a slave-purchaser's eye, and knew him, and said to her mistress,—"All that I saw in thy horoscope and foretold, is now in the course of fulfilment. God has brought Jemshíd hither to be thy spouse. Be not regardless of thy good fortune, and the Almighty will bless thee with a son, who will be the conqueror of the world. The signs and tokens of thy destiny I have already explained." The damsel had become greatly enamoured of the person of the stranger before she knew who he was, and now being told by her nurse that he was Jemshíd himself, her affection was augmented two-fold.

The happy tidings, blissful to her heart,
Increased the ardour of her love for him.

And now the picture was brought to the princess, who, finding the resemblance exact, put it into Jemshíd's hand. Jemshíd, in secretly recognising his own likeness, was forcibly reminded of his past glory and happiness, and he burst into tears.

> The memory of the diadem and throne
> No longer his, came o'er him, and his soul
> Was rent with anguish.

The princess said to him: "Why at the commencement of our friendship dost thou weep? Art thou discontented—dissatisfied, unhappy? and am I the cause?" Jemshíd replied: "No, it is simply this; those who have feeling, and pity the sufferings of others, weep involuntarily. I pity the misfortunes of Jemshíd, driven as he is by adversity from the splendour of a throne, and reduced to a state of destitution and ruin. But he must now be dead; devoured, perhaps, by the wolves and lions of the forest." The nurse and princess, however, were convinced, from the sweetness of his voice and discourse, that he could be no other than Jemshíd himself, and taking him aside, they said: "Speak truly, art thou not Jemshíd?" But he denied himself. Again, they observed: "What says this picture?" To this he replied; "It is not impossible that I may be like Jemshíd in feature; for surely there may be in the world two men like each other?" And notwithstanding all the efforts made by the damsel and her nurse to induce Jemshíd to confess, he still resolutely denied himself. Several times she assured him she would keep his secret, if he had one, but that she was certain of his being Jemshíd. Still he denied himself. "This nurse of mine, whom thou seest," said she, "has often repeated to me the good tidings that I should be united to Jemshíd, and bear him a son. My heart instinctively acknowledged thee at first sight: then wherefore this denial of the truth? Many kings have solicited my hand in marriage, but all have been rejected, as I am destined to be thine, and united to no other." Dismissing now all her attendants, she remained with the nurse and Jemshíd, and then resumed:—

> "How long hath sleep forsaken me? how long
> Hath my fond heart been kept awake by love?
> Hope still upheld me—give me one kind look,
> And I will sacrifice my life for thee;
> Come, take my life, for it is thine for ever."

Saying this, the damsel began to weep, and shedding a flood of tears, tenderly reproached him for not acknowledging the truth. Jemshíd was at length moved by her affection and sorrow, and thus addressed her:—"There are two considerations which at present prevent the truth being told. One of them is my having a powerful enemy, and Heaven forbid that he should obtain information of my place of refuge. The other is, I never intrust my secrets to a woman!

Fortune I dread, since fortune is my foe,
And womankind are seldom known to keep
Another's secret. To be poor and safe,
Is better far than wealth exposed to peril."
To this the princess: "Is it so decreed,
That every woman has two tongues, two hearts?
All false alike, their tempers all the same?
No, no! could I disloyally betray thee?
I who still love thee better than my life?"

Jemshíd found it impossible to resist the damsel's incessant entreaties and persuasive tenderness, mingled as they were with tears of sorrow. Vanquished thus by the warmth of her affections, he told her his name, and the history of his misfortunes. She then ardently seized his hand, overjoyed at the disclosure, and taking him privately to her own chamber, they were married according to the customs of her country.

Him to the secret bower with blushing cheek
Exultingly she led, and mutual bliss,
Springing from mutual tenderness and love.
Entranced their souls.

When Gúreng the king found that his daughter's visits to him became less frequent than usual, he set his spies to work, and was not long in ascertaining the cause of her continued absence. She had married without his permission, and he was in great wrath. It happened, too, at this time that the bride was pale and in delicate health.

The mystery soon was manifest,
And thus the king his child addrest,

Whilst anger darkened o'er his brow:—
"What hast thou done, ungrateful, now?
Why hast thou flung, in evil day,
Thy veil of modesty away?
That cheek the bloom of spring displayed,
Now all is withered, all decayed;
But daughters, as the wise declare,
Are ever false, if they be fair."

Incensed at words so sharp and strong,
The damsel thus repelled the wrong:—
"Me, father, canst thou justly blame?
I never, never, brought thee shame;
With me can sin and crime accord,
When Jemshíd is my wedded lord?"

After this precipitate avowal, the Kábul nurse, of many spells, instantly took up her defence, and informed the king that the prophecy she had formerly communicated to him was on the point of fulfilment, and that the Almighty having, in the course of destiny, brought Jemshíd into his kingdom, the princess, according to the same planetary influence, would shortly become a mother.

And now the damsel grovels on the ground
Before king Gúreng. "Well thou know'st," she cries,
"From me no evil comes. Whether in arms,
Or at the banquet, honour guides me still:
And well thou know'st thy royal will pronounced
That I should be unfettered in my choice,
And free to take the husband I preferred.
This I have done; and to the greatest king
The world can boast, my fortunes are united,
To Jemshíd, the most perfect of mankind."

With this explanation the king expressed abundant and unusual satisfaction. His satisfaction, however, did not arise from the circumstance of the marriage, and the new connection it established, but from the opportunity it afforded him of betraying Jemshíd, and treacherously sending him bound to Zohák, which he intended to do, in the hopes of being magnificently rewarded. Exulting with this anticipation, he said to her smiling:—

Glad tidings thou hast given to me,
My glory owes its birth to thee;
I bless the day, and bless the hour,
Which placed this Jemshíd in my power.
Now to Zohák, a captive bound,
I send the wanderer thou hast found;
For he who charms the monarch's eyes,
With this long-sought, this noble prize,
On solemn word and oath, obtains
A wealthy kingdom for his pains."

On hearing these cruel words the damsel groaned, and wept exceedingly before her father, and said to him: "O, be not accessory to the murder of such a king! Wealth and kingdoms pass away, but a bad name remains till the day of doom.

Turn thee, my father, from this dreadful thought,
And save his sacred blood: let not thy name
Be syllabled with horror through the world,
For such an act as this. When foes are slain,
It is enough, but keep the sword away
From friends and kindred; shun domestic crime.
Fear him who giveth life, and strength, and power,
For goodness is most blessed. On the day
Of judgment thou wilt then be unappalled.
But if determined to divide us, first
Smite off this head, and let thy daughter die."

So deep and violent was the grief of the princess, and her lamentations so unceasing, that the father became softened into compassion, and, on her account, departed from the resolution he had made. He even promised to furnish Jemshíd with possessions, with treasure, and an army, and requested her to give him the consolation he required, adding that he would see him in the morning in his garden.

The heart-alluring damsel instant flew
To tell the welcome tidings to her lord.

Next day king Gúreng proceeded to the garden, and had an interview with Jemshíd, to whom he expressed the warmest favour and affection; but notwithstanding all he said, Jemshíd could place no confidence in his professions, and was anxious to effect his escape. He was, indeed, soon convinced of his danger, for he had a private intimation that the king's vizírs were consulting together on the expedience of securing his person, under the apprehension that Zohák would be invading the country, and consigning it to devastation and ruin, if his retreat was discovered. He therefore took to flight.

Jemshíd first turned his steps towards Chín, and afterwards into Ind. He had travelled a great distance in that beautiful country, and one day came to a tower, under whose shadow he sought a little repose, for the thoughts of his melancholy and disastrous condition kept him almost constantly awake.

And am I thus to perish? Thus forlorn,
To mingle with the dust? Almighty God!
Was ever mortal born to such a fate,
A fate so sad as mine! O that I never
Had drawn the breath of life, to perish thus!

Exhausted by the keenness of his affliction Jemshíd at length fell asleep. Zohák, in the meanwhile, had despatched an envoy, with an escort of troops, to the Khakán of Chín, and at that moment the cavalcade happened to be passing by the tower where Jemshíd was reposing. The envoy, attracted to the spot, immediately recognized him, and awakening him to a sense of this new misfortune, secured the despairing and agonized wanderer, and sent him to Zohák.

He saw a person sleeping on the ground,
And knew that it was Jemshíd. Overjoyed,
He bound his feet with chains, and mounted him
Upon a horse, a prisoner.
What a world!
No place of rest for man! Fix not thy heart,
Vain mortal! on this tenement of life,
On earthly pleasures;—think of Jemshíd's fate;
His glory reached the Heavens, and now this world
Has bound the valiant monarch's limbs in fetters,
And placed its justice in the hands of slaves.

When Zohák received intelligence of the apprehension of his enemy, he ordered him to be brought before the throne that he might enjoy the triumph.

All fixed their gaze upon the captive king,
Loaded with chains; his hands behind his back;
The ponderous fetters passing from his neck
Down to his feet; oppressed with shame he stood,
Like the narcissus bent with heavy dew.
Zohák received him with a scornful smile,
Saying, "Where is thy diadem, thy throne,
Where is thy kingdom, where thy sovereign rule;
Thy laws and royal ordinances—where,
Where are they now? What change is this that fate
Has wrought upon thee?" Jemshíd thus rejoined:
"Unjustly am I brought in chains before thee,
Betrayed, insulted—thou the cause of all,
And yet thou wouldst appear to feel my wrongs!"
Incensed at this defiance, mixed with scorn,
Fiercely Zohák replied, "Then choose thy death;
Shall I behead thee, stab thee, or impale thee,
Or with an arrow's point transfix thy heart!
What is thy choice?"—
"Since I am in thy power,
Do with me what thou wilt—why should I dread
Thy utmost vengeance, why express a wish
To save my body from a moment's pain!"-

As soon as Zohák heard these words he resolved upon a horrible deed of vengeance. He ordered two planks to be brought, and Jemshíd being fastened down between them, his body was divided the whole length with a saw, making two figures of Jemshíd out of one!

Why do mankind upon this fleeting world
Place their affections, wickedness alone
Is nourished into freshness; sounds of death, too,
Are ever on the gale to wear out life.
My heart is satisfied—O Heaven! no more,
Free me at once from this continual sorrow.

It was not long before tidings of the foul proceedings, which put an end to the existence of the unfortunate Jemshíd, reached Zábulistán. The princess, his wife, on hearing of his fate, wasted away with inconsolable grief, and at last took poison to unburthen herself of insupportable affliction.

It is related that Jemshíd had two sisters, named Shahrnáz and Arnawáz. They had been both seized, and conveyed to Zohák by his people, and continued in confinement for some time in the King's harem, but they were afterwards released by Feridún.

The tyrant's cruelty and oppression had become intolerable. He was constantly shedding blood, and committing every species of crime.

> The serpents still on human brains were fed,
> And every day two youthful victims bled;
> The sword, still ready—thirsting still to strike,
> Warrior and slave were sacrificed alike.

The career of Zohák himself, however, was not unvisited by terrors. One night he dreamt that he was attacked by three warriors; two of them of large stature, and one of them small. The youngest struck him a blow on the head with his mace, bound his hands, and casting a rope round his neck, dragged him along in the presence of crowds of people. Zohák screamed, and sprung up from his sleep in the greatest horror. The females of his harem were filled with amazement when they beheld the terrified countenance of the king, who, in reply to their inquiries, said, trembling: "This is a dream too dreadful to be concealed." He afterwards called together the Múbids, or wise men of his court; and having communicated to them the particulars of what had appeared to him in his sleep, commanded them to give him a faithful interpretation of the dream. The Múbids foresaw in this vision the approaching declension of his power and dominion, but were afraid to explain their opinions, because they were sure that their lives would be sacrificed if the true interpretation was given to him. Three days were consumed under the pretence of studying more scrupulously all the signs and appearances, and still not one of them had courage to speak out. On the fourth day the king grew angry, and insisted upon the dream being interpreted. In this dilemma, the Múbids said, "Then, if the truth must be told, without evasion, thy life approaches to an end, and Feridún, though yet unborn, will be thy successor."—"But who was it," enquired Zohák impatiently, "that struck the blow on my head?" The Múbids declared, with fear and trembling, "it was the apparition of Feridún himself, who is destined to smite thee on the head."—"But why," rejoined Zohák, "does he wish to injure *me?*"—"Because, his father's blood being spilt by thee, vengeance falls into his hands." Hearing this interpretation of his dream, the king sunk senseless on the ground; and when he recovered, he could neither sleep nor take food, but continued overwhelmed with sorrow and misery. The light of his day was for ever darkened.

Abtín was the name of Feridún's father, and that of his mother Faránuk, of the race of Tahúmers. Zohák, therefore, stimulated to further cruelty by the prophecy, issued an order that every person belonging to the family of the Kais, wherever found, should be seized and fettered, and brought to him. Abtín had long avoided discovery, continuing to reside in the most retired and solitary places; but one day his usual circumspection forsook him, and he ventured beyond his limits. This imprudent step was dreadfully punished, for the spies of Zohák fell in with him, recognized him, and carrying him to the king, he was immediately put to death. When the mother of Feridún heard of this sanguinary catastrophe, she took up her infant and fled. It is said that Feridún was at that time only two months old. In her flight, the mother happened to arrive at some pasturage ground. The keeper of the pasture had a cow named Pur'máieh, which yielded abundance of milk, and he gave it away in charity. In consequence of the grief and distress of mind occasioned by the murder of her husband, Faránuk's milk dried up in her breasts, and she was therefore under the necessity of feeding the child with the milk from the cow. She remained there one night, and would have departed in the morning; but considering the deficiency of milk, and the misery in which she was involved, continually afraid of being discovered and known, she did not know what to do. At length she thought it best to leave Feridún with the keeper of the pasture, and resigning him to the protection of God, went herself to the mountain Alberz.* The keeper readily complied

* Alberz is the chain of mountains which divide Ghilán and Mazinderán

with the tenderest wishes of the mother, and nourished the child with the fondness and affection of a parent during the space of three years. After that period had elapsed, deep sorrow continuing to afflict the mind of Faránuk, she returned secretly to the old man of the pasture, for the purpose of reclaiming and conveying Feridún to a safer place of refuge upon the mountain Alberz. The keeper said to her: "Why dost thou take the child to the mountain? he will perish there;" but she replied that God Almighty had inspired a feeling in her heart that it was necessary to remove him. It was a divine inspiration, and verified by the event.

Intelligence having at length reached Zohák that the son of Abtín was nourished and protected by the keeper of the pasture, he himself proceeded with a large force to the spot, where he put to death the keeper and all his tribe, and also the cow which had supplied milk to Feridún, whom he sought for in vain.

> He found the dwelling of his infant-foe,
> And laid it in the dust; the very ground
> Was punished for the sustenance it gave him.

The ancient records relate that a dirvesh happened to have taken up his abode in the mountain Alberz, and that Faránuk committed her infant to his fostering care. The dirvesh generously divided with the mother and son all the food and comforts which God gave him, and at the same time he took great pains in storing the mind of Feridún with various kinds of knowledge. One day he said to the mother: "The person foretold by wise men and astrologers as the destroyer of Zohák and his tyranny, is thy son!

> This child to whom thou gavest birth,
> Will be the monarch of the earth;"

---

from Irák. Kai-kobad was the first king of the dynasty called Kaianidess and of the race of Feridún. Alberz is also famous for a number of temple, of the Magi.

and the mother, from several concurring indications and signs, held a similar conviction.

When Feridún had attained his sixteenth year, he descended from the mountain, and remained for a time on the plain beneath. He inquired of his mother why Zohák had put his father to death, and Faránuk then told him the melancholy story; upon hearing which, he resolved to be revenged on the tyrant. His mother endeavoured to divert him from his determination, observing that he was young, friendless, and alone, whilst his enemy was the master of the world, and surrounded by armies. "Be not therefore precipitate," said she. "If it is thy destiny to become a king, wait till the Almighty shall bless thee with means sufficient for the purpose."

Displeased, the youth his mother's caution heard,
And meditating vengeance on the head
Of him who robbed him of a father, thus
Impatiently replied :—"'Tis Heaven inspires me;
Led on by Heaven, this arm will quickly bring
The tyrant from his palace, to the dust."
"Imprudent boy!" the anxious mother said;
"Canst thou contend against imperial power?
Must I behold thy ruin? Pause awhile,
And perish not in this wild enterprize."

It is recorded that Zohák's dread of Feridún was so great, that day by day he became more irritable, wasting away in bitterness of spirit, for people of all ranks kept continually talking of the young invader, and were daily expecting his approach. At last he came, and Zohák was subdued, and his power extinguished.

KAVAH, THE BLACKSMITH.

Zohák having one day summoned together all the nobles and philosophers of the kingdom, he said to them: "I find that a young enemy has risen up against me; but notwithstanding his tender years, there is no safety even with an apparently insignificant foe. I hear, too, that though young, he is distinguished for his prowess and wisdom; yet I fear not him, but the change of fortune. I wish therefore to assemble a large army, consisting of Men, Demons, and Peris, that this enemy may be surrounded, and conquered. And, further, since a great enterprize is on the eve of being undertaken, it will be proper in future to keep a register or muster-roll of all the people of every age in my dominions, and have it revised annually." The register, including both old and young, was accordingly prepared.

At that period there lived a man named Kavah, a blacksmith, remarkably strong and brave, and who had a large family. Upon the day on which it fell to the lot of two of his children to be killed to feed the serpents, he rose up with indignation in presence of the king, and said:

"Thou art the king, but wherefore on my head
Cast fire and ashes? If thou hast the form
Of hissing dragon, why to me be cruel?
Why give the brains of my beloved children
As serpent-food, and talk of doing justice?"
At this bold speech the monarch was dismayed,
And scarcely knowing what he did, released
The blacksmith's sons. How leapt the father's heart,
How warmly he embraced his darling boys!
But now Zohák directs that Kavah's name
Shall be inscribed upon the register.
Soon as the blacksmith sees it written there,
Wrathful he turns towards the chiefs assembled,
Exclaiming loud: "Are ye then men, or what,
Leagued with a Demon!" All astonished heard,
And saw him tear the hated register,
And cast it under foot with rage and scorn

Kavah having thus reviled the king bitterly, and destroyed the register of blood, departed from the court, and took his children along with him. After he had gone away, the nobles said to the king:

"Why should reproaches, sovereign of the world,
Be thus permitted? Why the royal scroll
Torn in thy presence, with a look and voice
Of proud defiance, by the rebel blacksmith!
So fierce his bearing, that he seems to be
A bold confederate of this Feridún."
Zohák replied: "I know not what o'ercame me,
But when I saw him with such vehemence
Of grief and wild distraction, strike his forehead,
Lamenting o'er his children, doomed to death,
Amazement seized my heart, and chained my will.
What may become of this, Heaven only knows,
For none can pierce the veil of destiny."
  Kavah, meanwhile, with warning voice set forth
What wrongs the nation suffered, and there came
Multitudes round him, who called out aloud
For justice! justice! On his javelin's point
He fixed his leathern apron for a banner,
And lifting it on high, he went abroad
To call the people to a task of vengeance.
Wherever it was seen crowds followed fast,
Tired of the cruel tyranny they suffered.
"Let us unite with Feridún," he cried,
"And from Zohák's oppression we are free!"
And still he called aloud, and all obeyed
Who heard him, high and low. Anxious he sought
For Feridún, not knowing his retreat;
But still he hoped success would crown his search.
  The hour arrived, and when he saw the youth,
Instinctively he knew him, and thanked Heaven
For that good fortune. Then the leathern banner
Was splendidly adorned with gold and jewels,
And called the flag of Kavah. From that time
It was a sacred symbol; every king
In future, on succeeding to the throne,
Did honour to that banner, the true sign
Of royalty, in veneration held.

Feridún, aided by the directions and advice of the blacksmith, now proceeded against Zohák. His mother wept to see him depart, and continually implored the blessing of God upon him. He had two elder brothers, whom he took along with him. Desirous of having a mace formed like the head of a cow, he requested Kavah to make one of iron, and it was accordingly made in the shape he described. In his progress, he visited a shrine or place of pilgrimage frequented by the worshippers of God, where he besought inspiration and aid, and where he was taught by a radiant personage the mysteries of the magic art, receiving from him a key to every secret.

Bright beamed his eye, with firmer step he strode,
His smiling cheek with warmer crimson glowed.

When his two brothers saw his altered mien, the pomp and splendour of his appearance, they grew envious of his good fortune, and privately meditated his fall. One day they found him asleep at the foot of a mountain, and they immediately went to the top and rolled down a heavy fragment of rock upon him with the intention of crushing him to death; but the clattering noise of the stone awoke him, and, instantly employing the knowledge of sorcery which had been communicated to him, the stone was suddenly arrested by him in its course. The brothers beheld this with astonishment, and hastening down the mountain, cried aloud: "We know not how the stone was loosened from its place: God forbid that it should have done any injury to Feridún." Feridún, however, was well aware of this being the evil work of his brothers, but he took no notice of the conspiracy, and instead of punishing them, raised them to higher dignity and consequence.

They say that Kavah directed the route of Feridún over the mountainous tracts and plains which lie contiguous to the banks of the Dijleh, or Tigris, close to the city of Bagdád. Upon reaching that river, they called for boats, but got no answer from the ferryman; at which Feridún was enraged, and immediately plunged, on horseback, into the foaming stream. All his army followed without delay, and with the blessing of God arrived on the other side in safety. He then turned towards the Bait-el-Mukaddus, built by Zohák. In the Pahlavi language it was called Kunuk-duz-mokt. The tower of this edifice was so lofty that it might be seen at the distance of many leagues, and within that tower Zohák had formed a talisman of miraculous virtues. Feridún soon overthrew this talisman, and destroyed or vanquished successively with his mace all the enchanted monsters and hideous shapes which appeared before him. He captured the whole of the building, and released all the black-eyed damsels who were secluded there, and among them Shahrnáz and Arnawáz, the two sisters of Jemshíd before alluded to. He then ascended the empty throne of Zohák, which had been guarded by the talisman, and the Demons under his command; and when he heard that the tyrant had gone with an immense army towards Ind, in quest of his new enemy, and had left his treasury with only a small force at the seat of his government, he rejoiced, and appropriated the throne and the treasure to himself.

From their dark solitudes the Youth brought forth
The black-haired damsels, lovely as the sun,
And Jemshíd's sisters, long imprisoned there;
And gladly did the inmates of that harem
Pour out their gratitude on being freed
From that terrific monster; thanks to Heaven
Devoutly they expressed, and ardent joy.

Feridún inquired of Arnawáz why Zohák had chosen the route towards Ind; and she replied, "For two reasons: the first is, he expects to encounter thee in that quarter; and if he fails, he will subdue the whole country, which is the seat of sorcery, and thus obtain possession of a renowned magician who can charm thee into his power.

He wishes to secure within his grasp
That region of enchantment, Hindústan,
And then obtain relief from what he feels;
For night and day the terror of thy name
Oppresses him, his heart is all on fire,
And life is torture to him."

FERIDÚN.

Kandrú, the keeper of the talisman, having effected his escape, fled to Zohák, to whom he gave intelligence of the release of his women, the destruction of the talisman, and the conquest of his empire.

"The sign of retribution has appeared,
For sorrow is the fruit of evil deeds."
Thus Kandrú spoke: "Three warriors have advanced
Upon thy kingdom from a distant land,
One of them young, and from his air and mien
He seems to me of the Kaianian race.
He came, and boldly seized the splendid throne,
And all thy spells, and sorceries, and magic,
Were instantly dissolved by higher power,
And all who dwelt within thy palace walls,
Demon or man, all utterly destroyed,
Their severed heads cast weltering on the ground."
Then was Zohák confounded, and he shrunk
Within himself with terror, thinking now
His doom was sealed; but anxious to appear
In presence of his army, gay and cheerful,
Lest they too should despair, he dressed himself
In rich attire, and with a pleasant look,
Said carelessly: "Perhaps some gamesome guest
Hath in his sport committed this strange act."
"A guest, indeed!" Kandrú replied, "a guest,
In playful mood to batter down thy palace!
If he had been thy guest, why with his mace,
Cow-headed, has he done such violence?
Why did he penetrate thy secret chambers,
And bring to light the beautiful Shahrnáz,
And red-lipped Arnawáz?" At this, Zohák
Trembled with wrath—the words were death to him;
And sternly thus he spoke: "What hast thou fled
Through fear, betraying thy important trust?
No longer shalt thou share my confidence,
No longer share my bounty and regard."
To this the keeper tauntingly replied:
"Thy kingdom is overthrown, and nothing now
Remains for thee to give me; thou art lost."

The tyrant immediately turned towards his army, with the intention of making a strong effort to regain his throne, but he found that as soon as the soldiers and the people were made acquainted with the proceedings and success of Ferídún, rebellion arose among them, and shuddering with horror at the cruelty exercised by him in providing food for the accursed serpents, they preferred embracing the cause of the new king. Zohák, seeing that he had lost the affections of the army, and that universal revolt was the consequence, adopted another course, and endeavoured alone to be revenged upon his enemy. He proceeded on his journey, and arriving by night at the camp of Ferídún, hoped to find him off his guard and put him to death. He ascended a high place, himself unobserved, from which he saw Ferídún sitting engaged in soft dalliance with the lovely Shahrnáz. The fire of jealousy and revenge now consumed him more fiercely, and he was attempting to effect his purpose, when Ferídún was roused by the noise, and starting up struck a furious blow with his cow-headed mace upon the temples of Zohák, which crushed the bone, and he was on the point of giving him another; but a supernatural voice whispered in his ear,

"Slay him not now,—his time is not yet come,
His punishment must be prolonged awhile;
And as he cannot now survive the wound,
Bind him with heavy chains—convey him straight
Upon the mountain, there within a cave,
Deep, dark, and horrible—with none to soothe
His sufferings, let the murderer lingering die."
The work of heaven performing, Ferídún
First purified the world from sin and crime.
Yet Ferídún was not an angel, nor
Composed of musk or ambergris. By justice
And generosity he gained his fame.
Do thou but exercise these princely virtues,
And thou wilt be renowned as Ferídún.

FERIDÚN AND HIS THREE SONS.

Feridún had three sons. One of them was named Sílim, the other Túr, and the third Irij. When they had grown up, he called before him a learned person named Chundel, and said to him: "Go thou in quest of three daughters, born of the same father and mother, and adorned with every grace and accomplishment, that I may have my three sons married into one family. Chundel departed accordingly, and travelled through many countries in fruitless search, till he came to the King of Yemen, whose name was Sarú, and found that he had three daughters of the character and qualifications required. He therefore delivered Feridún's proposition to him, to which the King of Yemen agreed. Then Feridún sent his three sons to Yemen, and they married the three daughters of the king, who gave them splendid dowries in treasure and jewels. It is related that Feridún afterwards divided his empire among his sons. To Sílim he gave Rúm and Kháwer; to Túr, Túrán;* and to Irij, Irán or Persia. The sons then repaired to their respective kingdoms. Persia was a beautiful country, and the garden of spring, full of freshness and perfume; Túrán, on the contrary, was less cultivated, and the scene of perpetual broils and insurrections. The elder brother, Sílim, was therefore discontented with the unfair partition of the empire, and displeased with his father. He sent to Túr, saying: "Our father

* Ancient Scythia embraced the whole of Túrán and the northern part of Persia. The Túránians are the Scythians of the Greek Historians, who are said, about the year B.C. 639, to have invaded the kingdom of the Medes.

Túrán, which is the ancient name of the country of Turkistán, appears from Des Guignes, to be the source and fountain of all the celebrated Scythian nations, which, under the name of Goths and Vandals, subsequently overran the Roman empire. Irán and Túran, according to the Oriental historians, comprehended all that is comprised in upper Asia, with the exception of India and China. Every country beyond the pale of the Persian empire was considered barbarous. The great river called by the Arabs and Persians, Jihún or Amú, and by the Greeks and Romans, Oxus, divided these two great countries from each other.

has given to Irij the most delightful and productive kingdom, and to us, two wild uncultivated regions. I am the eldest son, and I am not satisfied with this distribution,—what sayest thou?" When this message was communicated to Túr, he fully concurred in the sentiments expressed by his brother, and determined to unite with him in any undertaking that might promise the accomplishment of their purpose, which was to deprive Irij of his dominions. But he thought it would be most expedient, in the first instance, to make their father acquainted with the dissatisfaction he had produced; "for," he thought to himself, "in a new distribution, he may assign Persia to me." Then he wrote to Sílim, advising that a messenger should be sent at once to Feridún to inform him of their dissatisfaction, and bring back a reply. The same messenger was dispatched by Sílim accordingly on that mission,

> Charged with unfilial language. "Give," he said,
> "This stripling Irij a more humble portion,
> Or we will, from the mountains of Túran,
> From Rúm, and Chín, bring overwhelming troops,
> Inured to wár, and shower disgrace and ruin
> On him and Persia."

When the messenger arrived at the court of Feridún, and had obtained permission to appear in the presence of the king, he kissed the ground respectfully, and by command related the purpose of his journey. Feridún was surprised and displeased, and said, in reply:

> "Have I done wrong, done evil? None, but good.
> I gave ye kingdoms, that was not a crime;
> But if ye fear not me, at least fear God.
> My ebbing life approaches to an end,
> And the possessions of this fleeting world
> Will soon pass from me. I am grown too old
> To have my passions roused by this rebellion;
> All I can do is, with paternal love,
> To counsel peace. Be with your lot contented;
> Seek not unnatural strife, but cherish peace."

After the departure of the messenger Feridún called Irij before him, and said: "Thy two brothers, who are older than thou art, have confederated together, and threaten to bring a large army against thee for the purpose of seizing thy kingdom, and putting thee to death. I have received this information from a messenger, who further says, that if I take thy part they will also wage war upon me." And after Irij had declared that in this extremity he was anxious to do whatever his father might advise, Feridún continued: "My son, thou art unable to resist the invasion of even one brother; it will, therefore, be impossible for thee to oppose both. I am now aged and infirm, and my only wish is to pass the remainder of my days in retirement and repose. Better, then, will it be for thee to pursue the path of peace and friendship, and like me throw away all desire for dominion.

For if the sword of anger is unsheathed,
And war comes on, thy head will soon be free!
From all the cares of government and life.
There is no cause for thee to quit the world,
The path of peace and amity is thine."

Irij agreed with his father, and declared that he would willingly sacrifice his throne and diadem rather than go to war with his brothers.

"Look at the Heavens, how they roll on;
And look at man, how soon he's gone.
A breath of wind, and then no more;
A world like this, should man deplore?"

With these sentiments Irij determined to repair immediately to his brothers, and place his kingdom at their disposal, hoping by this means to merit their favour and affection, and he said:

"I feel no resentment, I seek not for strife,
I wish not for thrones and the glories of life;
What is glory to man?—an illusion, a cheat;
What did it for Jemshíd, the world at his feet?
When I go to my brothers their anger may cease,
Though vengeance were fitter than offers of peace."

Feridún observed to him: "It is well that thy desire is for

reconciliation, as thy brothers are preparing for war." He then wrote a letter to his sons, in which he said: "Your younger brother considers your friendship and esteem of more consequence to him than his crown and throne. He has banished from his heart every feeling of resentment against you; do you, in the like manner, cast away hostility from your hearts against him. Be kind to him, for it is incumbent upon the eldest born to be indulgent and affectionate to their younger brothers. Although your consideration for my happiness has passed away, I still wish to please you." As soon as the letter was finished, Irij mounted his horse, and set off on his journey, accompanied by several of his friends, but not in such a manner, and with such an equipment, as might betray his rank or character. When he arrived with his attendants in Turkistán, he found that the armies of his two brothers were ready to march against him. Sílim and Túr, being apprized of the approach of Irij, went out of the city, according to ancient usage, to meet the deputation which was conveying to them their father's letter. Irij was kindly received by them, and accommodated in the royal residence.

It is said that Irij was in person extremely prepossessing, and that when the troops first beheld him, they exclaimed: "He is indeed fit to be a king!" In every place all eyes were fixed upon him, and wherever he moved he was followed and surrounded by the admiring army and crowds of people.

> In numerous groups the soldiers met, and blessed
> The name of Irij, saying in their hearts,
> This is the man to lead an armed host,
> And worthy of the diadem and throne.

The courtiers of the two brothers, alarmed by these demonstrations of attachment to Irij continually before their eyes, represented to Sílim and Túr that the army was disaffected towards them, and that Irij alone was considered deserving of the supreme authority. This intimation exasperated the malignant spirit of the two brothers: for although at first determined to put Irij to death, his youth and prepossessing appearance had in some degree subdued their animosity. They were therefore pleased with the intelligence, because it afforded a new and powerful reason for getting rid of him. "Look at our troops," said Sílim to Túr, "how they assemble in circles together, and betray their admiration of him. I fear they will never march against Persia. Indeed it is not improbable that even the kingdom of Túran may fall into his hands, since the hearts of our soldiers have become so attached to him.

> No time is this to deviate from our course,
> We must rush on; our armies plainly show
> Their love for Irij, and if we should fail
> To root up from its place this flourishing tree,
> Our cause is lost for ever."

Again, Sílim said to Túr: "Thou must put Irij to death, and then his kingdom will be thine." Túr readily undertook to commit that crime, and, on the following day, at an interview with Irij, he said to him: "Why didst thou consent to be the ruler of Persia, and fail in showing a proper regard for the interests of thy elder brothers? Whilst our barren kingdoms are constantly in a state of warfare with the Turks, thou art enjoying peace and tranquillity upon the throne of a fruitful country? Must we, thy elder brothers, remain thus under thy commands, and in subordinate stations?

> Must thou have gold and treasure,
> And thy heart be wrapt in pleasure,
> Whilst we, thy elder born,
> Of our heritage are shorn?
> Must the youngest still be nursed,
> And the elder branches cursed?
> And condemned, by stern command,
> To a wild and sterile land?"

When Irij heard these words from Túr, he immediately replied, saying:

> "I only seek tranquillity and peace;
> I look not on the crown of sovereignty.

Nor seek a name among the Persian host;
And though the throne and diadem are mine,
I here renounce them, satisfied to lead
A private life. For what hath ever been
The end of earthly power and pomp, but darkness?
I seek not to contend against my brothers;
Why should I grieve their hearts, or give distress
To any human being? I am young,
And Heaven forbid that I should prove unkind!"

Notwithstanding, however, these declarations of submission, and repeated assurances of his resolution to resign the monarchy of Persia, Túr would not believe one word. In a moment he sprung up, and furiously seizing the golden chair from which he had just risen, struck a violent blow with it on the head of Irij, calling aloud, "Bind him, bind him!" The youth, struggling on the ground, exclaimed: "O, think of thy father, and pity me! Have compassion on thy own soul! I came for thy protection, therefore do not take my life: if thou dost, my blood will call out for vengeance to the Almighty. I ask only for peace and retirement. Think of my father, and pity me!

Wouldst thou, with life endowed, take life away?
Torture not the poor ant, which drags the grain
Along the dust; it has a life, and life
Is sweet and precious. Did the innocent ant
Offend thee ever? Cruel must he be
Who would destroy a living thing so harmless!
And wilt thou, reckless, shed thy brother's blood,
And agonize the feelings of a father?
Pause, and avoid the wrath of righteous Heaven!"

But Túr was not to be softened by the supplications of his brother. Without giving any reply, he drew his dagger, and instantly dissevered the head of the youth from his body.

With musk and ambergris he first embalmed
The head of Irij, then to his old father
Dispatched the present with these cruel words:—
"Here is the head of thy beloved son,
Thy darling favourite, dress it with a crown
As thou wert wont; and mark the goodly fruit
Thou hast produced. Adorn thy ivory throne,
In all its splendour, for this worthy head,
And place it in full majesty before thee!"

In the mean time, Feridún had prepared a magnificent reception for his son. The period of his return had arrived, and he was in anxious expectation of seeing him, when suddenly he received intelligence that Irij had been put to death by his brothers. The mournful spectacle soon reached his father's house.

A scream of agony burst from his heart,
As wildly in his arms he clasped the face
Of his poor slaughtered son; then down he sank
Senseless upon the earth. The soldiers round
Bemoaned the sad catastrophe, and rent
Their garments in their grief. The souls of all
Were filled with gloom, their eyes with flowing tears,
For hope had promised a far different scene;
A day of heart-felt mirth and joyfulness,
When Irij to his father's house returned.

After the extreme agitation of Feridún had subsided, he directed all his people to wear black apparel, in honour of the murdered youth, and all his drums and banners to be torn to pieces. They say that subsequent to this dreadful calamity he always wore black clothes. The head of Irij was buried in a favourite garden, where he had been accustomed to hold weekly a rural entertainment. Feridún, in performing the last ceremony, pressed it to his bosom, and with streaming eyes exclaimed:

"O Heaven, look down upon my murdered boy;
His severed head before me, but his body
Torn by those hungry wolves! O grant my prayer,
That I may see, before I die, the seed
Of Irij hurl just vengeance on the heads
Of his assassins; hear, O hear my prayer."
—Thus he in sorrow for his favourite son
Obscured the light which might have sparkled still,
Withering the jasmine flower of happy days;
So that his pale existence looked like death.

MINÚCHIHR.

Feridún continued to cherish with the fondest affection the memory of his murdered son, and still looked forward with anxiety to the anticipated hour of retribution. He fervently hoped that a son might be born to take vengeance for his father's death. But it so happened that Mah-afrid, the wife of Irij, gave birth to a daughter. When this daughter grew up, Feridún gave her in marriage to Pishung, and from that union an heir was born who in form and feature resembled Irij and Feridún. He was called Minúchihr, and great rejoicings took place on the occasion of his birth.

> The old man's lips, with smiles apart,
> Bespoke the gladness of his heart.
> And in his arms he took the boy,
> The harbinger of future joy;
> Delighted that indulgent Heaven
> To his fond hopes this pledge had given.
> It seemed as if, to bless his reign,
> Irij had come to life again.

The child was nourished with great tenderness during his infancy, and when he grew up he was sedulously instructed in every art necessary to form the character, and acquire the accomplishments of a warrior. Feridún was accustomed to place him on the throne, and decorate his brows with the crown of sovereignty; and the soldiers enthusiastically acknowledged him as their king, urging him to rouse himself and take vengeance of his enemies for the murder of his grandfather. Having opened his treasury, Feridún distributed abundance of gold among the people, so that Minúchihr was in a short time enabled to embody an immense army, by whom he was looked upon with attachment and admiration.

When Sílim and Túr were informed of the preparations that were making against them, that Minúchihr, having grown to manhood, was distinguished for his valour and intrepidity, and that multitudes flocked to his standard with the intention on forwarding his purpose of revenge, they were seized with inexpressible terror, and anticipated an immediate invasion of their kingdoms. Thus alarmed, they counselled together upon the course it would be wisest to adopt.

"Should he advance, his cause is just,
And blood will mingle with the dust,
But heaven forbid our power should be
O'erwhelmed to give him victory;
Though strong his arm, and wild his ire,
And vengeance keen his heart inspire."

They determined, at length, to pursue pacific measures, and endeavour by splendid presents and conciliatory language to regain the good-will of Feridún. The elephants were immediately loaded with treasure, a crown of gold, and other articles of value, and a messenger was dispatched, charged with an acknowledgment of guilt and abundant expressions of repentance. "It was Iblís," they said, "who led us astray, and our destiny has been such that we are in every way criminal. But thou art the ocean of mercy; pardon our offences. Though manifold, they were involuntary, and forgiveness will cleanse our hearts and restore us to ourselves. Let our tears wash away the faults we have committed. To Minúchihr and to thyself we offer obedience and fealty, and we wait your commands, being but the dust of your feet."

When the messenger arrived at the court of Feridún he first delivered the magnificent presents, and the king, having placed Minúchihr on a golden chair by his side, observed to him, "These presents are to thee a prosperous and blessed omen—they shew that thy enemy is afraid of thee." Then the messenger was permitted to communicate the object of his mission.

He spoke with studied phrase, intent to hide,
Or mitigate the horror of their crime;
And with excuses plausible and bland
His speech was dressed. The brothers, he observed,
Desired to see their kinsman Minúchihr,—
And with the costliest gems they sought to pay
The price of kindred blood unjustly shed—

And they would willingly to him resign
Their kingdoms for the sake of peace and friendship.
The monarch marked him scornfully, and said,
"Canst thou conceal the sun? It is in vain
Truth to disguise with words of shallow meaning.
Now hear my answer. Ask thy cruel masters,
Who talk of their affection for the prince,
Where lies the body of the gentle Irij?
Him they have slain, the fierce, unnatural brothers,
And now they thirst to gain another victim.
They long to see the face of Minúchihr!
Yes, and they shall, surrounded by his soldiers,
And clad in steel, and they shall feel the edge
Of life-destroying swords. Yes, they shall see him!"

After uttering this indignant speech, Feridún shewed to the messenger his great warriors, one by one. He shewed him Kavah and his two sons, Shahpúr, and Shírúeh, and Kárun, and Sám,* and Narímán, and other chiefs—all of admirable courage and valour in war,—and thus resumed:

"Hence with your presents, hence, away,
Can gold or gems turn night to day?
Must kingly heads be bought and sold,
And shall I barter blood for gold?
Shall gold a father's heart entice,
Blood to redeem beyond all price?
Hence, hence with treachery; I have heard
Their glozing falsehoods, every word;
But human feelings guide my will,
And keep my honour sacred still.
True is the oracle we read:—
'Those who have sown oppression's seed
Reap bitter fruit; their souls, perplext,
Joy not in this world or the next.'
The brothers of my murdered boy,
Who could a father's hopes destroy,
An equal punishment will reap,
And lasting vengeance o'er them sweep.
They rooted up my favourite tree,
But yet a branch remains to me.

---

* Sám, Sám Suwár, was the son of Narímán. He is said to have vanquished or tamed a great number of animals and terrible monsters, amongst which was one remarkable for its ferocity. This furious animal was called Sohám, on account of its being of the colour and nature of fire. According to fabulous history, he made it his war-horse, in all his engagements against the Demons.

Now the young lion comes apace,
The glory of his glorious race;
He comes apace, to punish guilt,
Where brother's blood was basely spilt;
And blood alone for blood must pay;
Hence with your gold, depart, away!"

When the messenger heard these reproaches, mingled with poison, he immediately took leave, and trembling with fear, returned to Sílim and Túr with the utmost speed. He described to them in strong and alarming terms the appearance and character of Minúchihr, and his warriors; of that noble youth who with frowning eyebrows was only anxious for battle. He then communicated to them in what manner he had been received, and repeated the denunciations of Feridún, at which the brothers were exceedingly grieved and disappointed. But Sílim said to Túr:

"Let us be first upon the field, before
He marshals his array. It follows not,
That he should be a hero bold and valiant,
Because he is descended from the brave;
But it becomes us well to try our power,—
For speed, in war, is better than delay."

In this spirit the two brothers rapidly collected from both their kingdoms a large army, and proceeded towards Irán. On hearing of their progress, Feridún said: "This is well—they come of themselves. The forest game surrenders itself voluntarily at the foot of the sportsman." Then he commanded his army to wait quietly till they arrived; for skill and patience, he observed, will draw the lion's head into your toils.

As soon as the enemy had approached within a short distance, Minúchihr solicited Feridún to commence the engagement,—and the king having summoned his chief warriors before him, appointed them all, one by one, to their proper places.

The warriors of renown assembled straight
With ponderous clubs; each like a lion fierce,
Girded his loins impatient. In their front
The sacred banner of the blacksmith waved;
Bright scimitars were brandished in the air;

Beneath them pranced their steeds, all armed for fight,
And so incased in iron were the chiefs
From top to toe, their eyes were only seen.
When Kárun drew his hundred thousand troops
Upon the field, the battle-word was given,
And Minúchihr was, like the cypress tall,
Engaged along the centre of the hosts;
And like the moon he shone, amid the groups
Of congregated clouds, or as the sun
Glittering upon the mountain of Alberz.
The squadrons in advance Kabád commanded,
Garshasp the left, and Sám upon the right.
The shedders of a brother's blood had now
Brought their innumerous legions to the strife,
And formed them in magnificent array:
The picquet guards were almost thrown together,
When Túr sprung forward, and with sharp reproach,
And haughty gesture, thus addressed Kabád:
"Ask this new king, this Minúchihr, since Heaven
To Irij gave a daughter, who on him
Bestowed the mail, the battle-axe, and sword?"
To this insulting speech, Kabád replied:
"The message shall be given, and I will bring
The answer, too. Ye know what ye have done;
Have ye not murdered him who, trusting, sought
Protection from ye? All mankind for this
Must curse your memory till the day of doom;
If savage monsters were to fly your presence,
It would not be surprising. Those who die
In this most righteous cause will go to Heaven,
With all their sins forgotten!" Then Kabád
Went to the king, and told the speech of Túr:
A smile played o'er the cheek of Minúchihr
As thus he spoke: "A boaster he must be,
Or a vain fool, for when engaged in battle,
Vigour of arm and the enduring soul,
Will best be proved. I ask but for revenge—
Vengeance for Irij slain. Meanwhile, return;
We shall not fight to-day."
He too retired,
And in his tent upon the sandy plain,
Ordered the festive board to be prepared,
And wine and music whiled the hours away.

When morning dawned the battle commenced, and multitudes were slain on both sides.

The spacious plain became a sea of blood;
It seemed as if the earth was covered o'er
With crimson tulips; slippery was the ground,
And all in dire confusion.

The army of Minúchihr was victorious, owing to the bravery and skill of the commander. But Heaven was in his favour.

In the evening Sílim and Túr consulted together, and came to the resolution of effecting a formidable night attack on the enemy. The spies of Minúchihr, however, obtained information of this intention, and communicated the secret to the king. Minúchihr immediately placed the army in charge of Kárun, and took himself thirty thousand men to wait in ambuscade for the enemy, and frustrate his views. Túr advanced with a hundred thousand men; but as he advanced, he found every one on the alert, and aware of his approach. He had gone too far to retreat in the dark without fighting, and therefore began a vigorous conflict. Minúchihr sprung up from his ambuscade, and with his thirty thousand men rushed upon the centre of the enemy's troops, and in the end encountered Túr. The struggle was not long. Minúchihr dexterously using his javelin, hurled him from his saddle precipitately to the ground, and then with his dagger severed the head from his body. The body he left to be devoured by the beasts of the field, and the head he sent as a trophy to Feridún; after which, he proceeded in search of Sílim.

The army of the confederates, however, having suffered such a signal defeat, Sílim thought it prudent to fall back and take refuge in a fort. But Minúchihr went in pursuit, and besieged the castle. One day a warrior named Kakú made a sally out of the fort, and approaching the centre of the besieging army, threw a javelin at Minúchihr, which however fell harmless before it reached its aim. Then Minúchihr seized the enemy by the girdle, raised him up in air, and flung him from his saddle to the ground.

He grasped the foe-man by the girth,
And thundering drove him to the earth;
By wound of spear, and gory brand,
He died upon the burning sand.

The siege was continued for some time with the view of

weakening the power of Sílim; at last Minúchihr sent a message to him, saying: "Let the battle be decided between us. Quit the fort, and boldly meet me here, that it may be seen to whom God gives the victory." Sílim could not, without disgrace, refuse this challenge: he descended from the fort, and met Minúchihr. A desperate conflict ensued, and he was slain on the spot. Minúchihr's keen sword severed the royal head from the body, and thus quickly ended the career of Sílim. After that, the whole of the enemy's troops were defeated and put to flight in every direction.

The leading warriors of the routed army now sought protection from Minúchihr, who immediately complied with their solicitation, and by their influence all the forces of Sílim and Túr united under him. To each he gave rank according to his merits. After the victory, Minúchihr hastened to pay his respects to Feridún, who received him with praises and thanksgivings, and the customary honours. Returning from the battle, Feridún met him on foot; and the moment Minúchihr beheld the venerable monarch, he alighted and kissed the ground. They then, seated in the palace together, congratulated themselves on the success of their arms. In a short time after, the end of Feridún approached; when recommending Minúchihr to the care of Sám and Narimán, he said: "My hour of departure has arrived, and I place the prince under your protection." He then directed Minúchihr to be seated on the throne;

> And put himself the crown upon his head,
> And stored his mind with counsel good and wise.

Upon the death of Feridún, Minúchihr accordingly succeeded to the government of the empire, and continued to observe strictly all the laws and regulations of his great grandfather. He commanded his subjects to be constant in the worship of God.

> The army and the people gave him praise,
> Prayed for his happiness and length of days;
> Our hearts, they said, are ever bound to thee;
> Our hearts, inspired by love and loyalty

ZÁL, THE SON OF SÁM.

According to the traditionary histories from which Firdausí has derived his legends, the warrior Sám had a son born to him whose hair was perfectly white. On his birth the nurse went to Sám and told him that God had blessed him with a wonderful child, without a single blemish, excepting that his hair was white ; but when Sám saw him he was grieved :

> His hair was white as goose's wing,
> His cheek was like the rose of spring
> His form was straight as cypress tree—
> But when the sire was brought to see
> That child with hair so silvery white,
> His heart revolted at the sight.

His mother gave him the name of Zál, and the people said to Sám, "This is an ominous event, and will be to thee productive of nothing but calamity ;—it would be better if thou couldst remove him out of sight.

> No human being of this earth
> Could give to such a monster birth ;
> He must be of the Demon race,
> Though human still in form and face.
> If not a Demon, he, at least,
> Appears a party-coloured beast."

When Sám was made acquainted with these reproaches and sneers of the people, he determined, though with a sorrowful heart, to take him up to the mountain Alberz, and abandon him there to be destroyed by beasts of prey. Alberz was the abode of the Símurgh or Griffin,* and, whilst flying about in quest of food for his hungry young ones, that surprising animal

* The sex of this fabulous animal is not clearly made out ! It tells Zál that it had nursed him like a *father*, and therefore I have, in this place, adopted the masculine gender, though the preserver of young ones might authorise its being considered a female. The Símurgh is probably neither one nor the other, or both ! Some have likened the Símurgh to the Ippogrif or Griffin ; but the Símurgh is plainly a biped ; others again have supposed that the fable simply meant a holy recluse of the mountains, who nourished and educated the poor child which had been abandoned by its father.

discovered the child lying alone upon the hard rock, crying and sucking its fingers. The Símurgh, however, felt no inclination to devour him, but compassionately took him up in the air, and conveyed him to his own habitation.

> He who is blest with Heaven's grace
> Will never want a dwelling-place
> And he who bears the curse of Fate
> Can never change his wretched state.
> A voice, not earthly, thus addressed
> The Símurgh in his mountain nest—
> "To thee this mortal I resign,
> Protected by the power divine;
> Let him thy fostering kindness share,
> Nourish him with paternal care;
> For from his loins, in time, will spring
> The champion of the world, and bring
> Honour on earth, and to thy name;
> The heir of everlasting fame."

The young ones were also kind and affectionate to the infant, which was thus nourished and protected by the Símurgh for several years.

The Dream of Sám.

It is said that one night, after melancholy musings and reflecting on the miseries of this life, Sám was visited by a dream, and when the particulars of it were communicated to the interpreters of mysterious warnings and omens, they declared that Zál was certainly still alive, although he had been long exposed on Alberz, and left there to be torn to pieces by wild animals. Upon this interpretation being given the natural feelings of the father returned, and he sent his people to the mountain in search of Zál, but without success. On another night Sám dreamt a second time, when he beheld a young man of a beautiful countenance at the head of an immense army, with a banner flying before him, and a Múbid on his left hand. One of them addressed Sám, and reproached him thus :—

Unfeeling mortal, hast thou from thy eyes
Washed out all sense of shame? Dost thou believe
That to have silvery tresses is a crime?
If so, thy head is covered with white hair;
And were not both spontaneous gifts from Heaven?
Although the boy was hateful to thy sight,
The grace of God has been bestowed upon him;
And what is human tenderness and love
To Heaven's protection? Thou to him wert cruel,
But Heaven has blest him, shielding him from harm.

Sám screamed aloud in his sleep, and awoke greatly terrified. Without delay he went himself to Alberz, and ascended the mountain, and wept and prayed before the throne of the Almighty, saying :—

"If that forsaken child be truly mine,
And not the progeny of Demon fell,
O pity me! forgive the wicked deed,
And to my eyes, my injured son restore."

His prayer was accepted. The Símurgh, hearing the lamentations of Sám among his people, knew that he had come in quest of his son, and thus said to Zál :—"I have fed and protected thee like a kind nurse, and I have given thee the name of Dustán, like a father. Sám, the warrior, has just come upon the mountain in search of his child, and I must restore thee to him, and we must part." Zál wept when he heard of this unexpected separation, and in strong terms expressed his gratitude to his benefactor; for the Wonderful Bird had not omitted to teach him the language of the country, and to cultivate his understanding, removed as they were to such a distance from the haunts of mankind. The Símurgh soothed him by assuring him that he was not going to abandon him to misfortune, but to increase his prosperity; and, as a striking proof of affection, gave him a feather from his own wing, with these instructions :—"Whenever thou art involved in difficulty or danger, put this feather on the fire, and I will instantly appear to thee to ensure thy safety. Never cease to remember me.

> I have watched thee with fondness by day and by night,
> And supplied all thy wants with a father's delight;
> O forget not thy nurse—still be faithful to me—
> And my heart will be ever devoted to thee."

Zál immediately replied in a strain of gratitude and admiration; and then the Símurgh conveyed him to Sám, and said to him: "Receive thy son—he is of wonderful promise, and will be worthy of the throne and the diadem."

> The soul of Sám rejoiced to hear
> Applause so sweet to a parent's ear;
> And blessed them both in thought and word,
> The lovely boy, and the Wondrous Bird.

He also declared to Zál that he was ashamed of the crime of which he had been guilty, and that he would endeavour to obliterate the recollection of the past by treating him in future with the utmost respect and honour.

When Minúchihr heard from Zábul of these things, and of Sám's return, he was exceedingly pleased, and ordered his son, Naúder, with a splendid istakbál,* to meet the father and son on their approach to the city. They were surrounded by war-

* This custom is derived from the earliest ages of Persia, and has been continued down to the present times with no abatement of its pomp or splendour. Mr. Morier thus speaks of the progress of the Embassy to Persia :—

"An *Istakbál* composed of fifty horsemen of our Mehmandar's tribe, met us about three miles from our encampment; they were succeeded as we advanced by an assemblage on foot, who threw a glass vessel filled with sweetmeats beneath the Envoy's horse, a ceremony which we had before witnessed at Kauzeroon, and which we again understood to be an honour shared with the King and his sons alone. Then came two of the principal merchants of Shiraz, accompanied by a boy, the son of Mahomed Nebee Khan, the new Governor of Bushere. They, however, incurred the Envoy's displeasure by not dismounting from their horses, a form always observed in Persia by those of lower rank, when they meet a superior. We were thus met by three *Istakbáls* during the course of the day."

riors and great men, and Sám embraced the first moment to introduce Zál to the king.

> Zál humbly kissed the earth before the king,
> And from the hands of Minúchihr received
> A golden mace and helm. Then those who knew
> The stars and planetary signs, were told
> To calculate the stripling's destiny;
> And all proclaimed him of exalted fortune,
> That he would be prodigious in his might,
> Outshining every warrior of the age.

Delighted with this information, Minúchihr, seated upon his throne, with Kárun on one side and Sám on the other, presented Zál with Arabian horses, and armour, and gold, and splendid garments, and appointed Sám to the government of Kábul, Zábul, and Ind. Zál accompanied his father on his return; and when they arrived at Zábulistán, the most renowned instructors in every art and science were collected together to cultivate and enrich his young mind.

In the meantime Sám was commanded by the king to invade and subdue the Demon provinces of Ḳarugsár and Mazinderán;* and Zál was in consequence left by his father in charge of Zábulistán. The young nursling of the Símurgh is said to have performed the duties of sovereignty with admirable wisdom and discretion, during the absence of his father. He did not pass his time in idle exercises, but with zealous delight in the society of accomplished and learned men, for the purpose of becoming familiar with every species of knowledge and acquirement. The city of Zábul, however, as a constant residence, did not entirely satisfy him, and he wished to see more of the world; he therefore visited several other places, and proceeded as far as Kábul, where he pitched his tents, and remained for some time.

* The province of Mazinderán, of which the principal city is Amol, comprehends the whole of the southern coast of the Caspian sea. It was known to the ancients by the name of Hyrcania. At the period to which the text refers, the country was in the possession of demons.

RÚDÁBEH.

The chief of Kábul was descended from the family of Zohák. He was named Mihráb, and to secure the safety of his state, paid annual tribute to Sám. Mihráb, on the arrival of Zál, went out of the city to see him, and was hospitably entertained by the young hero, who soon discovered that he had a daughter of wonderful attractions.

Her name Rúdábeh; skreened from public view,
Her countenance is brilliant as the sun;
From head to foot her lovely form is fair
As polished ivory. Like the spring, her cheek
Presents a radiant bloom,—in stature tall,
And o'er her silvery brightness, richly flow
Dark musky ringlets clustering to her feet.
She blushes like the rich pomegranate flower;
Her eyes are soft and sweet as the narcissus,
Her lashes from the raven's jetty plume
Have stolen their blackness, and her brows are bent
Like archer's bow. Ask ye to see the moon?
Look at her face. Seek ye for musky fragrance?
She is all sweetness. Her long fingers seem
Pencils of silver, and so beautiful
Her presence, that she breathes of Heaven and love.

Such was the description of Rúdábeh,* which inspired the

* Firdausí is very exuberant in his account of Rúdábeh. Female beauty has always been a darling subject with the poets of all nations, and they have generally embellished it with all their powers of description.

In comparing the Greek and Persian notions of female beauty and its attributes, we find no important disparity, but a much closer resemblance than might be expected, considering the physical difference between the two countries. For the imagery of every genuine poet must be derived from what he is accustomed to see, from the natural objects and circumstances by which he is surrounded. Hence it is that every country must have what Dr. Johnson calls, "traditional imagery, and hereditary similes." The Odes of Hafiz have all the rich imagery of the Teian bard, besides an abundance of beautiful epithets, unknown to the Greek, drawn from the varied productions of a still more genial climate.

The following is a fuller description of the charms of Rúdábeh:—

If thou would'st make her charms appear,
Think of the Sun so bright and clear;

heart of Zál with the most violent affection, and imagination added to her charms.

Mihráb again waited on Zál, who received him graciously, and asked him in what manner he could promote his wishes. Mihráb said that he only desired him to become his guest at a banquet he intended to invite him to; but Zál thought proper to refuse, because he well knew, if he accepted an invitation of the kind from a relation of Zohák, that his father Sám and the King of Persia would be offended. Mihráb returned to Kábul disappointed, and having gone into his harem, his wife, Síndokht, inquired after the stranger from Zábul, the white-headed son of Sám. She wished to know what he was like, in form and feature, and what account he gave of his sojourn with the Símurgh. Mihráb described him in the warmest terms of admiration—he was valiant, he said, accomplished and handsome, with no other defect than that of white hair. And so boundless was his praise, that Rúdábeh, who was present, drank every word with avidity, and felt her own heart warmed into admira-

And brighter far, with softer light,
The maiden strikes the dazzled sight.
Think of her skin, with what compare!
Ivory was never half so fair!
Her stature like the Sabin tree;
Her eyes! so full of witchery,
Glow like the Nirgis * tenderly.
Her arching brows their magic fling,
Dark as the raven's glossy wing.
Soft o'er her blooming cheek is spread,
The rich pomegranate's vivid red.
Upon her bosom, white as snow,
Two vermil buds, in secret, blow.
Her musky ringlets, unconfined,
In clustering meshes roll behind.
Love ye the moon? Behold her face,
And there the lucid planet trace.
If breath of musky fragrance please,
Her balmy odours scent the breeze;
Possess'd of every sportive wile,
'Tis heaven, 'tis bliss, to see her smile!

This imagery is all familiar to European taste, not excepting even the allusion to the moon, which has usually been considered peculiar to the Poetry of Asia.

---

* The Narcissus, to which the eyes of beautiful women are usually compared.

tion and love. Full of emotion, she afterwards said privately to h attendants:

"To you alone the secret of my heart
I now unfold; to you alone confess
The deep sensations of my captive soul.
I love, I love; all day and night of him
I think alone—I see him in my dreams—
You only know my secret—aid me now,
And soothe the sorrows of my bursting heart."

The attendants were startled with this confession and intreaty, and ventured to remonstrate against so preposterous an attachment.

"What! hast thou lost all sense of shame,
All value for thy honoured name!
That thou, in loveliness supreme,
Of every tongue the constant theme,
Should choose, and on another's word,
The nursling of a Mountain Bird!
A being never seen before,
Which human mother never bore!
And can the hoary locks of age,
A youthful heart like thine engage?
Must thy enchanting form be prest
To such a dubious monster's breast?
And all thy beauty's rich array,
Thy peerless charms be thrown away?"

This violent remonstrance was more calculated to rouse the indignation of Rúdábeh than to induce her to change her mind. It did so. But she subdued her resentment, and again dwelt upon the ardour of her passion.

"My attachment is fixed, my election is made,
And when hearts are enchained 'tis in vain to upbraid.
Neither Kízar nor Faghfúr I wish to behold,
Nor the monarch of Persia with jewels and gold;
All, all I despise, save the choice of my heart,
And from his beloved image I never can part.
Call him aged, or young, 'tis a fruitless endeavour
To uproot a desire I must cherish for ever;
Call him old, call him young, who can passion controul?
Ever present, and loved, he entrances my soul.
'Tis for him I exist—him I worship alone,
And my heart it must bleed till I call him my own."

As soon as the attendants found that Rúdábeh's attachment was deeply fixed, and not to be removed, they changed their purpose, and became obedient to her wishes, anxious to pursue any measure that might bring Zál and their mistress together. Rúdábeh was delighted with this proof of their regard.

It was spring time, and the attendants repaired towards the halting-place of Zál, in the neighbourhood of the city. Their occupation seemed to be gathering roses along the romantic banks of a pellucid streamlet, and when they purposely strayed opposite the tent of Zál, he observed them, and asked his friends—why they presumed to gather roses in his garden. He was told that they were damsels sent by the moon of Kábulistán from the palace of Mihráb to gather roses, and upon hearing this his heart was touched with emotion. He rose up and rambled about for amusement, keeping the direction of the river, followed by a servant with a bow. He was not far from the damsels, when a bird sprung up from the water, which he shot, upon the wing, with an arrow. The bird happened to fall near the rose-gatherers, and Zál ordered his servant to bring it to him. The attendants of Rúdábeh lost not the opportunity, as he approached them, to inquire who the archer was. "Know ye not," answered the servant, "that this is Nímrúz, the son of Sám, and also called Dustán, the greatest warrior ever known." At this the damsels smiled, and said that they too belonged to a person of distinction—and not of inferior worth—to a star in the palace of Mihráb. "We have come from Kábul to the king of Zábulistán, and should Zál and Rúdábeh be of equal rank, her ruby lips may become acquainted with his, and their wished-for union be effected." When the servant returned, Zál was immediately informed of the conversation that had taken place, and in consequence presents were prepared.

They who to gather roses came—went back
With precious gems—and honorary robes;
And two bright finger-rings were secretly
Sent to the princess.

Then did the attendants of Rúdábeh exult in the success of their artifice, and say that the lion had come into their toils. Rúdábeh herself, however, had some fears on the subject. She anxiously sought to know exactly the personal appearance of Zál, and happily her warmest hopes were realized by the description she received. But one difficulty remained—how were they to meet? How was she to see with her own eyes the man whom her fancy had depicted in such glowing colours? Her attendants, sufficiently expert at intrigue, soon contrived the means of gratifying her wishes. There was a beautiful rural retreat in a sequestered situation, the apartments of which were adorned with pictures of great men, and ornamented in the most splendid manner. To this favourite place Rúdábeh retired, and most magnificently dressed, awaiting the coming of Zál, whom her attendants had previously invited to repair thither as soon as the sun had gone down. The shadows of evening were falling as he approached, and the enamoured princess thus addressed him from her balcony:—

"May happiness attend thee ever, thou,
Whose lucid features make this gloomy night
Clear as the day; whose perfume scents the breeze;
Thou who, regardless of fatigue, hast come
On foot too, thus to see me—"

Hearing a sweet voice, he looked up, and beheld a bright face in the balcony, and he said to the beautiful vision:—

"How often have I hoped that Heaven
Would, in some secret place display
Thy charms to me, and thou hast given
My heart the wish of many a day;
For now thy gentle voice I hear,
And now I see thee—speak again!
Speak freely in a willing ear,
And every wish thou hast obtain."

Not a word was lost upon Rúdábeh, and she soon accomplished her object. Her hair was so luxuriant, and of such a length, that casting it loose it flowed down from the balcony;

and, after fastening the upper part to a ring, she requested Zál to take hold of the other end and mount up. He ardently kissed the musky tresses, and by them quickly ascended.

Then hand in hand within the chambers they
Gracefully passed.—Attractive was the scene,
The walls embellished by the painter's skill,
And every object exquisitely formed,
Sculpture, and architectural ornament,
Fit for a king. Zál with amazement gazed
Upon what art had done, but more he gazed
Upon the witching radiance of his love,
Upon her tulip cheeks, her musky locks,
Breathing the sweetness of a summer garden;
Upon the sparkling brightness of her rings,
Necklace, and bracelets, glittering on her arms.
His mien too was majestic—on his head
He wore a ruby crown, and near his breast
Was seen a belted dagger. Fondly she
With side-long glances marked his noble aspect,
The fine proportions of his graceful limbs,
His strength and beauty. Her enamoured heart
Suffused her cheek with blushes, every glance
Increas'd the ardent transports of her soul.
So mild was his demeanour, he appeared
A gentle lion toying with his prey.
Long they remained rapt in admiration
Of each other. At length the warrior rose,
And thus addressed her:—"It becomes not us
To be forgetful of the path of prudence,
Though love would dictate a more ardent course,
How oft has Sám, my father, counselled me,
Against unseeming thoughts,—unseemly deeds,—
Always to choose the right, and shun the wrong.
How will he burn with anger when he hears
This new adventure; how will Minúchihr
Indignantly reproach me for this dream!
This waking dream of rapture! but I call
High Heaven to witness what I now declare—
Whoever may oppose my sacred vows,
I still am thine, affianced thine, for ever."
 And thus Rúdábeh:—"Thou hast won my heart,
And kings may sue in vain; to thee devoted,
Thou art alone my warrior and my love."
Thus they exclaimed,—then Zál with fond adieus
Softly descended from the balcony,
And hastened to his tent.

As speedily as possible he assembled together his counsellors and Múbids to obtain their advice on the present extraordinary occasion, and he represented to them the sacred importance of encouraging matrimonial alliances.

For marriage is a contract sealed by Heaven—
How happy is the Warrior's lot, amidst
His smiling children; when he dies, his son
Succeeds him, and enjoys his rank and name.
And is it not a glorious thing to say—
This is the son of Zál, or this of Sám,
The heir of his renowned progenitor?

He then related to them the story of his love and affection for the daughter of Mihráb; but the Múbids, well knowing that the chief of Kábul was of the family of Zohák, the serpent-king, did not approve the union desired, which excited the indignation of Zál. They, however, recommended his writing a letter to Sám, who might, if he thought proper, refer the matter to Minúchihr. The letter was accordingly written and dispatched, and when Sám received it, he immediately referred the question to his astrologers, to know whether the nuptials, if solemnized between Zál and Rúdábeh, would be prosperous or not. They foretold that the nuptials would be prosperous, and that the issue would be a son of wonderful strength and power, the conqueror of the world. This announcement delighted the heart of the old warrior, and he sent the messenger back with the assurance of his approbation of the proposed union, but requested that the subject might be kept concealed till he returned with his army from the expedition to Karugsár, and was able to consult with Minúchihr.

Zál, exulting at his success, communicated the glad tidings to Rúdábeh by their female emissary, who had hitherto carried on successfully the correspondence between them. But as she was conveying an answer to this welcome news, and some presents to Zál, Síndokht, the mother of Rúdábeh, detected her, and, examining the contents of the packet, she found sufficient evidence, she thought, of something wrong.

"What treachery is this? What have we here!
Sirbund and male attire! Thou, wretch, confess!
Disclose thy secret doings."

The emissary, however, betrayed nothing; but declared that she was a dealer in jewels and dresses, and had been only shewing her merchandize to Rúdábeh. Síndokht, in extreme agitation of mind, hastened to her daughter's apartment to ascertain the particulars of this affair, when Rúdábeh at once fearlessly acknowledged her unalterable affection for Zál.

"I love him so devotedly, all day,
All night my tears have flowed unceasingly;
And one hair of his head I prize more dearly
Than all the world beside; for him I live;
And we have met, and we have sat together,
And pledged our mutual love with mutual joy
And innocence of heart."

Rúdábeh further informed her of Sám's consent to their nuptials, which in some degree satisfied the mother. But when Mihráb was made acquainted with the arrangement, his rage was unbounded, for he dreaded the resentment of Sám and Minúchihr when the circumstances became fully known to them. Trembling with indignation he drew his dagger, and would have instantly rushed to Rúdábeh's chamber to destroy her, had not Síndokht fallen at his feet and restrained him. He insisted, however, on her being brought before him; and upon his promise not to do her any harm, Síndokht complied. Rúdábeh disdained to take off her ornaments to appear as an offender and a supplicant, but, proud of her choice, went into her father's presence, gaily adorned with jewels, and in splendid apparel. Mihráb received her with surprise.

"Why all this glittering finery? Is the devil
United to an angel? When a snake
Is met with in Arabia, it is killed!"

But Rúdábeh answered not a word, and was permitted to retire with her mother.

When Minúchihr was apprized of the proceedings between Zál and Rúdábeh, he was deeply concerned, anticipating nothing but confusion and ruin to Persia from the united influence of Zál and Mihráb. Ferídún had purified the world from the abominations of Zohák, and as Mihráb was a descendant of that merciless tyrant, he feared that some attempt would be made to resume the enormities of former times; Sám was therefore required to give his advice on the occasion.

The conqueror of Karugsár and Mazinderán was received on his return with cordial rejoicings, and he charmed the king with the story of his triumphant success. The monarch against whom he had fought was descended, on the mother's side, from Zohák, and his Demon army was more numerous than ants, or clouds of locusts, covering mountain and plain. Sám thus proceeded in his description of the conflict.

"And when he heard my voice, and saw what deeds
I had performed, approaching me, he threw
His noose; but downward bending I escaped,
And with my bow I showered upon his head
Steel-pointed arrows, piercing through the brain;
Then did I grasp his loins, and from his horse
Cast him upon the ground, deprived of life.
At this, the demons terrified and pale,
Shrunk back, some flying to the mountain wilds,
And others, taken on the battle-field,
Became obedient to the Persian king."

Minúchihr, gratified by this result of the expedition, appointed Sám to a new enterprize, which was to destroy Kábul by fire and sword, especially the house of Mihráb; and that ruler, of the serpent-race, and all his adherents were to be put to death. Sám, before he took leave to return to his own government at Zábul, tried to dissuade him from this violent exercise of revenge, but without making any sensible impression upon him.

Meanwhile the vindictive intentions of Minúchihr, which were soon known at Kábul, produced the greatest alarm and consternation in the family of Mihráb. Zál now returned to his father, and Sám sent a letter to Minúchihr, again to deprecate his wrath, and appointed Zál the messenger. In this letter Sám enumerates his services at Karugsár and Mazinderán, and especially dwells upon the destruction of a prodigious dragon.

"I am thy servant, and twice sixty years
Have seen my prowess. Mounted on my steed,
Wielding my battle-axe, o'erthrowing heroes,
Who equals Sám, the warrior? I destroyed
The mighty monster, whose devouring jaws
Unpeopled half the land, and spread dismay
From town to town. The world was full of horror,
No bird was seen in air, no beast of prey
In plain or forest; from the stream he drew
The crocodile; the eagle from the sky.
The country had no habitant alive,
And when I found no human being left,
I cast away all fear, and girt my loins,
And in the name of God went boldly forth,
Armed for the strife. I saw him towering rise,
Huge as a mountain, with his hideous hair
Dragging upon the ground; his long black tongue
Shut up the path; his eyes two lakes of blood;
And, seeing me, so horrible his roar,
The earth shook with affright, and from his mouth
A flood of poison issued. Like a lion
Forward I sprang, and in a moment drove
A diamond-pointed arrow through his tongue,
Fixing him to the ground. Another went
Down his deep throat, and dreadfully he writhed.
A third passed through his middle. Then I raised
My battle-axe, cow-headed, and with one
Tremendous blow, dislodged his venomous brain,
And deluged all around with blood and poison.
There lay the monster dead, and soon the world
Regained its peace and comfort. Now I'm old,
The vigour of my youth is past and gone,
And it becomes me to resign my station,
To Zál, my gallant son."

Mihráb continued in such extreme agitation, that in his own mind he saw no means of avoiding the threatened desolation of his country but by putting his wife and daughter to death. Síndokht however had a better resource, and suggested the expediency of waiting upon Sám herself, to induce him to forward her own views and the nuptials between Zál and Rúdábeh. To this Mihráb assented, and she proceeded, mounted on a richly caparisoned horse, to Zábul with most magnificent presents, consisting of three hundred thousand dínars; ten horses with golden, and thirty with silver, housings; sixty richly attired damsels, carrying golden trays of jewels and musk, and camphor, and wine, and sugar; forty pieces of figured cloth; a hundred milch camels, and a hundred others for burthen; two hundred Indian swords, a golden crown and throne, and four elephants. Sám was amazed and embarrassed by the arrival of this splendid array. If he accepted the presents, he would incur the anger of Minúchihr; and if he rejected them, Zál would be disappointed and driven to despair. He at length accepted them, and concurred in the wishes of Síndokht respecting the union of the two lovers.

When Zál arrived at the court of Minúchihr, he was received with honour, and the letter of Sám being read, the king was prevailed upon to consent to the pacific proposals that were made in favour of Mihráb, and the nuptials. He too consulted his astrologers, and was informed that the offspring of Zál and Rúdábeh would be a hero of matchless strength and valour. Zál, on his return through Kábul, had an interview with Rúdábeh, who welcomed him in the most rapturous terms:—

> Be thou for ever blest, for I adore thee,
> And make the dust of thy fair feet my pillow.

In short, with the approbation of all parties the marriage at length took place, and was celebrated at the beautiful summer-house where first the lovers met. Sám was present at Kábul on the happy occasion, and soon afterwards returned to Sístan, preparatory to resuming his martial labours in Karugsár and Mazinderán.

As the time drew near that Rúdábeh should become a mother, she suffered extremely from constant indisposition, and both Zál and Síndokht were in the deepest distress on account of her precarious state.

> The cypress leaf was withering; pale she lay,
> Unsoothed by rest or sleep, death seemed approaching.

At last Zál recollected the feather of the Símurgh, and followed the instructions which he had received, by placing it on the fire. In a moment darkness surrounded them, which was, however, immediately dispersed by the sudden appearance of the Símurgh. "Why," said the Símurgh, "do I see all this grief and sorrow? Why are the tear-drops in the warrior's eyes? A child will be born of mighty power, who will become the wonder of the world."

The Símurgh then gave some advice which was implicitly attended to, and the result was that Rúdábeh was soon out of danger. Never was beheld so prodigious a child. The father and mother were equally amazed. They called the boy Rustem. On the first day he looked a year old, and he required the milk of ten nurses. A likeness of him was immediately worked in silk, representing him upon a horse, and armed like a warrior, which was sent to Sám, who was then fighting in Mazínderán, and it made the old champion almost delirious with joy. At Kábul and Zábul there was nothing but feasting and rejoicing, as soon as the tidings were known, and thousands of dínars were given away in charity to the poor. When Rustem was five years of age, he ate as much as a man, and some say that even in his third year he rode on horseback. In his eighth year he was as powerful as any hero of the time.

In beauty of form and in vigour of limb,*
No mortal was ever seen equal to him.

---

* In the heroic ages of Persia, as in the early periods of every nation, feats of personal activity and muscular strength, constituted the most prominent features of a champion, and accordingly Firdausí has thought it necessary to give his hero extraordinary size and gigantic breadth of limb. Hercules had almost completed his eighth month before he strangled the serpents which Juno had sent to devour him; but Rustem, when a day old, was like a child of twelve months. When three years old he was fond of warlike pursuits and rode on horseback, and when ten, there was not a man in that country who could contend with him in battle. In wrestling, and other violent exercises, he was unequalled. Firdausí has thus, with a view of making him great, made him a prodigy. But Homer is not guiltless of similar extravagance, for he says of the giants Otus and Ephialtes:

The wondrous youths had scarce nine winters told
When high in air, tremendous to behold,
Nine ells aloft they reared their towering head,
And full nine cubits broad their shoulders spread;
Proud of their strength, and more than mortal size,
The gods they challenge, and affect the skies.

ODYSSEY, xi. 310. POPE.

Both Sám and Mihráb, though far distant from the scene of felicity, were equally anxious to proceed to Zábulistán to behold their wonderful grandson. Both set off, but Mihráb arrived first with great pomp, and a whole army for his suite, and went forth with Zál to meet Sám, and give him an honourable welcome. The boy Rustem was mounted on an elephant, wearing a splendid crown, and wanted to join them, but his father kindly prevented him undergoing the inconvenience of alighting. Zál and Mihráb dismounted as soon as Sám was seen at a distance, and performed the ceremonies of an affectionate reception. Sám was indeed amazed when he did see the boy, and showered blessings on his head.

Afterwards Sám placed Mihráb on his right hand, and Zal on his left, and Rustem before him, and began to converse with his grandson, who thus manifested to him his martial disposition.

> "Thou art the champion of the world, and I
> The branch of that fair tree of which thou art
> The glorious root: to thee I am devoted,
> But ease and leisure have no charms for me;
> Nor music, nor the songs of festive joy.
> Mounted and armed, a helmet on my brow,
> A javelin in my grasp, I long to meet
> The foe, and cast his severed head before thee."

Then Sám made a royal feast, and every apartment in his palace was richly decorated, and resounded with mirth and rejoicing. Mihráb was the merriest, and drank the most, and in his cups saw nothing but himself, so vain had he become from the countenance he had received. He kept saying:—

> "Now I feel no alarm about Sám or Zál-zer,
> Nor the splendour and power of the great Minúchihr;
> Whilst aided by Rustem, his sword, and his mace,
> Not a cloud of misfortune can shadow my face.
> All the laws of Zohák I will quickly restore,
> And the world shall be fragrant and blest as before."

This exultation plainly betrayed the disposition of his race;

and though Sám smiled at the extravagance of Mihráb, he looked up towards Heaven, and prayed that Rustem might not prove a tyrant, but be continually active in doing good, and humble before God.

Upon Sám departing, on his return to Karugsar and Mázinderán, Zál went with Rustem to Sístán, a province dependent on his government, and settled him there. The white elephant, belonging to Minúchihr, was kept at Sístán. One night Rustem was awakened out of his sleep by a great noise, and cries of distress, when starting up and inquiring the cause, he was told that the white elephant had got loose, and was trampling and crushing the people to death. In a moment he issued from his apartment, brandishing his mace; but was soon stopped by the servants, who were anxious to expostulate with him against venturing out in the darkness of night to encounter a ferocious elephant. Impatient at being thus interrupted he knocked down one of the watchmen, who fell dead at his feet, and the others running away, he broke the lock of the gate, and escaped. He immediately opposed himself to the enormous animal, which looked like a mountain, and kept roaring like the river Níl. Regarding him with a cautious and steady eye, he gave a loud shout, and fearlessly struck him a blow, with such strength and vigour, that the iron mace was bent almost double. The elephant trembled, and soon fell exhausted and lifeless in the dust. When it was communicated to Zál that Rustem had killed the animal with one blow, he was amazed, and fervently returned thanks to heaven. He called him to him, and kissed him, and said: "My darling boy, thou art indeed unequalled in valour and magnanimity."

Then it occurred to Zál that Rustem, after such an achievement, would be a proper person to take vengeance on the enemies of his grandfather Nárímán, who was sent by Feridún with a large army against an enchanted fort situated upon the mountain Sipund, and who whilst endeavouring to effect his object, was killed by a piece of rock thrown down from above by the besieged. The fort,* which was many miles high, inclosed beautiful lawns of the freshest verdure, and delightful gardens abounding with fruit and flowers; it was also full of treasure. Sám, on hearing of the fate of his father, was deeply afflicted, and in a short time proceeded against the fort himself; but he was surrounded by a trackless desert. He knew not what course to pursue; not a being was ever seen to enter or come out of the gates, and, after spending months and years in fruitless endeavours, he was compelled to retire from the appalling enterprize in despair. "Now," said Zál to Rustem, "the time is come, and the remedy is at hand; thou art yet unknown, and may easily accomplish our purpose." Rustem agreed to the proposed adventure, and according to his father's advice, assumed the dress and character of a salt-merchant, prepared a caravan of camels, and secreted arms for himself and companions among the loads of salt. Every thing being ready they set off, and it was not long before they reached the fort on the mountain Sipund. Salt being a precious article, and much wanted, as soon as the garrison knew that it was for sale, the gates were opened; and then was Rustem seen, together with his warriors, surrounded by men, women, and children, anxiously making their purchases, some giving clothes in exchange, some gold, and some silver, without fear or suspicion.

But when the night came on, and it was dark,
Rustem impatient drew his warriors forth,
And moved towards the mansion of the chief—
But not unheard. The unaccustomed noise,
Announcing warlike menace and attack,
Awoke the Kotwál, who sprung up to meet
The peril threatened by the invading foe.
Rustem meanwhile uplifts his ponderous mace,
And cleaves his head, and scatters on the ground

---

* The fort called Killah Suffeed, lies about seventy-six miles north-west of the city of Shiraz. It is of an oblong form, and encloses a level space at the top of the mountain, which is covered with delightful verdure, and watered by numerous springs. The ascent is near three miles, and for the last five or six hundred yards, the summit is so difficult of approach, that the slightest opposition, if well directed, must render it impregnable.

The reeking brains. And now the garrison
Are on the alert, all hastening to the spot
Where battle rages; midst the deepened gloom
Flash sparkling swords, which shew the crimson earth
Bright as the ruby.

Rustem continued fighting with the people of the fort all night, and, just as morning dawned, he discovered the chief and slew him. Those who survived, then escaped, and not one of the inhabitants remained within the walls alive. Rustem's next object was to enter the governor's mansion. It was built of stone, and the gate, which was made of iron, he burst open with his battle-axe, and advancing onward, he discovered a temple, constructed with infinite skill and science, beyond the power of mortal man, and which contained amazing wealth, in jewels and gold. All the warriors gathered for themselves as much treasure as they could carry away, and more than imagination can conceive; and Rustem wrote to Zál to know his further commands on the subject of the capture. Zál, overjoyed at the result of the enterprise, replied:

Thou hast illumed the soul of Náríman,
Now in the blissful bowers of Paradise,
By punishing his foes with fire and sword.

He then recommended him to load all the camels with as much of the invaluable property as could be removed, and bring it away, and then burn and destroy the whole place, leaving not a single vestige; and the command having been strictly complied with, Rustem retraced his steps to Zábulistán.

On his return Zál pressed him to his heart,
And paid him public honours. The fond mother
Kissed and embraced her darling son, and all
Uniting, showered their blessings on his head.

DEATH OF MINÚCHIHR.

To Minúchihr we now must turn again,
And mark the close of his illustrious reign.

The king had flourished one hundred and twenty years, when now the astrologers ascertained that the period of his departure from this life was at hand.

They told him of that day of bitterness,
Which would obscure the splendour of his throne;
And said—"The time approaches, thou must go,
Doubtless to Heaven. Think what thou hast to do;
And be it done before the damp cold earth
Inshrine thy body. Let not sudden death
O'ertake thee, ere thou art prepared to die!"
Warned by the wise, he called his courtiers round him,
And thus he counselled Nauder:—"O, my son!
Fix not thy heart upon a regal crown,
For this vain world is fleeting as the wind;
The pain and sorrows of twice sixty years
Have I endured, though happiness and joy
Have also been my portion. I have fought
In many a battle, vanquished many a foe;
By Ferídún's commands I girt my loins,
And his advice has ever been my guide.
I hurled just vengeance on the tyrant-brothers
Selim and Túr, who slew the gentle Irij;
And cities have I built, and made the tree
Which yielded poison, teem with wholesome fruit.
And now to thee the kingdom I resign,
That kingdom which belonged to Ferídún,
And thou wilt be the sovereign of the world!
But turn not from the worship of thy God,
That sacred worship Moses taught, the best
Of all the prophets; turn not from the path
Of purest holiness, thy father's choice.
"My son, events of peril are before thee;
Thy enemy will come in fierce array,
From the wild mountains of Túrán, the son
Of Poshang, the invader. In that hour
Of danger, seek the aid of Sám and Zál,
And that young branch just blossoming; Túrán
Will then have no safe buckler of defence,
None to protect it from their conquering arms."
Thus spoke the sire prophetic to his son,
And both were moved to tears. Again the king

Resumed his warning voice: "Nauder, I charge thee
Place not thy trust upon a world like this,*
Where nothing fixed remains. The caravan
Goes to another city, one to-day,
The next, to-morrow, each observes its turn
And time appointed—mine has come at last,
And I must travel on the destined road."

At the period Minúchihr uttered this exhortation, he was entirely free from indisposition, but he shortly afterwards closed his eyes in death.

NAUDER.

Upon the demise of Minúchihr, Nauder ascended the throne, and commenced his reign in the most promising manner; but before two months had passed, he neglected the counsels of his father, and betrayed the despotic character of his heart. To such an extreme did he carry his oppression, that to escape

---

* The Persian poets, and particularly Firdausí, are eminently distinguished for their apposite and striking reflections on fate and on the instability of worldly grandeur. The portion of the Sháh Námeh which contains the history of Jemshíd, abounds in beautiful and philosophical observations, conveyed in all the enchanting sweetness of harmonious versification. The declension of Jemshíd's glory, occasioned by his impious ambition to rival the Deity, and his subsequent wanderings, afforded a rich subject for our poet's peculiar vein. Sádi is also peculiarly successful in the same moral spirit. "When the pure and spotless soul is about to depart, of what importance is it whether we expire upon a throne or upon the bare ground!"

Thus Horace:

Pallida mors æquo pulsat pede pauperum tabernas,
Regumque turres. I. Od. iv. 13,

And Young:

What though we wade in wealth or soar in fame!
Earth's highest station ends in *here he lies!*
And *dust to dust* concludes her noblest song.

from his violence, the people were induced to solicit other princes to come and take possession of the empire. The courtiers laboured under the greatest embarrassment, their monarch being solely occupied in extorting money from his subjects, and amassing wealth for his own coffers. Nauder was not long in perceiving the dissatisfaction that universally prevailed, and, anticipating, not only an immediate revolt, but an invading army, solicited, according to his father's advice, the assistance of Sám, then at Mázinderán. The complaints of the people, however, reached Sám before the arrival of the messenger, and when he received the letter, he was greatly distressed on account of the extreme severity exercised by the new king. The champion, in consequence, proceeded forthwith from Mázinderán to Persia, and when he entered the capital, he was joyously welcomed, and at once entreated by the people to take the sovereignty upon himself. It was said of Nauder:

The gloom of tyranny has hid
  The light his father's counsel gave;
The hope of life is lost amid
  The desolation of the grave.

The world is withering in his thrall,
  Exhausted by his iron sway;
Do thou ascend the throne, and all
  Will cheerfully thy will obey.

But Sám said, "No; I should then be ungrateful to Minúchihr, a traitor, and deservedly offensive in the eyes of God. Nauder is the king, and I am bound to do him service, although he has deplorably departed from the advice of his father." He then soothed the alarm and irritation of the chiefs, and engaging to be a mediator upon the unhappy occasion, brought them to a more pacific tone of thinking. After this he immediately repaired to Nauder, who received him with great favour and kindness. "O king," said he, "only keep Feridún in remembrance, and govern the empire in such a manner that thy name may be honoured by thy subjects; for, be well assured, that he who has a just estimate of the world, will never look upon it as his place of rest. It is but an inn, where all travellers meet on their way to eternity, but must not remain. The wise consider those who fix their affections on this life, as utterly devoid of reason and reflection :

> Pleasure, and pomp, and wealth may be obtained—
> And every want luxuriously supplied :
> But suddenly, without a moment's warning,
> Death comes, and hurls the monarch from his throne,
> His crown and sceptre scattering in the dust.
> He who is satisfied with earthly joys,
> Can never know the blessedness of Heaven ;
> His soul must still be dark. Why do the good
> Suffer in this world, but to be prepared
> For future rest and happiness ? The name
> Of Feridún is honoured among men,
> Whilst curses load the memory of Zohák."

This intercession of Sám produced an entire change in the government of Nauder, who promised, in future, to rule his people according to the principles of Húsheng, and Feridún, and Minúchihr. The chiefs and captains of the army were, in consequence, contented, and the kingdom reunited itself under his sway.

In the mean time, however, the news of the death of Minúchihr, together with Nauder's injustice and severity, and the disaffection of his people, had reached Túrán, of which country Poshang, a descendant from Túr, was then the sovereign. Poshang, who had been unable to make a single successful hostile movement during the life of Minúchihr, at once conceived this to be a fit opportunity of taking revenge for the blood of Selim and Túr, and every appearance seeming to be in his favour, he called before him his heroic son Afrásiyáb, and explained to him his purpose and views. It was not difficult to inspire the youthful mind of Afrásiyáb with the sentiments he himself cherished, and a large army was immediately collected to take the field against Nauder. Poshang was proud of the chivalrous spirit and promptitude displayed by his son, who is said to have been as strong as a lion, or an elephant, and whose shadow extended miles. His tongue was like a bright sword, and his heart as bounteous as the ocean, and his hands like the clouds when rain falls to gladden the thirsty earth. Aghríras, the brother of Afrásiyáb, however, was not so precipitate. He cautioned his father to be prudent, for though Persia could no longer boast of the presence of Minúchihr, still the great warrior Sám, and Kárun, and Garsbásp, were living, and Poshang had only to look at the result of the wars in which Selim and Túr were involved, to be convinced that the existing conjuncture required mature deliberation. "It would be better," said he, "not to begin the contest at all, than to bring ruin and desolation on our own country." Poshang, on the contrary, thought the time peculiarly fit and inviting, and contended that, as Minúchihr took vengeance for the blood of his grandfather, so ought Afrásiyáb to take vengeance for his. "The grandson," he said, "who refuses to do this act of justice, is unworthy of his family. There is nothing to apprehend from the efforts of Nauder, who is an inexperienced youth, nor from the valour of his warriors. Afrásiyáb is brave and powerful in war, and thou must accompany him and share the glory." After this no further observation was offered, and the martial preparations were completed.

AFRÁSIYÁB MARCHES AGAINST NAUDER.

The brazen drums on the elephants were sounded as the signal of departure, and the army proceeded rapidly to its destination, overshadowing the earth in its progress. Afrásiyáb had penetrated as far as the Jihún before Nauder was aware of his approach. Upon receiving this intelligence of the activity of the enemy, the warriors of the Persian army immediately moved in that direction, and on their arrival at Dehstán, prepared for battle.

Afrásiyáb despatched thirty thousand of his troops under the command of Shimasas and Khazerván to Zábulistán, to act against Zál, having heard on his march of the death of the illustrious Sám, and advanced himself upon Dehstán with four hundred thousand soldiers, covering the ground like swarms of ants and locusts. He soon discovered that Nauder's forces did not exceed one hundred and forty thousand men, and wrote to Poshang, his father, in high spirits, especially on account of not having to contend against Sám, the warrior, and informed him that he had detached Shimasas against Zábulistán. When the armies had approached to within two leagues of each other, Bármán, one of the Túránian chiefs, offered to challenge any one of the enemy to single combat: but Aghríras objected to it, not wishing that so valuable a hero should run the hazard of discomfiture. At this Afrásiyáb was very indignant, and directed Bármán to follow the bent of his own inclinations.

> "'Tis not for us to shrink from Persian foe,
> Put on thy armour, and prepare thy bow."

Accordingly the challenge was given. Kárun looked round, and the only person who answered the call was the aged Kobád, his brother. Kárun and Kobád were both sons of Kávah, the blacksmith, and both leaders in the Persian army. No persuasion could restrain Kobád from the unequal conflict. He resisted all the entreaties of Kárun, who said to him,—

> "O, should thy hoary locks be stained with blood,
> Thy legions will be overwhelmed with grief,
> And, in despair, decline the coming battle."
> But what was the reply of brave Kobád?
> "Brother, this body, this frail tenement,
> Belongs to death. No living man has ever
> Gone up to Heaven—for all are doomed to die.—
> Some by the sword, the dagger, or the spear,
> And some, devoured by roaring beasts of prey;
> Some peacefully upon their beds, and others
> Snatched suddenly from life, endure the lot

Ordained by the Creator. If I perish,
Does not my brother live, my noble brother,
To bury me beneath a warrior's tomb,
And bless my memory?"

Saying this, he rushed forward, and the two warriors met in desperate conflict. The struggle lasted all day; at last Bármán threw a stone at his antagonist with such force, that Kobád in receiving the blow fell lifeless from his horse. When Kárun saw that his brother was slain, he brought forward his whole army to be revenged upon the enemy for the death of Kobád. Afrásiyáb himself advanced to the charge, and the encounter was dreadful. The soldiers who fell among the Túránians could not be numbered, but the Persians lost fifty thousand men.

Loud neighed the steeds, and their resounding hoofs,
Shook the deep caverns of the earth; the dust
Rose up in clouds and hid the azure heavens—
Bright beamed the swords, and in that carnage wide,
Blood flowed like water. Night alone divided
The hostile armies.

When the battle ceased Kárun fell back upon Dehstán, and communicated his misfortune to Nauder, who lamented the loss of Kobád, even more than that of Sám. In the morning Kárun again took the field against Afrásiyáb, and the conflict was again terrible. Nauder boldly opposed himself to the enemy, and singling out Afrásiyáb, the two heroes fought with great bravery till night again put an end to the engagement. The Persian army had suffered most, and Nauder retired to his tent disappointed, fatigued, and sorrowful. He then called to mind the words of Minúchihr, and called for his two sons, Tús and Gustahem. With melancholy forebodings he directed them to return to Irán, with his shubistan, or domestic establishment, and take refuge on the mountain Alberz, in the hope that some one of the race of Feridún might survive the general ruin which seemed to be approaching.

The armies rested two days. On the third the reverberating noise of drums and trumpets announced the recommencement of the battle. On the Persian side Shahpúr had been appointed in the room of Kobád, and Bármán and Shíwáz led the right and left of the Túránians under Afrásiyáb.

From dawn to sun-set, mountain, plain, and stream,
Were hid from view; the earth, beneath the tread
Of myriads, groaned; and when the javelins cast
Long shadows on the plain at even tide,
The Tartar host had won the victory;
And many a Persian chief fell on that day:—
Shahpúr himself was slain.

When Nauder and Kárun saw the unfortunate result of the battle, they again fell back upon Dehstán, and secured themselves in the fort. Afrásiyáb in the mean time dispatched Karúkhán' to Irán, through the desert, with a body of horsemen, for the purpose of intercepting and capturing the shubistan of Nauder. As soon as Kárun heard of this expedition he was all on fire, and proposed to pursue the squadron under Karúkhán, and frustrate at once the object which the enemy had in view; and though Nauder was unfavourable to this movement, Kárun, supported by several of the chiefs and a strong volunteer force, set off at midnight, without permission, on this important enterprize. It was not long before they reached the Duz-i-Supêd, or white fort, of which Gustahem was the governor, and falling in with Bármán, who was also pushing forward to Persia, Kárun, in revenge for his brother Kobád, sought him out, and dared him to single combat. He threw his javelin with such might, that his antagonist was driven furiously from his horse; and then, dismounting, he cut off his head, and hung it at his saddle-bow. After this he attacked and defeated the Tartar troops, and continued his march towards Irán.

Nauder having found that Kárun had departed, immediately followed, and Afrásiyáb was not long in pursuing him. The Túránians at length came up with Nauder, and attacked him with great vigour. The unfortunate king, unable to parry the onset, fell into the hands of his enemies, together with upwards of one thousand of his famous warriors.

> Long fought they, Nauder and the Tartar-chief,
> And the thick dust which rose from either host,
> Darkened the rolling Heavens. Afrásiyáb
> Seized by the girdle-belt the Persian king,
> And furious, dragged him from his foaming horse.
> With him a thousand warriors, high in name,
> Were taken on the field; and every legion,
> Captured whilst flying from the victor's brand.
> Such are the freaks of Fortune: friend and foe
> Alternate wear the crown. The world itself
> Is an ingenious juggler—every moment
> Playing some novel trick; exalting one
> In pomp and splendour, crushing down another,
> As if in sport,—and death the end of all!

After the achievement of this victory Afrásiyáb directed that Kárun should be pursued and attacked wherever he might be found; but when he heard that he had hurried on for the protection of the shubistan, and had conquered and slain Bármán, he gnawed his hands with rage. The reign of Nauder lasted only seven years. After him Afrásiyáb was the master of Persia.

AFRÁSIYÁB.

It has already been said that Shimasás and Khazerván were sent by Afrásiyáb with thirty thousand men against Kábul and Zábul, and when Zál heard of this movement he forthwith united with Mihráb the chief of Kábul, and having first collected a large army in Sístán, had a conflict with the two Tartar generals.

Zál promptly donned himself in war attire,
And, mounted like a hero, to the field
Hastened, his soldiers frowning on their steeds.
Now Khazerván grasps his huge battle-axe,
And, his broad shield extending, at one blow
Shivers the mail of Zál, who calls aloud
As, like a lion, to the fight he springs,
Armed with his father's mace. Sternly he looks
And with the fury of a dragon, drives
The weapon through his adversary's head,
Staining the ground with streaks of blood, resembling
The waving stripes upon a tiger's back.

At this time Rustem was confined at home with the small pox. Upon the death of Khazerván, Shimasás thirsted to be revenged; but when Zál meeting him raised his mace, and began to close, the chief became alarmed and turned back, and all his squadrons followed his example.

Fled Shimasás, and all his fighting train,
Like herds by tempests scattered o'er the plain.

Zál set off in pursuit, and slew a great number of the enemy; but when Afrásiyáb was made acquainted with this defeat, he immediately released Nauder from his fetters, and in his rage instantly deprived him of life.

He struck him and so deadly was the blow,
Breath left the body in a moment's space.

After this, Afrásiyáb turned his views towards Tús and Gustahem in the hope of getting them into his hands; but as soon as they received intimation of his object, the two brothers retired from Irán, and went to Sístán to live under the protection of Zál. The champion received them with due respect and honour. Kárum also went, with all the warriors and people who had been supported by Nauder, and co-operated with Zál, who encouraged them with the hopes of future success. Zál, however, considered that both Tús and Gustahem were still of a tender age—that a monarch of extraordinary wisdom and energy was required to oppose Afrásiyáb—that he himself was not of the blood of the Kaís, nor fit for the duties of sovereignty, and, therefore, he turned his thoughts towards Aghríras, the younger brother of Afrásiyáb, distinguished as he was for his valour, prudence, and humanity, and to whom Poshang, his father, had given the government of Raí. To him Zál sent an envoy, saying, that if he would proceed to Sístán, he should be supplied with ample resources to place him on the throne of Persia; that by the co-operation of Zál and all his warriors the conquest would be easy, and that there would be no difficulty in destroying the power of Afrásiyáb. Aghríras accepted the offer, and immediately proceeded from his kingdom of Raí towards Sístán. On his arrival at Bábel, Afrásiyáb heard of his ambitious plans, and lost no time in assembling his army and marching to arrest the progress of his brother. Aghríras, unable to sustain a battle, had recourse to negociation and a conference, in which Afrásiyáb said to him, "What rebellious conduct is this, of which thou art guilty? Is not the country of Raí sufficient for thee, that thou art thus aspiring to be a great king?" Aghríras replied: "Why reproach and insult me thus? Art thou not ashamed to accuse another of rebellious conduct?

> Shame might have held thy tongue; reprove not me
> In bitterness; God did not give thee power
> To injure man, and surely not thy kin."
> Afrásiyáb, enraged at this reproof,
> Replied by a foul deed—he grasped his sword,
> And with remorseless fury slew his brother!

When intelligence of this cruel catastrophe came to Zál's ears, he exclaimed: "Now indeed has the empire of Afrásiyáb arrived at its crisis:

> Yes, yes, the tyrant's throne is tottering now,
> And past is all his glory."

Then Zál bound his loins in hostility against Afrásiyáb, and gathering together all his warriors, resolved upon taking revenge for the death of Nauder, and expelling the tyrant from Persia. Neither Tús nor Gustahem being yet capable of sustaining the cares and duties of the throne, his anxiety was to obtain the assistance of some one of the race of Feridún.

These youths were for imperial rule unfit:
A king of royal lineage and worth
The state required, and none could he remember
Save Tahmasp's son, descended from the blood
Of Feridún.

ZAU.

At the time when Selim and Túr were killed, Tahmasp, the son of Selim, fled from the country and took refuge in an island, where he died, and left a son named Zau. Zál sent Kárun, the son of Kávah, attended by a proper escort, with overtures to Zau, who readily complied, and was under favourable circumstances seated upon the throne :

Speedily, in arms,
He led his troops to Persia, fought, and won
A kingdom, by his power and bravery—
And happy was the day when princely Zau
Was placed upon that throne of sovereignty;
All breathed their prayers upon his future reign,
And o'er his head (the customary rite)
Shower'd gold and jewels.

When he had subdued the country, he turned his arms against Afrásiyáb, who in consequence of losing the co-operation of the Persians, and not being in a state to encounter a superior force, thought it prudent to retreat, and return to his father. The reign of Zau lasted five years, after which he died, and was succeeded by his son Garshásp.

GARSHÁSP.

Garshásp, whilst in his minority, being unacquainted with the affairs of government, abided in all things by the judgment and counsels of Zál. When Afrásiyáb arrived at Túrán, his father was in great distress and anger on account of the inhuman murder of Aghriras; and so exceedingly did he grieve, that he would not endure his presence.

And when Afrásiyáb returned, his sire,
Poshang, in grief, refused to see his face.
To him the day of happiness and joy
Had been obscured by the dark clouds of night;
And thus he said: "Why didst thou, why didst *thou*
In power supreme, without pretence of guilt,
With thy own hand his precious life destroy?
Why hast thou shed thy innocent brother's blood?
In this life thou art nothing now to me;
Away, I must not see thy face again."

Afrásiyáb continued offensive and despicable in the mind of his father till he heard that Garshásp was unequal to rule over Persia, and then thinking he could turn the warlike spirit of Afrásiyáb to advantage, he forgave the crime of his son. He forthwith collected an immense army, and sent him again to effect the conquest of Irán, under the pretext of avenging the death of Selim and Túr.

Afrásiyáb a mighty army raised,
And passing plain and river, mountain high,
And desert wild, filled all the Persian realm
With consternation, universal dread.

The chief authorities of the country applied to Zál as their only remedy against the invasion of Afrásiyáb.

They said to Zál, "How easy is the task
For thee to grasp the world—then, since thou canst
Afford us succour, yield the blessing now;
For, lo! the King Afrásiyáb has come,
In all his power and overwhelming might."

Zál replied that he had on this occasion appointed Rustem to command the army, and to oppose the invasion of Afrásiyáb.

And thus the warrior Zál to Rustem spoke—
"Strong as an elephant thou art, my son,
Surpassing thy companions, and I now
Forewarn thee that a difficult emprize,
Hostile to ease or sleep, demands thy care.
Tis true, of battles thou canst nothing know,
But what am I to do? This is no time
For banquetting, and yet thy lips still breathe
The scent of milk, a proof of infancy;
Thy heart pants after gladness and the sweet
Endearments of domestic life; can I
Then send thee to the war to cope with heroes
Burning with wrath and vengeance?" Rustem said,—
"Mistake me not, I have no wish, not I,
For soft endearments, nor domestic life,
Nor home-felt joys. This chest, these nervous limbs,
Denote far other objects of pursuit,
Than a luxurious life of ease and pleasure."

Zál having taken great pains in the instruction of Rustem in warlike exercises, and the rules of battle, found infinite aptitude in the boy, and his activity and skill seemed to be superior to his own. He thanked God for the comfort it gave him, and was glad. Then Rustem asked his father for a suitable mace; and seeing the huge weapon which was borne by the great Sám, he took it up, and it answered his purpose exactly.

When the young hero saw the mace of Sám
He smiled with pleasure, and his heart rejoiced;
And paying homage to his father Zál,
The champion of the age, asked for a steed
Of corresponding power, that he might use
That famous club with added force and vigour.

Zál shewed him all the horses in his possession, and Rustem tried many, but found not one of sufficient strength to suit him. At last his eyes fell upon a mare followed by a foal of great promise, beauty, and strength.

Seeing that foal, whose bright and glossy skin
Was dappled o'er, like blossoms of the rose
Upon a saffron lawn, Rustem prepared
His noose, and held it ready in his hand.

The groom recommended him to secure the foal, as it was the offspring of Abresh, born of a Díw, or Demon, and called Rakush. The dam had killed several persons who attempted to seize her young one.

Now Rustem flings the noose, and suddenly
Rakush secures. Meanwhile the furious mare
Attacks him, eager with her pointed teeth
To crush his brain—but, stunned by his loud cry,
She stops in wonder. Then with clenched hand
He smites her on the head and neck, and down
She tumbles, struggling in the pangs of death.

Rakush, however, though with the noose round his neck, was not so easily subdued; but kept dragging and pulling Rustem, as if by a tether, and it was a considerable time before the animal could be reduced to subjection. At last, Rustem thanked Heaven that he had obtained the very horse he wanted.

"Now am I with my horse prepared to join
The field of warriors!" Thus the hero said,
And placed the saddle on his charger. Zál
Beheld him with delight,—his withered heart
Glowing with summer freshness. Open then
He threw his treasury,—thoughtless of the past
Or future—present joy absorbing all
His faculties, and thrilling every nerve.

In a short time Zál sent Rustem with a prodigious army against Afrásiyáb, and two days afterwards set off himself and joined his son. Afrásiyáb said, "The son is but a boy, and the father is old; I shall have no difficulty in recovering the empire of Persia." These observations having reached Zál, he pondered deeply, considering that Garshásp would not be able to contend against Afrásiyáb, and that no other prince of the race of Ferídún was known to be in existence. However, he dispatched people in every quarter to gather information on the subject, and at length Kai-kobád was understood to be residing in obscurity on the mountain Alberz, distinguished for his wisdom and valour, and his qualifications for the exercise of sovereign power. Zál therefore recommended Rustem to proceed to Alberz, and bring him from his concealment.

> Thus Zál to Rustem spoke, "Go forth, my son,
> And speedily perform this pressing duty,
> To linger would be dangerous. Say to him,
> 'The army is prepared—the throne is ready,
> And thou alone, of the Kaiánian race,
> Deemed fit for sovereign rule.'"

Rustem accordingly mounted Rakush, and accompanied by a powerful force, pursued his way towards the mountain Alberz; and though the road was infested by the troops of Afrásiyáb, he valiantly overcame every difficulty that was opposed to his progress. On reaching the vicinity of Alberz, he observed a beautiful spot of ground studded with luxuriant trees, and watered by glittering rills. There too, sitting upon a throne, placed in the shade on the flowery margin of a stream, he saw a young man, surrounded by a company of friends and attendants, and engaged at a gorgeous entertainment. Rustem, when he came near, was hospitably invited to partake of the feast: but this he declined, saying, that he was on an important mission to Alberz, which forbade the enjoyment of any pleasure till his task was accomplished; in short, that he was in search of Kai-kobád: but upon being told that he would there receive intelligence of him, he alighted and approached the bank of the stream where the company was assembled. The young man who was seated upon the golden throne took hold of the hand of Rustem, and filling up a goblet with wine, gave another to his guest, and asked him at whose command or suggestion he was in search of Kai-kobád. Rustem replied, that he was sent by his father Zál, and frankly communicated to him the special object they had in view. The young man, delighted with the information, immediately discovered himself, acknowledged that he was Kai-kobád, and then Rustem respectfully hailed him as the sovereign of Persia.

> The banquet was resumed again—
> And, hark, the softly warbled strain,

As harp and flute, in union sweet,
The voices of the singers meet.
The black-eyed damsels now display
Their art in many an amorous lay;
And now the song is loud and clear,
And speaks of Rustem's welcome here.
"This is a day, a glorious day,
That drives ungenial thoughts away;
This is a day to make us glad,
Since Rustem comes for Kai-kobád;
O, let us pass our time in glee,
And talk of Jemshíd's majesty,
The pomp and glory of his reign,
And still the sparkling goblet drain.—
Come, Sakí, fill the wine-cup high,
And let not even its brim be dry;
For wine alone has power to part
The rust of sorrow from the heart.
Drink to the king, in merry mood,
Since fortune smiles, and wine is good;
Quaffing red wine is better far
Than shedding blood in strife, or war;
Man is but dust, and why should he
Become a fire of enmity?
Drink deep, all other cares resign,
For what can vie with ruby wine?"

In this manner ran the song of the revellers. After which, and being rather merry with wine, Kai-kobád told Rustem of the dream that had induced him to descend from his place of refuge on Alberz, and to prepare a banquet on the occasion. He dreamt the night before that two white falcons from Persia placed a splendid crown upon his head, and this vision was interpreted by Rustem as symbolical of his father and himself, who at that moment were engaged in investing him with kingly power. The hero then solicited the young sovereign to hasten his departure for Persia, and preparations were made without delay. They travelled night and day, and fell in with several detachments of the enemy, which were easily repulsed by the valour of Rustem. The fiercest attack proceeded from Kelún, one of Afrásiyáb's warriors, near the confines of Persia, who in the encounter used his spear with great dexterity and address.

But Rustem with his javelin soon transfixed
The Tartar knight—who in the eyes of all
Looked like a spitted chicken—down he sunk,
And all his soldiers fled in wild dismay.
Then Rustem turned aside, and found a spot
Where verdant meadows smiled, and streamlets flowed,
Inviting weary travellers to rest.
There they awhile remained—and when the sun
Went down, and night had darkened all the sky,
The champion joyfully pursued his way,
And brought the monarch to his father's house.
—Seven days they sat in council—on the eighth
Young Kai-kobád was crowned—and placed upon
The ivory throne in presence of his warriors,
Who all besought him to commence the war
Against the Tartar prince, Afrásiyáb.

KAI-KOBÁD.

Kai-kobád having been raised to the throne at a council of the warriors, and advised to oppose the progress of Afrásiyáb, immediately assembled his army. Mihráb, the ruler of Kábul, was appointed to one wing, and Gustahem to the other—the centre was given to Kárun and Kishwád, and Rustem was placed in front, Zál with Kai-kobád remaining in the rear. The glorious standard of Kávah streamed upon the breeze.

On the other side, Afrásiyáb prepared for battle, assisted by his heroes Akbás, Wísah, Shimasás, and Gersíwaz; and so great was the clamour and confusion which proceeded from both armies, that earth and sky seemed blended together.* The clattering of hoofs, the shrill roar of trumpets, the rattle of

* The numerical strength of the Persian and Túránian forces appears prodigious on all occasions, but nothing when compared with the army under Xerxes at Thermopylæ, which, with the numerous retinue of servants, eunuchs, and women that attended it, is said to have amounted to no less than 5,283,220 souls.

brazen drums, and the vivid glittering of spear and shield, produced indescribable tumult and splendour.

Kárun was the first in action, and he brought many a her to the ground. He singled out Shimasás; and after a desperate struggle, laid him breathless on the field.. Rustem, stimulated by these exploits, requested his father, Zál, to point out Afrásiyáb, that he might encounter him; but Zál endeavoured to dissuade him from so hopeless an effort, saying,

> "My son, be wise, and peril not thyself;
> Black is his banner, and his cuirass black—
> His limbs are cased in iron—on his head
> He wears an iron helm—and high before him
> Floats the black ensign; equal in his might
> To ten strong men, he never in one place
> Remains, but everywhere displays his power.
> The crocodile has in the rolling stream
> No safety; and a mountain, formed of steel,
> Even at the mention of Afrásiyáb,
> Melts into water. Then, beware of him."
> Rustem replied:—"Be not alarmed for me—
> My heart, my arm, my dagger, are my castle,
> And Heaven befriends me—let him but appear,
> Dragon or Demon, and the field is mine."

Then Rustem valiantly urged Rakush towards the Túránian army, and called out aloud. As soon as Afrásiyáb beheld him, he inquired who he could be, and he was told, "This is Rustem, the son of Zál. Seest thou not in his hand the battle-axe of Sám? The youth has come in search of renown." When the combatants closed, they struggled for some time together, and at length Rustem seized the girdle-belt of his antagonist, and threw him from his saddle. He wished to drag the captive as a trophy to Kai-kobád, that his first great victory might be remembered, but unfortunately the belt gave way, and Afrásiyáb fell on the ground. Immediately the fallen chief was surrounded and rescued by his own warriors, but not before Rustem had snatched off his crown, and carried it away with the broken girdle which was left in his hand. And now a general engagement took place. Rustem being reinforced by the advance of the king, with Zál and Mihráb at his side,—

Both armies seemed so closely waging war,
Thou wouldst have said,* that they were mixed together.
The earth shook with the tramping of the steeds,
Rattled the drums; loud clamours from the troops
Echoed around, and from the iron grasp
Of warriors, many a life was spent in air.
With his huge mace, cow-headed, Rustem dyed
The ground with crimson—and wherever seen,
Urging impatiently his fiery horse,
Heads severed fell like withered leaves in autumn.
If, brandishing his sword, he struck the head,
Horseman and steed were downward cleft in twain—
And if his side-long blow was on the loins,
The sword passed through, as easily as the blade
Slices a cucumber. The blood of heroes
Deluged the plain. On that tremendous day,
With sword and dagger, battle-axe and noose,†
He cut, and tore, and broke, and bound the brave,
Slaying and making captive. At one swoop
More than a thousand fell by his own hand.

Zál beheld his son with amazement and delight. The Túránians left the fire-worshippers in possession of the field, and retreated towards the Jihún with precipitation, not a sound of drum or trumpet denoting their track. After halting three days in a state of deep dejection and misery, they continued their retreat along the banks of the Jihún. The Persian army,

* This mode of expression, so frequent in Firdausí, and which makes the reader a spectator of the scene described, is constantly to be met with in Homer. Longinus has pointed out its peculiar force and beauty, and gives the following observations on the subject. "A very powerful dramatic efficacy arises from a change of persons, which frequently makes the hearer or reader imagine himself engaged in the midst of danger:

"Thou wouldst have thought, so furious was their fire!
No force could tame them, and no toil could tire." ILIAD, XV. 844.

"And where the discourse is addressed to an individual; as in this example also:

"*Thou* hadst not known with whom Tydides fought." ILIAD, V. 85.

† Herodotus speaks of a people confederated with the army of Xerxes, who employed the noose. "Their principal dependance in action is upon cords made of twisted leather, which they use in this manner: when they engage an enemy, they throw out these cords, having a noose at the extremity; if they entangle in them either horse or man, they without difficulty put them to death."—Beloe's transl. Polymnia, Sec. 85.

upon the flight of the enemy, fell back with their prisoners of war, and Rustem was received by the king with distinguished honour. When Afrásiyáb returned to his father, he communicated to him, with a heavy heart, the misfortunes of the battle, and the power that had been arrayed against him, dwelling with wonder and admiration on the stupendous valour of Rustem.

> Seeing my sable banner,
> He to the fight came like a crocodile,
> Thou wouldst have said his breath scorched up the plain;
> He seized my girdle with such mighty force
> As if he would have torn my joints asunder;
> And raised me from my saddle—that I seemed
> An insect in his grasp—but presently
> The golden girdle broke, and down I fell
> Ingloriously upon the dusty ground;
> But I was rescued by my warrior train!
> Thou knowest my valour, how my nerves are strung,
> And may conceive the wondrous strength, which thus
> Sunk me to nothing. Iron is his frame,
> And marvellous his power; peace, peace, alone
> Can save us and our country from destruction.

Poshang, considering the luckless state of affairs, and the loss of so many valiant warriors, thought it prudent to acquiesce in the wishes of Afrásiyáb, and sue for peace. To this end Wísah was intrusted with magnificent presents, and the overtures which in substance ran thus:—"Minúchihr was revenged upon Túr and Selim for the death of Irij. Afrásiyáb again has revenged their death upon Náuder, the son of Minúchihr, and now Rustem has conquered Afrásiyáb. But why should we any longer keep the world in confusion—Why should we not be satisfied with what Feridún, in his wisdom, decreed? Continue in the empire which he appropriated to Irij, and let the Jihún be the boundary between us, for are we not connected by blood, and of one family? Let our kingdoms be gladdened with the blessings of peace."

When these proposals of peace reached Kai-kobád, the following answer was returned:

"Well dost thou know that I was not the first
To wage this war. From Túr, thy ancestor,
The strife began. Bethink thee how he slew
The gentle Irij—his own brother;—how,
In these our days, thy son, Afrásiyáb,
Crossing the Jihún, with a numerous force
Invaded Persia—think how Nauder died!
Not in the field of battle, like a hero,
But murdered by thy son—who, ever cruel,
Afterwards stabbed his brother, young Aghríras,
So deeply mourned by thee. Yet do I thirst not
For vengeance, or for strife. I yield the realm
Beyond the Jihún—let that river be
The boundary between us; but thy son,
Afrásiyáb, must take his solemn oath
Never to cross that limit, or disturb
The Persian throne again; thus pledged, I grant
The peace solicited."

The messenger without delay conveyed this welcome intelligence to Poshang, and the Túránian army was in consequence immediately withdrawn within the prescribed line of division. Rustem, however, expostulated with the king against making peace at a time the most advantageous for war, and especially when he had just commenced his victorious career; but Kai-kobád thought differently, and considered nothing equal to justice and tranquillity. Peace was accordingly concluded, and upon Rustem and Zál he conferred the highest honours, and his other warriors engaged in the late conflict also experienced the effects of his bounty and gratitude in an eminent degree.

Kai-kobád then moved towards Persia, and establishing his throne at Istakhar,* he administered the affairs of his government with admirable benevolence and clemency, and with un-

* Istakhar, also called Persepolis, and Chehel-minar, or the Forty Pillars. This city was said to have been laid in ruins by Alexander after the conquest or Darius; that,

Thais led the way,
And like another Helen fired another Troy.
DRYDEN. ALEX. FEAST.

But this, for the credit of Alexander, does not appear to be the fact. M. Langlés has shown that the destruction of this renowned city was owing, long afterwards, to the fanatic Arabs.

ceasing solicitude for the welfare of his subjects. In his eyes every one had an equal claim to consideration and justice. The strong had no power to oppress the weak. After he had continued ten years at Istakhar, building towns and cities, and diffusing improvement and happiness over the land, he removed his throne into Irán. His reign lasted one hundred years, which were passed in the continual exercise of the most princely virtues, and the most munificent liberality. He had four sons: Kai-káús, Arish, Poshín, and Aramín; and when the period of his dissolution drew nigh, he solemnly enjoined the eldest, whom he appointed his successor, to pursue steadily the path of integrity and justice, and to be kind and merciful in the administration of the empire left to his charge.

KAI-KÁÚS.

When Kai-káús* ascended the throne of his father, the whole world was obedient to his will; but he soon began to deviate from the wise customs and rules which had been recommended as essential to his prosperity and happiness. He feasted and drank wine continually with his warriors and chiefs, so that in the midst of his luxurious enjoyments he looked

* Kai-káús, the second King of Persia of the dynasty called Kaianides. He succeeded Kai kobad, about six hundred years B.C. According to Firdausí he was a foolish tyrannical prince. He appointed Rustem captain-general of the armies, to which the lieutenant-generalship and the administration of the state was annexed, under the title of "the champion of the world." He also gave him a taj, or crown of gold, which kings only were accustomed to wear, and granted him the privilege of giving audience seated on a throne of gold.

It is said that Kai-káús applied himself much to the study of astronomy, and that he founded two great observatories, the one at Babel, and the other on the Tigris. Perhaps his reputed fondness for astronomical studies gave rise to the fable of his aerial excursion recorded further on.

upon himself as superior to every being upon the face of the earth, and thus astonished the people, high and low, by his extravagance and pride.

One day a Demon, disguised as a musician, waited upon the monarch, and playing sweetly on his harp, sung a song in praise of Mázinderán.

And thus he warbled to the king—
"Mázinderán is the bower of spring,
My native home; the balmy air
Diffuses health and fragrance there;
So tempered is the genial glow,
Nor heat nor cold we ever know;
Tulips and hyacinths abound
On every lawn; and all around
Blooms like a garden in its prime,
Fostered by that delicious clime.
The bulbul sits on every spray,
And pours his soft melodious lay;
Each rural spot its sweets discloses,
Each streamlet is the dew of roses;
And damsels, idols of the heart,
Sustain a more bewitching part.
And mark me, that untravelled man
Who never saw Mázinderán,
And all the charms its bowers possess,
Has never tasted happiness!"

No sooner had Kai-káús heard this description of the country of Mázinderán than he determined to lead an army thither, declaring to his warriors that the splendour and glory of his reign should exceed that of either Jemshíd, Zohák, or Kai-kobád. The warriors however were alarmed at this precipitate resolution, thinking it certain destruction to make war against the Demons; but they had not courage or confidence enough to disclose their real sentiments. They only ventured to suggest, that if his majesty reflected a little on the subject, he might not ultimately consider the enterprize so advisable as he had at first imagined. But this produced no impression, and they then deemed it expedient to despatch a messenger to Zál, to inform him of the wild notions which the Evil One had put into the head of Kai-káús to effect his ruin, imploring Zál to allow of no delay, otherwise the eminent services so lately performed by him and Rustem for the state would be rendered utterly useless and vain. Upon this summons, Zál immediately set off from Sístán to Irán; and having arrived at the royal court, and been received with customary respect and consideration, he endeavoured to dissuade the king from the contemplated expedition into Mázinderán.

"O, could I wash the darkness from thy mind,
And show thee all the perils that surround
This undertaking! Jemshíd, high in power,
Whose diadem was brilliant as the sun,
Who ruled the demons—never in his pride
Dreamt of the conquest of Mázinderán!
Remember Feridún, he overthrew
Zohák—destroyed the tyrant, but he never
Thought of the conquest of Mázinderán!
This strange ambition never fired the souls
Of by-gone monarchs—mighty Minúchihr,
Always victorious, boundless in his wealth,
Nor Zau, nor Nauder, nor even Kai-kobád,
With all their pomp, and all their grandeur, ever
Dreamt of the conquest of Mázinderán!
It is the place of demon-sorcerers,
And all enchanted. Swords are useless there,
Nor bribery nor wisdom can obtain
Possession of that charm-defended land.
Then throw not men and treasure to the winds;
Waste not the precious blood of warriors brave,
In trying to subdue Mázinderán!"

Kai-káús, however, was not to be diverted from his purpose; and with respect to what his predecessors had not done, he considered himself superior in might and influence to either Feridún, Jemshíd, Minúchihr, or Kai-kobád, who had never aspired to the conquest of Mázinderán. He further observed, that he had a bolder heart, a larger army, and a fuller treasury than any of them, and the whole world was under his sway

And what are all these Demon-charms,
That they excite such dread alarms?
What is a Demon-host to me,
Their magic spells and sorcery?
One effort, and the field is won;
Then why should I the battle shun?

Be thou and Rustem (whilst afar
I wage the soul-appalling war),
The guardians of the kingdom; Heaven
To me hath its protection given;
And, when I reach the Demon's fort,
Their severed heads shall be my sport!

When Zál became convinced of the unalterable resolution of Kai-káús, he ceased to oppose his views, and expressed his readiness to comply with whatever commands he might receive for the safety of the state.

May all thy actions prosper—mayst thou never
Have cause to recollect my warning voice,
With sorrow or repentance. Heaven protect thee!

Zál then took leave of the king and his warrior friends, and returned to Sístán, not without melancholy forebodings respecting the issue of the war against Mázinderán.

As soon as morning dawned, the army was put in motion. The charge of the empire, and the keys of the treasury and jewel-chamber were left in the hands of Mílad, with injunctions, however, not to draw a sword against any enemy that might spring up, without the consent and assistance of Zál and Rustem. When the army had arrived within the limits of Mázinderán, Kai-káús ordered Gíw to select two thousand of the bravest men, the boldest wielders of the battle-axe, and proceed rapidly towards the city. In his progress, according to the king's instructions, he burnt and destroyed every thing of value, mercilessly slaying man, woman, and child. For the king said:

Kill all before thee, whether young or old,
And turn their day to night; thus free the world
From the magician's art.

Proceeding in his career of desolation and ruin, Gíw came near to the city, and found it arrayed in all the splendour of heaven; every street was crowded with beautiful women, richly adorned, and young damsels with faces as bright as the moon. The treasure-chamber was full of gold and jewels, and the country abounded with cattle. Information of this discovery was immediately sent to Kai-káús, who was delighted to find that Mázinderán was truly a blessed region, the very garden of beauty, where the cheeks of the women seemed to be tinted with the hue of the pomegranate flower, by the gate-keeper of Paradise.

This invasion filled the heart of the king of Mázinderán with grief and alarm, and his first care was to call the gigantic White Demon to his aid. Meanwhile Kai-káús, full of the wildest anticipations of victory, was encamped on the plain near the city in splendid state, and preparing to commence the final overthrow of the enemy on the following day. In the night, however, a cloud came, and deep darkness like pitch overspread the earth, and tremendous hail-stones poured down upon the Persian host, throwing them into the greatest confusion. Thousands were destroyed, others fled, and were scattered abroad in the gloom. The morning dawned, but it brought no light to the eyes of Kai-káús; and amidst the horrors he experienced, his treasury was captured, and the soldiers of his army either killed or made prisoners of war. Then did he bitterly lament that he had not followed the wise counsel of Zál. Seven days he was involved in this dreadful affliction, and on the eighth day he heard the roar of the White Demon, saying:

"O king, thou art the willow-tree, all barren,
With neither fruit, nor flower. What could induce
The dream of conquering Mázinderán?
Hadst thou no friend to warn thee of thy folly?
Hadst thou not heard of the White Demon's power—
Of him, who from the gorgeous vault of Heaven
Can charm the stars? From this mad enterprize
Others have wisely shrunk—and what hast thou
Accomplished by a more ambitious course?
Thy soldiers have slain many, dire destruction
And spoil have been their purpose—thy wild will
Has promptly been obeyed; but thou art now
Without an army, not one man remains
To lift a sword, or stand in thy defence;
Not one to hear thy groans and thy despair."

There were selected from the army twelve thousand of the demon-warriors, to take charge of and hold in custody the Iránian captives, all the chiefs, as well as the soldiers, being secured with bonds, and only allowed food enough to keep them alive. Arzang, one of the demon-leaders, having got possession of the wealth, the crown and jewels, belonging to Kai-káús, was appointed to escort the captive king and his troops, all of whom were deprived of sight, to the city of Mázinderán, where they were delivered into the hands of the monarch of that country. The White Demon, after thus putting an end to hostilities, returned to his own abode.

Kai-káús, strictly guarded as he was, found an opportunity of sending an account of his blind and helpless condition to Zál, in which he lamented that he had not followed his advice, and urgently requested him, if he was not himself in confinement, to come to his assistance, and release him from captivity. When Zál heard the melancholy story, he gnawed the very skin of his body with vexation, and turning to Rustem, conferred with him in private.

"The sword must be unsheathed, since Kai-káús
Is bound a captive in the dragon's den,
And Rakush must be saddled for the field,
And thou must bear the weight of this emprize;
For I have lived two centuries, and old age
Unfits me for the heavy toils of war.
Should'st thou release the king, thy name will be
Exalted o'er the earth.—Then don thy mail,
And gain immortal honour."

Rustem replied that it was a long journey to Mázinderán, and that the king had been six months on the road. Upon this Zál observed that there were two roads—the most tedious one was that which Kai-káús had taken; but by the other, which was full of dangers and difficulty, and lions, and demons, and sorcery, he might reach Mázinderán in seven days, if he reached it at all.

On hearing these words Rustem assented, and chose the short road, observing:

"Although it is not wise, they say,
With willing feet to track the way
To hell; though only men who've lost,
All love of life, by misery crossed,
Would rush into the tiger's lair,
And die, poor reckless victims, there;
I gird my loins, whate'er may be,
And trust in God for victory."

On the following day, resigning himself to the protection of Heaven, he put on his war attire, and with his favourite horse, Rakush, properly caparisoned, stood prepared for the journey. His mother, Rúdábeh, took leave of him with great sorrow; and the young hero departed from Sístán, consoling himself and his friends, thus:

"O'er him who seeks the battle-field,
Nobly his prisoned king to free,
Heaven will extend its saving shield,
And crown his arms with victory."

The HEFT-KHAN; or, SEVEN LABOURS of RUSTEM.

First Stage.—He rapidly pursued his way, performing two days' journey in one, and soon came to a forest full of wild asses. Oppressed with hunger, he succeeded in securing one of them, which he roasted over a fire, lighted by sparks produced by striking the point of his spear, and kept in a blaze with dried grass and branches of trees. After regaling himself, and satisfying his hunger, he loosened the bridle of Rakush, and allowed him to graze; and choosing a safe place for repose during the night, and taking care to have his sword under his head, he went to sleep among the reeds of that wilderness. In a short space a fierce lion appeared, and attacked Rakush with great violence; but Rakush very speedily with his teeth and heels put an end to his furious assailant. Rustem, awakened by the confusion, and seeing the dead lion before him, said to his favourite companion:—

"Ah! Rakush,* why so thoughtless grown,
To fight a lion thus alone;
For had it been thy fate to bleed,
And not thy foe, my gallant steed!
How could thy master have conveyed
His helm, and battle-axe, and blade,
Kamund, and bow, and buberyán,
Unaided, to Mázinderán?
Why didst thou fail to give the alarm,
And save thyself from chance of harm,
By neighing loudly in my ear;
But though thy bold heart knows no fear,
From such unwise exploits refrain,
Nor try a lion's strength again."

Saying this, Rustem laid down to sleep, and did not awake till the morning dawned. As the sun rose, he remounted Rakush, and proceeded on his journey towards Mázinderán.

* Though Rakush was a model of intelligence and sagacity, he could not speak, like Xanthus and Balius, the two horses of Achilles! The former, prophesied the doom of his master. There is nothing therefore extravagant in Rustem addressing his horse so familiarly.

"We may be assured, says Cowper, that it was customary for the Greeks occasionally to harangue their horses, for Homer was a poet too attentive to nature, to introduce speeches that would have appeared strange to his countrymen. Hector addresses his horses in the eighth book, and Antilochus, in the chariot race, whose horses were not only of terrestrial origin, but the slowest in the camp of Greece. That Achilles, then, should have spoken to his steeds, is not surprising, seeing that they were of celestial seed."

Aristotle and Pliny, write that these animals often deplore their masters lost in battle, and have shed tears for them—and Ælian relates the same of elephants, who, like the Swiss, overcome with the *maladie du pays*, weep in far-off captivity to think of their native forests. Suetonius, in the life of Cæsar, tells us that several horses which, at the passage of the Rubicon, had been consecrated to Mars, and turned loose on the banks, were observed some days after to abstain from feeding, and to weep abundantly. Virgil knew all this, and could not, therefore, forbear copying this beautiful circumstance in those fine lines on the horse of Pallas:

Post Bellator equus, positis insignibus, Æthon
It lacrymans, guttisque humectat grandibus ora.—ÆNEID, xi. 89.

SECOND STAGE.—After travelling rapidly for some time, he entered a desert, in which no water was to be found, and the sand was so burning hot, that it seemed to be instinct with fire. Both horse and rider were oppressed with the most maddening thirst. Rustem alighted, and vainly wandered about in search of relief, till almost exhausted, he put up a prayer to Heaven for protection against the evils which surrounded him, engaged as he was in an enterprize for the release of Kai-káús and the Persian army, then in the power of the demons. With pious earnestness he besought the Almighty to bless him in the great work; and whilst in a despairing mood he was lamenting his deplorable condition, his tongue and throat being parched with thirst, his body prostrate on the sand, under the influence of a raging sun, he saw a sheep pass by, which he hailed as the harbinger of good. Rising up and grasping his sword in his hand, he followed the animal, and came to a fountain of water, where he devoutly returned thanks to God for the blessing which had preserved his existence, and prevented the wolves from feeding on his lifeless limbs. Refreshed by the cool water, he then looked out for something to allay his hunger, and killing a gor, he lighted a fire and roasted it, and regaled upon its savoury flesh, which he eagerly tore from the bones.

When the period of rest arrived, Rustem addressed Rakush, and said to him angrily :—

> " Beware, my steed, of future strife.
> Again thou must not risk thy life;
> Encounter not with lion fell,
> Nor demon still more terrible;
> But should an enemy appear,
> Ring loud the warning in my ear.'

After delivering these injunctions, Rustem laid down to sleep, leaving Rakush unbridled, and at liberty to crop the herbage close by.

THIRD STAGE.—At midnight a monstrous dragon-serpent issued from the forest; it was eighty yards in length, and so fierce, that neither elephant, nor demon, nor lion, ever ventured to pass by its lair. It came forth, and seeing the champion asleep, and a horse near him, the latter was the first object of attack. But Rakush retired towards his master, and neighed and beat the ground so furiously, that Rustem soon awoke; looking round on every side, however, he saw nothing—the dragon had vanished, and he went to sleep again. Again the dragon burst out of the thick darkness, and again Rakush was at the pillow of his master, who rose up at the alarm: but anxiously trying to penetrate the dreary gloom, he saw nothing—all was a blank; and annoyed at this apparently vexatious conduct in his horse, he spoke sharply:—

"Why thus again disturb my rest,
When sleep had softly soothed my breast?
I told thee, if thou chanced to see
Another dangerous enemy,
To sound the alarm; but not to keep
Depriving me of needful sleep;
When nothing meets the eye nor ear,
Nothing to cause a moment's fear!
But if again my rest is broke,
On thee shall fall the fatal stroke,
And I myself will drag this load
Of ponderous arms along the road;
Yes, I will go, a lonely man,
Without thee, to Mázinderán."

Rustem again went to sleep, and Rakush was resolved this time not to move a step from his side, for his heart was grieved and afflicted by the harsh words that had been addressed to him. The dragon again appeared, and the faithful horse almost tore up the earth with his heels, to rouse his sleeping master. Rustem again awoke, and sprang to his feet, and was again angry; but fortunately at that moment sufficient light was providentially given for him to see the prodigious cause of alarm.

Then swift he drew his sword, and closed in strife
With that huge monster.—Dreadful was the shock
And perilous to Rustem; but when Rakush
Perceived the contest doubtful, furiously,

With his keen teeth, he bit and tore away
The dragon's scaly hide; whilst quick as thought
The Champion severed off the ghastly head,
And deluged all the plain with horrid blood.
Amazed to see a form so hideous
Breathless stretched out before him, he returned
Thanks to the Omnipotent for his success,
Saying—"Upheld by thy protecting arm,
What is a lion's strength, a demon's rage,
Or all the horrors of the burning desert,
With not one drop to quench devouring thirst?
Nothing, since power and might proceed from Thee.

Fourth Stage.—Rustem having resumed the saddle, continued his journey through an enchanted territory, and in the evening came to a beautifully green spot, refreshed by flowing rivulets, where he found, to his surprise, a ready-roasted deer, and some bread and salt. He alighted, and sat down near the enchanted provisions, which vanished at the sound of his voice, and presently a tambourine met his eyes, and a flask of wine. Taking up the instrument he played upon it, and chaunted a ditty about his own wanderings, and the exploits which he most loved. He said that he had no pleasure in banquets, but only in the field fighting with heroes and crocodiles in war. The song happened to reach the ears of a sorceress, who, arrayed in all the charms of beauty, suddenly approached him, and sat down by his side. The champion put up a prayer of gratitude for having been supplied with food and wine, and music, in the desert of Mázinderán, and not knowing that the enchantress was a demon in disguise, he placed in her hands a cup of wine in the name of God; but at the mention of the Creator, the enchanted form was converted into a black fiend. Seeing this, Rustem threw his kamund, and secured the demon; and, drawing his sword, at once cut the body in two!

Fifth Stage.

From thence proceeding onward, he approached
A region destitute of light, a void
Of utter darkness. Neither moon nor star

Peep'd through the gloom; no choice of path remained.
And therefore, throwing loose the rein, he gave
Rakush the power to travel on, unguided.
At length the darkness was dispersed, the earth
Became a scene, joyous and light, and gay,
Covered with waving corn—there Rustem paused
And quitting his good steed among the grass,
Laid himself gently down, and, wearied, slept;
His shield beneath his head, his sword before him.

When the keeper of the forest first saw the stranger and his horse, he went to Rustem, then asleep, and struck his staff violently on the ground, and having thus awakened the hero, he asked him, devil that he was, why he had allowed his horse to feed upon the green corn-field. Angry at these words, Rustem, without uttering a syllable, seized hold of the keeper by the ears, and wrung them off. The mutilated wretch, gathering up his severed ears, hurried away, covered with blood, to his master, Aúlád, and told him of the injury he had sustained from a man like a black demon, with a tiger-skin cuirass and an iron helmet; showing at the same time the bleeding witnesses of his sufferings. Upon being informed of this outrageous proceeding, Aúlád, burning with wrath, summoned together his fighting men, and hastened by the directions of the keeper to the place where Rustem had been found asleep. The champion received the angry lord of the land, fully prepared, on horseback, and heard him demand his name, that he might not slay a worthless antagonist, and why he had torn off the ears of his forest-keeper! Rustem replied that the very sound of his name would make him shudder with horror Aúlád then ordered his troops to attack Rustem, and they rushed upon him with great fury; but their leader was presently killed by the master-hand, and great numbers were also scattered lifeless over the plain. The survivors running away, Rustem's next object was to follow and secure, by his kamund, the person of Aúlád, and with admirable address and ingenuity, he succeeded in dismounting him and taking him alive. He then bound his hands, and said to him:—

"If thou wilt speak the truth unmixed with lies,
Unmixed with false prevaricating words,
And faithfully point out to me the caves
Of the White Demon and his warrior chiefs—
And where Káús is prisoned—thy reward
Shall be the kingdom of Mázinderán;
For I, myself, will place thee on that throne.
But if thou play'st me false—thy worthless blood
Shall answer for the foul deception."
"Stay,
Be not in wrath," Aúlád at once replied,—
"Thy wish shall be fulfilled—and thou shalt know
Where king Káús is prisoned—and, beside,
Where the White Demon reigns. Between two dark
And lofty mountains, in two hundred caves
Immeasurably deep, his people dwell.
Twelve hundred Demons keep the watch by night
Upon the mountain's brow;—their chiefs, Púlád,
And Baid, and Sinja. Like a reed, the hills
Tremble whenever the White Demon moves.
But dangerous is the way. A stony desert
Lies full before thee, which the nimble deer
Has never passed. Then a prodigious stream
Two farsangs wide obstructs thy path, whose banks
Are covered with a host of warrior-Demons,
Guarding the passage to Mázinderán;
And thou art but a single man—canst thou
O'ercome such fearful obstacles as these?
At this the Champion smiled. "Shew but the way,
And thou shalt see what one man can perform,
With power derived from God! Lead on, with speed,
To royal Káús." With obedient haste
Aúlád proceeded, Rustem following fast,
Mounted on Rakush. Neither dismal night
Nor joyous day they rested—on they went
Until at length they reached the fatal field,
Where Káús was o'ercome. At midnight hour,
Whilst watching with attentive eye and ear,
A piercing clamour echoed all around,
And blazing fires were seen, and numerous lamps
Burnt bright on every side. Rustem inquired
What this might be. "It is Mázinderán,"
Aúlád rejoined, "and the White Demon's chiefs
Are gathered there. Then Rustem to a tree
Bound his obedient guide—to keep him safe,
And to recruit his strength, laid down awhile
And soundly slept.
When morning dawned, he rose,
And mounting Rakush, put his helmet on,
The tiger-skin defended his broad chest,
And sallying forth, he sought the Demon chief,

Arzang, and summoned him with such a roar
That stream and mountain shook. Arzang sprang up,
Hearing a human voice, and from his tent
Indignant issued—him the champion met,
And clutched his arms and ears, and from his body
Tore off the gory head, and cast it far
Amidst the shuddering Demons, who with fear
Shrunk back and fled, precipitate, lest they
Should likewise feel that dreadful punishment.

SIXTH STAGE.—After this achievement Rustem returned to the place where he had left Aúlád, and having released him, sat down under the tree and related what he had done. He then commanded his guide to shew the way to the place where Kai-káús was confined; and when the champion entered the city of Mázinderán, the neighing of Rakush was so loud that the sound distinctly reached the ears of the captive monarch. Káús rejoiced, and said to his people: "I have heard the voice of Rakush, and my misfortunes are at an end;" but they thought he was either insane or telling them a dream. The actual appearance of Rustem, however, soon satisfied them. Gúdarz, and Tús, and Bahrám, and Gíw, and Gustahem, were delighted to meet him, and the king embraced him with great warmth and affection, and heard from him with admiration the story of his wonderful progress and exploits. But Káús and his warriors, under the influence and spells of the Demons, were still blind, and he cautioned Rustem particularly to conceal Rakush from the sight of the sorcerers, for if the White Demon should hear of the slaughter of Arzang, and the conqueror being at Mázinderán, he would immediately assemble an overpowering army of Demons, and the consequences might be terrible.

"But thou must storm the cavern of the Demons
And their gigantic chief—great need there is
For sword and battle-axe—and with the aid
Of Heaven, these miscreant sorcerers may fall
Victims to thy avenging might. The road
Is straight before thee—reach the Seven Mountains,
And there thou wilt discern the various groups,
Which guard the awful passage. Further on,

Within a deep and horrible recess,
Frowns the White Demon—conquer him—destroy
That fell magician, and restore to sight
Thy suffering king. and all his warrior train.
The wise in cures declare, that the warm blood
From the White Demon's heart, dropped in the eye,
Removes all blindness—it is, then, my hope,
Favoured by God, that thou wilt slay the fiend,
And save us from the misery we endure,
The misery of darkness without end."

Rustem accordingly, after having warned his friends and companions in arms to keep on the alert, prepared for the enterprise, and guided by Aúlád, hurried on till he came to the Haft-koh, or Seven Mountains. There he found numerous companies of Demons; and coming to one of the caverns, saw it crowded with the same awful beings. And now consulting with Aúlád, he was informed that the most advantageous time for attack would be when the sun became hot, for then all the Demons were accustomed to go to sleep, with the exception of a very small number who were appointed to keep watch. He therefore waited till the sun rose high in the firmament; and as soon as he had bound Aúlád to a tree hand and foot, with the thongs of his kamund, drew his sword, and rushed among the prostrate Demons, dismembering and slaying all that fell in his way. Dreadful was the carnage, and those who survived fled in the wildest terror from the champion's fury.

SEVENTH STAGE.—Rustem now hastened forward to encounter the White Demon.

Advancing to the cavern, he looked down
And saw a gloomy place, dismal as hell;
But not one cursed, impious sorcerer
Was visible in that infernal depth.
Awhile he stood—his falchion in his grasp,
And rubbed his eyes to sharpen his dim sight,
And then a mountain-form, covered with hair,
Filling up all the space, rose into view.
The monster was asleep, but presently
The daring shouts of Rustem broke his rest,
And brought him suddenly upon his feet,
When seizing a huge mill-stone, forth he came,
And thus accosted the intruding chief:

"Art thou so tired of life, that reckless thus
Thou dost invade the precincts of the Demons?
Tell me thy name, that I may not destroy
A nameless thing!" The champion stern replied,
"My name is Rustem—sent by Zál, my father,
Descended from the champion Sám Súwár,
To be revenged on thee—the King of Persia
Being now a prisoner in Mázinderán."
When the accursed Demon heard the name
Of Sám Súwár, he, like a serpent, writhed
In agony of spirit; terrified
At that announcement—then, recovering strength,
He forward sprang, and hurled the mill-stone huge
Against his adversary, who fell back
And disappointed the prodigious blow.
Black frowned the Demon, and through Rustem's heart
A wild sensation ran of dire alarm;
But, rousing up, his courage was revived,
And wielding furiously his beaming sword,
He pierced the Demon's thigh, and lopped the limb;
Then both together grappled, and the cavern
Shook with the contest—each, at times, prevailed;
The flesh of both was torn, and streaming blood
Crimsoned the earth. "If I survive this day,"
Said Rustem in his heart, in that dread strife,
"My life must be immortal." The White Demon,
With equal terror, muttered to himself:
"I now despair of life—sweet life; no more
Shall I be welcomed at Mázinderán."
And still they struggled hard—still sweat and blood
Poured down at every strain. Rustem, at last,
Gathering fresh power, vouchsafed by favouring Heaven
And bringing all his mighty strength to bear,
Raised up the gasping Demon in his arms,
And with such fury dashed him to the ground,
That life no longer moved his monstrous frame.
Promptly he then tore out the reeking heart,
And crowds of demons simultaneous fell
As part of him, and stained the earth with gore;
Others who saw this signal overthrow,
Trembled, and hurried from the scene of blood]
Then the great victor, issuing from that cave
With pious haste—took off his helm, and mail,
And royal girdle—and with water washed
His face and body—choosing a pure place
For prayer—to praise his Maker—Him who gave
The victory, the eternal source of good;
Without whose grace and blessing, what is man!
With it his armour is impregnable.

The Champion having finished his prayer, resumed his war

habiliments, and going to Aúlád, released him from the tree, and gave into his charge the heart of the White Demon. He then pursued his journey back to Káús at Mázinderán. On the way Aúlád solicited some reward for the services he had performed, and Rustem again promised that he should be appointed governor of the country.

> "But first the monarch of Mázinderán,
> The Demon-king, must be subdued, and cast
> Into the yawning cavern—and his legions
> Of foul enchanters, utterly destroyed."

Upon his arrival at Mázinderán, Rustem related to his sovereign all that he had accomplished, and especially that he had torn out and brought away the White Demon's heart, the blood of which was destined to restore Kai-káús and his warriors to sight. Rustem was not long in applying the miraculous remedy, and the moment the blood touched their eyes, the fearful blindness was perfectly cured.

> The champion brought the Demon's heart,
> And squeezed the blood from every part,
> Which, dropped upon the injured sight,
> Made all things visible and bright;
> One moment broke that magic gloom.
> Which seemed more dreadful than the tomb.

The monarch immediately ascended his throne surrounded by all his warriors, and seven days were spent in mutual congratulations and rejoicing. On the eighth day they all resumed the saddle, and proceeded to complete the destruction of the enemy. They set fire to the city, and burnt it to the ground, and committed such horrid carnage among the remaining magicians that streams of loathsome blood crimsoned all the place.

Káús afterwards sent Ferhád as an ambassador to the king of Mázinderán, suggesting to him the expediency of submission, and representing to him the terrible fall of Arzang, and of the White Demon with all his host, as a warning against resistance to the valour of Rustem. But when the king of Mázinderán heard from Ferhád the purpose of his embassy, he expressed great astonishment, and replied that he himself was superior in all respects to Káús; that his empire was more extensive, and his warriors more numerous and brave. "Have I not," said he, "a hundred war-elephants, and Káús not one? Wherever I move, conquest marks my way; why then should I fear the sovereign of Persia? Why should I submit to him?"

This haughty tone made a deep impression upon Ferhád, who returning quickly, told Káús of the proud bearing and fancied power of the ruler of Mázinderán. Rustem was immediately sent for; and so indignant was he on hearing the tidings, that "every hair on his body started up like a spear," and he proposed to go himself with a second despatch. The king was too much pleased to refuse, and another letter was written more urgent than the first, threatening the enemy to hang up his severed head on the walls of his own fort, if he persisted in his contumacy and scorn of the offer made.

As soon as Rustem had come within a short distance of the court of the king of Mázinderán, accounts reached his majesty of the approach of another ambassador, when a deputation of warriors was sent to receive him. Rustem observing them, and being in sight of the hostile army, with a view to shew his strength, tore up a large tree on the road by the roots, and dexterously wielded it in his hand like a spear. Tilting onwards, he flung it down before the wondering enemy, and one of the chiefs then thought it incumbent upon him to display his own prowess. He advanced, and offered to grasp hands with Rustem: they met; but the gripe of the champion was so excruciating that the sinews of his adversary cracked, and in agony he fell from his horse. Intelligence of this discomfiture was instantly conveyed to the king, who then summoned his most valiant and renowned chieftain, Kálahúr, and directed him to go and punish, signally, the warrior who had thus presumed to triumph over one of his heroes. Accordingly Kálahúr appeared, and boastingly stretched out his hand, which Rustem wrung with such grinding force, that the very nails dropped off, and blood started from his body. This was enough, and Kálahúr hastily returned to the king, and anxiously recommended him to submit to terms, as it would be in vain to oppose such invincible strength. The king was both grieved and angry at this situation of affairs, and invited the ambassador to his presence. After inquiring respecting Káús and the Persian army, he said :

> "And thou art Rustem, clothed with mighty power,
> Who slaughtered the White Demon, and now comest
> To crush the monarch of Mázinderán!"
> "No!" said the champion, "I am but his servant,
> And even unworthy of that noble station ;
> My master being a warrior, the most valiant
> That ever graced the world since time began.
> Nothing am I ; but what doth he resemble!
> What is a lion, elephant, or demon!
> Engaged in fight, he is himself a host!"

The ambassador then tried to convince the king of the folly of resistance, and of his certain defeat if he continued to defy the power of Káús and the bravery of Rustem ; but the effort was fruitless, and both states prepared for battle.

The engagement which ensued was obstinate and sanguinary, and after seven days of hard fighting, neither army was victorious, neither defeated. Afflicted at this want of success, Káús grovelled in the dust, and prayed fervently to the Almighty to give him the triumph. He addressed all his warriors, one by one, and urged them to increased exertions ; and on the eighth day, when the battle was renewed, prodigies of valour were performed. Rustem singled out, and encountered the king of Mázinderán, and fiercely they fought together with sword and javelin ; but suddenly, just as he was rushing on with overwhelming force, his adversary, by his magic art, transformed himself into a stony rock. Rustem and the Persian warriors were all amazement. The fight had been suspended for some time, when Káús came forward to enquire the cause ; and hearing with astonishment of the transformation, ordered his soldiers to drag the enchanted mass towards his own tent; but all the strength that could be applied was unequal to move so great a weight, till Rustem set himself to the task, and amidst the wondering army, lifted up the rock and conveyed it to the appointed place. He then addressed the work of sorcery, and said: "If thou dost not resume thy original shape, I will instantly break thee, flinty-rock as thou now art, into atoms, and scatter thee in the dust." The magician-king was alarmed by this threat, and re-appeared in his own form, and then Rustem, seizing his hand, brought him to Káús, who, as a punishment for his wickedness and atrocity, ordered him to be slain, and his body to be cut into a thousand pieces! The wealth of the country was immediately afterwards secured; and at the recommendation of Rustem, Aúlád was appointed governor of Mázinderán. After the usual thanksgivings and rejoicings on account of the victory, Káús and his warriors returned to Persia, where splendid honours and rewards were bestowed on every soldier for his heroic services. Rustem having received the highest acknowledgments of his merit, took leave, and returned to his father Zál at Zábulistán.

Suddenly an ardent desire arose in the heart of Káús to survey all the provinces and states of his empire. He wished to visit Túrán, and Chín, and Mikrán, and Berber, and Zirra. Having commenced his royal tour of inspection, he found the king of Berberistán in a state of rebellion, with his army prepared to dispute his authority. A severe battle was the consequence; but the refractory sovereign was soon compelled to retire, and the elders of the city came forward to sue for mercy and protection. After this triumph, Káús turned towards the mountain Káf, and visited various other countries, and in his progress became the guest of the son of Zál in Zábulistán, where he staid a month, enjoying the pleasures of the festive board and the sports of the field.

The disaffection of the king of Hámáverán, in league with the king of Misser and Shám, and the still hostile king of Berberistán, soon, however, drew him from Nímrúz, and quitting the principality of Rustem, his arms were promptly directed against his new enemy, who in the contest which ensued, made an obstinate resistance, but was at length overpowered, and obliged to ask for quarter. After the battle, Káús was informed that the shah had a daughter of great beauty, named Súdáveh, possessing a form as graceful as the tall cypress, musky ringlets, and all the charms of Heaven. From the description of this damsel he became enamoured, and through the medium of a messenger, immediately offered himself to be her husband. The father did not seem to be glad at this proposal, observing to the messenger, that he had but two things in life valuable to him, and those were his daughter and his property; one was his solace and delight, and the other his support; to be deprived of both would be death to him; still he could not gainsay the wishes of a king of such power, and his conqueror. He then sorrowfully communicated the overture to his child, who however readily consented; and in the course of a week, the bride was sent escorted by soldiers, and accompanied by a magnificent cavalcade, consisting of a thousand horses and mules, a thousand camels, and numerous female attendants. When Súdáveh descended from her litter, glowing with beauty, with her rich dark tresses flowing to her feet, and cheeks like the rose, Káús regarded her with admiration and rapture; and so impatient was he to possess that lovely treasure, that the marriage rites were performed according to the laws of the country without delay.

The sháh of Hámáverán, however, was not satisfied, and he continually plotted within himself how he might contrive to regain possession of Súdáveh, as well as be revenged upon the king. With this view he invited Káús to be his guest for a while; but Súdáveh cautioned the king not to trust to the treachery which dictated the invitation, as she apprehended from it nothing but mischief and disaster. The warning, however, was of no avail, for Káús accepted the proffered hospitality of his new father-in-law. He accordingly proceeded with his bride and his most famous warriors to the city, where he was received and entertained in the most sumptuous manner, seated on a gorgeous throne, and felt infinitely exhilarated with the magnificence and the hilarity by which he was surrounded. Seven days were passed in this glorious banqueting and delight; but on the succeeding night, the sound of trumpets and the war-cry was heard. The intrusion of soldiers changed the face of the scene; and the king, who had just been waited on, and pampered with such respect and devotion, was suddenly seized, together with his principal warriors, and carried off to a remote fortress, situated on a high mountain, where they were imprisoned, and guarded by a thousand valiant men. His tents were plundered, and all his treasure taken away. At this event his wife was inconsolable and deaf to all entreaties from her father, declaring that she preferred death to separation from her husband; upon which she was conveyed to the same dungeon, to mingle groans with the captive king.

> Alas! how false and fickle is the world,
> Friendship nor pleasure, nor the ties of blood,
> Can check the headlong course of human passions;
> Treachery still laughs at kindred;—who is safe
> In this tumultuous sphere of strife and sorrow?

The INVASION of IRÁN by AFRÁSIYÁB.

The intelligence of Káús's imprisonment was very soon spread through the world, and operated as a signal to all the inferior states to get possession of Irán. Afrásiyáb was the most powerful aspirant to the throne; and gathering an immense army, he hurried from Túrán, and made a rapid incursion into the country, which after three months he succeeded in conquering, scattering ruin and desolation where-ever he came.

Some of those who escaped from the field bent their steps towards Zábulistán, by whom Rustem was informed of the misfortunes in which Káús was involved; it therefore became necessary that he should again endeavour to effect the liberation of his sovereign; and accordingly, after assembling his troops from different quarters, the first thing he did was to dispatch a messenger to Hámáverán, with a letter, demanding the release of the prisoners; and in the event of a refusal, declaring the king should suffer the same fate as the White Demon and the magician-monarch of Mázinderán. Although this threat produced considerable alarm in the breast of the king of Hámáverán, he arrogantly replied, that if Rustem wished to be placed in the same situation as Káús, he was welcome to come as soon as he liked.

Upon hearing this defiance, Rustem left Zábulistán, and after an arduous journey by land and water, arrived at the confines of Hámáverán. The king of that country, roused by the noise and uproar, and bold aspect of the invading army, drew up his own forces, and a battle ensued, but he was unequal to stand his ground before the overwhelming courage of Rustem. His troops fled in confusion, and then almost in despair he anxiously solicited assistance from the chiefs of Berber and Misser, which was immediately given. Thus three kings and their armies were opposed to the power and resources of one man. Their formidable array covered an immense space.

Each proud his strongest force to bring,
The eagle of valour flapped his wing.

But when the king of Hámáverán beheld the person of Rustem in all its pride and strength, and commanding power, he paused with apprehension and fear, and intrenched himself well behind his own troops. Rustem, on the contrary, was full of confidence.

"What, though there be a hundred thousand men
Pitched against one, what use is there in numbers
When Heaven is on my side: with Heaven my friend,
The foe will soon be mingled with the dust."

Having ordered the trumpets to sound, he rushed on the enemy, mounted on Rakush, and committed dreadful havoc among them.

> It would be difficult to tell
> How many heads, dissevered, fell,
>   Fighting his dreadful way;
> On every side his falchion gleamed,
> Hot blood in every quarter streamed
>   On that tremendous day.

The chief of Hámáverán and his legions were the first to shrink from the conflict; and then the king of Misser, ashamed of their cowardice, rapidly advanced towards the champion with the intention of punishing him for his temerity, but had no sooner received one of Rustem's hard blows on his head, than he turned to flight, and thus hoped to escape the fury of his antagonist. That fortune, however, was denied him, for being instantly pursued, he was caught with the kamund, or noose, thrown round his loins, dragged from his horse, and safely delivered into the hands of Bahrám, who bound him, and kept him by his side.

> Ring within ring the lengthening kamund flew,
> And from his steed the astonished monarch drew.

Having accomplished this signal capture, Rustem proceeded against the troops under the sháh of Berberistán, which, valorously aided as he was, by Zúára, he soon vanquished and dispatched; and impelling Rakush impetuously forward upon the sháh himself, made him and forty of his principal chiefs prisoners of war. The king of Hámáverán, seeing the horrible carnage, and the defeat of all his expectations, speedily sent a messenger to Rustem, to solicit a suspension of the fight, offering to deliver up Káús and all his warriors, and all the regal property and treasure which had been plundered from him. The troops of the three kingdoms also urgently prayed for quarter and protection, and Rustem readily agreed to the proffered conditions.

"Káús to liberty restore,
With all his chiefs, I ask no more;
For him alone I conquering came;
Than him no other prize I claim."

The RETURN of KÁI-KÁÚS.

It was a joyous day when Káús and his illustrious heroes were released from their fetters, and removed from the mountain-fortress in which they were confined. Rustem forthwith reseated him on his throne, and did not fail to collect for the public treasury all the valuables of the three states which had submitted to his power. The troops of Misser, Berberistán, and Hámáverán, having declared their allegiance to the Persian king, the accumulated numbers increased Káús's army to upwards of three hundred thousand men, horse and foot, and with this immense force he moved towards Irán. Before marching, however, he sent a message to Afrásiyáb, commanding him to quit the country he had so unjustly invaded, and recommending him to be contented with the territory of Túrán.

"Hast thou forgotten Rustem's power,
When thou wert in that perilous hour
By him o'erthrown? Thy girdle broke,
Or thou hadst felt the conqueror's yoke.
Thy crowding warriors proved thy shield,
They saved and dragged thee from the field;
By them unrescued then, would'st thou
Have lived to vaunt thy prowess now?"

This message was received with bitter feelings of resentment by Afrásiyáb, who prepared his army for battle without delay, and promised to bestow his daughter in marriage and a kingdom upon the man who should succeed in taking Rustem alive. This proclamation was a powerful excitement: and when the engagement took place, mighty efforts were made for the reward; but those who aspired to deserve it were only the first to fall. Afrásiyáb beholding the fall of so many of his chiefs, dashed forward to cope with the champion: but his bravery was unavailing; for, suffering sharply under the overwhelming attacks of Rustem, he was glad to effect his escape, and retire from the field. In short, he rapidly retraced his steps to Túrán, leaving Káús in full possession of the kingdom.

With anguish stricken, he regained his home,
After a wild and ignominious flight;
The world presenting nothing to his lips
But poison-beverage; all was death to him.

Káús being again seated on the throne of Persia, he resumed the administration of affairs with admirable justice and liberality, and despatched some of his most distinguished warriors to secure the welfare and prosperity of the states of Mervi, and Balkh, and Níshapúr, and Hírát. At the same time he conferred on Rustem the title of Jaháni Pahlván, or, Champion of the World.

In safety now from foreign and domestic enemies, Káús turned his attention to pursuits very different from war and conquest. He directed the Demons to construct two splendid palaces on the mountain Alberz, and separate mansions for the accommodation of his household, which he decorated in the most magnificent manner. All the buildings were beautifully arranged both for convenience and pleasure; and gold and silver and precious stones were used so lavishly, and the brilliancy produced by their combined effect was so great, that night and day appeared to be the same.

Iblís, ever active, observing the vanity and ambition of the king, was not long in taking advantage of the circumstance, and he soon persuaded the Demons to enter into his schemes. Accordingly one of them, disguised as a domestic servant, was instructed to present a nosegay to Káús; and after respectfully kissing the ground, say to him;—

"Thou art great as king can be,
Boundless in thy majesty;
What is all this earth to thee,
    All beneath the sky?
Péris, mortals, demons, hear
Thy commanding voice with fear;
Thou art lord of all things here,
    But, thou canst not fly!

That remains for thee; to know
Things above, as things below,
    How the planets roll;
How the sun his light displays,
How the moon darts forth her rays;
How the nights succeed the days;
What the secret cause betrays,
    And who directs the whole!"

This artful address of the Demon satisfied Káús of the imperfection of his nature, and the enviable power which he had yet to obtain. To him, therefore, it became matter of deep concern, how he might be enabled to ascend the Heavens without wings, and for that purpose he consulted his astrologers, who presently suggested a way in which his desires might be successfully accomplished.

They contrived to rob an eagle's nest of its young, which they reared with great care, supplying them well with invigorating food, till they grew large and strong. A framework of aloes-wood was then prepared; and at each of the four corners was fixed perpendicularly, a javelin, surmounted on the point with flesh of a goat. At each corner again one of the eagles was bound, and in the middle Káús was seated in great pomp with a goblet of wine before him. As soon as the eagles became hungry, they endeavoured to get at the goat's flesh upon the javelins, and by flapping their wings and flying upwards, they quickly raised up the throne from the ground. Hunger still pressing them, and still being distant from their prey, they ascended higher and higher in the clouds, conveying the astonished king far beyond his own country; but after long and fruitless exertion their strength failed them, and unable to keep their way, the whole fabric came tumbling down from the sky, and fell upon a dreary solitude in the kingdom of Chín. There Káús was left, a prey to hunger, alone, and in utter despair, until he was discovered by a band of Demons, whom his anxious ministers had sent in search of him.

Rustem, and Gúdarz, and Tús, at length heard of what had befallen the king, and with feelings of sorrow not unmixed with indignation, set off to his assistance. "Since I was born," said Gúdarz, "never did I see such a man as Káús. He seems to be entirely destitute of reason and understanding; always in distress and affliction. This is the third calamity in which he has wantonly involved himself. First at Mázinderán, then at Hámáverán, and now he is being punished for attempting to discover the secrets of the Heavens!" When they reached the wilderness into which Káús had fallen, Gúdarz repeated to him the same observations, candidly telling him that he was fitter for a mad-house than a throne, and exhorting him to be satisfied with his lot and be obedient to God, the creator of all things. The miserable king was softened to tears, acknowledged his folly; and as soon as he was escorted back to his palace, he shut himself up, remaining forty days, unseen, prostrating himself in shame and repentance. After that he recovered his spirits, and resumed the administration of affairs with his former liberality, clemency, and justice, almost rivalling the glory of Ferídún and Jemshíd.

One day Rustem made a splendid feast; and whilst he and his brother warriors, Gíw and Gúdarz, and Tús, were quaffing their wine, it was determined upon to form a pretended hunting party, and repair to the sporting grounds of Afrásiyáb. The feast lasted seven days; and on the eighth, preparations were made for the march, an advance party being pushed on to reconnoitre the motions of the enemy. Afrásiyáb was soon informed of what was going on, and flattered himself with the hopes of getting Rustem and his seven champions into his thrall, for which purpose he called together his wise men and warriors, and said to them: "You have only to secure these invaders, and Káús will soon cease to be the sovereign of Persia." To accomplish this object, a Túránian army of thirty thousand veterans was assembled, and ordered to occupy all the positions and avenues in the vicinity of the sporting grounds. An immense clamour, and thick clouds of dust, which darkened the skies, announced their approach; and when intelligence of their numbers was brought to Rustem, the undaunted champion smiled, and said to Garáz: "Fortune favours me; what cause is there to fear the king of Túrán? his army does not exceed a hundred thousand men. Were I alone, with Rakush, with my armour, and battle-axe, I would not shrink from his legions. Have I not seven companions in arms, and is not one of them equal to five hundred Túránian heroes? Let Afrásiyáb dare to cross the boundary-river, and the contest will presently convince him that he has only sought his own defeat." Promptly at a signal the cup-bearer produced goblets of the red wine of Zábul; and in one of them Rustem pledged his royal master with loyalty, and Tús and Zúára joined in the convivial and social demonstration of attachment to the king.

The champion arrayed in his buburiyán, mounted Rakush, and advanced towards the Túránian army. Afrásiyáb, when he beheld him in all his terrible strength and vigour, was amazed and disheartened, accompanied, as he was, by Tús, and Gúdarz, and Gúrgín, and Gíw, and Bahrám, and Berzín, and Ferhád. The drums and trumpets of Rustem were now heard, and immediately the hostile forces engaged with dagger, sword, and javelin. Dreadful was the onset, and the fury with which the conflict was continued. In truth, so sanguinary and destructive was the battle, that Afrásiyáb exclaimed in grief and terror: "If this carnage lasts till the close of day, not a man of my army will remain alive. Have I not one warrior endued with sufficient bravery to oppose and subdue this mighty Rustem? What! not one fit to be rewarded with a diadem, with my own throne and kingdom, which I will freely give to the victor!" Pílsum heard the promise, and was ambitious of earning the reward; but fate decreed it otherwise. His prodigious efforts were of no avail. Alkús was equally unsuccessful, though the bravest of the brave among the Túránian warriors. Encountering Rustem, his brain was pierced by a javelin wielded by the Persian hero, and he fell dead from his saddle. This signal achievement astonished and terrified the Túránians, who, however, made a further despairing effort against the champion and his seven conquering companions, but with no better result than before, and nothing remained to them excepting destruction or flight. Choosing the latter they wheeled round, and endeavoured to escape from the sanguinary fate that awaited them.

Seeing this precipitate movement of the enemy, Rustem impelled Rakush forward in pursuit, addressing his favourite horse with fondness and enthusiasm :

"My valued friend—put forth thy speed,
This is a time of pressing need ;
Bear me away amidst the strife,
That I may take that despot's life ;
And with my ma e and javelin, flood
This dusty plain with foe-man's blood."

Excited by his master's cry,
  The war-horse bounded o'er the plain,
So swiftly that he seemed to fly,
Snorting with pride, and tossing high
  His streaming mane.

And soon he reached that despot's side,
"Now is the time !" the Champion cried,
  "This is the hour to victory given,"
And flung his noose—which bound the king
Fast for a moment in its ring ;
  But soon, alas ! the bond was riven.

Haply the Tartar-monarch slipt away,
Not doomed to suffer on that bloody day ;
And freed from thrall, he hurrying led
  His legions cross the boundary-stream,
Leaving his countless heaps of dead
  To rot beneath the solar beam.

Onward he rushed with heart opprest,
  And broken fortunes ; he had quaffed
Bright pleasure's cup,—but now, unblest,
  Poison was mingled with the draught !

The booty in horses, treasure, armour, pavilions, and tents, was immense; and when the whole was secured, Rustem and his companions fell back to the sporting-grounds already mentioned, from whence he informed Kai-káús by letter of the victory that had been gained. After remaining two weeks there, resting from the toils of war and enjoying the pleasures of hunting, the party returned home to pay their respects to the Persian king.

And this is life! Thus conquest and defeat,
Vary the lights and shades of human scenes,
And human thought. Whilst some, immersed in pleasure,
Enjoy the sweets, others again endure
The miseries of the world. Hope is deceived
In this frail dwelling; certainty and safety
Are only dreams which mock the credulous mind;
Time sweeps o'er all things; why then should the wise
Mourn o'er events which roll resistless on,
And set at nought all mortal opposition?

THE STORY OF SOHRÁB.

Now further mark the searchless ways of Heaven,
Father and son to mortal combat driven!
Alas! the tale of sorrow must be told,
The tale of tears, derived from minstrel old.

Firdausí relates that Rustem, being on a hunting excursion in the neighbourhood of Túrán, killed an onager, or wild ass,* which he roasted in the forest; and having allayed his hunger, went to sleep, leaving his horse, Rakush, at liberty to graze. In the mean time a band of Tartar wanderers appeared, and

* Hunting the Gor, or wild-ass, appears to have been a favourite sport in Persia. Bahram the Sixth was surnamed Gor, in consequence of his being peculiarly devoted to the chase of this animal, and which at last cost him his life.

seeing so fine an animal astray, succeeded in securing him with their kamunds, or nooses, and conveyed him home. When Rustem awoke from sleep he missed his favourite steed, and felt convinced from the surrounding traces of his footsteps that he had been captured and carried away. Accordingly he proceeded towards Samengán, a small principality on the borders of Túrán, and his approach being announced to the king, his majesty went on foot to receive him with due respect and consideration. Rustem, however, was in great wrath, and haughtily told the king that his horse had been stolen from him in his dominions, and that he had traced his footsteps to Samengán. The king begged that he would not be angry, but become his guest, and he would immediately order a search for the missing horse. Rustem was appeased by this conciliatory address, and readily accepted the proffered hospitality. Having in the first place dispatched his people in quest of Rakush, the king of Samengán prepared a magnificent feast for the entertainment of his illustrious guest, at which wine and music and dancing contributed their several charms. Rustem was delighted with the welcome he received; and when the hour of repose arrived, he was accommodated with a couch suitably provided and decorated. Soon after he had fallen asleep, he was awakened by a beautiful vision, which presented itself close to his pillow, accompanied by a slave girl with a lamp in her hand.

A moon-faced beauty rose upon his sight,
Like the sun sparkling, full of bloom and fragrance;
Her eye-brows bended like the archer's bow,
Her ringlets fateful as the warrior's kamund;
And graceful as the lofty cypress tree,
She moved towards the champion, who surprised
At this enchanting vision, asked the cause
Which brought her thither. Softly thus she spoke:—
"I am the daughter of the king, my name
Tahmíneh, no one from behind the screen
Of privacy has yet beheld me, none;
Nor even heard the echo of my voice.
But I have heard of thy prodigious deeds,
Of thy unequalled valour and renown—"

Rustem was still more astonished when he was apprized of the nature of this extraordinary adventure, and anxiously asked more particularly the object of her wishes. She replied that she had become enamoured of him, on account of the fame and the glory of his actions, and in consequence had vowed to God that she would espouse no other man. "I employed spies to seize upon Rakush and secure him to obtain a foal of his breed, and happily Almighty God has conducted thee to Samengán to fulfil my desires. I have been irresistibly impelled to make this disclosure, and now I depart; only, to-morrow, do thou solicit the consent of my father to our union, and he certainly will not refuse to bless us." Rustem acceded to the flattering proposal, and in the morning the nuptial engagement was sanctioned by the king.

> Joyous the monarch smiled, and gave his child,
> According to the customs of the kingdom,
> To that brave champion.

Rustem could not remain long with his bride, and when parting from her he said: "If the Almighty should bless thee with a daughter, place this amulet * in her hair; but if a son,

* It seems by the text that the Mohreh, or amulet, of Rustem was celebrated throughout the world for its wonderful virtues. The Mohrehi Suliman, Solomon's Seal, was a talisman of extraordinary power, said to be capable of rendering objects invisible, and of creating every kind of magical illusion. Josephus relates that he saw a certain Jew, named Eleazar, draw the devil out of an old woman's nostril, by the application of *Solomon's Seal* to her nose, in the presence of the Emperor Vespasian! But Mohreh is more properly an amulet, or spell, against misfortune. The wearer of one of them imagines himself safe under every situation of danger.

The application of the magical instrument to the mouth was often indispensable. Thus Angelica in the Orlando Furioso:

> Del dito se lo leva, e a mano a mano,
> Se'l chiude in bocca, e in men, che non balena,
> Così dagli occhi di Ruggier si cela,
> Come fa il Sol, quando la nube il vela. CANTO XI. St. 6.

> Then from her hand she took with eager haste,
> And twixt her lips, the shining circlet placed,
> And instant vanished from Rogero's sight!
> Like Phœbus when a cloud obscures his light. HOOLE.

bind it on his arm, and it will inspire him with the disposition and valour of Narímán." Having said these words, and Rakush being at the same time restored to him, he took leave, and went away to his own country.

> How wept that angel-face at parting, grief
> Subdued her heart; but when nine months had past,
> A boy was born as lovely as the moon,
> The image of his father, and of Sám,
> And Narímán—for in one little month
> He had attained the growth of a full year;
> His spreading chest was like the chest of Zál.
> When nine, there was not in that country round
> One who could equal him in feats of arms.

Hatim placed the talisman in his mouth when he plunged into the cauldron of boiling oil. [See Hatim Ta'í, a Persian Romance, full of magic, and the wild and marvellous adventures of Knight-errantry.] Aristotle speaks of the ring of Battus which inspired the wearer with GRATITUDE AND HONOR! Faith in rings and amulets prepared at particular seasons, under certain mysterious forms and circumstances, is an ancient superstition, but in Persia and India, there is hardly a man without his Bazúbund, or bracelet, to preserve him from the influence of the Demons. "The women of condition, in Persia, have small silver plates of a circular form, upon which are engraved sentences from the Koran; these, as well as the Talismans, they bind about their arms with pieces of red and green silk, and look upon them as never-failing charms against the fascinations of the devil, wicked spirits, &c." (Francklin's Tour to Persia.) Rustem had also a magic garment, or cloak, called according to the Burhani-katia, Buburiyán. Some say that he received it from his father Zál, and others, that it was made of the skin of Akwan Díw; others again say, that it was made of the skin of a leopard, or some similar animal, which Rustem killed on the mountain Sham. It had the property of resisting the impression of every weapon, it was proof against fire, and would not sink in water. Something like the charm in the curse of Kehama.

> I charm thy life,
> From the weapons of strife,
> From stone and from wood,
> From fire and from flood,
> From the serpent's tooth,
> And the beasts of blood.

Bubur is an animal of the tiger kind, said to be superior in strength to the lion. The famous heroes of antiquity usually wore the skins of wild beasts. Hercules wore the skin of the Nemæan lion. The skins of panthers and leopards were worn by the Greek and Trojan chiefs. Virgil says of Acestes,

> occurrit Acestes,
> Horridus in jaculis, et pelle Libystidos ursæ. ÆN. B. 5, v. 36.

The king of Samengán named him Sohráb; and when the youth was ten years old, he said to his mother: "People ask me who my father is, and want to know his name!" To this, Tahmíneh replied: "Thy father's name is Rustem,

> "Since the God of creation created the earth,
> To a hero like Rustem he never gave birth."

And she then described the valour and renown of his ancestors, which excited in the breast of Sohráb the desire of being immediately introduced to his father; but his mother endeavoured to repress his eagerness, and told him to beware—

> "For if he knows thou'rt his, he will remove thee
> From me, and thy sweet home; from thee divided,
> Thy mother's heart will break in agony!"

Rustem had sent a present of jewels and precious stones to Tahmíneh, with inquiries respecting her offspring, and the reply she returned was, that a daughter was the fruit of their union. This intelligence disappointed him, and he afterwards thought no more of Samengán. Tahmíneh again said to Sohráb: "Beware also of speaking too publicly of thy relationship to Rustem, for fear of Afrásiyáb depriving me of thee."—"Never," said he, "will I conceal the name of my father; nay, I will go to him myself:—

> Even now, I will oppose the Tartar host,
> Whate'er their numbers—Káús shall be hurled
> From his imperial throne, and Tús subdued—
> To Rustem I will give the crown and sceptre,
> And place him on the seat, whence Káús ruled
> His myriad subjects—I will seize the throne
> Of stern Afrásiyáb; my javelin's point
> Shall pierce the Heaven of Heavens. And since 'tis so—
> Between my glorious father and myself,
> No crowned tyrant shall remain unpunished."

Tahmíneh wept bitterly, but her entreaties were of no avail—the youth being unalterably fixed in his determination. One day he told her that he wanted a suitable war-horse, and immediately the royal stables were explored; but the only animal of sufficient size and vigour that could be found there, was the foal produced from Rakush, which was at length brought to him.

His nervė and action pleased the boy,
He stroked and patted him with joy;
And on his back the saddle placed,
The mouth and head the bridle graced,
And springing on th' impatient steed,
He proved his fitness and his speed.

Satisfied with the horse he had obtained, and the arms and armour with which he was supplied, he announced his resolution of going to war against Káús, and conquering the kingdom of Persia for Rustem! The news of Sohráb's preparations soon reached Afrásiyáb, who hailed the circumstance as peculiarly favourable to his own ambitious ends; and taking advantage of the youth's enthusiasm, sent an army to his assistance, declaring that Káús was also his enemy, and that he was anxious to share with him in the glory of overcoming the imperial despot. Sohráb readily accepted the offer, and the Tartar legions, his auxiliaries, were commanded by two noted warriors, Húmán and Bármán, to whom Afrásiyáb gave the following instructions: "It must be so contrived that Rustem and Sohráb shall not know each other's person or name. They must be brought together in battle. Sohráb is the youngest, and will no doubt overcome Rustem, in which case the conqueror may be easily dispatched by stratagem, and when both are destroyed, the empire of Persia will be all my own!" Furnished with these instructions, the Tartar leaders united with Sohráb, and commenced their march towards Persia. There was a fortress on the road, in which Hujír, a famous warrior, was stationed; and when Sohráb arrived at that fortress, he rushed out alone to oppose the progress of the invader, crying hastily—

"And who art thou? I am myself Hujír
The valiant champion, come to conquer thee,*
And to lop off that towering head of thine."

* This haughty manner was common among the heroes of antiquity. "And

Sohráb smiled at this fierce menace, and a sharp conflict ensued between the two combatants, in which the vain boaster was precipitately thrown from his horse, and afterwards made a prisoner by the stripling-warrior. Gurd-afríd, the daughter of Gustahem, perceiving this unhappy result, left the fort precipitately for the purpose of encountering the youth, and being revenged upon him.

When tidings reached her of the fate Hujír
Had thus provoked, she dressed herself in mail,
And, hastily, beneath her helmet hid
Her glossy ringlets ; down she, from the fort,
Came bravely like a lion, nobly mounted ;
And as she approached the hostile army, called
With an undaunted voice. Sohráb beheld
The gallant foe with smiles, believing her
A boy of tender years, and, wondering, saw
The vigour of the arm opposed to him ;
The force with which the pointed spear was thrown.
Assailed so bravely, he drew forth his noose,
And, casting it around the enemy, brought
Her headlong to the ground. Off flew her helm,
When her luxuriant tresses scattered loose,
And cheeks of radiant bloom, her sex betrayed !

When the astonishment produced by this unexpected discovery had subsided, Sohráb regarded her with tender emotion, and securely made her his captive ; but Gurd-afríd promptly addressed him, and said : "Allow me to return to the fort ; all the treasure and property it contains are at my command, and shall be given to thee as my ransom. My father is old, and his fondest hopes are centered in me. Be therefore considerate and merciful." Sohráb was too young and ardent not

the Philistine said to David, Come to me, and I will give thy flesh unto the fowls of the air, and to the beasts of the field." I. Samuel, xvii. 44. This is like the boast of Hujír. These denunciations are frequent in Homer as well as Firdausí. Thus Diomed to Glaucus :

If the fruits of earth,
Sustain thy life and human be thy birth ;
Bold as thou art, too prodigal of breath,
Approach and enter the dark gates of death !

POPE : ILIAD, vi. 42.

to be carried away by his feelings; he was affected by her beauty and her tears, and set her at liberty! As soon as the damsel had re-entered the fortress, a council was held to deliberate on the exigencies of the time, and the garrison resolved upon evacuating the place by secret passages during the ensuing night. When morning dawned, Sohráb approached the gate, and not a person was anywhere to be found. Grieved and disappointed, sorrow preyed deeply upon his heart, losing, as he had done, so foolishly, the lovely heroine of whom he had become enamoured.

The father, and daughter, and the garrison, shaped their course immediately to the court of Káús, to whom they related that a wonderful hero had come from Túrán, against whose courage it was in vain to contend, and said to be not more than fourteen years of age! What then would he be, they thought, when arrived at maturity! The capture of Hujír, and the accounts of Sohráb's amazing prowess, filled Káús with alarm, and the warrior Gíw was forthwith deputed to Zábulistán to call Rustem to his aid. The letter ran thus:—"A youthful warrior, named Sohráb, has invaded Persia from Túrán, and thou art alone able to avert his destructive progress;

"Thou art the sole support of Persia; thou—
Endued with nerve of more than human power;
Thou art the conqueror of Mázinderán;
And at Hámáverán thou didst restore
The king to liberty and life; thy sword
Makes the sun weep; thy glorious actions fling
Unequalled splendour o'er the kingly throne."

When the letter was received, Rustem inquired anxiously about the particular form and character of Sohráb, whom Gíw described as being like Sám and Narimán. This made him ponder, and he thought it might be his own son; but he recollected Tahmíneh had written from Samengán, that her child was a daughter! He, however, still pondered, although Gíw repeated the commands of the king that no time should be lost. Regardless of the summons, Rustem called for wine and music, and made a feast, which continued seven days. On the eighth he said, "This too must be a day of festivity;" and it was not till the ninth that he ordered Rakush to be saddled for the journey. He then departed with his brother Zúára and the Zábul troops, and at length arrived at the royal court. Káús was in great indignation at the delay that had occurred, and directed both Rustem and Gíw to be impaled alive for the offence they had committed in not attending to his instructions. Tús was commanded to execute this order; but when he stretched out his hand towards Rustem, the champion dashed it aside; and retiring from the assembly, and vaulting upon his horse, thus addressed the king:—

"Weak and insensate! take not to thy breast
Devouring fire; thy latest actions still
Outdo the past in baseness. Go, thyself,
And, if thou canst, impale Sohráb alive!
When wrath inflames my heart, what is Káús!
What, but a clod of earth? Him must I dread?
No, to the Almighty power alone I bend.
The warriors of the empire sought to place
The crown upon my head; but I was faithful,
And held the kingdom's laws and customs sacred.
Had I looked to the throne, thou would'st not now
Have had the power with which thou art surrounded,
To injure one who is thy safest friend.
But I deserve it all; for I have ever,
Ungrateful monarch! done thee signal service."

Saying this, Rustem withdrew; and as he went away, the hearts of all the courtiers and warriors sunk with the most painful anticipations of unavoidable ruin to the empire. Gúdarz afforded the only spark of hope, for he was in great favour with the king; and it fortunately so happened, that by his interposition, the blind anger of Káús was soon appeased. His next office was to follow Rustem, and to restore the harmony which had been destroyed. He said to him:—

"Thou know'st that Káús is a brainless king,
Wayward, capricious, and to anger prone;
But quickly he repents, and now he seeks
For reconciliation. If thou'rt deaf

To this good change in him, and nourishest
The scorn he has inspired, assuredly
The people of our nation will be butchered;
For who can now resist the Tartar brand?
Persia again will groan beneath the yoke
Of the Túránian despot. Must it be?
Have pity on thy countrymen, and never
Let it be bruited through the scornful world,
That Rustem feared to fight a beardless boy!"

The speech of Gúdarz had its due effect; and the champion, with altered feelings, returned to the court of the king; who, rising from his throne, received him with the highest honour and respect, and apologized for the displeasure into which he had been betrayed.

"Wrathful and wayward in my disposition,
I felt impatient at the long delay;
But now I see my error, and repentance
Must, for that insult unprovoked, atone."

Rustem, in reply, assured the king of his allegiance, and of his readiness to undertake whatever might be desired of him; but Káús said:—

"To-day let us feast; let us banquet to day,
And to-morrow to battle we'll hasten away."

Having feasted all night, in the morning Káús placed all his warriors, and his army, under the command of Rustem; who immediately set off to oppose the progress of Sohráb.

The countless thousands seemed to hide the earth;
The Heavens, too, were invisible; so great
And overspreading was the Persian host.
Thus they rolled on, until they reached the fort,
The barrier-fort, where still Sohráb remained.

When the stripling from the top of the fort first observed the approach of the Persians, he said to Húmán—"Look, on every side at the coming legions;" at which the Tartar chief turned pale. But the youth added—"Fear not, by the favour of Heaven I will soon disperse them;" and then called for a goblet of wine, full of confidence in his own might, and in the result of the expected battle. Descending from the walls, he proceeded to his pavilion, pitched on the plain in front of the fort, and sat in pomp among the chiefs of the Túránian army.

Rustem repaired thither in secret, and in disguise,* to watch the motions of his formidable enemy, and beheld him sitting drinking wine, surrounded by great men and heroes. Zindeh, a warrior, retiring from the banquet, saw the shadow of some one, and going nearer to the spot, found it to be a man in ambush. He said, "Who art thou?" when Rustem struck him a blow on the neck, which stretched him lifeless on the ground, and effected his escape. In a few minutes another person came, who seeing the body, brought a light, and discovered it to be Zindeh. When the fatal circumstance was communicated to Sohráb, the youth well knew that it must have been the work of the enemy, who had secretly entered his pavilion, and he solemnly vowed that next day he would be revenged on the Iránians, and especially on Káús, wherever he might be found.

In the mean time Rustem described to Káús the appearance and splendour of Sohráb:

"In stature perfect, as the cypress tree,
No Tartar ever boasted such a presence;
Túrán, nor even Persia, now can shew
A hero of his bold and gallant bearing;
Seeing his form thou would'st at once declare
That he is Sám, the warrior; so majestic
In mien and action!"

When morning dawned, Sohráb took Hujír to the top of

* It appears that in Rustem's time there was nothing dishonourable in the character of a spy. The adventure of Diomed and Ulysses in the tenth book of the Iliad shows a similar conclusion with respect to the Greeks. Alfred entered the hostile camp of the Danes, under "the disguise of a harper, and so entertained them with his music and facetious humours, that he met with a welcome reception."

the fortress, and speaking kindly to him, promised to release him if he would answer truly what he had to ask. Commencing his anxious inquiries, he then said :—"To whom belongs that pavilion surrounded by elephants?" Hujír replied—"It belongs to king Káús." Sohráb resumed—"To whom belongs the tent on the right?"—"To the warrior Tús." "To whom, then, belongs that crimson pavilion?"—"To Gúdarz." "Whose is that green pavilion, with the Gáváni banner flying over it, and in which a throne is seen?" Hujír knew that this was Rustem's tent; but he reflected that if he told the truth, Sohráb might in his wrath attack the champion unprepared, and slay him; better it would be, he thought, to deny his being present, and accordingly he said :—"That tent belongs to the chief of the troops sent by the Emperor of Chín in aid of king Káús." "Dost thou know his name?"—"No, I do not." Sohráb meditated, and said in his heart :—"I see here the plain indications of Rustem's presence, which my mother gave me—why am I deceived?" He again questioned Hujír, and received the same answer. "Then where is Rustem's tent?" he asked, impatiently. "It appears that he has not yet arrived from Zábulistán."

At this the stripling's heart was sunk in grief;
The tokens which his mother gave, were all
Conspicuous; yet his father was denied;
So Fate decreed it. Still he lingering hoped
By further question, and encouragement,
To win the important secret from Hujír.

Again he said, with persuasive gentleness, "Look well around; try if thou can'st find the tent of Rustem, and thou shalt be richly rewarded for thy trouble." "Rustem's tent may be in some degree similar to that; but it is not Rustem's." Hujír then went on in praise of the champion, and said :—

"When roused to fury in the battle-field,
What is a man, an elephant, or pard;
The strength of five-score valiant men exceeds not
Rustem's unwearied nerve and towering frame."

Then Sohráb said to him:—"Why dost thou praise Rustem in this manner to me? Where hast thou seen the strife of heroes?" Hujír became alarmed, and thought within himself, if I point out Rustem's tent, no doubt he will be killed by this ambitious youth, and then there will be no one to defend the Persian throne. Sohráb continued with emotion:—"Point out to me the tent of Rustem, this moment, or thou shalt die!" Hujír again paused, and said within himself:—"More honourable will it be to save the lives of Rustem and Káús than my own.—What is my life compared to theirs?—Nothing!" He then said aloud:—"Why thus seek for a pretext to shed my blood—why these pretences, since my life is in thy power!" Sohráb turned from him in despair, and descending from the rampart on which he stood, arrayed himself in armour, and prepared for battle. His first object was to attack the centre where Káús was posted; thither he proceeded, and called out aloud:—"I have sworn to be revenged on Káús for the murder of Zindeh; if he has any honour let him meet me in single combat." Sohráb stood alone on the plain, firm as the mountain Alberz, and such terror had seized upon the hearts of the warriors, that not a man had courage enough to advance a step against him. After a short space, Sohráb called out again:—"The king cannot be excused. It is not the custom of kings to be without honour, or to skulk away like foxes from the power of lions in battle. O, Káús, wherefore dost thou hesitate to enter the field?

"Why have they named thee, Kai-Káús, the king,
If thou'rt unfit to combat with the brave?"

Káús was appalled by the insulting boldness of the youth, and called to his friends to inform Rustem of the dilemma into which he was thrown, and the panic of his warriors, who seemed deprived of their senses. But Rustem had resolved not to fight on that day. "Let another chief," said he, "oppose the Tartar, and when he is overthrown it will be my turn." Káús then sent Tús to urge him to comply, and the champion being made acquainted with the distress and terror of the king, hurried on his armour, and left his tent. On the way, he said to himself: "This enemy must be of the demon-breed, otherwise why should such an impression have been made on the warriors, that they are afraid to oppose him." Then throwing aside all apprehension on his own account, and placing his trust in God, he appeared before Sohráb, who invited him to go to a little distance, and fight apart from the beholders. The invitation being accepted, Sohráb said: "No mortal has power to resist this arm—thou must perish!"—"Why this boasting? Thou art but a child, and where hast thou seen the conflicts of the valiant? I am myself an old experienced warrior; I slew the White Demon and all his Demon-host, and neither lion, nor dragon, nor tiger, can escape from me.

"Compassion rises in my heart,
I cannot slay thee—let us part!
Thy youth, thy gallantry, demand
A different fate than murderous brand."

"Perhaps," replied Sohráb, "thou art Rustem!"—"No, I am only the servant of Rustem." At this declaration,

Aspiring hope was turned to sad dismay,
And darkness quenched the joyous beam of day.

At first the two combatants fought with spears, which were soon shivered to pieces; then with swords, which became hacked like saws, and then with clubs. So fiercely they contended that their mail was torn in pieces, their weapons bent, and their horses almost exhausted. Blood and sweat poured down on the ground as they strugged, and their throats were parched with thirst. Both stood still for a while to breathe. Rustem said to himself: "I never saw man or Demon with such activity and strength;" and Sohráb thus addressed the champion gaily, "When thou art ready, come and try the effects of bow and arrow!" They then engaged with bows and arrows, but without any decisive result. Afterwards they used their hands and arms in wrestling, and Rustem applied as much force as might have shaken a mountain, to raise Sohráb from the ground, but he could not move him. Sohráb then endeavoured to lift up his antagonist, but in vain. Both were satisfied, and forsook each other's hold. Sohráb however had recourse to his mace, and struck a heavy blow on the head of Rustem, who reeled with the pain it inflicted. The laughing stripling, in consequence, spoke tauntingly to him, and Rustem said, "Night is coming on, we will resume the battle to-morrow." Sohráb replied, "Go, I have given thee enough, I will now let Káús feel the sharpness of my sword!" and, at the same moment that he proceeded against the Persian king, Rustem galloped forward to be revenged on the Túránians. But in the midst of his career, the unprotected situation of Káús struck his mind, and returning to his own army, found that Sohráb had slain a number of his warriors, and was still committing great havoc. He called to him, and said, "Let there be a truce to-night; but if thou art still for war, oppose thyself to me alone!" Sohráb was himself weary, and closed with the first proposal. Both accordingly retired to their tents.

In the night Káús sent for Rustem, and observed, that during the whole period of his life he had never witnessed or heard of such overwhelming valour as had been exhibited by the young invader; to which Rustem replied, "I know not, but he seems to be formed of iron. I have fought him with sword, and arrow, and mace, and he is still unhurt. In the warrior's art he is my superior, and Heaven knows what may be the result to-morrow." Having retired to his own place of rest, Rustem passed the night in petitions to the Almighty, and to his brother Zúára he said, "Alas! I have felt that the power of this youth's arm is prodigious. Should any thing untoward happen in the ensuing fight, go immediately to Zál, and think not of opposition to this triumphant Tartar, for certainly the whole of Persia will fall under his control."

Meanwhile Sohráb, having returned to his tent, said to Húmán, "This old man has the strength and the port of Rustem; God forbid that, if the signs which my mother gave be true, he should prove my father!" Húmán said, in answer: "I have often seen Rustem, and I know him; but this is not the champion of Persia—and though his horse is like Rakush, it is not the same." From this declaration of Húmán, Sohráb felt assured that this was not Rustem.

As soon as the morning dawned both the combatants were opposed to each other; and when the eye of Sohráb fell upon Rustem, an instinctive feeling of affection rose in his heart, and he wished to close the contest in peace.

> "Let us together sit and shun the strife,
> Which sternly seeks each other's valued life;
> Let others mix in fight, whilst we agree,
> And yield our hearts to peace and amity.
> Affection fills my breast with hopes and fears,
> For thee my cheeks are overflowed with tears;
> How have I ceaseless sought to know thy name,
> Oh, tell it now, thou man of mighty fame."

To this address, Rustem replied, that the words of the preceding evening were of a different import, and the agreement was to wrestle to-day. "I am not," said he, "a person of trick or artifice, nor a child, as thou art, but I am prepared to wrestle with thee." Sohráb finding every effort fruitless, all his hopes disappointed, and his views frustrated at every step, dismounted and prepared for the contest. Rustem was already on foot, tightening his girdle previous to the struggle.

> Like lions they together tugged, and strained
> Their nervous limbs;—and from their bodies flowed
> Streams of red blood and sweat. Sohráb with force
> Equal to a mad elephant's, raised up
> The champion, and upon the sandy plain
> Dashed him down backward. Then upon his breast,
> Fierce as a tiger on a prostrate elk,
> He sat, all ready to lop off the head.

But Rustem called out in time, and said, "According to the custom of my country, the first time a combatant in wrestling is thrown, his head is not severed from his body, but only after the second fall." As soon as Sohráb heard these words, he returned his dagger into the sheath, and allowed his antagonist to rise.

When the youth returned to his tent, and told Húmán what he had done, the Túránian chief lamented deeply the thoughtlessness of his conduct. "To ensnare the lion," said he, "and then set him at liberty to devour thee, was certainly a foolish thing!" But Sohráb said, "He is still in my power, being inferior to me in skill and strength, and I shall to-morrow be able to command the same advantage.' To this, Húmán replied, "The wise never look upon an enemy as weak and contemptible!"

When Rustem had escaped from the battle with Sohráb, he purified himself with water, and prostrated himself all night in devotion to the Almighty, praying that his former strength and power might be vouchsafed to him. It is said that in the first instance God gave him so much strength, that in placing his foot upon a rock it sunk to its centre. But as he was thus unable to walk, he prayed for a suitable diminution of power, and the prayer was accepted. With this diminished power, though still prodigious, he was now again favoured, and on the following day the fight was renewed. "What! here again?" said Sohráb, triumphantly.

Again their backs they wrestling bend,*
Again their limbs they seem to rend;
They seize each other's girdle-band,
And strain and grasp with foot and hand,
Doubt hanging still on either side,
From morn to sombre even-tide.

---

* Wrestling is a favourite sport in the east. From Homer down to Statius, the Greek and Roman poets have introduced wrestling in their Epic poems. Wrestlers, like the gladiators at Rome, are exhibited in India on a variety of occasions. Prize wrestlers were common in almost every European nation.

At length Rustem made a powerful effort, and got Sohráb under him. Apprehensive however that he had not strength enough to keep him there, he plunged his dagger in the side of the unhappy youth, and fatally prevented all further resistance. Groaning heavily, the dying Sohráb said: "Alas! I came here in anxious search of my father, and it has cost me my life. But if thou wert a fish, and sought refuge at the bottom of the ocean, or a star in the heavens, my father will be revenged on thee for this deed."—"What is thy father's name?" said the champion. "His name is Rustem, and my mother is the daughter of the king of Samengán." On hearing these words, the world faded before Rustem's eyes, and he fell senseless on the ground. After some time he rose up in deep agitation, and asked Sohráb what tokens he possessed to prove the truth of his assertion,—"for I am Rustem!" he said in agony. "Alas!" rejoined Sohráb, "the instinctive feeling was ever at my heart, but, wonderful to say, it received no mutual assurance from thine! If a token is required, ungird my mail, and there behold the amulet which my mother bound on my arm, and which Rustem gave to her, saying that it would be of extraordinary use on a future day." The sight of the amulet was an overwhelming blow to the father—he exclaimed in bitterness of soul: "O cruelly art thou slain my son! my son! What father ever thus destroyed his own offspring! I shall never be released from the horror of this dreadful crime, and therefore better will it be that I put an end to my own existence!" But Sohráb dissuaded him from this resolution. "It has been

The old poet Drayton in his Poly-Olbion alludes to this manly exercise in England.

> This isle in wrestling doth excel;
> With collars be they yoked, to prove the arm at length,
> Like bulls set head to head, with meer deliver strength:
> Or by the girdles grasp'd, they practice with the hip,
> The forward, backward, falx, the mar, the turn, the trip:
> When stript into their shirts each other they invade,
> Within a spacious ring, for the beholders made,
> According to the law.

my destiny thus to perish, it can be of no avail to kill thyself. Let me depart, alone—and thou remain for ever." Rustem, in utter despair, flung himself on the ground, and covered his head with dust and ashes; whilst Sohráb continued writhing and fluttering like a bird, from the anguish of his wound.

When the people of Káús perceived Rakush riderless, they reported to him that Rustem was dead, and a loud wail of sorrow arose from the whole army. The messenger who was sent to ascertain the particulars of the misfortune, found Rustem rolling in the dust in the deepest affliction, and Sohráb at the point of death; and raising up the head of the champion, asked him what had happened. "I have done that," said he, "which has made me weary of life. I have, in my old age, slain my son!" Zúára, his brother, hearing this, turned in sorrow to Sohráb, who said to him: "Such is my destiny, such the will of fortune. It was decreed that I should perish by the hand of my father. I came like a flash of lightning, and now I depart like the empty wind." Both Rustem and Zúára were inconsolable, but Sohráb again tried to soothe them, and said, "No person remains for ever in the world; then why this grief?" He then addressed Rustem, "O let not those who have followed my fortunes be put to trouble, or punished on my account,—they are not to blame." And Rustem set his mind entirely at rest about them.

Gúdarz was now sent by the champion to Káús to ask him for a cordial balm which he possessed of wonderful virtue, in the hope that it might restore Sohráb to life. But when the king heard the request, he said: "Doubtless the cordial will make him better, but I cannot forget the scandal and disgrace which this youth heaped upon me even in presence of my own army. Besides which, he threatened to deprive me of my crown, and give it to Rustem. I will not serve him."

When Gúdarz heard this cruel speech,
Which flinty heart alone could teach,
He hastened back and told the tale;
But though it was his fate to fail,

Rustem himself. the king might calm,
And gain the life-reviving balm!
Then Rustem to his sovereign went,
But scarcely had he reached the tent,
Ere news arrived that all was past,—
The warrior-youth had breathed his last!

Rustem returned with the utmost speed, and continued mourning intensely. "Son of the valiant! thou art gone, the descendant of heroes has departed. Right would it be were I to cut off both my hands, and sit for evermore in dust and darkness." The body of Sohráb was then placed on a bier, and there was nothing but lamentation.

Alas! for that valour, that wisdom of thine,
Alas! that sweet life thou wert doomed to resign;
Alas! for the anguish thy mother must feel,
And thy father's affliction, which time will not heal.

The champion now proceeded to his tent, and consigned all his property, warlike appurtenances, and armour, to the flames.

Why should affection cling to this vain world,
Still fleeting, never for a moment fixed?
Who that has reason or reflection ever
Can be deceived by life's delusive joys?

Káús himself now repaired to Rustem, and offered him the consolation he required:

"No one is free from sorrow, all
Who sojourn on this earthly ball,
Must weep o'er friends and kindred gone,
And some are left to mourn, alone.
'Twas ever thus since time began,
For sorrow is the lot of man."

Upon this Rustem observed: "Thus it is, the arrow has reached the mark. My son is dead! and after this, I shall never more gird my loins against the Túránians. Let me request that Húmán may be allowed to return with his army unmolested to his own country, and that peace be made with

Afrásiyáb." The king acceded to this solicitation, saying, "My heart bleeds for thee, and on thy account I will overlook the injuries and insults which I have received from my implacable enemy. Let them go." Zúára was appointed to see Húmán and the Tartar troops across the Jíhún, and at the same time Káús with his army returned to Irán.

Meanwhile Rustem accompanied the bier of Sohráb to Sístan, and was met by Zál, with his household and troops in mourning raiment, throwing ashes over their heads. He said to his father, "Alas! in this narrow coffin lies the very image of Sám Súwár!" and when the bier was conveyed into the house, loud and continued lamentations burst forth from the mother of Rustem and the women of her family. At length the body of Sohráb was honourably interred, and a lasting monument erected to his memory.

When the melancholy tidings of the stripling's fate arrived at Samengán, and were communicated to Tahmíneh, she lighted a fire and threw herself into it; and when rescued from the flames by her people, she burnt her flowing hair, and disfigured her body in the agony of desperation.

> With her clenched hand she tore her raven locks,
> Locks of ensnaring beauty, as these words,
> Uttered with frenzied look, and trembling accent,
> Fell from her lips: "My child, my darling child!
> Where art thou now, mixed with the worthless earth,
> In a remote, inhospitable land?
> Seeking thy father, what hast thou obtained?
> Death from a parent's hand! O how I loved thee,
> And watched thee night and day; whom can I now
> Clasp in these longing arms, to whom relate
> The agony I suffer! O my child!
> Where were the tokens which I gave to thee,
> Why didst thou not present them to his view?
> But wherefore did I madly stay behind,
> And not point out to thee thy mighty father?"
> Thus wildly she exclaimed, and all around
> Seeing her frantic grief, shed floods of tears.
> The stripling's horse was brought, and to her bosom
> She pressed the hoofs, and kissed the head and face,
> Bathing them with her tears. His mail, and helm,
> Bow, spear, and mace, his bridle, shield, and saddle,

Were all before her, and with these she beat
Her bursting head, as if she could not feel
Aught but the wounds of her maternal spirit.
Thus she unceasing raved and wept by turns,
Till one long year had passed—then, welcome death
Released her from the heavy load of life,
The pressure of unmitigated woe.

THE STORY OF SAIÁWUSH.

Early one morning as the cock crew, Tús arose, and accompanied by Gíw and Gúdarz and a company of horsemen, proceeded on a hunting excursion, not far from the banks of the Jíhún, where, after ranging about the forest for some time, they happened to fall in with a damsel of extreme beauty, with smiling lips, blooming cheeks, and fascinating mien. They said to her:

"Never was seen so sweet a flower,
In garden, vale, or fairy bower;
The moon is on thy lovely face,
Thy cypress-form is full of grace;
But why, with charms so soft and meek,
Dost thou the lonely forest seek?"

She replied that her father was a violent man, and that she had left her home to escape his anger. She had crossed the river Jíhún, and had travelled several leagues on foot, in consequence of her horse being too much fatigued to bear her farther. She had at that time been three days in the forest. On being questioned respecting her parentage, she said her father's name was Shíwer, of the race of Feridún. Many sovereigns had been suitors for her hand, but she did not approve of one of them. At last he wanted to marry her to Poshang, the ruler of Túrán, but she refused him on account of his ugliness and bad temper! This she said was the cause of her father's violence, and of her flight from home.

"But when his angry mood is o'er,
He'll love his daughter as before;
And send his horsemen far and near,
To take me to my mother dear;
Therefore, I would not further stray,
But here, without a murmur, stay."

The hearts of both Tús and Gíw were equally inflamed with love for the damsel, and each was equally determined to support his own pretensions, in consequence of which a quarrel arose between them. At length it was agreed to refer the matter to the king, and to abide by his decision. When, however, the king beheld the lovely object of contention, he was not disposed to give her to either claimant, but without hesitation took her to himself, after having first ascertained that she was of distinguished family and connection. In due time a son was born to him, who was, according to the calculations of the astrologers, of wonderful promise, and named Saiáwush. The prophecies about his surprising virtues, and his future renown, made Káús anxious that justice should be done to his opening talents, and he was highly gratified when Rustem agreed to take him to Zábulistán, and there instruct him in all the accomplishments which were suitable to his illustrious rank. He was accordingly taught horsemanship and archery, how to conduct himself at banquets, how to hunt with the falcon and the leopard, and made familiar with the manners and duty of kings, and the hardy chivalry of the age. His progress in the attainment of every species of knowledge and science was surprising, and in hunting he never stooped to the pursuit of animals inferior to the lion or the tiger. It was not long before the youth felt anxious to pay a visit to his father, and Rustem willingly complying with his wishes, accompanied his accomplished pupil to the royal court, where they were both received with becoming distinction, Saiáwush having fulfilled Káús expectations in the highest degree, and the king's gratitude to the champion being in proportion to the eminent merit of his services on the interesting occasion. After this, however, preceptors were continued to enlighten his mind seven years longer, and then he was emancipated from further application and study.

One day Súdáveh, the daughter of the Shah of Hámáverán, happening to see Saiáwush sitting with his father, the beauty of his person made an instantaneous impression on her heart.

> The fire of love consumed her breast,
> The thoughts of him denied her rest.
> For him alone she pined in grief,
> From him alone she sought relief,
> And called him to her secret bower,
> To while away the passing hour :
> But Saiáwush refused the call,
> He would not shame his father's hall.

The enamoured Súdáveh, however, was not to be disappointed without further effort, and on a subsequent day she boldly went to the king, and praising the character and attainments of his son, proposed that he should be united in marriage to one of the damsels of royal lineage under her care. For the pretended purpose therefore of making his choice, she requested he might be sent to the harem, to see all the ladies and fix on one the most suited to his taste. The king approved of the proposal, and intimated it to Saiáwush ; but Saiáwush was modest, timid, and bashful, and mentally suspected in this overture some artifice of Súdáveh. He accordingly hesitated, but the king overcame his scruples, and the youth at length repaired to the shubistán, as the retired apartments of the women are called, with fear and trembling. When he entered within the precincts of the sacred place, he was surprised by the richness and magnificence of every thing that struck his sight. He was delighted with the company of beautiful women, and he observed Súdáveh sitting on a splendid throne in an interior chamber, like Heaven in beauty and loveliness, with a coronet on her head, and her hair floating round her in musky ringlets. Seeing him she descended gracefully, and clasping him in her arms, kissed his eyes and face with such ardour and enthusiasm that he thought proper to retire from her endearments and mix among the other damsels, who placed him on a golden chair and kept him in agreeable conversation for some time. After this pleasing interview he returned to the king, and gave him a very favourable account of his reception, and the heavenly splendour of the retirement, worthy of Jemshíd, Ferídún, or Húsheng, which gladdened his father's heart. Káús repeated to him his wish that he would at once choose one of the lights of the harem for his wife, as the astrologers had prophesied on his marriage the birth of a prince. But Saiáwush endeavoured to excuse himself from going again to Súdáveh's apartments. The king smiled at his weakness, and assured him that Súdáveh was alone anxious for his happiness, upon which the youth found himself again in her power. She was surrounded by the damsels as before, but, whilst his eyes were cast down, they shortly disappeared, leaving him and the enamoured Súdáveh together. She soon approached him, and lovingly said:

> "O why the secret keep from one,
> Whose heart is fixed on thee alone!
> Say who thou art, from whom descended,
> Some Peri with a mortal blended.
> For every maid who sees that face,
> That cypress form replete with grace,
> Becomes a victim to the wiles
> Which nestle in those dimpled smiles;
> Becomes thy own adoring slave,
> Whom nothing but thy love can save."

To this Saiáwush made no reply. The history of the adventure of Káús at Hámáverán, and what the king and his warriors endured in consequence of the treachery of the father of Súdáveh, flashed upon his mind. He therefore was full of apprehension, and breathed not a word in answer to her fondness. Súdáveh observing his silence and reluctance, threw away from herself the veil of modesty,

And said: "O be my own, for I am thine,
And clasp me in thy arms!" And then she sprang
To the astonished boy, and eagerly
Kissed his deep crimsoned cheek, which filled his soul
With strange confusion. "When the king is dead,
O take me to thyself; see how I stand,
Body and soul devoted unto thee."
In his heart he said: "This never can be:
This is a demon's work—shall I be treacherous?
What! to my own dear father? Never, never;
I will not thus be tempted by the devil;
Yet must I not be cold to this wild woman,
For fear of further folly."

Saiáwush then expressed his readiness to be united in marriage to her daughter, and to no other; and when this intelligence was conveyed to Káús by Súdáveh herself, his majesty was extremely pleased, and munificently opened his treasury on the happy occasion. But Súdáveh still kept in view her own design, and still labouring for its success, sedulously read her own incantations to prevent disappointment, at any rate to punish the uncomplying youth if she failed. On another day she sent for him, and exclaimed:

"I cannot now dissemble; since I saw thee
I seem to be as dead—my heart all withered.
Seven years have passed in unrequited love—
Seven long, long years. O! be not still obdurate,
But with the generous impulse of affection,
Oh, bless my anxious spirit, or, refusing,
Thy life will be in peril; thou shalt die!"
"Never," replied the youth; "O, never, never;
Oh, ask me not, for this can never be."

Saiáwush then rose to depart precipitately, but Súdáveh observing him, endeavoured to cling round him and arrest his flight. The endeavour, however, was fruitless; and finding at length her situation desperate, she determined to turn the adventure into her own favour, by accusing Saiáwush of an atrocious outrage on her own person and virtue. She accordingly tore her dress, screamed aloud, and rushed out of her apartment to inform Káús of the indignity she had suffered. Among her women the most clamorous lamentations arose, and echoed on every side. The king, on hearing that Saiáwush had preferred Súdáveh to her daughter, and that he had meditated so abominable an offence, thought that death alone could expiate his crime. He therefore summoned him to his presence; but satisfied that it would be difficult, if not impossible, to ascertain the truth of the case from either party concerned, he had recourse to a test which he thought would be infallible and conclusive. He first smelt the hands of Saiáwush, and then his garments, which had the scent of rose-water; and then he took the garments of Súdáveh, which, on the contrary, had a strong flavour of wine and musk. Upon this discovery, the king resolved on the death of Súdáveh, being convinced of the falsehood of the accusation she had made against his son. But when his indignation subsided, he was induced on various accounts to forego that resolution. Yet he said to her, "I am sure that Saiáwush is innocent, but let that remain concealed." Súdáveh, however, persisted in asserting his guilt, and continually urged him to punish the reputed offender, but without being attended to.

At length he resolved to ascertain the innocence of Saiáwush by the ordeal of fire; and the fearless youth prepared to undergo the terrible trial to which he was sentenced, telling his father to be under no alarm.

"The truth (and its reward I claim),
Will bear me safe through fiercest flame."

A tremendous fire was accordingly lighted on the adjacent plain, which blazed to an immense distance. The youth was attired in his golden helmet and a white robe, and mounted on a black horse. He put up a prayer to the Almighty for protection, and then rushed amidst the conflagration, as collectedly as if the act had been entirely free from peril. When Súdáveh heard the confused exclamations that were uttered at that moment, she hurried upon the terrace of the palace and witnessed the appalling sight, and in the fondness of her heart, wished even that she could share his fate, the fate of him of whom she was so deeply enamoured. The king himself fell from his throne in horror on seeing him surrounded and enveloped in the flames, from which there seemed no chance of extrication; but the gallant youth soon rose up, like the moon from the bursting element, and went through the ordeal unharmed and untouched by the fire. Káús, on coming to his senses, rejoiced exceedingly on the happy occasion, and his severest anger was directed against Súdáveh, whom he now determined to put to death, not only for her own guilt, but for exposing his son to such imminent danger. The noble youth, however, interceded for her. Súdáveh, notwithstanding, still continued to practice her charms and incantations in secret, to the end that Saiáwush might be put out of the way; and in this pursuit she was indeed indefatigable.

Suddenly intelligence was received that Afrásiyáb had assembled another army, for the purpose of making an irruption into Irán; and Káús, seeing that a Tartar could neither be bound by promise nor oath, resolved that he would on this occasion take the field himself, penetrate as far as Balkh, and seizing the country, make an example of the inhabitants. But Saiáwush perceiving in this prospect of affairs an opportunity of becoming free from the machinations and witchery of Súdáveh, earnestly requested to be employed, adding that, with the advice and bravery of Rustem, he would be sure of success. The king referred the matter to Rustem, who candidly declared that there was no necessity whatever for his majesty proceeding personally to the war; and upon this assurance he threw open his treasury, and supplied all the resources of the empire to equip the troops appointed to accompany them. After one month the army marched towards Balkh, the point of attack.

On the other side Gersíwaz, the ruler of Balghar, joined the Tartar legions at Balkh, commanded by Bármán, who both sallied forth to oppose the Persian host, and after a conflict of three days were defeated, and obliged to abandon the fort. When the accounts of this calamity reached Afrásiyáb, he was seized with the utmost terror, which was increased by a dreadful dream. He thought he was in a forest abounding with serpents, and that the air was darkened by the appearance of countless eagles. The ground was parched up with heat, and a whirlwind hurled down his tent and overthrew his banners. On every side flowed a river of blood, and the whole of his army had been defeated and butchered in his sight. He was afterwards taken prisoner, and ignominiously conducted to Káús, in whose company he beheld a gallant youth, not more than fourteen years of age, who, the moment he saw him, plunged a dagger in his loins, and with the scream of agony produced by the wound, he awoke. Gersíwaz had in the meantime returned with the remnant of his force; and being informed of these particulars, endeavoured to console Afrásiyáb, by assuring him that the true interpretation of dreams was the reverse of appearances. But Afrásiyáb was not to be consoled in this manner. He referred to his astrologers, who, however, hesitated, and were unwilling to afford an explanation of the mysterious vision. At length one of them, upon the solicited promise that the king would not punish him for divulging the truth, described the nature of the warning implied in what had been witnessed.

"And now I throw aside the veil,
Which hides the darkly shadowed tale.
Led by a prince of prosperous star,
The Persian legions speed to war,
And in his horoscope we scan
The lordly victor of Túrán.
If thou shouldst to the conflict rush,
Opposed to conquering Saiáwush,
Thy Turkish cohorts will be slain,
And all thy saving efforts vain.
For if he, in the threatened strife,
Should haply chance to lose his life;
Thy country's fate will be the same,
Stripped of its throne and diadem."

Afrásiyáb was satisfied with this interpretation, and felt the prudence of avoiding a war so pregnant with evil consequences to himself and his kingdom. He therefore deputed Gersíwaz to the head-quarters of Saiáwush, with splendid presents, consisting of horses richly caparisoned, armour, swords, and other costly articles, and a written despatch, proposing a termination to hostilities.

In the meantime Saiáwush was anxious to pursue the enemy across the Jíhún, but was dissuaded by his friends. When Gersíwaz arrived on his embassy he was received with distinction, and the object of his mission being understood, a secret council was held upon what answer should be given. It was then deemed proper to demand: first, one hundred distinguished heroes as hostages; and secondly, the restoration of all the provinces which the Túránians had taken from Irán. Gersíwaz sent immediately to Afrásiyáb to inform him of the conditions required, and without the least delay they were approved. A hundred warriors were soon on their way; and Bokhára, and Samerkánd, and Haj, and the Punjáb, were faithfully delivered over to Saiáwush. Afrásiyáb himself retired towards Gungduz, saying, "I have had a terrible dream, and I will surrender whatever may be required from me, rather than go to war."

The negotiations being concluded, Saiáwush sent a letter to his father by the hands of Rustem. Rumour, however, had already told Káús of Afrásiyáb's dream, and the terror he had been thrown into in consequence. The astrologers in his service having prognosticated from it the certain ruin of the Túránian king, the object of Rustem's mission was directly contrary to the wishes of Káús; but Rustem contended that the policy was good, and the terms were good, and he thereby incurred his majesty's displeasure. On this account Káús appointed Tús the leader of the Persian army, and commanded him to march against Afrásiyáb, ordering Saiáwush at the same time to return, and bring with him his hundred hostages. At this command Saiáwush was grievously offended, and consulted with his chieftains, Báhrám, and Zinga, and Sháwerán, on the fittest course to be pursued, saying, "I have pledged my word to the fulfilment of the terms, and what will the world say if I do not keep my faith?" The chiefs tried to quiet his mind, and recommended him to write again to Káús, expressing his readiness to renew the war, and return the hundred hostages. But Saiáwush was in a different humour, and thought as Tús had been actually appointed to the command of the Persian army, it would be most advisable for him to abandon his country and join Afrásiyáb. The chiefs, upon hearing this singular resolution, unanimously attempted to dissuade him from pursuing so wild a course as throwing himself into the power of his enemy; but he was deaf to their entreaties, and in the stubbornness of his spirit, wrote to Afrásiyáb, informing him that Káús had refused to ratify the treaty of peace, that he was compelled to return the hostages, and even himself to seek protection in Túrán from the resentment of his father, the warrior Tús having been already entrusted with the charge of the army. This unexpected intelligence excited considerable surprise in the mind of Afrásiyáb, but he had no hesitation in selecting the course to be followed. The ambassadors, Zinga and Sháwerán, were soon furnished with a reply, which was to this effect: "I settled the terms of peace with thee, not with thy father. With him I have nothing to do. If thy choice be retirement and tranquillity, thou shalt have a peaceful and independent province allotted to thee; but if war be thy object, I will furnish thee with a large army: thy father is old and infirm, and with the aid of Rustem, Persia will be an easy conquest." Having thus obtained the promised favour and support of Afrásiyáb, Saiáwush gave in charge to Báhrám the city of Balkh, the army and treasure, in order that they might be delivered over to Tús on his arrival; and taking with him three hundred chosen horsemen, passed the Jíhún, in progress to the court of Afrásiyáb. On taking this decisive step, he again wrote to Káús, saying:

"From my youth upward I have suffered wrong
At first Súdáveh, false and treacherous,
Sought to destroy my happiness and fame;
And thou hadst nearly sacrificed my life

To glut her vengeance. The astrologers
Were all unheeded, who pronounced me innocent,
And I was doomed to brave devouring fire,
To testify that I was free from guilt;
But God was my deliverer! Victory now
Has marked my progress. Balkh, and all its spoils,
Are mine, and so reduced the enemy,
That I have gained a hundred hostages,
To guarantee the peace which I have made;
And what my recompense! a father's anger,
Which takes me from my glory. Thus deprived
Of thy affection, whither can I fly?
Be it to friend or foe, the will of fate
Must be my only guide—condemned by thee."

The reception of Saiáwush by Afrásiyáb was warm and flattering. From the gates of the city to the palace, gold and incense were scattered over his head in the customary manner, and exclamations of welcome uttered on every side.

"Thy presence gives joy to the land,
Which awaits thy command;
It is thine! it is thine!
All the chiefs of the state have assembled to meet thee,
All the flowers of the land are in blossom to greet thee!"

The youth was placed on a golden throne next to Afrásiyáb, and a magnificent banquet prepared in honour of the stranger, and music and the songs of beautiful women enlivened the festive scene. They chaunted the praises of Saiáwush, distinguished, as they said, among men for three things: first, for being of the line of Kai-kobád; secondly, for his faith and honour; and, thirdly, for the wonderful beauty of his person, which had gained universal love and admiration. The favourable sentiments which characterized the first introduction of Saiáwush to Afrásiyáb continued to prevail, and indeed the king of Túrán seemed to regard him with increased attachment and friendship, as the time passed away, and shewed him all the respect and honour to which his royal birth would have entitled him in his own country. After the lapse of a year, Pírán-wísah, one of Afrásiyáb's generals, said to him: "Young prince, thou art now high in the favour of the king, and at a great distance from Persia, and thy father is old; would it not therefore be better for thee to marry and take up thy residence among us for life?" The suggestion was a rational one, and Saiáwush readily expressed his acquiescence; accordingly, the lovely Gúlshaher, who was also named Jarira, having been introduced to him, he was delighted with her person, and both consenting to a union, the marriage ceremony was immediately performed.

> And many a warm delicious kiss,
> Told how he loved the wedded bliss.

Some time after this union, Pírán suggested another alliance, for the purpose of strengthening his political interest and power, and this was with Ferangís, the daughter of Afrásiyáb. But Saiáwush was so devoted to Gúlshaher that he first consulted with her on the subject, although the hospitality and affection of the king constituted such strong claims on his gratitude that refusal was impossible. Gúlshaher, however, was a heroine, and willingly sacrificed her own feelings for the good of Saiáwush, saying she would rather condescend to be the very handmaid of Ferangís than that the happiness and prosperity of her lord should be compromised. The second marriage accordingly took place, and Afrásiyáb was so pleased with the match that he bestowed on the bride and her husband the sovereignty of Khoten, together with countless treasure in gold, and a great number of horses, camels, and elephants. In a short time they proceeded to the seat of the new government.

Meanwhile Káús suffered the keenest distress and sorrow when he heard of the flight of Saiáwush into Túrán, and Rustem felt such strong indignation at the conduct of the king that he abruptly quitted the court, without permission, and retired to Sístán. Káús thus found himself in an embarrassed condition, and deemed it prudent to recall both Tús and the army from Balkh, and relinquish further hostile measures against Afrásiyáb.

The first thing that Saiáwush undertook after his arrival at Khoten, was to order the selection of a beautiful site for his residence, and Pírán devoted his services to fulfil that object, exploring all the provinces, hills, and dales, on every side. At last he discovered a beautiful spot, at the distance of about a month's journey, which combined all the qualities and advantages required by the anxious prince. It was situated on a mountain, and surrounded by scenery of exquisite richness and variety. The trees were fresh and green, birds warbled on every spray, transparent rivulets murmured through the meadows, the air was neither oppressively hot in summer, nor cold in winter, so that the temperature, and the attractive objects which presented themselves at every glance, seemed to realize the imagined charms and fascinations of Paradise. The inhabitants enjoyed perpetual health, and every breeze was laden with music and perfume. So lovely a place could not fail to yield pleasure to Saiáwush, who immediately set about building a palace there, and garden-temples, in which he had pictures painted of the most remarkable persons of his time, and also the portraits of ancient kings. The walls were decorated with the likenesses of Kai-kobád, of Kai-káús, Poshang, Afrásiyáb, and Sám, and Zál, and Rustem, and other champions of Persia and Túrán. When completed, it was a gorgeous retreat, and the sight of it sufficient to give youthful vigour to the withered faculties of age. And yet Saiáwush was not happy! Tears started into his eyes and sorrow weighed upon his heart, whenever he thought upon his own estrangement from home!

It happened that the lovely Gúlshaher, who had been left in the house of her father, was delivered of a son in due time, and he was named Ferúd.

Afrásiyáb, on being informed of the proceedings of Saiáwush, and of the heart-expanding residence he had chosen, was highly gratified; and to shew his affectionate regard, dispatched to him with the intelligence of the birth of a son, presents of great value and variety. Gersíwaz, the brother of Afrásiyáb, and who had from the first looked upon Saiáwush with a jealous and malignant eye, being afraid of his interfering with his own prospects in Túrán, was the person sent on this occasion. But he hid his secret thoughts under the veil of outward praise and approbation. Saiáwush was pleased with the intelligence and the presents, but failed to pay the customary respect to Gersíwaz on his arrival, and, in consequence, the lurking indignation and hatred formerly felt by the latter were considerably augmented. The attention of Saiáwush respecting his army and the concerns of the state, was unremitting, and noted by the visitor with a jealous and scrutinizing eye, so that Gersíwaz, on his return to the court of Afrásiyáb, artfully talked much of the pomp and splendour of the prince, and added: "Saiáwush is far from being the amiable character thou hast supposed; he is artful and ambitious, and he has collected an immense army; he is in fact dissatisfied. As a proof of his haughtiness, he paid me but little attention, and doubtless very heavy calamity will soon befall Túrán, should he break out, as I apprehend he will, into open rebellion.

For he is proud, and thou hast yet to learn
The temper of thy daughter Ferangís,
Now bound to him in duty and affection;
Their purpose is the same, to overthrow
The kingdom of Túrán, and thy dominion;
To merge the glory of this happy realm
Into the Persian empire!"

But plausible and persuasive as were the observations and positive declarations of Gersíwaz, Afrásiyáb would not believe the imputed ingratitude and hostility of Saiáwush. "He has sought my protection," said he; "he has thrown himself upon my generosity, and I cannot think him treacherous. But if he has meditated any thing unmerited by me, and unworthy of himself, it will be better to send him back to Kai-káús, his father." The artful Gersíwaz, however, was not to be diverted from his object: he said that Saiáwush had become personally acquainted with Túrán, its position, its weakness, its strength, and resources, and aided by Rustem, would soon be able to overrun the country if he was suffered to return, and therefore he recommended Afrásiyáb to bring him from Khoten by some artifice, and secure him. In conformity with this suggestion, Gersíwaz was again deputed to the young prince, and a letter of a friendly nature written for the purpose of blinding him to the real intentions of his father-in-law. The letter was no sooner read than Saiáwush expressed his desire to comply with the request contained in it, saying that Afrásiyáb had been a father to him, and that he would lose no time in fulfilling in all respects the wishes he had received.

This compliance and promptitude, however, was not in harmony with the sinister views of Gersíwaz, for he foresaw that the very fact of answering the call immediately would shew that some misrepresentation had been practised, and consequently it was his business now to promote procrastination, and an appearance of evasive delay. He therefore said to him privately that it would be advisable for him to wait a little, and not manifest such implicit obedience to the will of Afrásiyáb; but Saiáwush replied, that both his duty and affection urged him to a ready compliance. Then Gersíwaz pressed him more warmly, and represented how inconsistent, how unworthy of his illustrious lineage it would be to betray so meek a spirit, especially as he had a considerable army at his command, and could vindicate his dignity and his rights. And he addressed to him these specious arguments so incessantly and with such earnestness, that the deluded prince was at last induced to put off his departure, on account of his wife Ferangís pretending that she was ill, and saying that the moment she was better he would return to Túrán. This was quite enough for treachery to work upon; and as soon as the dispatch was sealed, Gersíwaz conveyed it with the utmost expedition to Afrásiyáb. Appearances, at least, were thus made strong against Saiáwush, and the tyrant of Túrán, now easily convinced of his falsehood, and feeling in consequence his former enmity renewed, forthwith assembled an army to punish his refractory son-in-law. Gersíwaz was appointed the leader of that army, which was put in motion without delay against the unoffending youth. The news of Afrásiyáb's warlike preparations satisfied the mind of Saiáwush that Gersíwaz had given him good advice, and that he had been a faithful monitor, for immediate compliance, he now concluded, would have been his utter ruin. When he communicated this unwelcome intelligence to Ferangís, she was thrown into the greatest alarm and agitation; but ever fruitful in expedients, suggested the course that it seemed necessary he should instantly adopt, which was to fly by a circuitous route back to Irán. To this he expressed no dissent, provided she would accompany him; but she said it was impossible to do so on account of the condition she was in. "Leave me," she added, "and save thy own life!" He therefore called together his three hundred Iránians, and requesting Ferangís, if she happened to be delivered of a son, to call him Kai-khosráu, set off on his journey.

> "I go, surrounded by my enemies;
> The hand of merciless Afrásiyáb
> Lifted against me."

It was not the fortune of Saiáwush, however, to escape so easily as had been anticipated by Ferangís. Gersíwaz was soon at his heels, and in the battle that ensued, all the Iránians were killed, and also the horse upon which the unfortunate prince rode, so that on foot he could make but little progress. In the meantime Afrásiyáb came up, and surrounding him, wanted to shoot him with an arrow, but he was restrained from the violent act by the intercession of his people, who recommended his being taken alive, and only kept in prison. Accordingly he was again attacked and secured, and still Afrásiyáb wished to put him to death; but Pílsam, one of his warriors, and the brother of Píran, induced him to relinquish that diabolical intention, and to convey him back to his own palace. Saiáwush was then ignominiously fettered and conducted to the royal residence, which he had himself erected and ornamented with such richness and magnificence. The sight of the city and its splendid buildings filled every one with wonder and admiration. Upon the arrival of Afrásiyáb, Ferangís hastened to him in a state of the deepest distress, and implored his clemency and compassion in favour of Saiáwush.

"O father, he is not to blame,
Still pure and spotless is his name;
Faithful and generous still to me,
And never—never false to thee.
This hate to Gersíwaz he owes,
The worst, the bitterest of his foes;
Did he not thy protection seek,
And wilt thou overpower the weak?
Spill royal blood thou shouldest bless,
In cruel sport and wantonness?
And earn the curses of mankind,
  Living, in this precarious state,
And dead, the torments of the mind,
  Which hell inflicts upon the great
Who revel in a murderous course,
And rule by cruelty and force.

It scarce becomes me now to tell,
What the accursed Zohák befel,
Or what the punishment which hurled
Selim and Túr from out the world.
And is not Káús living now,
With rightful vengeance on his brow?
And Rustem, who alone can make
Thy kingdom to its centre quake?
Gúdarz, Zúára, and Friburz,
And Tús, and Girgín, and Frámurz;
And others too of fearless might,
To challenge thee to mortal fight?
O, from this peril turn away,
Close not in gloom so bright a day;
Some heed to thy poor daughter give,
And let thy guiltless captive live."

The effect of this appeal, solemnly and urgently delivered, was only transitory. Afrásiyáb felt a little compunction at the moment, but soon resumed his ferocious spirit, and to ensure, without interruption, the accomplishment of his purpose, confined Ferangís in one of the remotest parts of the palace;

And thus to Gersíwaz unfeeling spoke :
"Off with his head, down with the enemy ;
But take especial notice that his blood
Stains not the earth, lest it should cry aloud
For vengeance on us. Take good care of that!"

Gersíwaz, who was but too ready an instrument, immediately directed Karú-zíra, a kinsman of Afrásiyáb, who had been also one of the most zealous in promoting the ruin of the Persian prince, to inflict the deadly blow ; and Saiáwush, whilst under the grasp of the executioner, had but time to put up a prayer to Heaven, in which he hoped that a son might be born to him to vindicate his good name, and be revenged on his murderer. The executioner then seized him by the hair, and throwing him on the ground, severed the head from the body. A golden vessel was ready to receive the blood, as commanded by Afrásiyáb ; but a few drops happened to be spilt on the soil, and upon that spot a tree grew up, which was afterwards called Saiáwush, and believed to possess many wonderful virtues! The blood was carefully conveyed to Afrásiyáb, the head fixed on the point of a javelin, and the body was buried with respect and affection by his friend Pílsam, who had witnessed the melancholy catastrophe. It is also related that a tremendous tempest occurred at the time this amiable prince was murdered, and that a total darkness covered the face of the earth, so that the people could not distinguish each other's faces. Then was the name of Afrásiyáb truly execrated and abhorred for the cruel act he had committed, and all the inhabitants of Khoten long cherished the memory of Saiáwush.

Ferangís was frantic with grief when she was told of the sad fate of her husband, and all her household uttered the loudest lamentations. Pílsam gave the intelligence to Pírán, and the proverb was then remembered: "It is better to be in hell, than under the rule of Afrásiyáb!" When the deep sorrow of Ferangís reached the ears of her father, he determined on a summary procedure, and ordered Gersíwaz to have her privately made away with, so that there might be no issue of her marriage with Saiáwush.

Pírán with horror heard this stern command,
And hasten'd to the king, and thus addressed him:
"What! would'st thou hurl thy vengeance on a woman,
That woman, too, thy daughter? Is it wise,
Or natural, thus to sport with human life?
Already hast thou taken from her arms
Her unoffending husband—that was cruel;
But thus to shed an innocent woman's blood,
And kill her unborn infant—that would be
Too dreadful to imagine! Is she not
Thy own fair daughter, given in happier time
To him who won thy favour and affection?
Think but of that, and from thy heart root out
This demon wish, which leads thee to a crime,
Mocking concealment; vain were the endeavour
To keep the murder secret, and when known,
The world's opprobrium would pursue thy name.
And after death, what would thy portion be!
No more of this—honour me with the charge,
And I will keep her with a father's care,
In my own mansion." Then Afrásiyáb
Readily answered: "Take her to thy home,
But when the child is born, let it be brought
Promptly to me—my will must be obeyed."

Pírán rejoiced at his success; and assenting to the command of Afrásiyáb, took Ferangís with him to Khoten, where in due time a child was born, and being a son, was called Kai-khosráu. As soon as he was born, Pírán took measures to prevent his being carried off to Afrásiyáb, and committed him to the care of some peasants on the mountain Kalún. On the same night Afrásiyáb had a dream, in which he received intimation of the birth of Kai-khosráu; and upon this intimation he sent for Pírán to know why his commands had not been complied with. Pírán replied, that he had cast away the child in the wilderness: "And why was he not sent to me?" inquired the despot. "Because," said Pírán, "I considered thy own future happiness; thou hast unjustly killed the father, and God forbid that thou shouldst also kill the son!" Afrásiyáb was abashed, and it is said that ever after the atrocious murder of Saiáwush, he had been tormented with the most terrible and harrowing dreams. Gersíwaz now became hateful to his sight, and he began at last deeply to repent of his violence and inhumanity.

Kai-khosráu grew up under the fostering protection of the peasants, and showed early marks of surprising talent and activity. He excelled in manly exercises; and hunting ferocious animals was his peculiar delight. Instructors had been provided to initiate him in all the arts and pursuits cultivated by the warriors of those days, and even in his twelfth year accounts were forwarded to Pírán of several wonderful feats which he had performed.

> Then smiled the good old man, and joyful said:
> "'Tis ever thus—the youth of royal blood
> Will not disgrace his lineage, but betray
> By his superior mien and gallant deeds
> From whence he sprung. 'Tis by the luscious fruit
> We know the tree, and glory in its ripeness!"

Pírán could not resist paying a visit to the youth in his mountainous retreat, and, happy to find him, beyond all expectation, distinguished for the elegance of his external appearance, and the superior qualities of his mind, related to him the circumstances under which he had been exposed, and the rank and misfortunes of his father. An artifice then occurred to him which promised to be of ultimate advantage. He afterwards told Afrásiyáb that the offspring of Ferangís, thrown by him into the wilderness to perish, had been found by a peasant and brought up, but that he understood the boy was little better than an idiot. Afrásiyáb, upon this information, desired that he might be sent for, and in the meantime Pírán took especial care to instruct Kai-khosráu how he should act; which was to seem in all respects insane, and he accordingly appeared before the king in the dress of a prince with a golden crown on his head, and the royal girdle round his loins. Kai-khosráu proceeded on horseback to the court of Afrásiyáb, and having performed the usual salutations, was suitably received, though with strong feelings of shame and remorse on the part of the tyrant. Afrásiyáb put several questions to him, which were answered in a wild and incoherent manner, entirely at variance with the subject proposed. The king could not help smiling, and supposing him to be totally deranged, allowed him to be sent with presents to his mother, for no harm, he thought, could possibly be apprehended from one so forlorn in mind. Pírán triumphed in the success of his scheme, and lost no time in taking Kai-khosráu to his mother. All the people of Khoten poured blessings on the head of the youth, and imprecations on the merciless spirit of Afrásiyáb. The city built by Saiáwush had been razed to the ground by the exterminating fury of his enemies, and wild animals and reptiles occupied the place on which it stood. The mother and son visited the spot where Saiáwush was barbarously killed, and the tree, which grew up from the soil enriched by his blood, was found verdant and flourishing, and continued to possess in perfection its marvellous virtues.

The tale of Saiáwush is told;
And now the pages bright unfold,
Rustem's revenge—Súdáveh's fate—
Afrásiyáb's degraded state,
And that terrific curse and ban
Which fell at last upon Túrán!

When Kai-káús heard of the fate of his son, and all its horrible details were pictured to his mind, he was thrown into the deepest affliction. His warriors, Tús, and Gúdarz, and Báhrám, and Fríburz, and Ferhád, felt with equal keenness the loss of the amiable prince, and Rustem, as soon as the dreadful intelligence reached Sistán, set off with his troops to the court of the king, still full of indignation at the conduct of Káús, and oppressed with sorrow respecting the calamity which had occurred. On his arrival he thus addressed the weeping and disconsolate father of Saiáwush, himself at the same time drowned in tears:

"How has thy temper turned to nought, the seed
Which might have grown, and cast a glorious shadow;
How is it scattered to the barren winds!
Thy love for false Súdáveh was the cause
Of all this misery; she, the Sorceress,
O'er whom thou hast so oft in rapture hung,
Enchanted by her charms;* she was the cause
Of this destruction. Thou art woman's slave!
Woman, the bane of man's felicity!
Who ever trusted woman? Death were better
Than being under woman's influence;
She places man upon the foamy ridge
Of the tempestuous wave, which rolls to ruin.
Who ever trusted woman?—Woman! woman!"
Káús looked down with melancholy mien,
And, half consenting, thus to Rustem said:—
"Súdáveh's blandishments absorbed my soul,
And she has brought this wretchedness upon me."
Rustem rejoined—"The world must be revenged
Upon this false Súdáveh;—she must die."
Káús was silent; but his tears flowed fast,
And shame withheld resistance. Rustem rushed
Without a pause towards the shubistan;
Impatient, nothing could obstruct his speed
To slay Súdáveh;—her he quickly found,
And rapidly his sanguinary sword
Performed its office. Thus the Sorceress died.
Such was the punishment her crimes received.

Having thus accomplished the first part of his vengeance, he proceeded with the Persian army against Afrásiyáb, and all the Iránian warriors followed his example. When he had penetrated as far as Túrán, the enemy sent forward thirty thousand men to oppose his progress; and in the conflict which ensued, Ferámurz took Sarkhá, the son of Afrásiyáb, prisoner. Rustem delivered him over to Tús to be put to death precisely in

* So Shakespeare:

Nay, but this dotage of our general's
O'erflows the measure: those his goodly eyes
That o'er the files and musters of the war
Have glowed like plated Mars, now bend, now turn,
The office and devotion of their view
Upon a tawny front: his captain's heart,
Which in the scuffles of great fights hath burst
The buckles on his breast, reneges all temper
And is become the bellows and the fan
To cool a gipsy's lust. ANTONY AND CLEOPATRA, I., 1.

the same manner as Saiáwush; but the captive represented himself as the particular friend of Saiáwush, and begged to be pardoned on that account. Rustem, however, had sworn that he would take his revenge, without pity or remorse, and accordingly death was inflicted upon the unhappy prisoner, whose blood was received in a dish, and sent to Káús, and the severed head suspended over the gates of the king's palace. Afrásiyáb hearing of this catastrophe, which sealed the fate of his favourite son, immediately collected together the whole of the Túránian army, and hastened himself to resist the conquering career of the enemy.

> As on they moved; with loud and dissonant clang;
> His numerous troops shut out the prospect round;
> No sun was visible by day; no moon,
> Nor stars by night. The tramp of men and steeds,
> And rattling drums, and shouts, were only heard,
> And the bright gleams of armour only seen.

Ere long the two armies met, when Pílsam, the brother of Pírán, was ambitious of opposing his single arm against Rustem, upon which Afrásiyáb said:—"Subdue Rustem, and thy reward shall be my daughter, and half my kingdom." Pírán, however, observed that he was too young to be a fit match for the experience and valour of the Persian champion, and would have dissuaded him from the unequal contest, but the choice was his own, and he was consequently permitted by Afrásiyáb to put his bravery to the test. Pílsam accordingly went forth and summoned Rustem to the fight; but Gív, hearing the call, accepted the challenge himself, and had nearly been thrown from his horse by the superior activity of his opponent. Ferámurz luckily saw him at the perilous moment, and darting forward, with one stroke of his sword shattered Pílsam's javelin to pieces, and then a new strife began. Pílsam and Ferámurz fought together with desperation, till both were almost exhausted, and Rustem himself was surprised to see the display of so much valour. Perceiving the wearied state of the two warriors he pushed forward

Rakush, and called aloud to Pílsam :—"Am I not the person challenged ?" and immediately the Túránian chief proceeded to encounter him, striking with all his might at the head of the champion ; but though the sword was broken by the blow, not a hair of his head was disordered.

Then Rustem urging on his gallant steed,
Fixed his long javelin in the girdle band
Of his ambitious foe, and quick unhorsed him ;
Then dragged him on towards Afrásiyáb,
And, scoffing, cast him at the despot's feet.
"Here comes the glorious conqueror," he said ;
"Now give to him thy daughter and thy treasure,
Thy kingdom and thy soldiers ; has he not
Done honour to thy country ?—Is he not
A jewel in thy crown of sovereignty ?
What arrogance inspired the fruitless hope !
Think of thy treachery to Saiáwush ;
Thy savage cruelty, and never look
For aught but deadly hatred from mankind ;
And in the field of fight defeat and ruin."
Thus scornfully he spoke, and not a man,
Though in the presence of Afrásiyáb,
Had soul to meet him ; fear o'ercame them all
Monarch and warriors, for a time. At length
Shame was awakened, and the king appeared
In arms against the champion. Fiercely they
Hurled their sharp javelins—Rustem's struck the head
Of his opponent's horse, which floundering fell,
And overturned his rider. Anxious then
The champion sprang to seize the royal prize ;
But Húmán rushed between, and saved his master,
Who vaulted on another horse and fled.

Having thus rescued Afrásiyáb, the wary chief exercised all his cunning and adroitness to escape himself, and at last succeeded. Rustem pursued him, and the Túránian troops, who had followed the example of the king ; but though thousands were slain in the chase which continued for many farsangs, no further advantage was obtained on that day. Next morning, however, Rustem resumed his pursuit ; and the enemy hearing of his approach, retreated into Chinese Tartary, to secure, among other advantages, the person of Kai-khosráu ; leaving the kingdom of Túrán at the mercy of the invader, who mounted the throne, and ruled there, it is said, about seven years, with memorable severity, proscribing and putting to death every person who mentioned the name of Afrásiyáb. In the mean time he made splendid presents to Tús and Gúdarz, suitable to their rank and services; and Zúára, in revenge for the monstrous outrage committed upon Saiáwush, burnt and destroyed every thing that came in his way; his wrath being exasperated by the sight of the places in which the young prince had resided, and recreated himself with hunting and other sports of the field. The whole realm, in fact, was delivered over to plunder and devastation; and every individual of the army was enriched by the appropriation of public and private wealth. The companions of Rustem, however, grew weary of residing in Túrán, and they strongly represented to him the neglect which Kai-káús had suffered for so many years, recommending his return to Persia, as being more honourable than the exile they endured in an ungenial climate. Rustem's abandonment of the kingdom was at length carried into effect; and he and his warriors did not fail to take away with them all the immense property that remained in jewels and gold; part of which was conveyed by the champion to Zábul and Sistán, and a goodly proportion to the king of kings in Persia.

When to Afrásiyáb was known
The plunder of his realm and throne,
That the destroyer's reckless hand
With fire and sword had seathed the land,
Sorrow and anguish filled his soul,
And passion raged beyond control;
And thus he to his warriors said :—
"At such a time, is valour dead?
The man who hears the mournful tale,
And is not by his country's bale
Urged on to vengeance, cannot be
Of woman born; accursed is he!
The time will come when I shall reap
The harvest of resentment deep;
And till arrives that fated hour,
Farewell to joy in hall or bower."

Rustem, in taking revenge for the murder of Saiáwush, had

not been unmindful of Kai-khosráu, and had actually sent to the remote parts of Tartary in quest of him.

It is said that Gúdarz beheld in a dream the young prince, who pointed out to him his actual residence, and intimated that of all the warriors of Káús, Gíw was the only one destined to restore him to the world and his birth-right. The old man immediately requested his son Gíw to go to the place where the stranger would be found. Gíw readily complied, and in his progress provided himself at every stage successively with a guide, whom he afterwards slew to prevent discovery, and in this manner he proceeded till he reached the boundary of Chín, enjoying no comfort by day, or sleep by night. His only food was the flesh of the wild ass, and his only covering the skin of the same animal. He went on traversing mountain and forest, enduring every privation, and often did he hesitate, often did he think of returning, but honour urged him forward in spite of the trouble and impediments with which he was continually assailed. Arriving in a desert one day, he happened to meet with several persons, who upon being interrogated, said that they were sent by Pírán Wísah in search of Kai-káús. Gíw kept his own secret, saying that he was amusing himself with hunting the wild ass, but took care to ascertain from them the direction in which they were going. During the night the parties separated, and in the morning Gíw proceeded rapidly on his route, and after some time discovered a youth sitting by the side of a fountain, with a cup in his hand, whom he supposed to be Kai-khosráu. The youth also spontaneously thought "This must be Gíw;" and when the traveller approached him, and said, "I am sure thou art the son of Saiáwush;" the youth observed, "I am equally sure that thou art Gíw, the son of Gúdarz." At this Gíw was amazed, and falling at his feet, asked how, and from what circumstance, he recognized him. The youth replied that he knew all the warriors of Káús; Rustem, and Kishwád, and Tús, and Gúdarz, and the rest, from their portraits in his father's gallery, they being deeply impressed on his mind. He then asked in what way

Gíw had discovered him to be Kai-khosráu, and Gíw answered, "Because I perceived something kingly in thy countenance. But let me again examine thee!" The youth, at this request, removed his garments, and Gíw beheld that mark on his body which was the heritage of the race of Kai-kobád. Upon this discovery he rejoiced, and congratulating himself and the young prince on the success of his mission, related to him the purpose for which he had come. Kai-khosráu was soon mounted on horseback, and Gíw accompanied him respectfully on foot. They, in the first instance, pursued their way towards the abode of Ferangís, his mother. The persons sent by Pírán Wísah did not arrive at the place where Kai-khosráu had been kept till long after Gíw and the prince departed; and then they were told that a Persian horseman had come and carried off the youth, upon which they immediately returned, and communicated to Pírán what had occurred. Ferangís, in recovering her son, mentioned to Gíw, with the fondness of a mother, the absolute necessity of going on without delay, and pointed out to him the meadow in which some of Afrásiyáb's horses were to be met with, particularly one called Behzád, which once belonged to Saiáwush, and which her father had kept in good condition for his own riding. Gíw, therefore, went to the meadow, and throwing his kamund, secured Behzád and another horse; and all three being thus accommodated, hastily proceeded on their journey towards Irán.

Tidings of the escape of Kai-khosráu having reached Afrásiyáb, he dispatched Kulbád with three hundred horsemen after him; and so rapid were his movements that he overtook the fugitives in the vicinity of Bulgharia. Khosráu and his mother were asleep, but Gíw being awake, and seeing an armed force evidently in pursuit of his party, boldly put on his armour, mounted Behzád, and before the enemy came up, advanced to the charge. He attacked the horsemen furiously with sword and mace, for he had heard the prophecy, which declared that Kai-khosráu was destined to be the king of kings, and therefore he braved the direst peril with confidence, and the certainty of success. It was this feeling which enabled him to perform such a prodigy of valour, in putting Kulbád and his three hundred horsemen to the route. They all fled defeated, and dispersed precipitately before him. After this surprising victory, he returned to the halting place, and told Kai-khosráu what he had done. The prince was disappointed at not having been awakened to participate in the exploit, but Gíw said, "I did not wish to disturb thy sweet slumbers unnecessarily. It was thy good fortune and prosperous star, however, which made me triumph over the enemy." The three travellers then resuming their journey:

> Through dreary track, and pathless waste,
> And wood and wild, their way they traced.

The return of the defeated Kulbád excited the greatest indignation in the breast of Pírán. "What! three hundred soldiers to fly from the valour of one man! Had Gíw possessed even the activity and might of Rustem and Sám, such a shameful discomfiture could scarcely have happened." Saying this, he ordered the whole force under his command to be got ready, and set off himself to overtake and intercept the fugitives, who, fatigued with the toilsome march, were only able to proceed one stage in the day. Pírán, therefore, who travelled at the rate of one hundred leagues a day, overtook them before they had passed through Bulgharia. Ferangís, who saw the enemy's banner floating in the air, knew that it belonged to Pírán, and instantly awoke the two young men from sleep. Upon this occasion, Khosráu insisted on acting his part, instead of being left ignominiously idle; but Gíw was still resolute and determined to preserve him from all risk, at the peril of his own life. "Thou art destined to be the king of the world; thou art yet young, and a novice, and hast never known the toils of war; Heaven forbid that any misfortune should befall thee: indeed, whilst I live, I will never suffer thee to go into battle!" Khosráu then proposed to give him assistance; but Gíw said he wanted no assistance, not even from Rustem;

"for," he added, "in art and strength we are equal, having frequently tried our skill together." Rustem had given his daughter in marriage to Gíw, he himself being married to Gíw's sister. "Be of good cheer," resumed he, "get upon some high place, and witness the battle between us.

Fortune will still from Heaven descend,
The god of victory is my friend."

As soon as he took the field, Pírán thus addressed him: "Thou hast once, singly, defeated three hundred of my soldiers; thou shalt now see what punishment awaits thee at my hands.

For should a warrior be a rock of steel,
A thousand ants, gathered on every side,
In time will make him but a heap of dust."

In reply, Gíw said to Pírán, "I am the man who bound thy two women, and sent them from China to Persia—Rustem and I are the same in battle. Thou knowest, when he encountered a thousand horsemen, what was the result, and what he accomplished! Thou wilt find me the same: is not a lion enough to overthrow a thousand kids?

If but a man survive of thy proud host,
Brand me with coward—say I'm not a warrior.
Already have I triumphed o'er Kulbád,
And now I'll take thee prisoner, yea, alive!
And send thee to Káús—there thou wilt be
Slain to avenge the death of Saiáwush;
Túrán shall perish, and Afrásiyáb,
And every earthly hope extinguished quite."
Hearing this awful threat, Pírán turned pale
And shook with terror,—trembling like a reed;
And saying: "Go, I will not fight with thee!"
But Gíw asked fiercely: "Why?" And on he rushed
Against the foe, who fled—but 'twas in vain.
The kamund round the old man's neck was thrown,
And he was taken captive. Then his troops
Showered their sharp arrows on triumphant Gíw,
To free their master, who was quickly brought
Before Kai-khosráu, and the kamund placed
Within his royal hands. This service done,
Gíw sped against the Tartars, and full soon
Defeated and dispersed them.

On his return, Gíw expressed his astonishment that Pírán was still alive; when Ferangís interposed, and weeping, said how much she had been indebted to his interposition and the most active humanity on various occasions, and particularly in saving herself and Kai-khosráu from the wrath of Afrásiyáb after the death of Saiáwush. "If," said she, "after so much generosity he has committed one fault, let it be forgiven.

> Let not the man of many virtues die,
> For being guilty of one trifling error.
> Let not the friend who nobly saved my life,
> And more, the dearer life of Kai-khosráu,
> Suffer from us. O, he must never, never,
> Feel the sharp pang of foul ingratitude,
> From a true prince of the Kaiánian race."

But Gíw paused, and said, "I have sworn to crimson the earth with his blood, and I must not pass from my oath." Khosráu then suggested to him to pierce the lobes of Pírán's ears, and drop the blood on the ground to stain it, in order that he might not depart from his word; and this humane fraud was accordingly committed. Khosráu further interceded; and instead of being sent a captive to Káús, the good old man was set at liberty.

When the particulars of this event were described to Afrásiyáb by Pírán Wísah, he was exceedingly sorrowful, and lamented deeply that Kai-khosráu had so successfully effected his escape. But he had recourse to a further expedient, and sent instructions to all the ferrymen of the Jihún, with a minute description of the three travellers, to prevent their passing that river, announcing at the same time that he himself was in pursuit of them. Not a moment was lost in preparing his army for the march, and he moved forward with the utmost expedition, night and day. At the period when Gíw arrived on the banks of the Jihún, the stream was very rapid and formidable, and he requested the ferrymen to produce their certificates to show themselves equal to their duty. They pretended that their certificates were lost, but demanded for their fare the black horse upon which Gíw rode. Gíw replied, that he could not part with his favourite horse; and they rejoined, "Then give us the damsel who accompanies you." Gíw answered, and said, "This is not a damsel, but the mother of that youth!"—"Then," observed they, "give us the youth's crown." But Gíw told them that he could not comply with their demand; yet he was ready to reward them with money to any extent. The pertinacious ferrymen, who were not anxious for money, then demanded his armour, and this was also refused; and such was their independence or their effrontery, that they replied, "If not one of these four things you are disposed to grant, cross the river as best you may." Gíw whispered to Kai-khosráu, and told him that there was no time for delay. "When Kávah, the blacksmith," said he, "rescued thy great ancester, Feridún, he passed the stream in his armour without impediment; and why should we, in a cause of equal glory, hesitate for a moment?" Under the inspiring influence of an auspicious omen, and confiding in the protection of the Almighty, Kai-khosráu at once impelled his foaming horse into the river; his mother, Feringís, followed with equal intrepidity, and then Gíw; and notwithstanding the perilous passage, they all successfully overcame the boiling surge, and landed in safety, to the utter amazement of the ferrymen, who of course had expected they would be drowned.

It so happened that at the moment they touched the shore, Afrásiyáb with his army arrived, and had the mortification to see the fugitives on the other bank, beyond his reach. His wonder was equal to his disappointment.

"What spirits must they have to brave
The terrors of that boiling wave—
With steed and harness, riding o'er
The billows to the further shore."
—It was a cheering sight, they say,
To see how well they kept their way,
How Ferangís impelled her horse
Across that awful torrent's course,
Guiding him with heroic hand,
To reach unhurt the friendly strand.

Afrásiyáb continued for some time mute with astonishment and vexation, and when he recovered, ordered the ferrymen to get ready their boats to pass him over the river; but Húmán dissuaded him from that measure, saying that they could only convey a few troops, and they would doubtless be received by a large force of the enemy on the other side. At these words, Afrásiyáb seemed to devour his own blood with grief and indignation, and immediately retracing his steps, returned to Túrán.

As soon as Gíw entered within the boundary of the Persian empire, he poured out thanksgivings to God for his protection, and sent intelligence to Káús of the safe arrival of the party in his dominions. The king rejoiced exceedingly, and appointed an honorary deputation under the direction of Gúdarz, to meet the young prince on the road. On first seeing him, the king moved forward to receive him; and weeping affectionately, kissed his eyes and face, and had a throne prepared for him exactly like his own, upon which he seated him; and calling the nobles and warriors of the land together, commanded them to obey him. All readily promised their allegiance, excepting Tús, who left the court in disgust, and repairing forthwith to the house of Fríburz, one of the sons of Káús, told him that he would only pay homage and obedience to him, and not to the infant whom Gíw had just brought out of a desert. Next day the great men and leaders were again assembled to declare publicly by an official act their fealty to Kai-khosráu, and Tús was also invited to the banquet, which was held on the occasion, but he refused to go. Gíw was deputed to repeat the invitation; and he then said, "I shall pay homage to Fríburz, as the heir to the throne, and to no other.

> "For is he not the son of Kai-káús,
> And worthy of the regal crown and throne?
> I want not any of the race of Poshang—
> None of the proud Túránian dynasty—
> Fruitless has been thy peril, Gíw, to bring
> A silly child among us, to defraud
> The rightful prince of his inheritance!"

Gíw, in reply, vindicated the character and attainments of Khosráu, but Tús was not to be appeased. He therefore returned to his father and communicated to him what had occurred. Gúdarz was roused to great wrath by this resistance to the will of the king, and at once took twelve thousand men and his seventy-eight kinsmen, together with Gíw, and proceeded to support his cause by force of arms. Tús, apprized of his intentions, prepared to meet him, but was reluctant to commit himself by engaging in a civil war, and said, internally:

"If I unsheath the sword of strife,
Numbers on either side will fall,
I would not sacrifice the life
Of one who owns my sovereign's thrall.

My country would abhor the deed,
And may I never see the hour
When Persia's sons are doomed to bleed,
But when opposed to foreign power.

The cause must be both good and true,
And if their blood in war must flow,
Will it not seem of brighter hue,
When shed to crush the Tartar foe?"

Possessing these sentiments, Tús sent an envoy to Gúdarz, suggesting the suspension of any hostile proceedings until information on the subject had been first communicated to the king. Káús was extremely displeased with Gúdarz for his precipitancy and folly, and directed both him and Tús to repair immediately to court. Tús there said frankly, "I now owe honour and allegiance to king Káús; but should he happen to lay aside the throne and the diadem, my obedience and loyalty will be due to Fríburz his heir, and not to a stranger." To this, Gúdarz replied, "Saiáwush was the eldest son of the king, and unjustly murdered, and therefore it becomes his majesty to appease and rejoice the soul of the deceased, by putting Kai-khosráu in his place. Kai-khosráu, like Ferídún, is worthy of empire; all the nobles of the land are of this opinion, excepting thyself, which must arise from ignorance and vanity.

From Nauder certainly thou art descended,
Not from a stranger, not from foreign loins;
But though thy ancestor was wise and mighty,
Art thou of equal merit? No, not thou!
Regarding Khosráu, thou hast neither shewn
Reason nor sense—but most surprising folly!"
To this contemptuous speech, Tús thus replied:
"Ungenerous warrior! wherefore thus employ
Such scornful words to me? Who art thou, pray!
Who, but the low descendant of a blacksmith?
No Khosráu claims thee for his son, no chief
Of noble blood; whilst I can truly boast
Kindred to princes of the highest worth,
And merit not to be obscured by thee!"
To him then Gúdarz: "Hear me for this once,
Then shut thy ears for ever. Need I blush
To be the kinsman of the glorious Kávah?
It is my humour to be proud of him.
Although he was a blacksmith;—that same man,
Who, when the world could little boast of valour,
Tore up the name-roll of the fiend Zohák,
And gave the Persians freedom from the fangs
Of the devouring serpents. He it was,
Who raised the banner, and proclaimed aloud,
Freedom for Persia! Need I blush for him?
To him the empire owes its greatest blessing,
The prosperous rule of virtuous Feridún."
Tús wrathfully rejoined: "Old man! thy arrow
May pierce an anvil—mine can pierce the heart
Of the Káf mountain! If thy mace can break
A rock asunder—mine can strike the sun!"

The anger of the two heroes beginning to exceed all proper bounds, Káús commanded silence; when Gúdarz came forward, and asked permission to say one word more: "Call Khosráu and Fríburz before thee, and decide impartially between them which is the most worthy of sovereignty—let the wisest and the bravest only be thy successor to the throne of Persia." Káús replied:

"The father has no choice among his children,
He loves them all alike—his only care
Is to prevent disunion; to preserve
Brotherly kindness and respect among them."

After a pause, he requested the attendance of Fríburz and Khosráu, and told them that there was a demon-fortress in the vicinity of his dominions called Bahmen, from which fire was continually issuing. "Go, each of you," said he, "against this fortress, supported by an army with which you shall each be equally provided, and the conqueror shall be the sovereign of Persia." Fríburz was not sorry to hear of this probationary scheme, and only solicited to be sent first on the expedition. He and Tús looked upon the task as perfectly easy, and promised to be back triumphant in a short time.

But when the army reached that awful fort,
The ground seemed all in flames on every side;
One universal fire raged round and round,
And the hot wind was like the scorching breath
Which issues from red furnaces, where spirits
Infernal dwell. Full many a warrior brave,
And many a soldier perished in that heat,
Consumed to ashes. Nearer to the fort
Advancing, they beheld it in mid-air,
But not a living thing—nor gate, nor door;
Yet they remained one week, hoping to find
Some hidden inlet, suffering cruel loss
Hour after hour—but none could they descry.
At length, despairing, they returned, worn out,
Scorched, and half-dead with watching, care, and toil.
And thus Fríburz and Tús, discomfited
And sad, appeared before the Persian king.
Then was it Khosráu's turn, and him Káús
Dispatched with Gíw, and Gúdarz, and the troops
Appointed for that enterprise, and blessed them.
When the young prince approached the destined scene
Of his exploit, he saw the blazing fort
Reddening the sky and earth, and well he knew
This was the work of sorcery, the spell
Of demon-spirits. In a heavenly dream,
He had been taught how to destroy the charms
Of fell magicians, and defy their power,
Though by the devil, the devil himself, sustained.
He wrote the name of God, and piously
Bound it upon his javelin's point, and pressed
Fearlessly forward, showing it on high;
And Gíw displayed it on the magic walls
Of that proud fortress—breathing forth a prayer
Craving the aid of the Almighty arm;
When suddenly the red fires died away,
And all the world was darkness. Khosráu's troops
Following the orders of their prince, then shot
Thick clouds of arrows from ten thousand bows,
In the direction of the enchanted tower,

The arrows fell like rain, and quickly slew
A host of demons,—presently bright light
Dispelled the gloom, and as the mist rolled off
In sulphury circles, the surviving fiends
Were seen in rapid flight; the fortress, too,
Distinctly shone, and its prodigious gate,
Through which the conquerors passed. Great wealth they
found,
And having sacked the place, Khosráu erected
A lofty temple, to commemorate
His name and victory there, then back returned
Triumphantly to gladden king Káús,
Whose heart expanded at the joyous news.

The result of Kai-khosráu's expedition against the enchanted castle, compared with that of Fríburz, was sufficient of itself to establish the former in the king's estimation, and accordingly it was announced to the princes and nobles and warriors of the land, that he should succeed to the throne, and be crowned on a fortunate day. A short time afterwards the coronation took place with great pomp and splendour; and Khosráu conducted himself towards men of every rank and station with such perfect kindness and benevolence, that he gained the affections of all and never failed daily to pay a visit to his grandfather Káús, and to familiarize himself with the affairs of the kingdom which he was destined to govern.

Justice he spread with equal hand,
Rooting oppression from the land;
And every desert, wood, and wild,
With early cultivation smiled;
And every plain, with verdure clad,
And every Persian heart was glad.

KAI-KHOSRÁU.

The tidings of Khosráu's accession to the throne were received at Sístan by Zál and Rustem with heartfelt pleasure, and they forthwith hastened to court with rich presents, to pay him their homage, and congratulate him on the occasion of his elevation. The heroes were met on the road with suitable honours, and Khosráu embracing Rustem affectionately, lost no time in asking for his assistance in taking vengeance for the death of Saiáwush. The request was no sooner made than granted, and the champion having delivered his presents, then proceeded with his father Zál to wait upon Káús, who prepared a royal banquet, and entertained Khosráu and them in the most sumptuous manner. It was there agreed to march a large army against Afrásiyáb ; and all the warriors zealously came forward with their best services, except Zál, who on account of his age requested to remain tranquilly in his own province. Khosráu said to Káús :

> "The throne can yield no happiness for me,
> Nor can I sleep the sleep of health and joy
> Till I have been revenged on that destroyer.
> The tyrant of Túrán ; to please the spirit
> Of my poor butchered father."

Káús, on delivering over to him the imperial army, made him acquainted with the character and merits of every individual of importance. He appointed Fríburz, and a hundred warriors, who were the prince's friends and relatives, to situations of trust and command, and Tús was among them. Gúdarz and his seventy-eight sons and grandsons were placed on the right, and Gustahem, the brother of Tús, with an immense levy on the left. There were also close to Khosráu's person, in the centre of the hosts, thirty-three warriors of the race of Poshang, and a separate guard under Byzun.

In their progress Khosráu said to Fríburz and Tús, "Ferúd, who is my brother, has built a strong fort in Bokhara, called

Kulláb, which stands on the way to the enemy, and there he resides with his mother, Gúlshaher. Let him not be molested, for he is also the son of Saiáwush, but pass on one side of his possessions." Fríburz did pass on one side as requested ; but Tús, not liking to proceed by the way of the desert, and prefering a cultivated and pleasant country, went directly on through the places which led to the very fort in question. When Ferúd was informed of the approach of Tús with an armed force, he naturally concluded that he was coming to fight him, and consequently determined to oppose his progress. Tús, however, sent Ríú, his son-in-law, to explain to Ferúd that he had no quarrel or business with him, and only wished to pass peaceably through his province ; but Ferúd thought this was merely an idle pretext, and proceeding to hostilities, Ríú was killed by him in the conflict that ensued. Tús, upon being informed of this result, drew up his army, and besieged the fort into which Ferúd had precipitately retired. When Ferúd, however, found that Tús himself was in the field, he sallied forth from his fastness, and assailed him with his bow and arrows. One of the darts struck and killed the horse of Tús, and tumbled his rider to the ground. Upon this occurrence Gíw rushed forward in the hopes of capturing the prince ; but it so happened that he was unhorsed in the same way. Byzun, the son of Gíw, seeing with great indignation this signal overthrow, wished to be revenged on the victor ; and though his father endeavoured to restrain him, nothing could control his wrath. He sprung speedily forward to fulfil his menace, but by the bravery and expertness of Ferúd, his horse was killed, and he too was thrown headlong from his saddle. Unsubdued, however, he rose upon his feet, and invited his antagonist to single combat. In consequence of this challenge, they fought a short time with spears till Ferúd deemed it advisable to retire into his fort, from the lofty walls of which he cast down so many stones, that Byzun was desperately wounded, and compelled to leave the place. When he informed Tús of the misfortune which had befallen him, that warrior vowed that on the following day not a man should remain alive in the fort. The mother of Ferúd, who was the daughter of Wísah, had at this period a dream which informed her that the fortress had taken fire, and that the whole of the inhabitants had been consumed to death. This dream she communicated to Ferúd, who said in reply :

"Mother! I have no dread of death;
What is there in this vital breath?
My sire was wounded, and he died;
And fate may lay me by his side!
Was ever man immortal?—never!
We cannot, mother, live for ever.
Mine be the task in life to claim
In war a bright and spotless name.
What boots it to be pale with fear,
And dread each grief that waits us here?
Protected by the power divine,
Our lot is written—why repine?

Tús, according to his threat, attacked the fort, and burst open the gates. Ferúd defended himself with great valour against Byzun ; and whilst they were engaged in deadly battle, Bahrám, the hero, sprang up from his ambuscade, and striking furiously upon the head of Ferúd, killed that unfortuuate youth on the spot. The mother, the beautiful Gúlshaher, seeing what had befallen her sou, rushed out of the fort in a state of frenzy, and flying to him, clasped him in her arms in an agony of grief. Unable to survive his loss, she plunged a dagger in her own breast, and died at his feet. The Persians then burst open the gates, and plundered the city. Bahrám, when he saw what had been done, reproached Tús with being the cause of this melancholy tragedy, and asked him what account he would give of his conduct to Kai-khosráu. Tús was extremely concerned, and remaining three days at that place, erected a lofty monument to the memory of the unfortunate youth, and scented it with musk and camphor. He then pushed forward his army to attack another fort. That fort gave way, the commandant being killed in the attack ; and he then hastened on towards Afrásiyáb, who had ordered Nizád with thirty thousand horsemen to meet him. Byzun distinguished himself in the contest which followed, but would have fallen into the hands of the enemy if he had not been rescued by his men, and conveyed from the field of battle. Afrásiyáb pushed forward another force of forty thousand horsemen under Pírán Wísah, who suffered considerable loss in an engagement with Gíw; and in consequence fell back for the purpose of retrieving himself by a shubkhún, or night attack. The resolution proved to be a good one; for when night came on, the Persians were found off their guard, many of them being intoxicated, and the havoc and destruction committed among them by the Tartars was dreadful. The survivors were in a miserable state of despondency, but it was not till morning dawned that Tús beheld the full extent of his defeat and the ruin that surrounded him. When Kai-khosráu heard of this heavy reverse, he wrote to Fríburz, saying, "I warned Tús not to proceed by the way of Kulláb, because my brother and his mother dwelt in that place, and their residence ought to have been kept sacred. He has not only despised my orders, but he has cruelly occasioned the untimely death of both. Let him be bound, and sent to me a prisoner, and do thou assume the command of the army." Fríburz accordingly placed Tús in confinement, and sent him to Khosráu, who received and treated him with reproaches and wrath, and consigned him to a dungeon. He then wrote to Pírán, reproaching him for resorting to a night attack so unworthy of a brave man, and challenging him to resume the battle with him. Pírán said that he would meet him after the lapse of a month, and at the expiration of that period both armies were opposed to each other. The contest commenced with arrows, then swords, and then with javelins; and Gíw and Byzun were the foremost in bearing down the warriors of the enemy, who suffered so severely that they turned aside to attack Fríburz, against whom they hoped to be more successful. The assault which they made was overwhelming, and vast numbers were slain, so that Fríburz, finding himself driven to extremity, was obliged to shelter himself and his remaining troops on the skirts of a mountain. In the meantime Gúdarz and Gíw determined to keep their ground or perish, and sent Byzun to Fríburz to desire him to join them, or if that was impracticable, to save the imperial banner by dispatching it to their care. To this message, Fríburz replied: "The traitors are triumphant over me on every side, and I cannot go, nor will I give up the imperial banner, but, tell Gúdarz to come to my aid." Upon receiving this answer, Byzun struck the standard-bearer dead, and snatching up the Derafsh Gávahní, conveyed it to Gúdarz, who, raising it on high, directed his troops against the enemy; and so impetuous was the charge, that the carnage on both sides was prodigious. Only eight of the sons of Gúdarz remained alive, seventy of his kindred having been slain on that day, and many of the family of Káús were also killed. Nor did the relations of Afrásiyáb and Pírán suffer in a less degree, nine hundred of them, warriors and cavaliers, were sent out of the world; yet victory remained with the Túránians.

When Afrásiyáb was informed of the result of this battle, he sent presents and honorary dresses to his officers, saying, "We must not be contented with this triumph; you have yet to obscure the martial glory of Rustem and Khosráu." Pírán replied, "No doubt that object will be accomplished with equal facility."

After the defeat of the Persian army, Fríburz retired under the cover of night, and at length arrived at the court of Khosráu, who was afflicted with the deepest sorrow, both on account of his loss in battle and the death of his brother Ferúd. Rustem was now as usual applied to for the purpose of consoling the king, and extricating the empire from its present misfortunes. Khosráu was induced to liberate Tús from his confinement, and requested Rustem to head the army against Pírán, but Tús promptly offered his services, and the champion observed, "He is fully competent to oppose the arms of Pírán; but if Afrásiyáb takes the field, I will myself instantly follow to the war." Khosráu accordingly deputed Tús and Gúdarz with a large army, and the two hostile powers were soon placed in opposition to each other. It is said that they were engaged seven days and nights, and that on the eighth Húmán came forward, and challenged several warriors to fight singly, all of whom he successively slew. He then called upon Tús, but Gúdarz not permitting him to accept the challenge, sent Gíw in his stead. The combatants met; and after being wounded and exhausted by their struggles for mastery, each returned to his own post. The armies again engaged with arrows, and again the carnage was great, but the battle remained undecided.

Pírán had now recourse to supernatural agency, and sent Barú, a renowned magician, perfect in his art, upon the neighbouring mountains, to involve them in darkness, and produce by his conjuration tempestuous showers of snow and hail. He ordered him to direct all their intense severity against the enemy, and to avoid giving any annoyance to the Túránian army. Accordingly when Húmán and Pírán Wísah made their attack, they had the co-operation of the elements, and the consequence was a desperate overthrow of the Persian army.

So dreadful was the carnage, that the plain
Was crimsoned with the blood of warriors slain.

In this extremity, Tús and Gúdarz piously put up a prayer to God, earnestly soliciting protection from the horrors with which they were surrounded.

O Thou! the clement, the compassionate,
We are thy servants, succour our distress,
And save us from the sorcery that now
Yields triumph to the foe. In thee alone
We place our trust; graciously hear our prayer!

Scarcely had this petition been uttered, when a mysterious person appeared to Rehám from the invisible world, and pointed to the mountain from whence the tempest descended. Rehám immediately attended to the sign, and galloped forward to the mountain, where he discovered the magician upon its summit, deeply engaged in incantations and witchcraft. Forthwith he drew his sword and cut off this wizard's arms.

Suddenly a whirlwind arose, which dissipated the utter darkness that prevailed; and then nothing remained of the preternatural gloom, not a particle of the hail or snow was to be seen: Rehám, however, brought him down from the mountain and after presenting him before Tús, put an end to his wicked existence. The armies were now on a more equal footing: they beheld more clearly the ravages that had been committed by each, and each had great need of rest. They acccordingly retired till the following day, and then again opposed each other with renewed vigour and animosity. But fortune would not smile on the exertions of the Persian hosts, they being obliged to fall back upon the mountain Hamáwun and in the fortress situated there Tús deposited all his sick and wounded, continuing himself in advance to ensure their protection. Pírán seeing this, ordered his troops to besiege the place where Tús had posted himself. This was objected to by Húmán, but Pírán was resolved upon the measure, and had several conflicts with the enemy without obtaining any advantage over them. In the mountain-fortress there happened to be wells of water and abundance of grain and provisions, so that the Persians were in no danger of being reduced by starvation. Khosráu, however, being informed of their situation, sent Rustem, accompanied by Fríburz, to their assistance, and they were both welcomed, and received with rejoicing, and cordial satisfaction. The fortress gates were thrown open, and Rustem was presently seen seated upon a throne in the public hall, deliberating on the state of affairs, surrounded by the most distinguished leaders of the army.

In the mean while Pírán Wísah had written to Afrásiyáb, informing him that he had reduced the Persian army to great distress, had forced them to take refuge in a mountain fort, and requested a further reinforcement to complete the victory, and make them all prisoners. Afrásiyáb in consequence dispatched three illustrious confederates from different regions. There was Shinkul of Sugsar, the Khakán of Chín, whose crown was the starry heavens, and Kámús of Kushán, a hero of high renown and wondrous in every deed.

For when he frowned, the air grew freezing cold ;
And when he smiled, the genial spring showered down
Roses and hyacinths, and all was brightness !

Pírán went first to pay a visit to Kámús, to whom he, almost trembling, described the amazing strength and courage of Rustem : but Kámús was too powerful to express alarm ; on the contrary, he said :

"Is praise like this to Rustem due ?
And what, if all thou say'st be true ?
Are his large limbs of iron made ?
Will they resist my trenchant blade ?
His head may now his shoulders grace,
But will it long retain its place ?
Let me but meet him in the fight,
And thou shalt see Kámús's might !"

Pírán's spirits rose at this bold speech, and encouraged by its effects, he repaired to the Khakán of Chín, with whom he settled the necessary arrangements for commencing battle on the following day. Early in the morning the different armies under Kámús, the Khakán, and Pírán Wísah, were drawn out, and Rustem was also prepared with the troops under his command for the impending conflict. He saw that the force arrayed against him was prodigious, and most tremendous in aspect ; and offering a prayer to the Creator, he plunged into the battle.

'Twas at midday the strife began,
With steed to steed and man to man ;
The clouds of dust which rolled on high,
Threw darkness o'er the earth and sky.
Each soldier on the other rushed,
And every blade with crimson blushed ,
And valiant hearts were trod upon,
  Like sand beneath the horse's feet,
And when the warrior's life was gone,
  His mail became his winding sheet.

The first leader who advanced conspicuously from among the Tartar army was Ushkabús, against whom Rehám boldly opposed himself; but after a short conflict, in which he had some difficulty in defending his life from the assaults of his antagonist, he thought it prudent to retire. When Ushkabús saw this, he turned round with the intention of rejoining his own troops; but Rustem having witnessed the triumph over his friend, sallied forth on foot, taking up his bow, and placing a few arrows in his girdle, and asked him whither he was going.

Astonished, Ushkabús cried, "Who art thou?
What kindred hast thou to lament thy fall?"
Rustem replied: "Why madly seek to know
That which can never yield thee benefit?
My name is death to thee, thy hour is come!"
"Indeed! and thou on foot, mid mounted warriors,
To talk so bravely!"—"Yes," the champion said;
"And hast thou never heard of men on foot,
Who conquered horsemen? I am sent by Tús,
To take for him the horse of Ushkabús."
"What! and unarmed?" inquired the Tartar chief;
"No!" cried the champion, "Mark, my bow and arrow!
Mark, too, with what effect they may be used!"
So saying, Rustem drew the string, and straight
The arrow flew, and faithful to its aim,
Struck dead the foeman's horse. This done, he laughed,
But Ushkabús was wroth, and showered upon
His bold antagonist his quivered store—
Then Rustem raised his bow, with eager eye
Choosing a dart, and placed it on the string,
A thong of elk-skin; to his ear he drew
The feathered notch, and when the point had touched
The other hand, the bended horn recoiled,
And twang the arrow sped, piercing the breast
Of Ushkabús, who fell a lifeless corse,
As if he never had been born! Erect,
And firm, the champion stood upon the plain,
Towering like mount Alberz, immoveable,
The gaze and wonder of the adverse host!

When Rustem, still unknown to the Túránian forces, returned to his own army, the Tartars carried away the body of Ushkabús, and took it to the Khakán of Chín, who ordered the arrow to be drawn out before him; and when he and Kámús saw how deeply it had penetrated, and that the feathered end was wet with blood, they were amazed at the immense power which had driven it from the bow; they had never witnessed or heard of any thing so astonishing. The fight was, in consequence, suspended till the following day. The Khakán of Chín then inquired who was disposed or ready to be revenged on the enemy for the death of Ushkabús, when Kámús advanced, and, soliciting permission, urged forward his horse to the middle of the plain. He then called aloud for Rustem, but a Kábul hero, named Alwund, a pupil of Rustem's asked his master's permission to oppose the challenger, which being granted, he rushed headlong to the combat. Luckless however were his efforts, for he was soon overthrown and slain, and then Rustem appeared in arms before the conqueror, who hearing his voice, cried: "Why this arrogance and clamour! I am not like Ushkabús, a trembler in thy presence." Rustem replied:

"When the lion sees his prey,
Sees the elk-deer cross his way,
Roars he not? The very ground
Trembles at the dreadful sound.
And art thou from terror free,
When opposed in fight to me?"

Kámús now examined him with a stern eye, and was satisfied that he had to contend against a powerful warrior: he therefore with the utmost alacrity threw his kamund, which Rustem avoided, but it fell over the head of his horse Rakush. Anxious to extricate himself from this dilemma, Rustem dexterously caught hold of one end of the kamund, whilst Kámús dragged and strained at the other; and so much strength was applied that the line broke in the middle, and Kámús in consequence tumbled backwards to the ground. The boaster had almost succeeded in remounting his horse, when he was secured round the neck by Rustem's own kamund, and conveyed a prisoner to the Persian army, where he was put to death!

The fate of Kámús produced a deep sensation among the Túránians, and Pírán Wísah, partaking of the general alarm, and thinking it impossible to resist the power of Rustem, proposed to retire from the contest, but the Khakán of Chín was of a different opinion, and offered himself to remedy the evil which threatened them all. Moreover the warrior, Chingush, volunteered to fight with Rustem; and having obtained the Khakán's permission, he took the field, and boldly challenged the champion. Rustem received the foe with a smiling countenance, and the struggle began with arrows. After a smart attack on both sides, Chingush thought it prudent to fly from the overwhelming force of Rustem, who, however, steadily pursued him, and adroitly seizing the horse by the tail, hurled him from his saddle.

> He grasped the charger's flowing tail,
> And all were struck with terror pale,
> To see a sight so strange; the foe,
> Dismounted by one desperate blow;
> The captive asked for life in vain,
> His recreant blood bedewed the plain.
> His head was from his shoulders wrung,
> His body to the vultures flung.

Rustem, after this exploit, invited some other hero to single combat; but at the moment not one replied to his challenge. At last Húmán came forward, not however to fight, but to remonstrate, and make an effort to put an end to the war which threatened total destruction to his country. "Why such bitter enmity? why such a whirlwind of resentment?" said he; "to this I ascribe the calamities under which we suffer; but is there no way by which this sanguinary career of vengeance can be checked or moderated?" Rustem, in answer, enumerated the aggressions and the crimes of Afrásiyáb, and especially dwelt on the atrocious murder of Saiáwush, which he declared could never be pardoned. Húmán wished to know his name; but Rustem refused to tell him, and requested Pírán Wísah might be sent to him, to whom he would communicate his thoughts, and the secrets of his heart freely. Húmán accordingly returned, and informed Pírán of the champion's wishes.

> "This must be Rustem, stronger than the pard,
> The lion, or the Egyptian crocodile,
> Or fell Iblís; dreams never painted hero
> Half so tremendous on the battle plain."

The old man said to him;

> "If this be Rustem, then the time has come,
> Dreaded so long—for what but fire and sword,
> Can now await us? Every town laid waste,
> Soldier and peasant, husband, wife, and child,
> Sharing the miseries of a ravaged land!"

With tears in his eyes and a heavy heart, Pírán repaired to the Khakán, who, after some discussion, permitted him in these terms to go and confer with Rustem.

> "Depart then speedful on thy embassy,
> And if he seeks for peace, adjust the terms,
> And presents to be sent us. If he talks
> Of war and vengeance, and is clothed in mail,
> No sign of peace, why we must trust in Heaven
> For strength to crush his hopes of victory.
> He is not formed of iron, nor of brass,
> But flesh and blood, with human nerves and hair,
> He does not in the battle tread the clouds,
> Nor can he vanish, like the demon race,—
> Then why this sorrow, why these marks of grief?
> He is not stronger than an elephant;
> Not he, but I will show him what it is
> To fight or gambol with an elephant!
> Besides, for every man his army boasts,
> We have three hundred—wherefore then be sad?"

Notwithstanding these expressions of confidence, Pírán's heart was full of alarm and terror; but he hastened to the Persian camp, and made himself known to the champion of the host, who frankly said, after he had heard Pírán's name, "I am Rustem of Zábul, armed as thou seest for battle!" Upon which Pírán respectfully dismounted, and paid the usual homage to his illustrious rank and distinction.

Rustem said to him, "I bring thee the blessings of Kai-khosráu and Ferangís, his mother, who nightly see thy face in their dreams."

"Blessings from me, upon that royal youth!"
Exclaimed the good old man. "Blessings on her,
The daughter of Afrásiyáb, his mother,
Who saved my life—and blessings upon thee,
Thou matchless hero! Thou hast come for vengeance,
In the dear name of gallant Saiáwush,
Of Saiáwush, the husband of my child,
(The beautiful Gúlshaher), of him who loved me
As I had been his father. His brave son,
Ferúd, was slaughtered, and his mother too,
And Khosráu was his brother, now the king,
By whom he fell, or if not by his word,
Whose was the guilty hand? Has punishment
Been meted to the offender? I protected,
In mine own house, the princess Ferangís;
And when her son was born, Kai-khosráu, still
I, at the risk of my existence, kept them
Safe from the fury of Afrásiyáb,
Who would have sacrificed the child, or both!
And night and day I watched them, till the hour
When they escaped and crossed the boundary-stream.
Enough of this! Now let us speak of peace,
Since the confederates in this mighty war
Are guiltless of the blood of Saiáwush!"

Rustem, in answer to Pírán, observed, that in negotiating the terms of pacification, several important points were to be considered, and several indispensable matters to be attended to. No peace could be made unless the principal actors in the bloody tragedy of Saiáwush's death were first given up, particularly Gersíwaz; vast sums of money were also required to be presented to the king of kings; and, moreover, Rustem said he would disdain making peace at all, but that it enabled Pírán to do service to Kai-khosráu. Pírán saw the difficulty of acceding to these demands, but he speedily laid them before the Khakán, who consulted his confederates on the subject, and after due consideration, their pride and shame resisted the overtures, which they thought ignominious. Shinkul, a king of Ind, was a violent opposer of the terms, and declared against peace on any such conditions. Several other warriors expressed their readiness to contend against Rustem, and they flattered themselves that by a rapid succession of attacks, one after the the other, they would easily overpower him. The Khakán was pleased with this conceit and permitted Shinkul to begin the struggle. Accordingly he entered the plain, and summoned Rustem to renew the fight. The champion came and struck him with a spear, which, penetrating his breast, threw him off his horse to the ground. The dagger was already raised to finish his career, but he sprang on his feet, and quickly ran away to tell his misfortune to the Khakán of Chín.

And thus he cried, in look forlorn,
"This foe is not of mortal born;
A furious elephant in fight,
A very mountain to the sight;
No warrior of the human race,
That ever wielded spear or mace,
Alone this dragon could withstand,
Or live beneath his conquering brand!"

The Khakán reminded him how different were his feelings and sentiments in the morning, and having asked him what he now proposed to do, he said that without a considerable force it would be useless to return to the field; five thousand men were therefore assigned to him, and with them he proceeded to engage the champion. Rustem had also been joined by his valiant companions, and a general battle ensued. The heavens were obscured by the dust which ascended from the tramp of the horses, and the plain was crimsoned with the blood of the slain. In the midst of the contest, Sáwa, a relation of Kámús, burst forward and sought to be revenged on Rustem for the fate of his friend. The champion raised his battle-axe, and giving Rakush the rein, with one blow of his mace removed him to the other world. No sooner had he dispatched this assailant than he was attacked by another of the kindred of Kámús, named Kahár, whom he also slew, and thus humbled the pride of the Kushanians. Elated with his success, and having further displayed his valour among the enemy's troops, he vowed that he would now encounter the Khakán himself, and despoil him of all his pomp and treasure. For this purpose he selected a thousand horsemen, and thus supported, approached the kulubgah, or head-quarters of the monarch of Chín. The clamour of the cavalry, and the clash of spears and swords, resounded afar. The air became as dark as the visage of an Ethiopian, and the field was covered with several heads, broken armour, and the bodies of the slain. Amidst the conflict Rustem called aloud to the Khakán :

> "Surrender to my arms those elephants,
> That ivory throne, that crown, and chain of gold ;
> Fit trophies for Kai-khosráu, Persia's king ;
> For what hast thou to do with diadem
> And sovereign power ! My noose shall soon secure thee,
> And I will send thee living to his presence ;
> Since, looking on my valour and my strength,
> Life is enough to grant thee. If thou wilt not
> Resign thy crown and throne—thy doom is sealed."

The Khakán, filled with indignation at these haughty words, cautioned Rustem to parry off his own danger, and then commanded his troops to assail the enemy with a shower of arrows. The attack was so tremendous and terrifying, even beyond the picturings of a dream, that Gúdarz was alarmed for the safety of Rustem, and sent Rehám and G'w to his aid. Rustem said to Rehám :—"I fear that my horse Rakush is becoming weary of exertion, in which case what shall I do in this conflict with the enemy ? I must attack on foot the Khakán of Chín, though he has an army here as countless as legions of ants or locusts ; but if Heaven continues my friend, I shall stretch many of them in the dust, and take many prisoners. The captives I will send to Khosráu, and all the spoils of Chín." Saying this he pushed forward, roaring like a tiger, towards the Khakán, and exclaiming with a stern voice :—"The Túrks are allied to the devil, and the wicked are always unprosperous. Thou hast not yet fallen in with Rustem, or thy brain would have been bewildered. He is a never-dying dragon, always seeking the strongest in battle. But thou hast not yet had enough of even me!" He then drew his kamund from the saddle-strap, and praying to God to grant him victory over his foes, urged on Rakush, and wherever he threw the noose, his aim was successful. Great was the slaughter, and the Khakán, seeing from the back of his white elephant the extent of his loss, and beginning to be apprehensive about his own safety, ordered one of his warriors, well acquainted with the language of Irán, to solicit from the enemy a cessation of hostilities.

"Say whence this wrath on us, this keen revenge?
We never injured Saiáwush; the kings
Of Ind and Chín are guiltless of his blood;
Then why this wrath on strangers? Spells and charms,
Used by Afrásiyáb,—the cause of all—
Have brought us hither to contend against
The champion Rustem; and since peace is better
Than war and bloodshed, let us part in peace."

The messenger having delivered his message, Rustem replied:—

"My words are few. Let him give up his crown,
His golden collar, throne, and elephants;
These are the terms I grant. He came for plunder,
And now he asks for peace. Tell him again,
Till all his treasure and his crown are mine,
His throne and elephants, he seeks in vain
For peace with Rustem, or the Persian king!"

When the Khakán was informed of these reiterated conditions, he burst out into bitter reproaches and abuse; and with so loud a voice, that the wind conveyed them distinctly to Rustem's ear. The champion immediately prepared for the attack; and approaching the enemy, flung his kamund, by which he at once dragged the Khakán from his white elephant. The hands of the captured monarch were straightway bound behind his back. Degraded and helpless he stood, and a single stroke deprived him of his crown, and throne, and life.

Such are, since time began, the ways of Heaven ;
Such the decrees of fate ! Sometimes raised up,
And sometimes hunted down by enemies,
Men, struggling, pass through this precarious life,
Exalted now to sovereign power ; and now
Steeped in the gulph of poverty and sorrow.
To one is given the affluence of Karún ;
Another dies in want. How little know we
What hue our future fortune may assume !
The world is all deceit, deception all !

Pirán Wísah beheld the disasters of the day, he saw the Khakán of Chín delivered over to Tús, his death, and the banners of the confederates overthrown ; and sorrowing said :—"This day is the day of flight, not of victory to us ! This is no time for son to protect father, nor father son—we must fly !" In the meanwhile Rustem, animated by feelings of a very different kind, gave a banquet to his warrior friends, in celebration of the triumph.

When the intelligence of the overthrow and death of Kámús and the Khakán of Chín, and the dispersion of their armies, reached Afrásiyáb, he was overwhelmed with distress and consternation, and expressed his determination to be revenged on the conquerors. Not an Iránian, he said, should remain alive ; and the doors of his treasury were thrown open to equip and reward the new army, which was to consist of a hundred thousand men.

Rustem having communicated to Kai-khosráu, through Fríburz, the account of his success, received the most satisfactory marks of his sovereign's applause ; but still anxious to promote the glory of his country, he engaged in new exploits. He went against Kafúr, the king of the city of Bídád, a cannibal, who feasted on human flesh, especially on the young women of his country, and those of the greatest beauty, being the richest morsels, were first destroyed. He soon overpowered and slew the monster, and having given his body to be devoured by dogs, plundered and razed his castle to the ground. After this he invaded and ravaged the province of Khoten, one of the dependencies of Túrán, and recently the possession of Saiáwush, which was a new affliction to Afrásiyáb, who, alarmed about his own empire, dispatched a trusty person secretly to Rustem's camp, to obtain private intelligence of his hostile movements. The answer of the spy added considerably to his distress, and in the dilemma he consulted with Pírán Wisah, that he might have the benefit of the old man's experience and wisdom. Pírán told him that he had failed to make an impression upon the Persians, even assisted by Kámús the Kashánian, and the Khakán of Chín; both had been slain in battle, and therefore it would be in vain to attempt further offensive measures without the most powerful aid. There was, he added, a neighbouring king, named Púladwund, who alone seemed equal to contend with Rustem. He was of immense stature, and of prodigious strength, and might, by the favour of heaven, be able to subdue him. Afrásiyáb was pleased with this information, and immediately invited Púladwund, by letter, to assist him in exterminating the champion of Persia. Púladwund was proud of the honour conferred upon him, and readily complied; hastening the preparation of his own army to co-operate with that of Afrásiyáb. He presently joined him, and the whole of the combined forces rapidly marched against the enemy. The first warrior he encountered was Gíw, whom he caught with his kamund. Rehám and Byzun seeing this, instantly rushed forward to extricate their brother and champion in arms; but they too were also secured in the same manner! In the struggle, however, the kamunds gave way, and then Púladwund drew his sword, and by several strokes wounded them all. The father, Gúdarz, apprised of this disaster, which had unfortunately happened to three of his sons, applied to Rustem for succour. The champion, the refuge, the protector of all, was, as usual, ready to repel the enemy. He forthwith advanced, liberated his friends, and dreadful was the conflict which followed. The club was used with great dexterity on both sides; but at length Púladwund struck his antagonist such a blow that the sound of it was heard by the troops at a distance, and Rustem, stunned by its severity, thought himself opposed with so much vigour, that he prayed to the Almighty for a prosperous issue to the engagement.

"Should I be in this struggle slain,
What stay for Persia will be left?
None to defend Kai-khosráu's reign,
Of me, his warrior-chief, bereft.
Then village, town, and city gay,
Will feel the cruel Tartar's sway!"

Púladwund wishing to follow up the blow by a final stroke of his sword, found to his amazement that it recoiled from the armour of Rustem, and thence he proposed another mode of fighting, which he hoped would be more successful. He wished to try his power in wrestling. The challenge was accepted. By agreement both armies retired, and left the space of a farsang between them, and no one was allowed to afford assistance to either combatant. Afrásiyáb was present, and sent word to Púladwund, the moment he got Rustem under him, to plunge a sword in his heart. The contest began, but Púladwund had no opportunity of fulfilling the wishes of Afrásiyáb. Rustem grasped him with such vigour, lifted him up in his arms, and dashed him so furiously on the plain, that the boaster seemed to be killed on the spot. Rustem indeed thought he had put a period to his life; and with that impression left him, and remounted Rakush: but the crafty Púladwund only pretended to be dead; and as soon as he found himself released, sprang up and escaped, flying like an arrow to his own side. He then told Afrásiyáb how he had saved his life by counterfeiting death, and assured him that it was useless to contend against Rustem. The champion having witnessed this subterfuge, turned round in pursuit, and the Tartars received him with a shower of arrows; but the attack was well answered, Púladwund being so alarmed that, without saying a word to Afrásiyáb, he fled from the field. Pirán now counselled Afrásiyáb to escape also to the remotest part of Tartary. As the flight of Púladwund had disheartened the Túránian troops, and there was no chance of profiting by further resistance, Afrásiyáb took his advice, and so precipitate was his retreat, that he entirely abandoned his standards, tents, horses, arms, and treasure to an immense amount. The most valuable booty was sent by Rustem to the king of Irán, and a considerable portion of it was divided among the chiefs and the soldiers of the army. He then mounted Rakush, and proceeded to the court of Kai-khosráu, where he was received with the highest honours and with unbounded rejoicings. The king opened his jewel chamber, and gave him the richest rubies, and vessels of gold filled with musk and aloes, and also splendid garments; a hundred beautiful damsels wearing crowns and ear-rings, a hundred horses, and a hundred camels. Having thus terminated triumphantly the campaign, Rustem carried with him to Zábul the blessings and admiration of his country.

AKWÁN DÍW.

And now we come to Akwán Díw,
Whom Rustem next in combat slew.

One day as Kai-khosráu was sitting in his beautiful garden, abounding in roses and the balmy luxuriance of spring, surrounded by his warriors, and enjoying the pleasures of the banquet with music and singing, á peasant approached, and informed him of a most mysterious apparition. A wild ass, he said, had come in from the neighbouring forest; it had at least the external appearance of a wild ass, but possessed such supernatural strength, that it had rushed among the horses in the royal stables with the ferocity of a lion or a demon, doing extensive injury, and in fact appeared to be an evil spirit! Kai-khosráu felt assured that it was something more than it seemed to be, and looked round among his warriors to know what should be done. It was soon found that Rustem was the only person capable of giving effectual assistance in this emergency, and accordingly a message was forwarded to request his services. The champion instantly complied, and it was not long before he occupied himself upon the important enterprise. Guided by the peasant, he proceeded in the first place towards the spot where the mysterious animal had been seen; but it was not till the fourth day of his search that he fell in with him, and then, being anxious to secure him alive, and send him as a trophy to Kai-khosráu, he threw his kamund; but it was in vain: the wild ass in a moment vanished out of sight! From this circumstance Rustem observed, "This can be no other than Akwán Díw, and my weapon must now be either dagger or sword." The next time the wild ass appeared he pursued him with his drawn sword; but on lifting it up to strike, nothing was to be seen. He tried again, when he came near him, both spear and arrow: still the animal vanished, disappointing his blow; and thus three days and nights he continued fighting, as it were against a shadow. Wearied at length with his exertions, he dismounted, and leading Rakush to a green spot near a limpid fountain or rivulet of spring water, allowed him to graze, and then went to sleep. Akwán Díw seeing from a distance that Rustem had fallen asleep, rushed towards him like a whirlwind, and rapidly digging up the ground on every side of him, took up the plot of ground and the champion together, placed them upon his head, and walked away with them. Rustem being awakened with the motion, he was thus addressed by the giant-demon:

"Warrior! now no longer free!
Tell me what thy wish may be;
Shall I plunge thee in the sea,
  Or leave thee on the mountain drear,
  None to give thee succour, near?
Tell thy wish to me!"

Rustem, thus deplorably in the power of the demon, began

to consider what was best to be done, and recollecting that it was customary with that supernatural race to act by the rule of contraries, in opposition to an expressed desire, said in reply, for he knew that if he was thrown into the sea there would be a good chance of escape :—

> " O, plunge me not in the roaring sea,
> The maw of a fish is no home for me ;
> But cast me forth on the mountain ; there
> Is the lion's haunt and the tiger's lair ;
> And for them I shall be a morsel of food,
> They will eat my flesh and drink my blood ;
> But my bones will be left, to shew the place
> Where this form was devoured by the feline race ;
> Yes, something will then remain of me,
> Whilst nothing escapes from the roaring sea ! "

Akwán Díw having heard this particular desire of Rustem, determined at once to thwart him, and for this purpose he raised him up with his hands, and flung him from his lofty position headlong into the deep and roaring ocean. Down he fell, and a crocodile speedily darted upon him with the eager intention of devouring him alive ; but Rustem drew his sword with alacrity, and severed the monster's head from his body. Another came, and was put to death in the same manner, and the water was crimsoned with blood. At last he succeeded in swimming safely on shore, and instantly returned thanks to Heaven for the signal protection he had experienced.

> Breasting the wave, with fearless skill
> He used his glittering brand ;
> And glorious and triumphant still,
> He quickly reached the strand.

He then moved towards the fountain where he had left Rakush ; but, to his great alarm and vexation his matchless horse was not there. He wandered about for some time, and in the end found him among a herd of horses belonging to Afrásiyáb. Having first caught him, and resumed his seat in the saddle, he resolved upon capturing and driving away the whole herd, and conveying them to Kai-khosráu. He was carrying into effect this resolution when the noise awoke the keepers specially employed by Afrásiyáb, and they, indignant at this outrageous proceeding, called together a strong party to pursue the aggressor. When they had nearly reached him, he turned boldly round, and said aloud :—"I am Rustem, the descendant of Sám. I have conquered Afrásiyáb in battle, and after that dost thou presume to oppose me?" Hearing this, the keepers of the Tartar stud instantly turned their backs, and ran away.

It so happened that at this period Afrásiyáb paid his annual visit to his nursery of horses, and on his coming to the meadows in which they were kept, neither horses nor keepers were to be seen. In a short time, however, he was informed by those who had returned from the pursuit, that Rustem was the person who had carried off the herd, and upon hearing of this outrage, he proceeded with his troops at once to attack him. Impatient at the indignity, he approached Rustem with great fury, but was presently compelled to fly to save his life, and thus allow his herd of favourite steeds, together with four elephants, to be placed in the possession of Kai-khosráu. Rustem then returned to the meadows and the fountain near the habitation of Akwán Díw; and there he again met with the demon, who thus accosted him :—

"What! art thou then aroused from death's dark sleep?
Hast thou escaped the monsters of the deep?
And dost thou seek upon the dusty plain
To struggle with a demon's power again?
Of flint, or brass, or iron is thy form?
Or canst thou, like the demons, raise the dreadful battle
storm?"

Rustem, hearing this taunt from the tongue of Akwán Díw, prepared for fight, and threw his kamund with such precision and force, that the demon was entangled in it, and then he struck him such a mighty blow with his sword, that it severed the head from the body. The severed head of the unclean monster he transmitted as a trophy to Kai-khosráu, by whom it was regarded with amazement, on account of its hideous expression and its vast size. After this extraordinary feat, Rustem paid his respects to the king, and was received as usual with distinguished honour and affection; and having enjoyed the magnificent hospitality of the court for some time, he returned to Zábulistán, accompanied part of the way by Kai-khosráu himself and a crowd of valiant warriors, ever anxious to acknowledge his superior worth and prodigious strength.

THE STORY OF BYZUN AND MANÍJEH, THE DAUGHTER OF AFRÁSIYÁB.

One day the people of Armán petitioned Kai-khosráu to remove from them a grievous calamity. The country they inhabited was overrun with herds of wild boars, which not only destroyed the produce of their fields, but the fruit and flowers in their orchards and gardens, and so extreme was the ferocity of the animals that it was dangerous to go abroad; they therefore solicited protection from this disastrous visitation, and hoped for relief. The king was at the time enjoying himself amidst his warriors at a banquet, drinking wine, and listening to music and the songs of bewitching damsels.

> The glance of beauty, and the charm
> Of heavenly sounds, so soft and thrilling,
> And ruby wine, must ever warm
> The heart, with love and rapture filling.
> Can aught more sweet, more genial prove,
> Than melting music, wine, and love?

The moment he was made acquainted with the grievances endured by the Armánians, he referred the matter to the consideration of his counsellors and nobles, in order that a remedy might be immediately applied. Byzun, when he heard what was required, and had learned the disposition of the king, rose up at once with all the enthusiasm of youth, and offered to undertake the extermination of the wild boars himself. But Gíw objected to so great a hazard, for he was too young, he said; a hero of greater experience being necessary for such an arduous enterprise. Byzun, however, was not to be rejected on this account, and observed, that though young, he was mature in judgment and discretion, and he relied on the liberal decision of the king, who at length permitted him to go, but he was to be accompanied by the veteran warrior Girgín. Accordingly Byzun and Girgín set off on the perilous expedition; and after a journey of several days arrived at the place situated between Irán and Túrán, where the wild boars were the most destructive. In a short time a great number were hunted down and killed, and Byzun, utterly to destroy the sustenance of the depredators, set fire to the forest, and reduced the whole of the cultivation to ashes. His exertions were, in short, entirely successful, and the country was thus freed from the visitation which had occasioned so much distress and ruin. To give incontestable proof of this exploit, he cut off the heads of all the wild boars, and took out the tusks, to send to Kai-khosráu. When Girgín had witnessed the intrepidity and boldness of Byzun, and found him determined to send the evidence of his bravery to Kai-khosráu, he became envious of the youth's success, and anticipated by comparison the ruin of his own name and the gratification of his foes. He therefore attempted to dissuade him from sending the trophies to the king, and having failed, he resolved upon getting him out of the way. To effect this purpose he worked upon the feelings and the passions of Byzun with consummate art, and whilst his victim was warm with wine, praised him beyond all the warriors of the age. He then told him he had heard that at no great distance from them there was a beautiful place, a garden of perpetual spring, which was visited every vernal season by Maníjeh, the lovely daughter of Afrásiyáb.

"It is a spot beyond imagination
Delightful to the heart, where roses bloom.
And sparkling fountains murmur—where the earth
Is rich with many-coloured flowers; and musk
Floats on the gentle breezes, hyacinths
And lilies add their perfume—golden fruit
Weigh down the branches of the lofty trees,
The glittering pheasant moves in stately pomp,
The bulbul warbles from the cypress bough,
And love-inspiring damsels may be seen
O'er hill and dale, their lips all winning smiles,
Their cheeks like roses—in their sleepy eyes
Delicious languor dwelling. Over them
Presides the daughter of Afrásiyáb,
The beautiful Manijeh; should we go,
('Tis but a little distance), and encamp
Among the lovely groups—in that retreat
Which blooms like Paradise—we may secure
A bevy of fair virgins for the king!"

Byzun was excited by this description; and impatient to realize what it promised, repaired without delay, accompanied by Girgín, to the romantic retirement of the princess. They approached so close to the summer-tent in which she dwelt that she had a full view of Byzun, and immediately becoming deeply enamoured of his person, dispatched a confidential domestic, her nurse, to inquire who he was, and from whence he came.

"Go, and beneath that cypress tree,
Where now he sits so gracefully,
Ask him his name, that radiant moon,
And he may grant another boon!
Perchance he may to me impart
The secret wishes of his heart!
Tell him he must, and further say,
That I have lived here many a day;
That every year, whilst spring discloses
The fragrant breath of budding roses,
I pass my time in rural pleasure;
But never—never such a treasure,
A mortal of such perfect mould,
Did these admiring eyes behold!
Never, since it has been my lot
To dwell in this sequestered spot,
A youth by nature so designed
To soothe a love-lorn damsel's mind!
His wondrous looks my bosom thrill
Can Saiáwush be living still?"

The nurse communicated faithfully the message of Maníjeh, and Byzun's countenance glowed with delight when he heard it. "Tell thy fair mistress," he said in reply, "that I am not Saiáwush, but the son of Gíw. I came from Irán, with the express permission of the king, to exterminate a terrible and destructive herd of wild boars in this neighbourhood; and I have cut off their heads, and torn out their tusks to be sent to Kai-khosráu, that the king and his warriors may fully appreciate the exploit I have performed. But having heard afterwards of thy mistress's beauty and attractions, home and my father were forgotten, and I have preferred following my own desires by coming hither. If thou wilt therefore forward my views; if thou wilt become my friend by introducing me to thy mistress, who is possessed of such matchless charms, these precious gems are thine and this coronet of gold. Perhaps the daughter of Afrásiyáb may be induced to listen to my suit." The nurse was not long in making known the sentiments of the stranger, and Maníjeh was equally prompt in expressing her consent. The message was full of ardour and affection.

"O gallant youth, no farther roam,
This summer-tent shall be thy home;
Then will the clouds of grief depart
From this enamoured, anxious heart.
For thee I live—thou art the light
Which makes my future fortune bright.
Should arrows pour like showers of rain
Upon my head—'twould be in vain;
Nothing can ever injure me,
Blessed with thy love—possessed of thee!"

Byzun therefore proceeded unobserved to the tent of the princess, who on meeting and receiving him, pressed him to her bosom; and taking off his Kaiání girdle, that he might be more at his ease, asked him to sit down and relate the particulars of his enterprise among the wild boars of the forest. Having done so, he added that he had left Girgín behind him.

"Enraptured, and impatient to survey
Thy charms, I brook'd no pause upon the way."

He was immediately perfumed with musk and rose-water, and refreshments of every kind were set before him; musicians played their sweetest airs, and dark-eyed damsels waited upon him. The walls of the tent were gorgeously adorned with amber, and gold, and rubies; and the sparkling old wine was drank out of crystal goblets. The feast of joy lasted three nights and three days, Byzun and Maníjeh enjoying the precious moments with unspeakable rapture. Overcome with wine and the felicity of the scene, he at length sunk into repose, and on the fourth day came the time of departure; but the princess, unable to relinquish the society of her lover, ordered a narcotic draught to be administered to him, and whilst he continued in a state of slumber and insensibility, he was conveyed secretly and in disguise into Túrán. He was taken even to the palace of Afrásiyáb, unknown to all but to the emissaries and domestics of the princess, and there he awoke from the trance into which he had been thrown, and found himself clasped in the arms of his idol. Considering, on coming to his senses, that he had been betrayed by some witchery, he made an attempt to get out of the seclusion: above all, he was apprehensive of a fatal termination to the adventure; but Maníjeh's blandishments induced him to remain, and for some time he was contented to be immersed in continual enjoyment,—such pleasure as arises from the social banquet and the attractions of a fascinating woman.

"Grieve not my love—be not so sad,
'Tis now the season to be glad;
There is a time for war and strife,
A time to soothe the ills of life.
Drink of the cup which yields delight,
The ruby glitters in thy sight;
Steep not thy heart in fruitless care,
But in the wine-flask sparkling there."

At length, however, the love of the princess for a Persian youth was discovered, and the keepers and guards of the palace were in the greatest terror, expecting the most signal punishment for their neglect or treachery. Dreadful indeed was the rage of the king when he was first told the tidings; he trembled like a reed in the wind, and the colour fled from his cheeks. Groaning, he exclaimed:

> "A daughter, even from a royal stock,
> Is ever a misfortune—hast thou one?
> The grave will be thy fittest son-in-law!
> Rejoice not in the wisdom of a daughter;
> Who ever finds a daughter good and virtuous?
> Who ever looks on woman-kind for aught
> Save wickedness and folly? Hence how few
> Ever enjoy the bliss of Paradise:
> Such the sad destiny of erring woman!"

Afrásiyáb consulted the nobles of his household upon the measures to be pursued on this occasion, and Gersíwaz was in consequence deputed to secure Byzun, and put him to death. The guilty retreat was first surrounded by troops, and then Gersíwaz entered the private apartments, and with surprise and indignation saw Byzun in all his glory, Maníjeh at his side, his lips stained with wine, his face full of mirth and gladness, and encircled by the damsels of the shubistán. He accosted him in severe terms, and was promptly answered by Byzun, who, drawing his sword, gave his name and family, and declared that if any violence or insult was offered, he would slay every man that came before him with hostile intentions. Gersíwaz, on hearing this, thought it prudent to change his plan, and conduct him to Afrásiyáb, and he was permitted to do so on the promise of pardon for the alleged offence. When brought before Afrásiyáb, he was assailed with further opprobrium, and called a dog and a wicked remorseless demon.

> "Thou caitiff wretch, of monstrous birth,
> Allied to hell, and not of earth!"

But he thus answered the king:

> "Listen awhile, if justice be thy aim,
> And thou wilt find me guiltless. I was sent

From Persia to destroy herds of wild boars,
Which laid the country waste. That labour done,
I lost my way, and weary with the toil,
Weary with wandering in a wildering maze,
Haply reposed beneath a shady cypress;
Thither a Perí came, and whilst I slept,
Lifted me from the ground, and quick as thought
Conveyed me to a summer-tent, where dwelt
A princess of incomparable beauty.
From thence, by hands unknown, I was removed,
Still slumbering in a litter—still unconscious;
And when I woke, I found myself reclining
In a retired pavilion of thy palace,
Attended by that soul-entrancing beauty!
My heart was filled with sorrow, and I shed
Showers of vain tears, and desolate I sate,
Thinking of Persia, with no power to fly
From my imprisonment, though soft and kind,
Being the victim of a sorcerer's art.
Yes, I am guiltless, and Maníjeh too,
Both by some magic influence pursued,
And led away against our will or choice!"

Afrásiyáb listened to this speech with distrust, and hesitated not to charge him with falsehood and cowardice. Byzun's indignation was roused by this insulting accusation; and he said to him aloud, "Cowardice, what! cowardice! I have encountered the tusks of the formidable wild boar and the claws of the raging lion. I have met the bravest in battle with sword and arrow; and if it be thy desire to witness the strength of my arm, give me but a horse and a battle-axe, and marshal twice five hundred Túránians against me, and not a man of them shall survive the contest. If this be not thy pleasure, do thy worst, but remember my blood will be avenged. Thou knowest the power of Rustem!" The mention of Rustem's name renewed all the deep feelings of resentment and animosity in the mind of Afrásiyáb, who, resolved upon the immediate execution of his purpose, commanded Gersíwaz to bind the youth, and put an end to his life on the gallows tree. The good old man Pírán Wísah happened to be passing by the place to which Byzun had just been conveyed to suffer death; and seeing a great concourse of people, and a lofty dar erected, from which hung a noose, he inquired for whom it was intended. Gersíwaz heard the question, and replied that it was for a Persian, an enemy of Túrán, a son of Gíw, and related to Rustem. Pírán straightway rode up to the youth, who was standing in deep affliction, almost naked, and with his hands bound behind his back, and he said to him :—

> "Why didst thou quit thy country, why come hither,
> Why choose the road to an untimely grave?"

Upon this Byzun told him his whole story, and the treachery of Girgín. Pírán wept at the recital, and remembering the circumstances under which he had encountered Gíw, and how he had been himself delivered from death by the interposition of Ferangís, he requested the execution to be stayed until he had seen the king, which was accordingly done. The king received him with honour, praised his wisdom and prudence, and conjecturing from his manner that something was heavy at his heart, expressed his readiness to grant any favour which he might have come to solicit. Pírán said: "Then, my only desire is this: do not put Byzun to death; do not repeat the tragedy of Saiáwush, and again consign Túrán and Írán to all the horrors of war and desolation. Remember how I warned thee against taking the life of that young prince; but malignant and evil advisers exerted their influence, were triumphant, and brought upon thee and thy kingdom the vengeance of Káús, of Rustem, and all the warriors of the Persian empire. The swords now sleeping in their scabbards are ready to flash forth again, for assuredly if the blood of Byzun be spilt the land will be depopulated by fire and sword. The honour of a king is sacred; when that is lost, all is lost." But Afrásiyáb replied: "I fear not the thousands that can be brought against me. Byzun has committed an offence which can never be pardoned; it covers me with shame, and I shall be universally despised if I suffer him to live. Death were better for me than life in disgrace. He must die."—"That is not necessary," rejoined Pirán, "let him be imprisoned in a deep cavern; he will never be heard of more, and then thou canst not be accused of having shed his blood." After some deliberation, Afrásiyáb altered his determination, and commanded Gersíwaz to bind the youth with chains from head to foot, and hang him within a deep pit with his head downwards, that he might never see sun or moon again; and he sentenced Maníjeh to share the same fate: and to make their death more sure, he ordered the enormous fragment of rock which Akwán Díw had dragged out of the ocean and flung upon the plain of Tartary, to be placed over the mouth of the pit. In respect to Byzun, Gersíwaz did as he was commanded; but the lamentations in the shubistán were so loud and distressing upon Maníjeh being sentenced to the same punishment, that the tyrant was induced to change her doom, allowing her to dwell near the pit, but forbidding, by proclamation, any one going to her or supplying her with food. Gersíwaz conducted her to the place; and stripping her of her rich garments and jewels, left her bare-headed and bare-footed, weeping torrents of tears.

He left her—the unhappy maid;
Her head upon the earth was laid,
In bitterness of grief, and lone,
Beside that dreadful demon-stone.

There happened, however, to be a fissure in the huge rock that covered the mouth of the pit, which allowed of Byzun's voice being heard, and bread and water was let down to him, so that they had the melancholy satisfaction of hearing each other's woes.

The story now relates to Girgín, who finding after several days that Byzun had not returned, began to repent of his treachery; but what is the advantage of such repentance? it is like the smoke that rises from a conflagration.

When flames have done their worst, thick clouds arise
Of lurid smoke, which useless mount the skies.

He sought everywhere for him; went to the romantic retreat where the daughter of Afrásiyáb resided; but the place was deserted, nothing was to be seen, and nothing to be heard. At length he saw Byzun's horse astray, and securing him with his kamund, thought it useless to remain in Túrán, and therefore proceeded in sorrow back to Irán. Gíw, finding that his son had not returned with him from Armán, was frantic with grief; he tore his garments and his hair, and threw ashes over his head; and seeing the horse which his son had rode, caressed it in the fondest manner, demanding from Girgín a full account of what he knew of his fate. "O Heaven forbid," said he, "that my son should have fallen into the power of the merciless demons!" Girgín could not safely confess the truth, and therefore told a falsehood, in the hope of escaping from the consequences of his own guilt. "When we arrived at Armán," said he, "we entered a large forest, and cutting down the trees, set them on fire. We then attacked the wild boars, which were found in vast numbers; and as soon as they were all destroyed, left the place on our return. Sporting all the way, we fell in with an elk, of a most beautiful and wonderful form. It was like the Símúrgh; it had hoofs of steel, and the head and ears and tail of a horse. It was strong as a lion and fleet as the wind, and came fiercely before us, yet seemed to be a thing of air. Byzun threw his kamund over him; and when entangled in the noose, the animal became furious and sprung away, dragging Byzun after him. Presently the prospect was enveloped in smoke, the earth looked like the ocean, and Byzun and the phantom-elk disappeared. I wandered about in search of my companion, but found him not: his horse only remained. My heart was rent with anguish, for it seemed to me that the furious elk must have been the White Demon." But Gíw was not to be deceived by this fabricated tale; on the contrary, he felt convinced that treachery had been at work, and in his rage seized Girgín by the beard, dragged him to and fro, and inflicted on him two hundred strokes with a scourge. The unhappy wretch, from the wounds he had received, fell senseless on the ground. Gíw then hastened to Kai-khosráu to inform him of his misfortune; and though the first resolve was to put the traitor to death, the king was contented to load him with chains and cast him into prison. The astrologers being now consulted, pronounced that Byzun was still living, and Gíw was consoled and cheered by the promptitude with which the king dispatched troops in every quarter in search of his son.

"Weep no longer, warrior bold,
Thou shalt soon thy son behold.
In this Cup, this mirror bright,
All that's dark is brought to light;
All above and under ground,
All that's lost is quickly found."
Thus spake the monarch, and held up
Before his view that wondrous Cup
Which first to Jemshíd's eye revealed
All that was in the world concealed.
And first before him lay exposed
All that the seven climes enclosed,
Whether in ocean or amid
The stars the secret things were hid,
Whether in rock or cavern placed,
In that bright Cup were clearly traced.
And now his eye Karugsar surveys,
The Cup the province wide displays.
He sees within that dismal cave
Byzun the good, the bold, the brave;
And sitting on that demon-stone
Lovely Manfjeh sad and lone.
And now he smiles and looks on Gíw,
And cries: "My prophecy was true.
Thy Byzun lives; no longer grieve,
I see him there, my words believe;
And though bound fast in fetters, he
Shall soon regain his liberty."

Kai-khosráu, thinking the services of Rustem requisite on this occasion, dispatched Gíw with an invitation to him, explaining the circumstance of Byzun's capture. Rustem had made up his mind to continue in peace and tranquillity at his Zábul principality, and not to be withdrawn again from its comforts by any emergency; but the reported situation of his near relative altered his purpose, and he hesitated not to give his best aid to restore him to freedom. Gíw rejoiced at this, and both repaired without delay to the royal residence, where Khosráu gratified the champion with the most cordial welcome, placing him on a throne before him. The king asked him what force he would require, and he replied that he did not require any army; he preferred going in disguise as a merchant. Accordingly the necessary materials were prepared; a thousand camels were laden with jewels and brocades, and other merchandise, and a thousand warriors were habited like camel-drivers. Girgín had prayed to be released from his bonds, and by the intercession of Rustem was allowed to be of the party; but his children were kept in prison as hostages and security for his honourable conduct. When the champion, with his kafila, arrived within the territory of the enemy, and approached the spot where Byzun was imprisoned, a loud clamour arose that a caravan of merchandise had come from Irán, such as was never seen before. The tidings having reached the ear of Maníjeh, she went immediately to Rustem, and inquired whether the imprisonment of Byzun was yet known at the Persian court? Rustem replied in anger: "I am a merchant employed in traffic, what can I know of such things? Go away, I have no acquaintance with either the king or his warriors." This answer overwhelmed Maníjeh with disappointment and grief, and she wept bitterly. Her tears began to soften the heart of Rustem, and he said to her in a soothing voice:—"I am not an inhabitant of the city in which the court is held, and on that account I know nothing of these matters; but tell me the cause of thy grief." Maníjeh sighed deeply, and endeavoured to avoid giving him any reply, which increased the curiosity of the champion; but she at length complied. She told him who she was, the daughter of Afrásiyáb, the story of her love, and the misfortunes of Byzun, and pointed out to him the pit in which he was imprisoned and bound down with heavy chains.

"For the sake of him has been my fall
From royal state, and bower, and hall,

And hence this pale and haggard face,
This saffron hue thy eye may trace,
Where bud of rose was wont to bloom,
But withered now and gone;
And I must sit in sorrow's gloom
Unsuccoured and alone."

Rustem asked with deep interest if any food could be conveyed to him, and she said that she had been accustomed to supply him with bread and water through a fissure in the huge stone which covered the mouth of the pit. Upon receiving this welcome information, Rustem brought a roasted fowl, and inclosing in it his own seal-ring, gave it to Maníjeh to take to Byzun. The poor captive, on receiving it, inquired by whom such a blessing could have been sent, and when she informed him that it had been given to her by the chief of a caravan from Irán, who had manifested great anxiety about him, his smiles spoke the joyous feelings of his heart, for the name of Rustem was engraved on the ring. Maníjeh was surprised to see him smile, considering his melancholy situation, and could not imagine the cause. "If thou wilt keep my secret," said he, "I will tell the cause." "What!" she replied, "have I not devoted my heart and soul to thee?—have I not sacrificed everything for thy love, and is my fidelity now to be suspected?

"Can I be faithless, then, to thee,
The choice of this fond heart of mine;
Why sought I bonds, when I was free,
But to be thine—for ever thine?"

"True, true! then hear me:—the chief of the caravan is Rustem, who has undoubtedly come to release me from this dreadful pit. Go to him, and concert with him the manner in which my deliverance may be soonest effected." Maníjeh accordingly went and communicated with the champion; and it was agreed between them that she should light a large fire to guide him on his way. He was prompt as well as valiant, and repaired in the middle of the following night, accompanied by seven of his warriors, directed by the blaze, to the place where

Byzun was confined. The neighbourhood was infested by demons with long nails, and long hair on their bodies like the hair of a goat, and horny feet, and with heads like dogs, and the chief of them was the son of Akwán Díw. The father having been slain by Rustem, the son nourished the hope of revenge, and perpetually longed for an opportunity of meeting him in battle. Well knowing that the champion was engaged in the enterprize to liberate Byzun, he commanded his demons to give him intelligence of his approach. His height was tremendous, his face was black, his mouth yawned like a cavern, his eyes were fountains of blood, his teeth like those of a wild boar, and the hair on his body like needles. The monster advanced, and reproaching Rustem disdainfully for having slain Akwán Díw, and many other warriors in the Túránian interest, pulled up a tree by the roots and challenged him to combat. The struggle began, but the Demon frequently escaped the fury of the champion by vanishing into air. At length Rustem struck a fortunate blow, which cut the body of his towering adversary in two. His path being now free from interruption, he sped onward, and presently beheld the prodigious demon-stone which covered the mouth of the pit, in which Byzun was imprisoned.

> And praying to the Almighty to infuse
> Strength through his limbs, he raised it up, and flung
> The ponderous mass of rock upon the plain,
> Which shuddered to receive that magic load!

The mouth of the cavern being thus exposed, Rustem applied himself to the extrication of Byzun from his miserable condition, and letting down his kamund, he had soon the pleasure of drawing up the unfortunate captive, whom he embraced with great affection; and instantly stripped off the chains with which he was bound. After mutual congratulations had been exchanged, Rustem proposed that Byzun and Maníjeh should go immediately to Irán, whilst he and his companions in arms attacked the palace of Afrásiyáb; but though wasted as he was by long suffering, Byzun could not on any consideration consent to avoid the perils of the intended assault, and determined, at all hazards, to accompany his deliverer.

> "Full well I know thy super-human power
> Needs no assistance from an arm like mine;
> But grateful as I am for this great service,
> I cannot leave thee now, and shrink from peril,
> That would be baseness which I could not bear."

It was on the same night that Rustem and Byzun, and seven of his warriors, proceeded against that part of the palace in which the tyrant slept. He first put to death the watchman, and also killed a great number of the guard, and a loud voice presently resounded in the chamber of the king:—"Awake from thy slumbers, Afrásiyáb, Byzun has been freed from his chains." Rustem now entered the royal palace, and openly declaring his name, exclaimed:—"I am come, Afrásiyáb, to destroy thee, and Byzun is also here to do thee service for thy cruelty to him." The death-note awoke the trembling Afrásiyáb, and he rose up, and fled in dismay. Rustem and his companions rushed into the inner apartments, and captured all the blooming damsels of the shubistán, and all the jewels and golden ornaments which fell in their way. The moon-faced beauties were sent to Zábul; but the jewels and other valuable property were reserved for the king.

In the morning Afrásiyáb hastily collected together his troops and marched against Rustem, who, with Byzun and his thousand warriors, met him on the plain prepared for battle. The champion challenged any one who would come forward to single combat; but though frequently repeated, no attention was paid to the call. At length Rustem said to Afrásiyáb:—"Art thou not ashamed to avoid a contest with so inferior a force, a hundred thousand against one thousand? We two, and our armies, have often met, and dost thou now shrink from the fight?" The reproach had its effect,

> For the tyrant at once, and his heroes, began
> Their attack like the demons of Mázinderán.

But the valour and the bravery of Rustem were so eminently shewn, that he overthrew thousands of the enemy.

In the tempest of battle, disdaining all fear,
With his kamund, and khanjer, his garz, and shamshír,
How he bound, stabbed, and crushed, and dissevered the foe,
So mighty his arm, and so fatal his blow.*

And so dreadful was the carnage, that Afrásiyáb, unable to resist his victorious career, was compelled to seek safety in flight.

The field was red with blood, the Tartar banners
Cast on the ground, and when, with grief, he saw
The face of Fortune turned, his cohorts slain,
He hurried back, and sought Túrán again.

Rustem having obtained another triumph, returned to Irán with the spoils of his conquest, and was again honoured with the smiles and rewards of his sovereign. Maníjeh was not forgotten; she, too, received a present worthy of the virtue and fidelity she had displayed, and of the magnanimity of her spirit; and the happy conclusion of the enterprise was celebrated with festivity and rejoicing.

BARZÚ, AND HIS CONFLICT WITH RUSTEM.

Afrásiyáb after his defeat pursued his way in despair towards Chín and Má-chín, and on the road happened to fall in with a man of huge and terrific stature. Amazed at the sight of so

* This is a favourite passage in the original. My old Múnshi used to be delighted with it, thinking the description and effects of each weapon so truly admirable; the entangling of the noose, the stabbing of the dagger, the crushing of the mace, and the cutting of the sword being brought together within so small a compass.

extraordinary a being, he asked him who and what he was." "I am a villager," replied the stranger. "And thy father?" —"I do not know my father. My mother has never mentioned his name, and my birth is wrapped in mystery." Afrásiyáb then addressed him as follows:—"It is my misfortune to have a bitter and invincible enemy, who has plunged me into the greatest distress. If he could be subdued, there would be no impediment to my conquest of Irán; and I feel assured that thou, apparently endued with such prodigious strength, hast the power to master him. His name is Rustem." "What!" rejoined Barzú, "is all this concern and affliction about one man—about one man only?" "Yes," answered Afrásiyáb; "but that one man is equal to a hundred strong men. Upon him neither sword, nor mace, nor javelin has any effect. In battle he is like a mountain of steel." At this Barzú exclaimed in gamesome mood:—"A mountain of steel!—I can reduce to dust a hundred mountains of steel!—What is a mountain of steel to me!" Afrásiyáb rejoiced to find such confidence in the stranger, and instantly promised him his own daughter in marriage, and the monarchy of Chín and Ma-chín, if he succeeded in destroying Rustem. Barzú replied:

"Thou art but a coward slave,
Thus a stranger's aid to crave.
And thy soldiers, what are they?
Heartless on the battle-day.
Thou, the prince of such a host!
What, alas! hast thou to boast?
Art thou not ashamed to wear
The regal crown that glitters there?
And dost thou not disgrace the throne
Thus to be awed, and crushed by one;
By one, whate'er his name or might,
Thus to be put to shameful flight!"

Afrásiyáb felt keenly the reproaches which he heard; but, nevertheless, solicited the assistance of Barzú, who declared that he would soon overpower Rustem, and place the empire of Irán under the dominion of the Tartar king. He would, he said, overflow the land of Persia with blood, and take possession of the throne! The despot was intoxicated with delight, and expecting his most sanguine wishes would be realised, made him the costliest presents, consisting of gold and jewels, and horses, and elephants, so that the besotted stranger thought himself the greatest personage in all the world. But his mother, when she heard these things, implored him to be cautious:—

"My son, these presents, though so rich and rare,
Will be thy winding-sheet; beware, beware!
They'll drive to madness thy poor giddy brain,
And thou wilt never be restored again.
Never; for wert thou bravest of the brave,
They only lead to an untimely grave.
Then give them back, nor such a doom provoke,
Beware of Rustem's host-destroying stroke.
Has he not conquered demons!—and, alone,
Afrásiyáb's best warriors overthrown!
And canst thou equal them?—Alas! the day
That thy sweet life should thus be thrown away."

Barzú, however, was too much dazzled by the presents he had received, and too vain of his own personal strength to attend to his mother's advice. "Certainly," said he, "the disposal of our lives is in the hands of the Almighty, and as certain it is that my strength is superior to that of Rustem. Would it not then be cowardly to decline the contest with him?" The mother still continued to dissuade him from the enterprise, and assured him that Rustem was above all mankind distinguished for the art, and skill, and dexterity with which he attacked his enemy, and defended himself; and that there was no chance of his being overcome by a man entirely ignorant of the science of fighting; but Barzú remained unmoved: yet he told the king what his mother had said; and Afrásiyáb, in consequence, deemed it proper to appoint two celebrated masters to instruct him in the use of the bow, the sword, and the javelin, and also in wrestling and throwing the noose. Every day, clothed in armour, he tried his skill and strength with the warriors, and after ten days he was sufficiently accomplished to overthrow eighteen of them at one time. Proud of the progress he had made, he told the king that he would seize and bind eighteen of his stoutest and most experienced teachers, and bring them before him, if he wished, when all the assembly exclaimed :—"No doubt he is fully equal to the task ;

> He does not seem of human birth, but wears
> The aspect of the Evil One ; and looks
> Like Alberz mountain, clad in folds of mail ;
> Unwearied in the fight he conquers all."

Afrásiyáb's satisfaction was increased by this testimony to the merit of Barzú, and he heaped upon him further tokens of his good-will and munificence. The vain, newly-made warrior was all exultation and delight, and said impatiently :

> "Delays are ever dangerous—let us meet
> The foe betimes, this Rustem and the king,
> Kai-khosráu. If we linger in a cause
> Demanding instant action, prompt appliance,
> And rapid execution, we are lost.
> Advance, and I will soon lop off the heads
> Of this belauded champion and his king,
> And cast them, with the Persian crown and throne
> Trophies of glory, at thy royal feet ;
> So that Túrán alone shall rule the world."

Speedily ten thousand experienced horsemen were selected and placed under the command of Barzú ; and Húmán and Barmán were appointed to accompany him ; Afrásiyáb himself intending to follow with the reserve.

When the intelligence of this new expedition reached the court of Kai-khosráu, he was astonished, and could not conceive how, after so signal a defeat and overthrow, Afrásiyáb had the means of collecting another army, and boldly invading his kingdom. To oppose this invasion, however, he ordered Tús and Fríburz, with twelve thousand horsemen, and marched after them himself with a large army. As soon as Tús fell in with the enemy the battle commenced, and lasted, with great carnage, a whole day and night, and in the end Barzú was victorious. The warriors of the Persian force fled, and left Tús and Fríburz alone on the field, where they were encountered by the conqueror, taken prisoners, and bound, and placed in the charge of Húmán. The tidings of the result of this conflict were received with as much rejoicing by Afrásiyáb, as with sorrow and consternation by Kai-khosráu. And now the emergency, on the Persian side, demanded the assistance of Rustem, whose indignation was roused, and who determined on revenge for the insult that had been given. He took with him Gustahem, the brother of Tús, and at midnight thought he had come to the tent of Barzú, but it proved to be the pavilion of Afrásiyáb, who was seen seated on his throne, with Barzú on his right hand, and Pírán-Wísah on his left, and Tús and Fríburz standing in chains before them. The king said to the captive warriors :—"To-morrow you shall both be put to death in the manner I slew Saiáwush." He then retired. Meanwhile Rustem returned thanks to Heaven that his friends were still alive, and requesting Gustahem to follow cautiously, he waited awhile for a fit opportunity, till the watchman was off his guard, and then killing him, he and Gustahem took up and conveyed the two prisoners to a short distance, where they knocked off their chains, and then conducted them back to Kai-khosráu.

When Afrásiyáb arose from sleep, he found his warriors in close and earnest conversation, and was told that a champion from Persia had come and killed the watchman, and carried off the prisoners. Pírán exclaimed :—"Then assuredly that champion is Rustem, and no other." Afrásiyáb writhed with anger and mortification at this intelligence, and sending for Barzú, dispatched his army to attack the enemy, and challenge Rustem to single combat. Rustem was with the Persian troops, and, answering the summons, said :—"Young man, if thou art calling for Rustem, behold I come in his place to lay thee prostrate on the earth." "Ah!" rejoined Barzú, "and why this threat? It is true I am but of tender years, whilst thou art aged and experienced. But if thou art fire, I am water, and able to quench thy flames." Saying this he wielded his bow, and fixed the arrow in its notch, and commenced the strife.

Rustem also engaged with bow and arrows; and then they each had recourse to their maces, which from repeated strokes were soon bent as crooked as their bows, and they were themselves nearly exhausted. Their next encounter was by wrestling, and dreadful were the wrenches and grasps they received from each other. Barzú finding no advantage from this struggle, raised his mace, and struck Rustem such a prodigious blow on the head, that the champion thought a whole mountain had fallen upon him. One arm was disabled, but though the wound was desperate, Rustem had the address to conceal its effects, and Barzú wondered that he had made apparently so little impression on his antagonist. "Thou art," said he, "a surprizing warrior, and seemingly invulnerable. Had I struck such a blow on a mountain, it would have been broken into a thousand fragments, and yet it makes no impression upon thee. Heaven forbid!" he continued to himself, "that I should ever receive so bewildering a stroke upon my own head!" Rustem having successfully concealed the anguish of his wound, artfully observed that it would be better to finish the combat on the following day, to which Barzú readily agreed, and then they both parted.

Barzú declared to Afrásiyáb that his extraordinary vigour and strength had been of no account, for both his antagonist and his horse appeared to be composed of materials as hard as flint. Every blow was without effect; and "Heaven only knows," added he, "what may be the result of to-morrow's conflict." On the other hand Rustem shewed his lacerated arm to Khosráu, and said:—"I have escaped from him; but who else is there now to meet him, and finish the struggle? Ferámurz, my son, cannot fulfil my promise with Barzú, as he, alas! is fighting in Hindústan. Let me, however, call him hither, and in the meanwhile, on some pretext or other, delay the engagement." The king, in great sorrow and affliction, sanctioned his departure, and then said to his warriors:—"I will fight this Barzú myself to-morrow;" but Gúdarz would not consent to it, saying:—"As long as we live, the king must not be exposed to such hazard. Gíw and Byzun, and the other chiefs, must first successively encounter the enemy."

When Rustem reached his tent, he told his brother Zúara to get ready a litter, that he might proceed to Sístán for the purpose of obtaining a remedy for his wound from the Símurgh. Pain and grief kept him awake all night, and he prayed incessantly to the Supreme Being. In the morning early, Zúara brought him intelligence of the welcome arrival of Ferámurz, which gladdened his heart; and as the youth had undergone great fatigue on his long journey, Rustem requested him to repose awhile, and he himself, freed from anxiety, also sought relief in a sound sleep.

A few hours afterwards both armies were again drawn up, and Barzú, like a mad elephant, full of confidence and pride, rode forward to resume the combat; whilst Rustem gave instructions to Ferámurz how he was to act. He attired him in his own armour, supplied him with his own weapons, and mounted him on Rakush, and told him to represent himself to Barzú as the warrior who had engaged him the day before. Accordingly Ferámurz entered the middle space, clothed in his father's mail, raised his bow, ready bent, and shot an arrow at Barzú, crying:—"Behold thy adversary!—I am the man come to try thy strength again.—Advance!" To this Barzú replied:—"Why this hilarity, and great flow of spirits? Art thou reckless of thy life?" "In the eyes of warriors," said Ferámurz, "the field of fight is the mansion of pleasure. After I yesterday parted from thee I drank wine with my companions, and the impression of delight still remains on my heart.

"Wine exhilarates the soul,
Makes the eye with pleasure roll;
Lightens up the darkest mien,
Fills with joy the dullest scene;
Hence it is I meet thee now
With a smile upon my brow."

Barzú, however, thought that the voice and action of his adversary were not the same as he had heard and seen the preceding day, although there was no difference in the armour or the horse, and therefore he said :—"Perhaps the cavalier whom I encountered yesterday is wounded or dead, that thou hast mounted his charger, and attired thyself in his mail." "Indeed, rejoined Ferámurz, perhaps thou hast lost thy wits; I am certainly the person who engaged thee yesterday, and almost extinguished thee; and with God's favour thou shalt be a dead man to-day." "What is thy name?" "My name is Rustem, descended from a race of warriors, and my pleasure consists in contending with the lions of battle, and shedding the blood of heroes." Thus saying, Ferámurz rushed on his adversary, struck him several blows with his battle-axe, and drawing his noose from the saddle-strap with the quickness of lightning, secured his prize. He might have put an end to his existence in a moment, but preferred taking him alive, and shewing him as a captive. Afrásiyáb seeing the perilous condition of Barzú, came up with his whole army to his rescue; but Kai-khosráu was equally on the alert, accompanied by Rustem, who advancing to the support of Ferámurz, threw another noose round the neck of the already-captured Barzú, to prevent the possibility of his escape. Both armies now engaged, and the Túránians made many desperate efforts to recover their gigantic leader, but all their manœuvres were fruitless. The struggle continued fiercely, and with great slaughter, till it was dark, and then ceased; the two kings returning back to the respective positions they had taken up before the conflict took place. The Túránians were in the deepest grief for the loss of Barzú; and Pírán-Wisah having recommended an immediate retreat across the Jíhún, Afrásiyáb followed his counsel, and precipitately quitted Persia with all his troops.

Kai-khosráu ordered a grand banquet on the occasion of the victory; and when Barzú was brought before him, he commanded his immediate execution; but Rustem, seeing that he was very young, and thinking that he had not yet been corrupted and debased by the savage example of the Túránians, requested that he might be spared, and given to him to send into Sístán; and his request was promptly complied with.

When the mother of Barzú, whose name was Shah-rú, heard that her son was a prisoner, she wept bitterly, and hastened to Irán, and from thence to Sístán. There happened to be in Rustem's employ a singing-girl,* an old acquaintance of her's, to whom she was much attached, and to whom she made large presents, calling her by the most endearing epithets, in order that she might be brought to serve her in the important matter she had in contemplation. Her object was soon explained, and the preliminaries at once adjusted, and by the hands of this singing-girl she secretly sent some food to Barzú, in which she concealed a ring, to apprise him of her being near him. On finding the ring, he asked who had supplied him with the food, and her answer was:—"A woman recently arrived from Má-chín." This was to him delightful intelligence, and he could not help exclaiming, "That woman is my mother, I am grateful for thy services, but another time bring me, if thou canst, a large file, that I may be able to free myself from these chains." The singing-girl promised her assistance; and having told Shah-rú what her son required, conveyed to him a file, and resolved to accompany him in his flight. Barzú then requested that three fleet horses might be provided and kept ready under the walls, at a short distance; and this being also done, in the night, he and his mother, and the singing-girl, effected their escape, and pursued their course towards Túrán.

It so happened that Rustem was at this time in progress between Irán and Sístán, hunting for his own pleasure the elk or wild ass, and he accidentally fell in with the refugees, who made an attempt to avoid him, but, unable to effect their purpose, thought proper to oppose him with all their might,

* Theocritus introduces a Greek singing-girl in Idyllium, xv. at the festival of Adonis. In the Arabian Nights, the Kaliph is represented at his feasts surrounded by troops of the most beautiful females playing on various instruments.

and a sharp contest ensued. Both parties becoming fatigued, they rested awhile, when Rustem asked Barzú how he had obtained his liberty. "The Almighty freed me from the bondage I endured."—"And who are these two women ?"—"One of them," replied Barzú, "is my mother, and that is a singing-girl of thy own house." Rustem went aside, and called for breakfast, and thinking in his own mind that it would be expedient to poison Barzú, mixed up a deleterious substance in some food, and sent it to him to eat. He was just going to take it, when his mother cried, "My son, beware!" and he drew his hand from the dish. But the singing-girl did eat part of it, and died on the spot. Upon witnessing this appalling scene, Barzú sprung forward with indignation, and reproached Rustem for his treachery in the severest terms.

> "Old man! hast thou mid warrior-chiefs a place,
> And dost thou practice that which brings disgrace?
> Hast thou no fear of a degraded name,
> No fear of lasting obloquy and shame?
> O, thou canst have no hope in God, when thou
> Stand'st thus defiled,—dishonoured, false, as now;
> Unfair, perfidious, art thou too, in strife,
> By any pretext thou would'st take my life!"

He then in a menacing attitude exclaimed :—"If thou art a man, rise and fight!" Rustem felt ashamed on being thus detected, and rose up frowning in scorn. They met, brandishing their battle-axes, and looking as black as the clouds of night. They then dismounted to wrestle, and fastening the bridles, each to his own girdle, furiously grasped each others' loins and limbs, straining and struggling for the mastery. Whilst they were thus engaged, their horses betrayed equal animosity, and attacked each other with great violence. Rakush bit and kicked Barzú's steed so severely that he strove to gallop away, dragging his master, who was at the same time under the excruciating gripe of Rustem. "O, release me for a moment till I am disentangled from my horse," exclaimed Barzú; but Rustem heeding him not, now pressed him down beneath him, and was preparing to give him the finishing blow by cutting off his head, when the mother seeing the fatal moment approach, shrieked, and cried out, "Forbear, Rustem! this youth is the son of Sohráb, and thy own grandchild! Forbear, and bring not on thyself the devouring anguish which followed the death of his unhappy father.

> "Think of Sohráb! take not the precious life
> Of sire and son—unnatural is the strife;
> Restrain, for mercy's sake, that furious mood,
> And pause before thou shedd'st a kinsman's blood."

"Ah!" rejoined Rustem, "can that be true?" upon which Shah-rú showed him Sohráb's brilliant finger-ring and he was satisfied. He then pressed Barzú warmly and affectionately to his breast, and kissed his head and eyes, and took him along with him to Sístán, where he placed him in a station of honour, and introduced him to his great grandfather Zál, who received and caressed him with becoming tenderness and regard.

SÚSEN THE SORCERESS, AND AFRÁSIYÁB.

Soon after Afrásiyáb had returned defeated into Túrán, grievously lamenting the misfortune which had deprived him of the assistance of Barzú, a woman named Súsen, deeply versed in magic and sorcery, came to him, and promised by her potent art to put him in the way of destroying Rustem and his whole family.

> "Fighting disappointment brings,
> Sword and mace are useless things;
> If thou would'st a conqueror be,
> Monarch! put thy trust in me;
> Soon the mighty chief shall bleed,—
> Spells and charms will do the deed!"

Afrásiyáb at first refused to avail himself of her power, but was presently induced, by a manifestation of her skill, to consent to what she proposed. She required that a distinguished warrior should be sent along with her, furnished with abundance of treasure, honorary tokens and presents, so that none might be aware that she was employed on the occasion. Afrásiyáb appointed Pílsam, duly supplied with the requisites, and the warrior and the sorceress set off on their journey, people being stationed conveniently on the road to hasten the first tidings of their success to the king. Their course was towards Sístán, and arriving at a fort, they took possession of a commodious residence, in which they placed the wealth and property they had brought, and, establishing a house of entertainment, all travellers who passed that way were hospitably and sumptuously regaled by them.

For sparkling wine, and viands rare,
And mellow fruit, abounded there.

It is recorded that Rustem had invited to a magnificent feast at his palace in Sístán a large company of the most celebrated heroes of the kingdom, and amongst them happened to be Tús, whom the king had deputed to the champion on some important state affairs. Gúdarz was also present; and between him and Tús, ever hostile to each other, a dispute as usual took place. The latter, always boasting of his ancestry, reviled the old warrior and said, "I am the son of Nauder, and the grandson of Feridún, whilst thou art but the son of Kavah, the blacksmith;—why then dost thou put thyself on a footing with me?" Gúdarz, in reply, poured upon him reproaches equally irritating, accused him of ignorance and folly, and roused the anger of the prince to such a degree that he drew his dagger to punish the offender, when Rehám started up and prevented the intended bloodshed. This interposition increased his rage, and in serious dudgeon he retired from the banquet, and set off on his return to Irán.

Rustem was not present at the time, but when he heard of

the altercation and the result of it, he was very angry, saying that Gúdarz was a relation of the family, and Tús his guest, and therefore wrong had been done, since a guest ought always to be protected. "A guest," he said, "ought to be held as sacred as the king, and it is the custom of heroes to treat a guest with the most scrupulous respect and consideration.

For a guest is the king of the feast."

He then requested Gúdarz to go after Tús, and by fair words and proper excuses bring him back to his festive board. Accordingly Gúdarz departed. No sooner had he gone than Gíw rose up, and said, "Tús is little better than a madman, and my father of a hasty temper; I should therefore wish to follow, to prevent the possibility of further disagreement." To this Rustem consented. Byzun was now also anxious to go, and he too got permission. When all the three had departed, Rustem began to be apprehensive that something unpleasant would occur, and thought it prudent to send Ferámurz to preserve the peace. Zál then came forward, and thinking that Tús, the descendant of the Kaís and his revered guest, might not be easily prevailed upon to return either by Gúdarz, Gíw, Byzun, or Ferámurz, resolved to go himself and soothe the temper which had been so injudiciously and rudely ruffled at the banquet.

When Tús, on his journey from Rustem's palace, approached the residence of Súsen the sorceress, he beheld numerous cooks and confectioners on every side, preparing all kinds of rich and rare dishes of food, and every species of sweetmeat; and enquiring to whom they belonged, he was told that the place was occupied by the wife of a merchant from Túrán, who was extremely wealthy, and who entertained in the most sumptuous manner every traveller who passed that way. Hungry, and curious to see what was going on, Tús dismounted, and leaving his horse with the attendants, entered the principal apartment, where he saw a fascinating female, and was transported with joy.—She was

Tall as the graceful cypress, and as bright,
As ever struck a lover's ravished sight;
Why of her musky locks or ringlets tell?
Each silky hair itself contained a spell.
Why of her face so beautifully fair?
Wondering he saw the moon's refulgence there.

As soon as his transports had subsided he sat down before her, and asked her who she was, and upon what adventure she was engaged; and she answered that she was a singing-girl, that a wealthy merchant some time ago had fallen in love with and married her, and soon afterwards died; that Afrásiyáb, the king, had since wished to take her into his harem, which alarmed her, and she had in consequence fled from his country; she was willing, however, she said, to become the hand-maid of Kai-khosráu, he being a true king, and of a sweet and gentle temper.

"A persecuted damsel I,
Thus the detested tyrant fly,
And hastening from impending woes,
In happy Persia seek repose;
For long as cherished life remains,
Pleasure must smile where Khosráu reigns.
Thence did I from my home depart,
To please and bless a Persian heart."

The deception worked effectually on the mind of Tús, and he at once entered into the notion of escorting her to Kai-khosráu. But he was immediately supplied with charmed viands and goblets of rich wine, which he had not the power to resist, till his senses forsook him, and then Pílsam appeared, and, binding him with cords, conveyed him safely and secretly into the interior of the fort. In a short time Gúdarz arrived, and he too was received and treated in the same manner. Then Gíw and Byzun were seized and secured; and after them came Zál: but notwithstanding the enticements that were used, and the attractions that presented themselves, he would neither enter the enchanted apartment, nor taste the enchanted food or wine.

The witching cup was filled to the brim,
But the magic draught had no charms for him.

A person whispered in his ear that the woman had already wickedly got into her power several warriors, and he felt assured that they were his own friends. To be revenged for this treachery he rushed forward, and would have seized hold of the sorceress, but she fled into the fort and fastened the gate. He instantly sent a messenger to Rustem, explaining the perplexity in which he was involved, and exerting all his strength, broke down the gate that had just been closed against him. As soon as the passage was opened, out rushed Pílsam, who with his mace commenced a furious battle with Zál, in which he nearly overpowered him, when Ferámurz reached the spot, and telling the venerable old warrior to stand aside, took his place, and fought with Pílsam without intermission all day, and till they were parted by the darkness of night.

Early in the morning Rustem, accompanied by Barzú, arrived from Sístán, and entering the fort, called aloud for Pílsam. He also sent Ferámurz to Kai-khosráu to inform him of what had occurred. Pílsam at length issued forth, and attacked the champion. They first fought with bows and arrows, with javelins next, and then successively with maces, and swords, and daggers. The contest lasted the whole day; and when at night they parted, neither had gained the victory. The next morning immense clouds of dust were seen, and they were found to be occasioned by Afrásiyáb and his army marching to the spot. Rustem appointed Barzú to proceed with his Zábul troops against him, whilst he himself encountered Pílsam. The strife between the two was dreadful. Rustem struck him several times furiously upon the head, and at length stretched him lifeless on the sand. He then impelled Rakush towards the Túránian army, and aided by Zál and Barzú, committed tremendous havoc among them.

> So thick the arrows fell, helmet, and mail,
> And shield, pierced through, looked like a field of reeds.

In the meantime Súsen, the sorceress, escaped from the fort, and fled to Afrásiyáb.

Another cloud of dust spreading from earth to heaven, was observed in the direction of Persia, and the waving banners becoming more distinct, presently showed the approach of the king, Kai-khosráu.

> The steely javelins sparkled in the sun,
> Helmet and shield, and joyous seemed the sight.
> Banners, all gorgeous, floating on the breeze,
> And horns shrill echoing, and the tramp of steeds,
> Proclaimed to dazzled eye and half-stunned ear,
> The mighty preparation.

The hostile armies soon met, and there was a sanguinary conflict, but the Túránians were obliged to give way. Upon this common result, Pírán Wísah declared to Afrásiyáb that perseverance was as ridiculous as unprofitable. "Our army has no heart, nor confidence, when opposed to Rustem; how often have we been defeated by him—how often have we been scattered like sheep before that lion in battle! We have just lost the aid of Barzú, and now is it not deplorable to put any trust in the dreams of a singing-girl, to accelerate on her account the ruin of the country, and to hazard thy own personal safety.

> What! risk an empire on a woman's word!"

Afrásiyáb replied, "So it is;" and instantly urged his horse into the middle of the plain, where he loudly challenged Kai-khosráu to single combat, saying, "Why should we uselessly shed the blood of our warriors and people. Let us ourselves decide the day. God will give the triumph to him who merits it." Kai-khosráu was ashamed to refuse this challenge, and descending from his elephant, mounted his horse and prepared for the onset. But his warriors seized the bridle, and would not allow him to fight. He declared, however, that he would himself take revenge for the blood of Saiáwush, and struggled to overcome the friends who were opposing his progress. "Forbear awhile," said Rustem, "Afrásiyáb is expert in all the arts of the warrior, fighting with the sword, the dagger, in archery, and wrestling. When I wrestled with him, and held him down, he could not have escaped, excepting by the exercise of the most consummate dexterity. Allow thy warriors to fight for thee." But the king was angry, and said, "The monarch who does not fight for himself, is unworthy of the crown." Upon hearing this, Rustem wept tears of blood. Barzú now took hold of the king's stirrup, and knocked his forehead against it, and drawing his dagger, threatened to put an end to himself, saying, "My blood will be upon thy neck, if thou goest;" and he continued in a strain so eloquent and persuasive that Khosráu relaxed in his determination, and observed to Rustem: "There can be no doubt that Barzú is descended from thee." Barzú now respectfully kissed the ground before the king, and vaulting on his saddle with admirable agility, rushed onwards to the middle space where Afrásiyáb was waiting, and roared aloud. Afrásiyáb burned with indignation at the sight, and said in his heart: "It seems that I have nurtured and instructed this ingrate, to shed my own blood. Thou wretch of demon-birth, thou knowest not thy father's name! and yet thou comest to wage war against me! Art thou not ashamed to look upon the king of Túrán after what he has done for thee?" Barzú replied: "Although thou didst protect me, thou spilt the blood of Saiáwush and Aghríras unjustly. When I ate thy salt, I served thee faithfully, and fought for thee. I now eat the salt of Kai-khosráu, and my allegiance is due to him."

He spoke, and raised his battle-axe, and rushed,
Swift as a demon of Mázinderan,
Against Afrásiyáb, who, frowning, cried:—
"Approach not like a furious elephant,
Heedless what may befall thee—nor provoke
The wrath of him whose certain aim is death."
Then placed he on the string a pointed dart,
And shot it from the bow; whizzing it flew,
And pierced the armour of the wondering youth,
Inflicting on his side a painful wound,
Which made his heart with trepidation throb;
High exultation marked the despot's brow,
Seeing the gush of blood his loins distain.

Barzú was now anxious to assail Afrásiyáb with his mace,

instead of arrows; but whenever he tried to get near enough, he was disappointed by the adroitness of his adversary, whom he could not reach. He was at last compelled to lay aside the battle-axe, and have recourse to his bow, but every arrow was dexterously received by Afrásiyáb on his shield; and Barzú, on his part, became equally active and successful. Afrásiyáb soon emptied his quiver, and then he grasped his mace with the intention of extinguishing his antagonist at once, but at the moment Húmán came up, and said: "O, king! do not bring thyself into jeopardy by contending against a person of no account; thy proper adversary is Kai-khosráu, and not him, for if thou gainest the victory, it can only be a victory over a fatherless soldier, and if thou art killed, the whole of Túrán will be at the feet of Persia." Both Pírán and Húmán dissuaded the king from continuing the engagement singly, and directed the Túránians to commence a general attack. Afrásiyáb told them that if Barzú was not slain, it would be a great misfortune to their country; in consequence, they surrounded him, and inflicted on him many severe wounds. But Rustem and Ferámurz, beholding the dilemma into which Barzú was thrown, hastened to his support, and many of the enemy were killed by them, and great carnage followed by the advance of the Persian army.

> The noise of clashing swords, and ponderous maces
> Ringing upon the iron mail, seemed like
> The busy work-shop of an armourer;
> Tumultuous as the sea the field appeared,
> All crimsoned with the blood of heroes slain.

Kai-khosráu himself hurried to the assistance of Barzú, and the powerful force which he brought along with him soon put the Túránians to flight. Afrásiyáb too made his escape in the confusion that prevailed. The king wished to pursue the enemy, but Rustem observed that their defeat and dispersion was enough. The battle having ceased, and the army being in the neighbourhood of Sístán, the champion solicited permission to return to his home; "for I am now," said he, "four hundred years old, and require a little rest. In the meantime Ferámurz and Barzú may take my place." The king consented, and distributing his favours to each of his distinguished warriors for their prodigious exertions, left Zál and Rustem to proceed to Sístán, and returned to the capital of his kingdom.

THE EXPEDITION OF GÚDARZ AGAINST AFRÁSIYÁB.

The overthrow of the sovereign of Túrán had only a temporary effect, as it was not long before he was enabled to collect further supplies, and another army for the defence of his kingdom; and Kai-khosráu's ambition to reduce the power of his rival being animated by new hopes of success, another expedition was entrusted to the command of Gúdarz. Rustem, he said, had done his duty in repeated campaigns against Afrásiyáb, and the extraordinary gallantry and wisdom with which they were conducted, entitled him to the highest applause. "It is now, Gúdarz, thy turn to vanquish the enemy." Accordingly Gúdarz, accompanied by Gíw, and Tús and Byzun, and an immense army, proceeded towards Túrán. Ferámurz was directed previously to invade and conquer Hindústan, and from thence to march to the borders of Chín and Machín, for the purpose of uniting and co-operating with the army under Gúdarz, and, finally, to capture Afrásiyáb.

As soon as it was known in Túrán that Gúdarz was in motion to resume hostilities against the king, Húmán was appointed with a large force to resist his progress, and a second army of reserve was gathered together under the command of Pírán. The first conflict which occurred was between the troops of Gúdarz and Húmán. Gúdarz directed Byzun to attack Húmán. The two chiefs joined in battle, when Húmán fell under the sword of his adversary, and his army, being defeated, retired, and united in the rear with the legions of Pírán. The enemy thus became of formidable strength, and in consequence it was thought proper to communicate the inequality to Kaí-khosráu, that reinforcements might be sent without loss of time. The king immediately complied, and also wrote to Sístán to request the aid of Rustem. The war lasted two years, the army on each side being continually recruited as necessity required, so that the numbers were regularly kept up, till a great battle took place, in which the venerable Pírán was killed, and nearly the whole of his army destroyed. This victory was obtained without the assistance of Rustem, who, notwithstanding the message of the king, had still remained in Sístán. The loss of Pírán, the counsellor and warrior, proved to be a great affliction to Afrásiyáb: he felt as if his whole support was taken away, and deemed it the signal of approaching ruin to his cause.

> "Thou wert my refuge, thou my friend and brother;
> Wise in thy counsel, gallant in the field,
> My monitor and guide—and thou art gone!
> The glory of my kingdom is eclipsed,
> Since thou hast vanished from this world, and left me
> All wretched to myself. But food, nor sleep
> Nor rest will I indulge in, till just vengeance
> Has been inflicted on the cruel foe."

When the news of Pírán's death reached Kai-khosráu, he rapidly marched forward, crossed the Jíhún without delay, and passed through Samerkand and Bokhara, to encounter the Túránians. Afrásiyáb, in the meantime, had not been neglectful. He had all his hidden treasure dug up, with which he assembled a prodigious army, and appointed his son Shydah-Poshang to the command of a hundred thousand horsemen. To oppose this force, Khosráu appointed his young relative, Lohurásp, with eight thousand horsemen, and passing through

Sístán, desired Rustem, on account of Lohurásp's tender age and inexperience, to afford him such good counsel as he required. When Afrásiyáb heard this, he added to the force of Shydah another hundred thousand men, but first sent his son to Kai-khosráu in the character of an ambassador to offer terms of peace. "Tell him," said he, "that to secure this object, I will deliver to him one of my sons as a hostage, and a number of troops for his service, with the sacred promise never to depart from my engagements again.—But, a word in thy ear, Shydah; if Khosráu is not disposed to accept these terms, say, to prevent unnecessary bloodshed, he and I must personally decide the day by single combat. If he refuses to fight with me, say that thou wilt meet him; and shouldst thou be slain in the strife, I will surrender to him the kingdom of Túrán, and retire myself from the world." He further commanded him to propound these terms with a gallant and fearless bearing, and not to betray the least apprehension. Shydah entered fully into the spirit of his father's instructions, and declared that he would devote his life to the cause, that he would boldly before the whole assembly dare Kai-khosráu to battle; so that Afrásiyáb was delighted with the valorous disposition he displayed.

Kai-khosráu smiled when he heard of what Afrásiyáb intended, and viewed the proposal as a proof of his weakness. "But never," said he, "will I consent to a peace till I have inflicted on him the death which Saiáwush was made to suffer. When Shydah arrived, and with proper ceremony and respect had delivered his message, Kai-khosráu invited him to retire to his chamber and go to rest, and he would send an answer by one of his people. Shydah accordingly retired, and the king proceeded to consult his warrior-friends on the offers that had been made. "Afrásiyáb tells me," said he, "that if I do not wish for peace, I must fight either him or his son. I have seen Shydah—his eyes are red and blood-shot, and he has a fierce expression of feature; if I do not accept his terms, I shall probably soon have a dagger lodged in my breast."

Saying this, he ordered his mail to be got ready; but Rustem and all the great men about him exclaimed, unanimously: "This must not be allowed; Afrásiyáb is full of fraud, artifice, and sorcery, and notoriously faithless to his engagements. The sending of Shydah is all a trick, and his letter of proposal all deceit: his object is simply to induce thee to fight him alone.

If thou shouldst kill this Shydah—what of that!
There would be one Túránian warrior less,
To vex the world withal; would that be triumph?
And to a Persian king? But if it chanced,
That thou should'st meet with an untimely death,
By dart or javelin, at the stripling's hands,
What scathe and ruin would this realm befall!"

By the advice of Rustem, Kai-khosráu gave Shydah permission to depart, and said that he would send his answer to Afrásiyáb by Kárun. "But," observed the youth, "I have come to fight thee!" which touched the honour of the king, and he replied: "Be it so, let us then meet to-morrow."

In the mean time Khosráu prepared his letter to Afrásiyáb, in which he said:

"Our quarrel now is dark to view,
It bears the fiercest, gloomiest hue;
And vain have speech and promise been
To change for peace the battle scene;
For thou art still to treachery prone,
Though gentle now in word and tone;
But that imperial crown thou wearest,
That mace which thou in battle bearest,
Thy kingdom, all, thou must resign;
Thy army too—for all are mine!
Thou talk'st of strength, and might, and power,
When revelling in a prosperous hour;
But know, that strength of nerve and limb
We owe to God—it comes from Him!
And victory's palm, and regal sway,
Alike the will of Heaven obey.
Hence thy lost throne, no longer thine,
Will soon, perfidious king! be mine!"

In giving this letter to Kárun, Kai-khosráu directed him, in the first place, to deliver a message from him to Shydah, to the following effect:

> "Driven art thou out from home and life,
> Doomed to engage in mortal strife,
> For deeply lours misfortune's cloud;
> That gay attire will be thy shroud;
> Blood from thy father's eyes will gush,
> As Káús wept for Saiáwush."

In the morning Khosráu went to the appointed place, and when he approached Shydah, the latter said, "Thou hast come on foot, let our trial be in wrestling;" and the proposal being agreed to, both applied themselves fiercely to the encounter, at a distance from the troops.

> The youth appeared with joyous mien,
> And bounding heart, for life was new;
> By either host the strife was seen,
> And strong and fierce the combat grew.

Shydah exerted his utmost might, but was unable to move his antagonist from the ground; whilst Khosráu lifted him up without difficulty, and, dashing him on the plain,

> He sprang upon him as the lion fierce
> Springs on the nimble gor, then quickly drew
> His deadly dagger, and with cruel aim,
> Thrust the keen weapon through the stripling's heart.

Khosráu, immediately after slaying him, ordered the body to be washed with musk and rose-water, and, after burial, a tomb to be raised to his memory.

When Kárun reached the court of Afrásiyáb with the answer to the offer of peace, intelligence had previously arrived that Shydah had fallen in the combat, which produced in the mind of the father the greatest anguish. He gave no reply to Kárun, but ordered the drums and trumpets to be sounded, and instantly marched with a large army against the enemy. The two hosts were soon engaged, the anger of the Túránians being so much roused and sharpened by the death of the prince, that they were utterly regardless of their lives. The battle, therefore, was fought with unusual fury.

Two sovereigns in the field, in desperate strife,
Each by a grievous cause of wrath, urged on
To glut revenge ; this, for a father's life
Wantonly sacrificed ; that for a son
Slain in his prime.—The carnage has begun,
And blood is seen to flow on every side ;
Thousands are slaughtered ere the day is done,
And weltering swell the sanguinary tide ;
And why? To soothe man's hate, his cruelty, and pride.

The battle terminated in the discomfiture and defeat of the Túránians, who fled from the conquerors in the utmost con fusion. The people seized hold of the bridle of Afrásiyáb's horse, and obliged him to follow his scattered army.

Kai-khosráu having dispatched an account of his victory to Káús, went in pursuit of Afrásiyáb, traversing various countries and provinces, till he arrived on the borders of Chín. The Khakán, or sovereign of that state, became in consequence greatly alarmed, and presented to him large presents to gain his favour, but the only object of Khosráu was to secure Afrásiyáb, and he told the ambassador that if his master dared to afford him protection, he would lay waste the whole kingdom. The Khakán therefore withdrew his hospitable services, and the abandoned king was compelled to seek another place of refuge.

The DEATH of AFRÁSIYÁB.

Melancholy and afflicted, Afrásiyáb penetrated through wood and desert, and entered the province of Mikrán, whither he was followed by Kai-khosráu and his army. He then quitted Mikrán, but his followers had fallen off to a small number and to whatever country or region he repaired for rest and protection, none was given, lest the vengeance of Kai-khosráu should be hurled upon the offender. Still pursued and hunted like a wild beast, and still flying from his enemies, the small retinue which remained with him at last left him, and he was left alone, dejected, destitute, and truly forlorn. In this state of desertion he retired into a cave, where he hoped to continue undiscovered and unseen.

It chanced, however, that a man named Húm, of the race of Feridún, dwelt hard by. He was remarkable for his strength and bravery, but had peacefully taken up his abode upon the neighbouring mountain, and was passing a religious life without any communication with the busy world. His dwelling was a little way above the cave of Afrásiyáb. One night he heard a voice of lamentation below, and anxious to ascertain from whom and whence it proceeded, he stole down to the spot and listened. The mourner spoke in the Túrkish language, and said:—"O king of Túrán and Chín, where is now thy pomp and power! How has Fortune cast away thy throne and thy treasure to the winds?" Hearing these words Húm conjectured that this must be Afrásiyáb; and as he had suffered severely from the tyranny of that monarch, his feelings of vengeance were awakened, and he approached nearer to be certain that it was he. The same lamentations were repeated, and he felt assured that it was Afrásiyáb himself. He waited patiently, however, till morning dawned, and then he called out at the mouth of the cave:—"O, king of the world! come out of thy cave, and obtain thy desires! I have left the invisible sphere to accomplish thy wishes.—Appear!" Afrásiyáb thinking this a spiritual call, went out of the cave and was instantly recognized by Húm, who at the same moment struck him a severe blow on the forehead, which felled him to the earth, and then secured his hands behind his back. When the monarch found himself in fetters and powerless, he complained of the cruelty inflicted upon him, and asked Húm why he had treated a stranger in that manner. Húm replied:—"How many a prince of the race of Feridún hast thou sacrificed to thy ambition? How many a heart hast thou broken?—I, too, am one who was compelled to fly from thy persecutions, and take refuge here on this desert mountain, and constantly have I prayed for thy ruin that I might be released from this miserable mode of existence, and be permitted to return to my paternal home. My prayer has been heard at last, and God has delivered thee into my hands. But how camest thou hither, and by what strange vicissitudes art thou thus placed before me?" Afrásiyáb communicated to him the story of his misfortunes, and begged of him rather to put him to death on the spot than convey him to Kai-khosráu. But Húm was too much delighted with having the tyrant under his feet to consider either his safety or his feelings, and was not long in bringing him to the Persian king. Kaí-khosráu received the prisoner with exultation, and made Húm a magnificent present. He well recollected the basin and the dagger used in the murder of Saiáwush, and commanded the presence of the treacherous Gersíwaz, that he and Afrásiyáb might suffer, in every respect, the same fate together. The basin was brought, and the two victims were put to death, like two goats, their heads being chopped off from their bodies.

After this sanguinary catastrophe, Kai-khosráu returned to Irán, leaving Rustem to proceed to his own principality. Kai-káús quitted his palace, according to his established custom, to welcome back the conqueror. He kissed his head and face, and showered upon him praises and blessings for the valour he had displayed, and the deeds he had done, and especially for having so signally revenged the cruel murder of his father Saiáwush

THE DEATH OF KAI-KHOSRÁU.

Kai-khosráu at last became inspired by an insurmountable attachment to a religious life, and thought only of devotion to God. Thus influenced by a disposition peculiar to ascetics, he abandoned the duties of sovereignty, and committed all state affairs to the care of his ministers. The chiefs and warriors remonstrated respectfully against this mode of government, and trusted that he would devote only a few hours in the day to the transactions of the kingdom, and the remainder to prayer and religious exercises; but this he refused, saying:—"One heart is not equal to both duties; my affections indeed are not for this transitory world, and I trust to be an inhabitant of the world to come." The nobles were in great sorrow at this declaration, and anxiously applied to Zál and Rustem, in the hopes of working some change in the king's disposition. On their arrival the people cried to them:—

"Some evil eye has smote the king;—Iblís
By wicked wiles has led his soul astray,
And withered all life's pleasures. O release
Our country from the sorrow, the dismay
Which darkens every heart:—his ruin stay.
Is it not mournful thus to see him cold
And gloomy, casting pomp and joy away?
Restore him to himself; let us behold
Again the victor-king, the generous, just and bold."

Zál and Rustem went to the palace of the king in a melancholy mood, and Khosráu having heard of their approach, enquired of them why they had left Sístán. They replied that the news of his having relinquished all concern in the affairs of the kingdom had induced them to wait upon him. "I am weary of the troubles of this life," said he composedly, "and anxious to prepare for a future state." "But death," observed Zál, "is a great evil. It is dreadful to die!" Upon this the king said:—"I cannot endure any longer the deceptions and the perfidy of mankind. My love of heaven is so great that I cannot exist one moment without devotion and prayer. Last night a mysterious voice whispered in my ear :—The time of thy departure is nigh, prepare the load for thy journey, and neglect not thy warning angel, or the opportunity will be lost." When Zál and Rustem saw that Khosráu was resolved, and solemnly occupied in his devotions, they were for some time silent. But Zál was at length moved, and said :—"I will go into retirement and solitude with the king, and by continual prayer, and through his blessing, I too may be forgiven." "This, indeed," said the king, "is not the place for me. I must seek out a solitary cell, and there resign my soul to heaven." Zál and Rustem wept, and quitted the palace, and all the warriors were in the deepest affliction.

The next day Kai-khosráu left his apartment, and called together his great men and warriors, and said to them :—

"That which I sought for, I have now obtained.
Nothing remains of worldly wish, or hope,
To disappoint or vex me. I resign
The pageantry of kings, and turn away
From all the pomp of the Kaiánian throne,
Sated with human grandeur.—Now, farewell!
Such is my destiny. To those brave friends,
Who, ever faithful, have my power upheld,
I will discharge the duty of a king,
Paying the pleasing debt of gratitude."

He then ordered his tents to be pitched in the desert, and opened his treasury, and for seven days made a sumptuous feast, and distributed food and money among the indigent, the widows, and orphans, and every destitute person was abundantly supplied with the necessaries of life, so that there was no one left in a state of want throughout the empire. He also attended to the claims of his warriors. To Rustem he gave Zábul, and Kábul, and Ním-rúz. He appointed Lohurásp, the son-in-law of Kai-Káús, successor to his throne, and directed all his people to pay the same allegiance to him as they had done to himself; and they unanimously consented, declaring their firm attachment to his person and government. He appointed Gúdarz the chief minister, and Gív to the chief command of the armies. To Tús he gave Khorassán; and he said to Fríburz, the son of Káús:—"Be thou obedient, I beseech thee, to the commands of Lohurásp, whom I have instructed, and brought up with paternal care; for I know of no one so well qualified in the art of governing a kingdom." The warriors of Irán were surprised, and murmured together, that the son of Kai-káús should be thus placed under the authority of Lohurásp. But Zál observed to them:—"If it be the king's will, it is enough!" The murmurs of the warriors having reached Kai-khosráu, he sent for them, and addressed them thus:—"Fríburz is well known to be unequal to the functions of sovereignty; but Lohurásp is enlightened, and fully comprehends all the duties of regal sway. He is a descendant of Húsheng, wise and merciful, and God is my witness, I think him pefectly calculated to make a nation happy." Hearing this eulogium on the character of the new king from Kai-khosráu, all the warriors expressed their satisfaction, and anticipated a glorious reign. Khosráu further said:—"I must now address you on another subject. In my dreams a fountain has been pointed out to me; and when I visit that fountain, my life will be resigned to its Creator." He then bid farewell to all the people around him, and commenced his journey; and when he had accomplished one stage he pitched his tent. Next day he resumed his task, and took leave of Zál and Rustem; who wept bitterly as they parted from him.

"Alas!" they said, "that one on whom
 Heaven has bestowed a mind so great,
A heart so brave, should seek the tomb,
 And not his hour in patience wait.
The wise in wonder gaze, and say,
 No mortal being ever trod
Before, the dim supernal way,
 And living, saw the face of God!"

After Zál and Rustem, then Khosráu took leave of Gúdarz and Gív and Tús, and Gustahem, but unwilling to go back, they continued with him. He soon arrived at the promised fountain, in which he bathed. He then said to his followers:—"Now is the time for our separation;—you must go;" but they still remained. Again he said:—"You must go quickly; for presently heavy showers of snow will fall, and a tempestuous wind will arise, and you will perish in the storm." Saying this, he went into the fountain, and vanished!

> And not a trace was left behind,
>   And not a dimple on the wave;
> All sought, but sought in vain, to find
>   The spot which proved Kai-khosráu's grave!

The king having disappeared in this extraordinary manner, a loud lamentation ascended from his followers; and when the paroxysm of amazement and sorrow had ceased, Fríburz said:—"Let us now refresh ourselves with food, and rest awhile." Accordingly those that remained ate a little, and were soon afterwards overcome with sleep. Suddenly a great wind arose, and the snow fell and clothed the earth in white, and all the warriors and soldiers who accompanied Kai-khosráu to the mysterious fountain, and amongst them Tús and Fríburz, and Gíw, were while asleep overwhelmed in the drifts of snow. Not a man survived. Gúdarz had returned when about half-way on the road; and not hearing for a long time any tidings of his companions, sent a person to ascertain the cause of their delay. Upon proceeding to the fatal place, the messenger, to his amazement and horror, found them all stiff and lifeless under the snow!

LOHURÁSP.

The reputation of Lohurásp was of the highest order, and it is said that his administration of the affairs of his kingdom was more just and paternal than even that of Kai-khosráu. "The counsel which Khosráu gave me," said he, "was wise and admirable; but I find that I must go beyond him in moderation and clemency to the poor." Lohurásp had four sons, two by the daughter of Kai-káús, one named Ardshír, and the other Shydasp; and two by another woman, and they were named Gushtásp and Zarír. But Gushtásp was intrepid, acute, and apparently marked out for sovereignty, and on account of his independent conduct, no favourite with his father; in defiance of whom, with a rebellious spirit, he collected together a hundred thousand horsemen, and proceeded with them towards Hindústán of his own accord. Lohurásp sent after him his brother Zarír, with a thousand horsemen, in the hopes of influencing him to return; but when Zarír overtook him and endeavoured to persuade him not to proceed any further, he said to him, with an animated look:—

"Proceed no farther!—Well thou know'st
We've no Kaiánian blood to boast,
And, therefore, but a minor part
In Lohurásp's paternal heart.
Nor thou, nor I, can ever own
From him the diadem or throne.
The brothers of Káús's race
By birth command the brightest place,
Then what remains for us? We must
To other means our fortunes trust.
We cannot linger here, and bear
A life of discontent—despair."

Zarír, however, reasoned with him so winningly and effectually, that at last he consented to return; but only upon the condition that he should be nominated heir to the throne, and treated with becoming respect and ceremony. Zarír agreed to interpose his efforts to this end, and brought him back to his father; but it was soon apparent that Lohurásp had no inclination to promote the elevation of Gushtásp in preference to the claims of his other sons; and indeed shortly afterwards manifested to what quarter his determination on this subject was directed. It was indeed enough that his determination was unfavourable to the views of Gushtásp, who now, in disgust, fled from his fathers' house, but without any attendants, and shaped his course towards Rúm. Lohurásp again sent Zarír in quest of him; but the youth, after a tedious search, returned without success. Upon his arrival in Rúm, Gushtásp chose a solitary retirement, where he remained some time, and was at length compelled by poverty and want, to ask for employment in the establishment of the sovereign of that country, stating that he was an accomplished scribe, and wrote a beautiful hand. He was told to wait a few days, as at that time there was no vacancy. But hunger was pressing, and he could not suffer delay; he therefore went to the master of the camel-drivers and asked for service, but he too had no vacancy. However, commiserating the distressed condition of the applicant, he generously supplied him with a hearty meal. After that, Gushtásp went into a blacksmith's shop, and asked for work, and his services were accepted. The blacksmith put the hammer into his hands, and the first blow he struck was given with such force, that he broke the anvil to pieces. The blacksmith was amazed and angry, and indignantly turned him out of his shop, uttering upon him a thousand violent reproaches.

Wounded in spirit, broken-hearted,
  Misfortune darkening o'er his head,
To other lands he then departed,
  To seek another home for bread.

Disconsolate and wretched, he proceeded on his journey, and observing a husbandman standing in a field of corn, he approached the spot and sat down. The husbandman seeing a strong muscular youth, apparently a Túránian, sitting in sorrow and tears, went up to him and asked him the cause of his grief, and he soon became acquainted with all the circumstances of the stranger's life. Pitying his distress, he took him home and gave him some food.

After having partaken sufficiently of the refreshments placed before him, Gushtásp inquired of his host to what tribe he belonged, and from whom he was descended. "I am descended from Feridún," rejoined he, "and I belong to the Kaiánian tribe. My occupation in this retired spot is, as thou seest, the cultivation of the ground, and the customs and duties of husbandry." Gushtásp said, "I am myself descended from Húsheng, who was the ancestor of Feridún ; we are, therefore, of the same origin." In consequence of this connection, Gushtásp and the husbandman lived together on the most friendly footing for a considerable time. At length the star of his fortune began to illumine his path, and the favour of Heaven became manifest.

It was the custom of the king of Rúm, when his daughters came of age, to give a splendid banquet, and to invite to it all the youths of illustrious birth in the kingdom, in order that each might select one of them most suited to her taste, for her future husband. His daughter Kitabún was now of age, and in conformity with the established practice, the feast was prepared, and the youths of royal descent invited ; but it so happened that not one of them was sufficiently attractive for her choice, and the day passed over unprofitably. She had been told in a dream that a youth of a certain figure and aspect had arrived in the kingdom from Irán, and that to him she was destined to be married. But there was not one at her father's banquet who answered to the description of the man she had seen in her dream, and in consequence she was disappointed. On the following day the feast was resumed. She had again dreamt of the youth to whom she was to be united. She had presented to him a bunch of roses, and he had given her a rose-branch, and each regarded the other with smiles of mutual satisfaction. In the morning Kitabún issued a proclamation, inviting all the young men of royal extraction, whether natives of the kingdom or strangers, to her father's feast. On that day Gushtásp and the husbandman had come into the city from the country, and hearing the proclamation the latter said : "Let us go, for in this lottery the prize may be drawn in thy name." They accordingly went. Kitabún's handmaid was in waiting at the door, and kept every young man standing awhile, that her mistress might mark him well before she allowed him to pass into the banquet. The keen eyes of Kitabún soon saw Gushtásp, and her heart instantly acknowledged him as her promised lord, for he was the same person she had seen in her dream.

> As near the graceful stripling drew,
> She cried :—" My dream, my dream is true !
> Fortune from visions of the night
> Has brought him to my longing sight.
> Truth has pourtrayed his form divine ;
> He lives—he lives—and he is mine ! "

She presently descended from her balcony, and gave him a bunch of roses, the token by which her choice was made known, and then retired. The king, when he heard of what she had done, was exceedingly irritated, thinking that her affections were placed on a beggar, or some nameless stranger of no birth or fortune, and his first impulse was to have her put to death. But his people assembled around him, and said :—" What can be the use of killing her ?—It is in vain to resist the flood of destiny, for what will be, will be.

> The world itself is governed still by Fate,
> Fate rules the warrior's and the monarch's state ;
> And woman's heart, the passions of her soul,
> Own the same power, obey the same control ;
> For what can love's impetuous force restrain ?
> Blood may be shed, but what will be thy gain?

After this remonstrance he desired enquiries to be made into the character and parentage of his proposed son-in-law, and was told his name, the name of his father, and of his ancestors, and the causes which led to his present condition. But he would not believe a word of the narration. He was then informed of his daughter's dream, and other particulars : and he so far relented as to sanction the marriage ; but indignantly drove her from his house, with her husband, without a dowry, or any money to supply themselves with food.

Gushtásp and his wife took refuge in a miserable cell, which they inhabited, and when necessity pressed, he used to cross the river, and bring in an elk or wild ass from the forest, gave half of it to the ferryman for his trouble, and kept the remainder for his own board, so that he and the ferryman became great friends by these mutual obligations. It is related that a person of distinction, named Mabrín, solicited the king's second daughter in marriage; and Ahrun, another man of rank, was anxious to be espoused to the third, or youngest; but the king was unwilling to part with either of them, and openly declared his sentiments to that effect. Mabrín, however, was most assiduous and persevering in his attentions, and at last made some impression on the father, who consented to permit the marriage of the second daughter, but only on the following conditions: "There is," said he, "a monstrous wolf in the neighbouring forest, extremely ferocious, and destructive to my property. I have frequently endeavoured to hunt him down, but without success. If Mabrín can destroy the animal, I will give him my daughter." When these conditions were communicated to Mabrín, he considered it impossible that they could be fulfilled, and looked upon the proposal as an evasion of the question. One day, however, the ferryman having heard of Mabrín's disappointment, told him that there was no reason to despair, for he knew a young man, married to one of the king's daughters, who crossed the river every day, and though only a pedestrian, brought home regularly an elk-deer on his back. "He is truly," added he, "a wonderful youth, and if you can by any means secure his assistance, I have no doubt but that his activity and strength will soon put an end to the wolf's depredations, by depriving him of life."

This intelligence was received with great pleasure by Mabrín, who hastened to Gushtásp, and described to him his situation, and the conditions required. Gushtásp in reply said, that he would be glad to accomplish for him the object of his desires, and at an appointed time proceeded towards the forest, accompanied by Mabrín and the ferryman. When the party arrived at the borders of the wilderness which the wolf frequented, Gushtásp left his companions behind, and advanced alone into the interior, where he soon found the dreadful monster, in size larger than an elephant, and howling terribly, ready to spring upon him. But the hand and eye of Gushtásp were too active to allow of his being surprised, and in an instant he shot two arrows at once into the foaming beast, which, irritated by the deep wound, now rushed furiously upon him, without, however, doing him any serious injury; then with the rapidity of lightning, Gushtásp drew his sharp sword, with one tremendous stroke cut the wolf in two, deluging the ground with bubbling blood. Having performed this prodigious exploit, he called Mabrín and the ferryman to see what he had done, and they were amazed at his extraordinary intrepidity and muscular power, but requested, in order that the special object of the lover might be obtained, that he would conceal his name, for a time at least. Mabrín, satisfied on this point, then repaired to the emperor, and claimed his promised bride, as the reward for his labour. The king of Rúm little expected this result, and to assure himself of the truth of what he had heard, bent his way to the forest, where he was convinced, seeing with astonishment and delight that the wolf was really killed. He had now no further pretext, and therefore fulfilled his engagement, by giving his daughter to Mabrín.

It was now Ahrun's turn to repeat his solicitations for the youngest daughter. The king of Rúm had another evil to root out, so that he was prepared to propose another condition. This was to destroy a hideous dragon that had taken possession of a neighbouring mountain. Ahrun, on hearing the condition was in as deep distress as Mabrín had been, until he accidentally became acquainted with the ferryman, who described to him the generosity and fearless bravery of Gushtásp. He immediately applied to him, and the youth readily undertook the enterprise, saying:—"No doubt the monster's teeth are long and sharp, bring me therefore a dagger, and fasten round it a number of knives." Ahrun did so accordingly, and Gushtásp proceeded to the mountain. As soon as the dragon smelt the approach of a human being, flames issued from his nostrils, and he darted forward to devour the intruder, but was driven back by a number of arrows, rapidly discharged into his head and mouth. Again he advanced, but Gushtásp dodged round him, and continued driving arrows into him to the extent of forty, which subdued his strength, and made him writhe in agony. He then fixed the dagger, which was armed at right angles with knives, upon his spear, and going nearer, thrust it down his gasping throat

> Dreadful the weapon, each two-edged blade
> Cut deep into the jaws on either side,
> And the fierce monster, thinking to dislodge it,
> Crushed it between his teeth with all his strength,
> Which pressed it deeper in the flesh, when blood
> And poison issued from the gaping wounds;
> Then, as he floundered on the earth exhausted,
> Seizing the fragment of a flinty rock,
> Gushtásp beat out the brains, and soon the beast
> In terrible struggles died. Two deadly fangs
> Then wrenched he from the jaws, to testify
> The wonderful exploit he had performed.

When he descended from the mountain, these two teeth were delivered to Ahrun, and they were afterwards conveyed to the king, who could not believe his own eyes, but ascended the mountain himself to ascertain the fact, and there he beheld with amazement the dragon lifeless, and covered with blood. "And didst thou thyself kill this terrific dragon?" said he. "Yes," replied Ahrun. "And wilt thou swear to God that this is thy own achievement? It must be either the exploit of a demon, or of a certain Kaiánian, who resides in this neighbourhood." But there was no one to disprove his assertion, and therefore the king could no longer refuse to surrender to him his youngest daughter.

And now between Gushtásp, and Mabrín, and Ahrun, the warmest friendship subsisted. Indeed they were seldom parted; and the three sisters remained together with equal affection. One day Kitabún, the wife of Gushtásp, in conversation with some of her female acquaintance, let out the secret that her husband was the person who killed the wolf and the dragon.

No sooner was this story told, than it spread, and in the end reached the ears of the queen, who immediately communicated it to the king, saying :—"This is the work of Gushtásp, thy son-in-law, of him thou hast banished from thy presence—of him who nobly would not disclose his name, before Mabrín and Ahrun had attained the object of their wishes." The king said in reply that it was just as he had suspected; and sending for Gushtásp, conferred upon him great honour, and appointed him to the chief command of his army.

Having thus possessed himself of a leader of such skill and intrepidity, he thought it necessary to turn his attention to external conquest, and accordingly addressed a letter to Aliás, the ruler of Khuz, in which he said :—"Thou hast hitherto enjoyed thy kingdom in peace and tranquillity; but thou must now resign it to me, or prepare for war." Aliás on receiving this imperious and haughty menace collected his forces together, and advanced to the contest, and the king of Rúm assembled his own troops with equal expedition, under the direction of Gushtásp. The battle was fought with great valour on both sides, and blood flowed in torrents. Gushtásp challenged Aliás to single combat, and the warriors met; but in a short time the enemy was thrown from his horse, and dragged by the young conqueror, in fetters, before the king. The troops witnessing the prowess of Gushtásp, quickly fled; and the king commencing a hot pursuit, soon entered their city victoriously, subdued the whole kingdom, and plundered it of all its property and wealth. He also gained over the army, and with this powerful addition to his own forces, and with the booty he had secured, returned triumphantly to Rúm.

In consequence of this brilliant success, the king conferred additional honours on Gushtásp, who now began to display the ambition which he had long cherished. Aspiring to the sovereignty of Irán, he spoke to the Rúmí warriors on the subject of an invasion of that country, but they refused to enter into his schemes, conceiving that there was no chance of success. At this Gushtásp took fire, and declared that he knew the power and resources of his father perfectly, and that the conquest would be attended with no difficulty. He then went to the king, and said: "Thy chiefs are afraid to fight against Lohurásp; I will myself undertake the task with even an inconsiderable army." The king was overjoyed, and kissed his head and face, and loaded him with presents, and ordered his secretary to write to Lohurásp in the following terms: "I am anxious to meet thee in battle, but if thou art not disposed to fight, I will permit thee to remain at peace, on condition of surrendering to me half thy kingdom. Should this be refused, I will myself deprive thee of the whole sovereignty." When this letter was conveyed by the hands of Kabús to Irán, Lohurásp, upon reading it, was moved to laughter, and exclaimed, "What is all this? The king of Rúm has happened to obtain possession of the little kingdom of Khuz, and he has become insane with pride!" He then asked Kabús by what means he accomplished the capture of Khuz, and how he managed to kill Aliás. The messenger replied, that his success was owing to a youth of noble aspect and invincible courage, who had first destroyed a ferocious wolf, then a dragon, and had afterwards dragged Aliás from his horse, with as much ease as if he had been a chicken, and laid him prostrate at the feet of the king of Rúm. Lohurásp enquired his name, and he answered, Gushtásp. "Does he resemble in feature any person in this assembly?" Kabús looked round about him, and pointed to Zarír, from which Lohurásp concluded that it must be his own son, and sat silent. But he soon determined on what answer to send, and it was contained in the following words: "Do not take me for an Aliás, nor think that one hero of thine is competent to oppose me. I have a hundred equal to him. Continue, therefore, to pay me tribute, or I will lay waste thy whole country." With this letter he dismissed Kabús; and as soon as the messenger had departed, addressed himself to Zarír, saying: "Thou must go in the character of an ambassador from me to the king of Rúm, and represent to him the justice and propriety of preserving peace. After thy conference with him repair to the house of Gushtásp, and in my name ask his forgiveness for what I have done. I was not before aware of his merit, and day and night I think of him with repentance and sorrow. Tell him to pardon his old father's infirmities, and come back to Irán, to his own country and home, that I may resign to him my crown and throne, and like Kai-khosráu, take leave of the world. It is my desire to deliver myself up to prayer and devotion, and to appoint Gushtásp my successor, for he appears to be eminently worthy of that honour." Zarír acted scrupulously, in conformity with his instructions; and having first had an interview with the king, hastened to the house of his brother, by whom he was received with affection and gladness. After the usual interchange of congratulations and enquiry, he stated to him the views and the resolutions of his father, who on the faith of his royal word promised to appoint him his successor, and thought of him with the most cordial attachment. Gushtásp was as much astonished as delighted with this information, and his anxiety being great to return to his own country, he that very night, accompanied by his wife Kitabún, and Zarír, set out for Irán. Approaching the city, he was met by an istakbal, or honorary deputation of warriors, sent by the king; and when he arrived at court, Lohurásp descended from his throne and embraced him with paternal affection, shedding tears of contrition for having previously treated him not only with neglect but severity. However he now made him ample atonement, and ordering a golden chair of royalty to be constructed and placed close to his own, they both sat together, and the people by command tendered to him unanimously their respect and allegiance. Lohurásp repeatedly said to him :—

"What has been done was Fate's decree,
Man cannot strive with destiny.
To be unfeeling once was mine,
At length to be a sovereign thine."

Thus spoke the king, and kissed the crown,
And gave it to his valiant son.

Soon afterwards he relinquished all authority in the empire, assumed the coarse habit of a recluse, and retired to a celebrated place of pilgrimage in those days near Balkh. There, in a solitary cell, he devoted the remainder of his life to prayer and the worship of God. The period of Lohurásp's government lasted one hundred and twenty years.

GUSHTÁSP, AND THE FAITH OF ZERDUSHT.

I've said preceding sovereigns worshipped God,
By whom their crowns were given to protect
The people from oppressors; Him they served,
Acknowledging His goodness—for to Him,
The pure, unchangeable, the Holy One:
They owed their greatness and their earthly power.
But after times produced idolatry,
And Pagan faith, and then His name was lost
In adoration of created things.

Gushtásp had by his wife Kitabún, the daughter of the king of Rúm, two sons named Isfendiyár and Bashútan, who were remarkable for their piety and devotion to the Almighty. Being the great king, all the minor sovereigns paid him tribute, excepting Arjásp, the ruler of Chín and Ma-chín, whose army consisted of Díws, and Perís, and men; for considering him of superior importance, he sent him yearly the usual tributary present. In those days lived Zerdusht, the Guber, who was highly accomplished in the knowledge of divine things; and having waited upon Gushtásp, the king became greatly pleased with his learning and piety, and took him into his confidence. The philosopher explained to him the doctrines of the fire-worshippers, and by his art he reared a tree before the house of Gushtásp, beautiful in its foliage and branches, and whoever ate of the leaves of that tree became learned and accomplished in the mysteries of the future world, and those who ate of the fruit thereof became perfect in wisdom and holiness.

In consequence of the illness of Lohurásp, who was nearly at the point of death, Zerdusht went to Balkh for the purpose of administering relief to him, and he happily succeeded in restoring him to health. On his return he was received with additional favour by Gushtásp, who immediately afterwards became his disciple. Zerdusht then told him that he was the prophet of God, and promised to show him miracles. He said he had been to heaven and to hell. He could send any one, by prayer, to heaven; and whomsoever he was angry with he could send to hell. He had seen the seven mansions of the celestial regions, and the thrones of sapphires, and all the secrets of heaven were made known to him by his attendant angel. He said that the sacred book, called Zendavesta, descended from above expressly for him, and that if Gushtásp followed the precepts in that blessed volume, he would attain celestial felicity. Gushtásp readily became a convert to his principles, forsaking the pure adoration of God for the religion of the fire-worshippers. The philosopher further said that he had prepared a ladder, by which he had ascended into heaven and had seen the Almighty. This made the disciple still more obedient to Zerdusht. One day he asked Gushtásp why he condescended to pay tribute to Arjásp; "God is on thy side," said he, "and if thou desirest an extension of territory, the whole country of Chín may be easily conquered." Gushtásp felt ashamed at this reproof, and to restore his character, sent a dispatch to Arjásp, in which he said, "Former kings who paid thee tribute did so from terror only, but now the empire is mine; and it is my will, and I have the power, to resist the payment of it in future." This letter gave great offence to Arjásp; who at once suspected that the fire-worshipper, Zerdusht, had poisoned his mind, and seduced him from his pure and ancient religion, and was attempting to circumvent and lead him to his ruin. He answered him thus; "It is well known that thou hast now forsaken the right path, and involved thyself in darkness. Thou hast chosen a guide possessed of the attributes of Iblís, who with the art of a magician has seduced thee from the worship of the true God, from that God who gave thee thy kingdom and thy grandeur. Thy father feared God, and became a holy Dírvesh, whilst thou hast lost thy way in wickedness and impiety. It will therefore be a meritorious action in me to vindicate the true worship and oppose thy blasphemous career with all my demons. In a month or two I will enter thy kingdom with fire and sword, and destroy thy authority and thee. I would give thee good advice; do not be influenced by a wicked counsellor, but return to thy former religious practices. Weigh well, therefore, what I say." Arjásp sent this letter by two of his demons, familiar with sorcery; and when it was delivered into the hands of Gushtásp, a council was held to consider its contents, to which Zerdusht was immediately summoned. Jamásp, the minister, said that the subject required deep thought, and great prudence was necessary in framing a reply; but Zerdusht observed, that the only reply was obvious—nothing but war could be thought of. At this moment Isfendiyár gallantly offered to lead the army, but Zarír, his uncle, objected to him on account of his extreme youth, and proposed to take the command himself, which Gushtásp agreed to, and the two demon-envoys were dismissed. The answer was briefly as follows:

> "Thy boast is that thou wilt in two short months
> Ravage my country, scathe with fire and sword
> The empire of Irán; but on thyself
> Heap not destruction; pause before thy pride
> Hurries thee to thy ruin. I will open
> The countless treasures of the realm; my warriors,
> A thousand thousand, armed with shining steel,
> Shall over-run thy kingdom; I myself
> Will crush that head of thine beneath my feet."

The result of these menaces was the immediate prosecution of the war, and no time was lost by Arjásp in hastening into Irán.

Plunder and devastation marked his course,
The villages were all involved in flames,
Palace of pride, low cot, and lofty tower;
The trees dug up, and root and branch destroyed.
Gushtásp then hastened to repel his foes;
But to his legions they seemed wild and strange,
And terrible in aspect, and no light
Could struggle through the gloom they had diffused,
To hide their progress.

Zerdusht said to Gushtásp, "Ask thy vizir, Jamásp, what is written in thy horoscope, that he may relate to thee the dispensations of heaven." Jamásp, in reply to the inquiry, took the king aside and whispered softly to him:—"A great number of thy brethren, thy relations, and warriors will be slain in the conflict, but in the end thou wilt be victorious." Gushtásp deeply lamented the coming event, which involved the destruction of his kinsmen, but did not shrink from the battle, for he exulted in the anticipation of obtaining the victory. The contest was begun with indescribable eagerness and impetuosity.

Approaching, each a prayer addrest
To Heaven, and thundering forward prest;
Thick showers of arrows gloomed the sky,
The battle-storm raged long and high;
Above, black clouds their darkness spread,
Below, the earth with blood was red.

Ardshír, the son of Lohurásp, and descended from Kai-káús, was one of the first to engage; he killed many, and was at last killed himself. After him, his brother Shydasp was killed. Then Bishú, the son of Jamásp, urged on his steed, and with consummate bravery destroyed a great number of warriors. Zarír, equally bold and intrepid, also rushed amidst the host, and whether demons or men opposed him, they were all laid lifeless on the field. He then rode up towards Arjásp, scattered the ranks, and penetrated the head-quarters, which put the king into great alarm: for he exclaimed:—"What, have ye no courage, no shame! whoever kills Zarír shall have a magnificent reward." Bai-derafsh, one of the demons, animated by this offer, came forward, and with remorseless fury attacked Zarír. The onset was irresistible, and the young prince was soon overthrown and bathed in his own blood. The news of the unfortunate catastrophe deeply affected Gushtásp, who cried, in great grief: "Is there no one to take vengeance for this?" when Isfendiyár presented himself, kissed the ground before his father, and anxiously asked permission to engage the demon. Gushtásp assented, and told him that if he killed the demon and defeated the enemy, he would surrender to him his crown and throne.

> "When we from this destructive field return,
> Isfendiyár, my son, shall wear the crown,
> And be the glorious leader of my armies."

Saying this, he dismounted from his famous black horse, called Behzad, the gift of Kai-khosráu, and presented it to Isfendiyár. The greatest clamour and lamentation had arisen among the Persian army, for they thought that Baiderafsh had committed such dreadful slaughter, the moment of utter defeat was at hand, when Isfendiyár galloped forward, mounted on Behzad, and turned the fortunes of the day. He saw the demon with the mail of Zarír on his breast, foaming at the mouth with rage, and called aloud to him, "Stand, thou murderer!" The stern voice, the valour, and majesty of Isfendiyár, made the demon tremble, but he immediately discharged a blow with his dagger at his new opponent, who however seized the weapon with his left hand, and with his right plunged a spear into the monster's breast, and drove it through his body. Isfendiyár then cut off his head, remounted his horse, and that instant was by the side of Bishú, the son of the vizír, into whose charge, he gave the severed head of Baiderafsh, and the armour of Zarír. Bishú now attired himself in his father's mail, and fastening the head on his horse, declared that he would take his post close by Isfendiyár, whatever might betide. Firshaid, another Iránian warrior, came to the spot at the same moment, and expressed the same resolution, so that all three, thus accidentally met, determined to encounter Arjásp and capture him. Isfendiyár led the way, and the other two followed. Arjásp, seeing that he was singled out by three warriors, and that the enemy's force was also advancing to the attack in great numbers, gave up the struggle, and was the first to retreat. His troops soon threw away their arms and begged for quarter, and many of them were taken prisoners by the Iránians. Gushtásp now approached the dead body of Zarír, his son, and lamenting deeply over his unhappy fate, placed him in a coffin, and built over him a lofty monument, around which lights were ever afterwards kept burning, night and day; and he also taught the people the worship of fire, and was anxious to establish everywhere the religion of Zerdusht.

Jamásp appointed officers to ascertain the number of killed in the battle. Of Iránians there were thirty thousand, among whom were eight hundred chiefs; and the enemy's loss amounted to nine hundred thousand, and also eleven hundred and sixty-three chiefs. Gushtásp rejoiced at the glorious result, and ordered the drums to be sounded to celebrate the victory, and he increased his favour upon Zerdusht, who originated the war, and told him to call his triumphant son, Isfendiyár, near him.

The gallant youth the summons hears,
And midst the royal court appears,
Close by his father's side,
The mace, cow-headed, in his hand;
His air and glance express command,
And military pride.

Gushtásp beholds with heart elate,
The conqueror so young, so great,
And places round his brows the crown,
The promised crown, the high reward,
Proud token of a mighty king's regard,
Conferred upon his own.

After Gushtásp had crowned his son as his successor, he told him that he must not now waste his time in peace and private gratification, but proceed to the conquest of other countries. Zerdusht was also deeply interested in his further operations, and recommended him to subdue kingdoms for the purpose of diffusing everywhere the new religion, that the whole world might be enlightened and edified. Isfendiyár instantly complied, and the first kingdom he invaded was Rúm. The sovereign of that country having no power nor means to resist the incursions of the enemy, readily adopted the faith of Zerdusht, and accepted the sacred book named Zendavesta, as his spiritual instructor. Isfendiyár afterwards invaded Hindústan and Arabia, and several other countries, and successfully established the religion of the fire-worshippers in them all.

Where'er he went he was received
With welcome, all the world believed,
And all with grateful feelings took
The Holy Zendavesta-book,
Proud their new worship to declare,
The worship of Isfendiyár.

The young conqueror communicated by letters to his father the success with which he had disseminated the religion of Zerdusht, and requested to know what other enterprises required his aid. Gushtásp rejoiced exceedingly, and commanded a grand banquet to be prepared. It happened that Gurzam a warrior, was particularly befriended by the king, but retaining secretly in his heart a bitter enmity to Isfendiyár, now took an opportunity to gratify his malice, and privately told Gushtásp that he had heard something highly atrocious in the disposition of the prince. Gushtásp was anxious to know what it was; and he said, "Isfendiyár has subdued almost every country in the world: he is a dangerous person at the head of an immense army, and at this very moment meditates taking Balkh, and making even thee his prisoner!

Thou know'st not that thy son Isfendiyár
Is hated by the army. It is said
Ambition fires his brain, and to secure

The empire to himself, his wicked aim
Is to rebel against his generous father.
This is the sum of my intelligence;
But thou'rt the king, I speak but what I hear."

These malicious accusations by Gurzam insidiously made, produced great vexation in the mind of Gushtásp. The banquet went on, and for three days he drank wine incessantly, without sleep or rest because his sorrow was extreme. On the fourth day he said to his minister: "Go with this letter to Isfendiyár, and accompany him hither to me." Jamásp, the minister, went accordingly on the mission, and when he arrived, the prince said to him, "I have dreamt that my father is angry with me."—"Then thy dream is true," replied Jamásp, "thy father is indeed angry with thee."—"What crime, what fault have I committed?

Is it because I have with ceaseless toil
Spread wide the Zendavesta, and converted
Whole kingdoms to that faith? Is it because
For him I conquered those far-distant kingdoms,
With this good sword of mine? Why clouds his brow
Upon his son—some demon must have changed
His temper, once affectionate and kind,
Calling me to him thus in anger! Thou
Hast ever been my friend, my valued friend
Say, must I go? Thy counsel I require."

"The son does wrong who disobeys his father,
Despising his command," Jamásp replied.

"Yet," said Isfendiyár, "why should I go?
He is in wrath, it cannot be for good."

"Know'st thou not that a father's wrath is kindness?
The anger of a father to his child
Is far more precious than the love and fondness
Felt by that child for him. 'Tis good to go,
Whatever the result, he is the king,
And more—he is thy father!"

Isfendiyár immediately consented, and appointed Bahman, his eldest son, to fill his place in the army during his absence. He had four sons: the name of the second was Mihrbús; of the third, Avir; and of the fourth, Núsháhder; and these three he took along with him on his journey.

Before he had arrived at Balkh, Gushtásp had concerted measures to secure him as a prisoner, with an appearance of justice and impartiality. On his arrival, he waited on the king respectfully, and was thus received: "Thou hast become the great king! Thou hast conquered many countries, but why am I unworthy in thy sight? Thy ambition is indeed excessive." Isfendiyár replied: "However great I may be, I am still thy servant, and wholly at thy command." Upon hearing this, Gushtásp turned towards his courtiers, and said, "What ought to be done with that son, who in the lifetime of his father usurps his authority, and even attempts to eclipse him in grandeur? What! I ask, should be done with such a son!"

"Such a son should either be
Broken on the felon tree,
Or in prison bound with chains,
Whilst his wicked life remains,
Else thyself, this kingdom, all
Will be ruined by his thrall!"

To this heavy denunciation Isfendiyár replied: "I have received all my honours from the king, by whom I am appointed to succeed to the throne; but at his pleasure I willingly resign them." However, concession and remonstrance were equally fruitless, and he was straightway ordered to be confined in the tower-prison of the fort situated on the adjacent mountain, and secured with chains.

Dreadful the sentence: all who saw him wept;
And sternly they conveyed him to the tower,
Where to four columns, deeply fixed in earth,
And reaching to the skies, of iron formed,
They bound him; merciless they were to him
Who had given splendour to a mighty throne.
Mournful vicissitude! Thus pain and pleasure
Successive charm and tear the heart of man;
And many a day in that drear solitude,
He lingered, shedding tears of blood, till times
Of happier omen dawned upon his fortunes.

Having thus made Isfendiyár secure in the mountain-prison, and being entirely at ease about the internal safety of the empire, Gushtásp was anxious to pay a visit to Zál and Rustem at Sístán, and to convert them to the religion of Zerdusht. On his approach to Sístán he was met and respectfully welcomed by Rustem, who afterwards in open assembly received the Zendavesta and adopted the new faith, which he propagated throughout his own territory; but, according to common report it was fear of Gushtásp alone which induced him to pursue this course. Gushtásp remained two years his guest, enjoying all kinds of recreation, and particularly the sports of the field and the forests.

When Bahman, the son of Isfendiyár, heard of the imprisonment of his father, he, in grief and alarm, abandoned his trust, dismissed the army, and proceeded to Balkh, where he joined his two brothers, and wept over the fate of their unhappy father.

In the mean time the news of the confinement of Isfendiyár, and the absence of Gushtásp at Sístán, and the unprotected state of Balkh, stimulated Arjásp to a further effort, and he dispatched his son Kahram with a large army towards the capital of the enemy, to carry into effect his purpose of revenge. Lohurásp was still in religious retirement at Balkh. The people were under great apprehension, and being without a leader, anxiously solicited the old king to command them, but he said that he had abandoned all earthly concerns, and had devoted himself to God, and therefore could not comply with their entreaties. But they would hear no denial, and, as it were, tore him from his place of refuge and prayer. There were assembled only about one thousand horsemen, and with these he advanced to battle; but what were they compared to the hundred thousand whom they met, and by whom they were soon surrounded. Their bravery was useless. They were at once overpowered and defeated, and Lohurásp himself was unfortunately among the slain.

Upon the achievement of this victory, Kahram entered

Balkh in triumph, made the people prisoners, and destroyed all the places of worship belonging to the Gubers. He also killed the keeper of the altar, and burnt the Zendavesta, which contained the formulary of their doctrines and belief.

One of the women of Gushtásp's household happened to elude the grasp of the invader, and hastened to Sístán to inform the king of the disaster that had occurred. "Thy father is killed, the city is taken, and thy women and daughters in the power of the conqueror." Gushtásp received the news with consternation, and prepared with the utmost expedition for his departure. He invited Rustem to accompany him, but the champion excused himself at the time, and afterwards declined altogether on the plea of sickness. Before he had yet arrived at Balkh, Kahram hearing of his approach, went out to meet him with his whole army, and was joined on the same day by Arjásp and his demon-legions.

Great was the uproar, loud the brazen drums
And trumpets rung, the earth shook, and seemed rent
By that tremendous conflict, javelins flew
Like hail on every side, and the warm blood
Streamed from the wounded and the dying men.
The claim of kindred did not check the arm
Lifted in battle—mercy there was none,
For all resigned themselves to chance or fate,
Or what the ruling Heavens might decree.

At last the battle terminated in the defeat of Gushtásp, who was pursued till he was obliged to take refuge in a mountain-fort. He again consulted Jamásp to know what the stars foretold, and Jamásp replied that he would recover from the defeat through the exertions of Isfendiyár alone. Pleased with this interpretation, he on that very day sent Jamásp to the prison with a letter to Isfendiyár, in which he hoped to be pardoned for the cruelty he had been guilty of towards him, in consequence, he said, of being deceived by the arts and treachery of those who were only anxious to effect his ruin. He declared too that he would put those enemies to death in his presence, and replace the royal crown upon his head. At the same time he confined in chains Gurzam, the wretch who first practised upon his feelings. Jamásp rode immediately to the prison, and delivering the letter, urged the prince to comply with his father's entreaties, but Isfendiyár was incredulous and not so easily to be moved.

> "Has he not at heart disdained me?
> Has he not in prison chained me?
> Am I not his son, that he
> Treats me ignominiously?
>
> Why should Gurzam's scorn and hate
> Rouse a loving father's wrath?
> Why should he, the foul ingrate,
> Cast destruction in my path?"

Jamásp, however, persevered in his anxious solicitations, describing to him how many of his brethren and kindred had fallen, and also the perilous situation of his own father if he refused his assistance. By a thousand various efforts he at length effected his purpose, and the blacksmith was called to take off his chains; but in removing them, the anguish of the wounds they had inflicted was so great that Isfendiyár fainted away. Upon his recovery he was escorted to the presence of his father, who received him with open arms, and the strongest expressions of delight. He begged to be forgiven for his unnatural conduct to him, again resigned to him the throne of the empire, and appointed him to the command of the imperial armies. He then directed Gurzam, upon whose malicious counsel he had acted, to be brought before him, and the wicked minister was punished with death on the spot, and in the presence of the injured prince.

> Wretch! more relentless even than wolf or pard,
> Thou hast at length received thy just reward!

When Arjásp heard that Isfendiyár had been reconciled to his father, and was approaching at the head of an immense army, he was affected with the deepest concern, and forthwith sent his son Kahram to endeavour to resist the progress of the enemy. At the same time Kurugsar, a gladiator of the demon race, requested that he might be allowed to oppose Isfendiyár; and permission being granted, he was the very first on the field, where instantly wielding his bow, he shot an arrow at Isfendiyár, which pierced through the mail, but fortunately for him did no serious harm. The prince drew his sword with the intention of attacking him, but seeing him furious with rage, and being doubtful of the issue, thought it more prudent and safe to try his success with the noose. Accordingly he took the kamund from his saddle-strap, and dexterously flung it round the neck of his arrogant foe, who was pulled headlong from his horse; and, as soon as his arms were bound behind his back, dragged a prisoner in front of the Persian ranks. Isfendiyár then returned to the battle, attacked a body of the enemy's auxiliaries, killed a hundred and sixty of their warriors, and made the division of which Kahram was the leader fly in all directions. His next feat was to attack another force, which had confederated against him.

> With slackened rein he galloped o'er the field;
> Blood gushed from every stroke of his sharp sword,
> And reddened all the plain; a hundred warriors
> Eighty and five, in treasure rich and mail,
> Sunk underneath him, such his mighty power.

His remaining object was to assail the centre, where Arjásp himself was stationed; and thither he rapidly hastened. Arjásp, angry and alarmed at this success, cried out, "What! is one man allowed to scathe all my ranks, cannot my whole army put an end to his dreadful career?" The soldiers replied, "No! he has a body of brass, and the vigour of an elephant: our swords make no impression upon him, whilst with his sword he can cut the body of a warrior, cased in mail, in two, with the greatest ease. Against such a foe, what can we do?" Isfendiyár rushed on; and after an overwhelming attack, Arjásp was compelled to quit his ground and effect his escape. The Iránian troops were then ordered to pursue the fugitives, and in revenge for the death of Lohurásp, not to leave a man alive. The carnage was in consequence terrible, and the remaining Túránians were in such despair that they flung themselves from their exhausted horses, and placing straw in their mouths to show the extremity of their misfortune, called aloud for quarter. Isfendiyár was moved at last to compassion, and put an end to the fight; and when he came before Gushtásp, the mail on his body, from the number of arrows sticking in it, looked like a field of reeds; about a thousand arrows were taken out of its folds. Gushtásp kissed his head and face, and blessed him, and prepared a grand banquet, and the city of Balkh resounded with rejoicings on account of the great victory.

Many days had not elapsed before a further enterprise was to be undertaken. The sisters of Isfendiyár were still in confinement, and required to be released. The prince readily complied with the wishes of Gushtásp, who now repeated to him his desire to relinquish the cares of sovereignty, and place the reins of government in his hands, that he might devote himself entirely to the service of God.

> "To thee I yield the crown and throne,
> Fit to be held by thee alone;
> From worldly care and trouble free,
> A hermit's cell is enough for me."

But Isfendiyár replied, that he had no desire to be possessed of the power; he rather wished for the prosperity of the king, and no change.

> O, may thy life be long and blessed,
> And ever by the good caressed;
> For 'tis my duty still to be
> Devoted faithfully to thee!
> I want no throne, nor diadem;
> My soul has no delight in them.
> I only seek to give thee joy,
> And gloriously my sword employ.

I thirst for vengeance on Arjásp:
To crush him in my iron grasp,
That from his thrall I may restore
My sisters to their home again,
Who now their heavy fate deplore,
And toiling drag a slavish chain."
"Then go!" the smiling monarch said,
Invoking blessings on his head,
"And may kind Heaven thy refuge be,
And lead thee on to victory."

Isfendiyár now told his father that his prisoner Kurugsar was continually requesting him to represent his condition in the royal ear, saying, "Of what use will it be to put me to death? No benefit can arise from such a punishment. Spare my life, and you will see how largely I am able to contribute to your assistance." Gushtásp expressed his willingness to be merciful, but demanded a guarantee on oath from the petitioner that he would heart and soul be true and faithful to his benefactor. The oath was sworn, after which his bonds were taken from his hands and feet, and he was set at liberty. The king then called him, and pressed him with goblets of wine, which made him merry. "I have pardoned thee," said Gushtásp, "at the special entreaty of Isfendiyár—be grateful to him, and be attentive to his commands." After that, Isfendiyár took and conveyed him to his own house, that he might have an opportunity of experiencing and proving the promised fidelity of his new ally.

THE HEFT-KHAN OF ISFENDIYÁR.

Rustem had seven great labours, wondrous power
Nerved his strong arm in danger's needful hour;
And now Firdausí's legend-strains declare
The seven great labours of Isfendiyár.

The prince, who had determined to undertake the new expedition, and appeared confident of success, now addressed himself to Kurugsar, and said, "If I conquer the kingdom of Arjásp, and restore my sisters to liberty, thou shalt have for thyself any principality thou mayst choose within the boundaries of Irán and Túrán, and thy name shall be exalted; but beware of treachery or fraud, for falsehood shall certainly be punished with death." To this Kurugsar replied, "I have already sworn a solemn oath to the king, and at thy intercession he has spared my life—why then should I depart from the truth, and betray my benefactor?"

"Then tell me the road to the brazen fortress, and how far it is distant from this place?" said Isfendiyár.

"There are three different routes," replied Kurugsar. "One will occupy three months; it leads through a beautiful country, adorned with cities, and gardens, and pastures, and is pleasant to the traveller. The second is less attractive, the prospects less agreeable, and will only employ two months; the third, however, may be accomplished in seven days, and is thence called the Heft-khan, or seven stages; but at every stage some monster, or terrible difficulty, must be overcome. No monarch, even supported by a large army, has ever yet ventured to proceed by this route; and if it is ever attempted, the whole party will be assuredly lost.

Nor strength, nor juggling, nor the sorcerer's art
Can help him safely through that awful path,
Beset with wolves and dragons, wild and fierce,
From whom the fleetest have no power to fly.
There an enchantress, doubly armed with spells,
The most accomplished of that magic brood,
Spreads wide her snares to charm and to destroy,
And ills of every shape, and horrid aspect,
Cross the tired traveller at every step."

At this description of the terrors of the Heft-khan, Isfendiyár became thoughtful for a while, and then, resigning himself to the providence of God, resolved to take the shortest route. "No man can die before his time," said he; "heaven is my protector, and I will fearlessly encounter every difficulty on the road." "It is full of perils," replied Kurugsar, and endeavoured to dissuade him from the enterprise. "But with the blessing of God," rejoined Isfendiyár, "it will be easy." The prince then ordered a sumptuous banquet to be served, at which he gave Kurugsar abundant draughts of wine, and even in a state of intoxication the demon-guide still warned him against his proposed journey. "Go by the route which takes two months," said he, "for that will be convenient and safe;" but Isfendiyár replied:—"I neither fear the difficulties of the route, nor the perils thou hast described."

And though destruction spoke in every word,
Enough to terrify the stoutest heart,
Still he adhered to what he first resolved.
"Thou wilt attend me," said the dauntless prince;
And thus Kurugsar, without a pause, replied:
"Undoubtedly, if by the two months' way,
And do thee ample service; but if this
Heft-khan be thy eleetion; if thy choiee
Be fixed on that whieh leads to eertain death,
My presenee must be useless. Can *I* go
Where bird has never dared to wing its flight?"

Isfendiyár, upon hearing these words, began to suspect the fidelity of Kurugsar, and thought it safe to bind him in chains. The next day as he was going to take leave of his father, Kurugsar called out to him, and said: "After my promises of allegiance, and my solemn oath, why am I thus kept in chains?" "Not out of anger assuredly; but out of compassion and kindness, in order that I may take thee along with me on the enterprise of the Heft-khan; for wert thou not bound, thy faint heart might induce thee to run away.

Safe thou art when bound in ehains,
  Fettered foot can never fly.
Whilst thy body here remains,
  We may on thy faith rely.
Terror will in vain assail thee;
For these bonds shall never fail thee.
Guarded by a potent eharm,
They will keep thee free from harm."

Isfendiyár having received the parting benediction of Gushtásp, was supplied with a force consisting of twelve thousand chosen horsemen, and abundance of treasure, to enable him to proceed on his enterprise, and conquer the kingdom of Arjásp.

First Stage.—Isfendiyár placed Kurugsar in bonds among his retinue, and took with him his brother Bashútan. But the demon-guide complained that he was unable to walk, and in consequence he was mounted on a horse, still bound, and the bridle given into the hands of one of the warriors. In this manner they proceeded, directed from time to time by Kurugsar, till they arrived at the uttermost limits of the kingdom, and entered a desert wilderness. Isfendiyár now asked what they would meet with, and the guide answered, "Two monstrous wolves are in this quarter, as large as elephants, and whose teeth are of immense length." The prince told his people, that as soon as they saw the wolves, they must at once attack them with arrows. The day passed away, and in the evening they came to a forest and a murmuring stream, when suddenly the two enormous wolves appeared, and rushed towards the legions of Isfendiyár. The people seeing them advance, poured upon them a shower of arrows. Several men, however, were wounded, but they were themselves much exhausted by the arrows which had penetrated their bodies. At this moment Bashútan attacked one of them, and Isfendiyár the other; and so vigorous was their charge, that both the monsters were soon laid lifeless in the dust. After this signal overthrow, Isfendiyár turned to Kurugsar, and exclaimed: "Thus, through the favour of Heaven, the first obstacle has been easily extinguished!" The guide regarded him with amazement, and said: "I am indeed astonished at the intrepidity and valour that has been displayed."

> Seeing the bravery of Isfendiyár,
> Amazement filled the soul of Kurugsar.

The warriors and the party now dismounted, and regaled themselves with feasting and wine. They then reposed till the following morning.

SECOND STAGE.—Proceeding on the second journey, Isfendiyár inquired what might now be expected to oppose their progress, and Kurugsar replied: "This stage is infested by lions." "Then," rejoined Isfendiyár, "thou shalt see with what facility I can destroy them." At about the close of the day they met with a lion and a lioness. Bashútan said: "Take one and I will engage the other." But Isfendiyár observed, that the animals seemed very wild and ferocious, and he preferred attacking them both himself, that his brother might not be exposed to any harm. He first sallied forth against the lion, and with one mighty stroke put an end to his life. He then approached the lioness, which pounced upon him with great fury, but was soon compelled to desist, and the prince rapidly wielding his sword, in a moment cut off her head. Having thus successfully accomplished the second day's task, he alighted from his horse, and refreshments being spread out, the warriors and the troops enjoyed themselves with great satisfaction, exhilarated by plenteous draughts of ruby wine. Again Isfendiyár addressed Kurugsar, and said: "Thou seest with what facility all opposition is removed, when I am assisted by the favour of Heaven!" "But there are other and more terrible difficulties to surmount, and amazing as thy achievements certainly have been, thou wilt have still greater exertions to make before thy enterprise is complete." "What is the next evil I have to subdue?" "An enormous dragon,

With power to fascinate, and from the deep
To lure the finny tribe, his daily food.
Fire sparkles round him; his stupendous bulk
Looks like a mountain. When incensed, his roar
Makes the surrounding country shake with fear.
White poison-foam drops from his hideous jaws,
Which yawning wide, display a dismal gulf,
The grave of many a hapless being, lost
Wandering amidst that trackless wilderness."

Kurugsar described or magnified the ferocity of the animal in such a way, that Isfendiyár thought it necessary to be cautious, and with that view he ordered a curious apparatus to be constructed on wheels, something like a carriage, to which he fastened a large quantity of pointed instruments, and harnessed horses to it to drag it on the road. He then tried its motion, and found it admirably calculated for his purpose. The people were astonished at the ingenuity of the invention, and lauded him to the skies.

THIRD STAGE.—Away went the prince, and having travelled a considerable distance, Kurugsar suddenly exclaimed: "I now begin to smell the stench of the dragon." Hearing this, Isfendiyár dismounted, ascended the machine, and shutting the door fast, took his seat and drove off. Bashútan and all the warriors upon witnessing this extraordinary act, began to weep and lament, thinking that he was hurrying himself to certain destruction, and begged that for his own sake, as well as theirs, he would come out of the machine. But he replied: "Peace, peace! what know ye of the matter;" and as the warlike apparatus was so excellently contrived, that he could direct the movements of the horses himself, he drove on with increased velocity, till he arrived in the vicinity of the monster.

The dragon from a distance heard
 The rumbling of the wain,
And snuffing every breeze that stirred
 Across the neighbouring plain,

Smelt something human in his power,
 A welcome scent to him;
For he was eager to devour
 Hot reeking blood, or limb.

And darkness now is spread around,
 No pathway can be traced;
The fiery horses plunge and bound
 Amid the dismal waste.

And now the dragon stretches far
 His cavern throat, and soon
Licks in the horses and the car,
 And tries to gulp them down.

But sword and javelin, sharp and keen,
 Wound deep each sinewy jaw;
Midway, remains the huge machine,
 And chokes the monster's maw.

In agony he breathes, a dire
  Convulsion fires his blood,
And struggling, ready to expire,
  Ejects a poison-flood!

And then disgorges wain and steeds,
  And swords and javelins bright;
Then, as the dreadful dragon bleeds,
  Up starts the warrior-knight,

And from his place of ambush leaps,
  And, brandishing his blade,
The weapon in the brain he steeps,
  And splits the monster's head.

But the foul venom issuing thence,
  Is so o'erpowering found,
Isfendiyár, deprived of sense,
  Falls staggering to the ground!

Upon seeing this result, and his brother in so deplorable a situation, Bashútan and the troops also were in great alarm, apprehending the most fatal consequences. They sprinkled rose-water over his face, and administered other remedies, so that after some time he recovered; then he bathed, purifying himself from the filth of the monster, and poured out prayers of thankfulness to the merciful Creator for the protection and victory he had given him. But it was matter of great grief to Kurugsar that Isfendiyár had succeeded in his exploit, because under present circumstances, he would have to follow him in the remaining arduous enterprises; whereas, if the prince had been slain, his obligations would have ceased for ever.

"What may be expected to-morrow?" inquired Isfendiyár. "To-morrow," replied the demon-guide, "thou wilt meet with an enchantress, who can convert the stormy sea into dry land, and the dry land again into the ocean. She is attended by a gigantic ghoul, or apparition." "Then thou shalt see how easily this enchantress and her mysterious attendant can be vanquished."

FOURTH STAGE.—On the fourth day Isfendiyár and his companions proceeded on the destined journey, and coming to a pleasant meadow, watered by a transparent rivulet, the party alighted, and they all refreshed themselves heartily with various kinds of food and wine. In a short space of time the enchantress appeared, most beautiful in feature and elegant in attire, and approaching our hero with a sad but fascinating expression of countenance, said to him (the ghoul, her pretended paramour, being at a little distance):

> "I am a poor unhappy thing,
> The daughter of a distant king.
> This monster with deceit and fraud,
> By a fond parent's power unawed,
> Seduced me from my royal home,
> Through wood and desert wild to roam;
> And surely Heaven has brought thee now
> To cheer my heart, and smooth my brow,
> And free me from his loathed embrace,
> And bear me to a fitter place,
> Where, in thy circling arms more softly prest,
> I may at last be truly loved, and blest."

Isfendiyár immediately called her to him, and requested her to sit down. The enchantress readily complied, anticipating a successful issue to her artful stratagems; but the intended victim of her sorcery was too cunning to be imposed upon. He soon perceived what she was, and forthwith cast his kamund over her, and in spite of all her entreaties, bound her too fast to escape. In this extremity, she successively assumed the shape of a cat, a wolf, and a decrepit old man: and so perfect were her transformations, that any other person would have been deceived, but Isfendiyár detected her in every variety of appearance; and, vexed by her continual attempts to cheat him, at last took out his sword and cut her in pieces. As soon as this was done, a thick dark cloud of dust and vapour arose, and when it subsided, a black apparition of a demon burst upon his sight, with flames issuing from its mouth. Determined to destroy this fresh antagonist, he rushed forward, sword in hand, and though the flames, in the attack, burnt his cloth-armour and dress, he succeeded in cutting off the threatening monster's head. "Now," said he to Kurugsar, "thou hast seen that with the favour of Heaven, both enchantress and ghoul are exterminated, as well as the wolves, the lions, and the dragon." "Very well," replied Kurugsar, "thou hast achieved this prodigious labour, but to-morrow will be a heavy day, and thou canst hardly escape with life. To-morrow thou wilt be opposed by the Símurgh, whose nest is situated upon a lofty mountain. She has two young ones, each the size of an elephant, which she conveys in her beak and claws from place to place." "Be under no alarm," said Isfendiyár, "God will make the labour easy."

Fifth Stage.—On the fifth day, Isfendiyár resumed his journey, travelling with his little army over desert, plain, mountain, and wilderness, until he reached the neighbourhood of the Símurgh. He then adopted the same stratagem which he had employed before, and the machine supplied with swords and spears, and drawn by horses, was soon in readiness for the new adventure. The Símurgh, seeing with surprise an immense vehicle, drawn by two horses, approach at a furious rate, and followed by a large company of horsemen, descended from the mountain, and endeavoured to take up the whole apparatus in her claws to carry it away to her own nest; but her claws were lacerated by the sharp weapons, and she was then obliged to try her beak. Both beak and claws were injured in the effort, and the animal became extremely weakened by the loss of blood. Isfendiyár seizing the happy moment, sprang out of the carriage, and with his trenchant sword divided the Símurgh in two parts; and the young ones, after witnessing the death of their parent, precipitately fled from the fatal scene. When Bashútan, with the army, came to the spot, they were amazed at the prodigious size of the Símurgh, and the valour by which it had been subdued. Kurugsar turned pale with astonishment and sorrow. "What will be our next adventure?" said Isfendiyár to him. "To-morrow more pressing ills will surround thee. Heavy snow will fall, and there will be a violent tempest of wind, and it will be wonderful if even one man of thy legions remains alive. That will not be like fighting against lions, a dragon, or the Símurgh, but against the elements, against the Almighty, which never can be successful. Thou hadst better, therefore, return unhurt." The people on hearing this warning were alarmed, and proposed to go back; "for if the advice of Kurugsar is not taken, we shall all perish like the companions of Kai-khosráu, and be buried under drifts of snow.

"Let us return then, whilst we may;
Why should we throw our lives away?"

But Isfendiyár replied that he had already overcome five of the perils of the road, and had no fear about the remaining two. The people, however, were still discontented, and still murmured aloud; upon which the prince said, "Return then, and I will go alone.

I never can require the aid
Of men so easily dismayed."

Finding their leader immoveable, the people now changed their tone, and expressed their devotion to his cause; declaring that whilst life remained, they would never forsake him, no never.

SIXTH STAGE.—On the following morning, the sixth, Isfendiyár continued his labours, and hurried on with great speed. Towards evening he arrived on the skirts of a mountain, where there was a running stream, and upon that spot, he pitched his tents.

Presently from the mountain there rushed down
A furious storm of wind, then heavy showers
Of snow fell, covering all the earth with whiteness,
And making desolate the prospect round.
Keen blew the blast, and pinching was the cold;
And to escape the elemental wrath,
Leader and soldier, in the caverned rock
Scooped out by mouldering time, took shelter, there
Continuing three long days. Three lingering days
Still fell the snow, and still the tempest raged,
And man and beast grew faint for want of food.

Isfendiyár and his warriors, with heads exposed, now prostrated themselves in solemn prayer to the Almighty, and implored his favour and protection from the calamity which had befallen them. Happily their prayers were heard, Heaven was compassionate, and in a short space the snow and the mighty wind entirely ceased. By this fortunate interference of Providence, the army was enabled to quit the caves of the mountain; and then Isfendiyár again addressed Kurugsar triumphantly: "Thus the sixth labour is accomplished. What have we now to fear?" The demon-guide answered him and said: "From hence to the Brazen Fortress it is forty farsangs. That fortress is the residence of Arjásp; but the road is full of peril. For three farsangs the sand on the ground is as hot as fire, and there is no water to be found during the whole journey." This information made a serious impression upon the mind of Isfendiyár; who said to him sternly: "If I find thee guilty of falsehood, I will assuredly put thee to death." Kurugsar replied: "What! after six trials? Thou hast no reason to question my veracity. I shall never depart from the truth, and my advice is, that thou hadst better return; for the seventh stage is not to be ventured upon by human strength.

Along those plains of burning sand
No bird can move, nor ant, nor fly;
No water slakes the fiery land,
Intensely glows the flaming sky.

No tiger fierce, nor lion ever
Could breath that pestilential air;
Even the unsparing vulture never
Ventures on blood-stained pinions there.

At the distance of three farsangs beyond this inaccessible belt of scorching country lies the Brazen Fortress, to which there is no visible path; and if an army of a hundred thousand strong were to attempt its reduction, there would not be the least chance of success."

SEVENTH STAGE.—When Isfendiyár heard these things, enough to alarm the bravest heart, he turned towards his people to ascertain their determination; when they unanimously repeated their readiness to sacrifice their lives in his service, and to follow wherever he might be disposed to lead the way. He then put Kurugsar in chains again, and prosecuted his journey, until he reached the place said to be covered with burning sand. Arrived on the spot, he observed to the demon-guide: "Thou hast described the sand as hot, but it is not so." "True; and it is on account of the heavy showers of snow that have fallen and cooled the ground, a proof that thou art under the protection of the Almighty." Isfendiyár smiled, and said: "Thou art all insincerity and deception, thus to play upon my feelings with false or imaginary terrors." Saying this he urged his soldiers to pass rapidly on, so as to leave the sand behind them, and they presently came to a great river. Isfendiyár was now angry with Kurugsar, and said: "Thou hast declared that for the space of forty farsangs there was no water, every drop being everywhere dried up by the burning heat of the sun, and here we find water! Why didst thou also idly fill the minds of my soldiers with groundless fears?" Kurugsar replied: "I will confess the truth. Did I not swear a solemn oath to be faithful, and yet I was still doubted, and still confined in irons, though the experience of six days of trial had proved the correctness of my information and advice. For this reason I was disappointed and displeased; and I must confess that I did, therefore, exaggerate the dangers of the last day, in the hopes too of inducing thee to return and release me from my bonds.

For what have I received from thee,
But scorn, and chains, and slavery."

Isfendiyár now struck off the irons from the hands and feet of his demon-guide and treated him with favour and kindness, repeating to him his promise to reward him at the close of his victorious career with the government of a kingdom. Kurugsar was grateful for this change of conduct to him, and again acknowledging the deception he had been guilty of, hoped for pardon, engaging at the same time to take the party in safety across the great river which had impeded their progress. This was accordingly done, and the Brazen Fortress was now at no great distance. At the close of the day they were only one farsang from the towers, but Isfendiyár preferred resting till the next morning. "What is thy counsel now?" said he to his guide. "What sort of a fortress is this which fame describes in such dreadful colours?" "It is stronger than imagination can conceive, and impregnable."—"Then how shall I get to Arjásp?

How shall I cleave the oppressor's form asunder,
The murderer of my grandsire, Lohurásp?
The bravest heroes of Túrán shall fall
Under my conquering sword; their wives and children
Led captive to Irán; and desolation
Scathe the whole realm beneath the tyrant's sway."

But these words only roused and exasperated the feelings of Kurugsar, who bitterly replied:

"Then may calamity be thy reward,
Thy stars malignant, and thy life all sorrow;
And may'st thou perish, weltering in thy blood,
And the bare desert be thy lonely grave
For that inhuman thought, that cruel menace."

Isfendiyár, upon hearing this unexpected language, became furious with indignation, and instantaneously punished the offender on the spot; with one stroke of his sword he cleft Kurugsar in twain.

When the clouds of night had darkened the sky, Isfendiyár, with a number of his warriors, proceeded towards the Brazen Fortress, and secretly explored it on every side. He found it constructed entirely of iron and brass; and, notwithstanding a strict examination at every point, discovered no accessible part for attack. It was three farsangs high, and forty wide; and such a place as was never before beheld by man.

CAPTURE OF THE BRAZEN FORTRESS, AND DEATH OF ARJÁSP.

Isfendiyár returned from reconnoitring the fortress with acute feelings of sorrow and despair. He was at last convinced that Kurugsar had spoken the truth; for there seemed to be no chance whatever of taking the place by any stratagem he could invent. Revolving the enterprise seriously in his mind, he now began to repent of his folly, and the overweening confidence which had led him to undertake the journey. Returning thus to his tent in a melancholy mood, he saw a Fakír sitting down on the road, and him he anxiously accosted. "What may be the number of the garrison in this fort?" "There are a hundred thousand veteran warriors in the service of Arjásp in the fort, with abundance of supplies of every kind, and streams of pure water, so that nothing is wanted to foil an enemy." This was very unwelcome intelligence to Isfendiyár, who now assembled his officers to consider what was best to be done. They all agreed that the reduction of the fortress was utterly impracticable, and that the safest course for him would be to return. But he could not bring himself to acquiesce in this measure, saying: "God is almighty, and beneficent, and with him is the victory." He then reflected deeply and long, and finally determined upon entering the fort disguised as a merchant. Having first settled the mode of proceeding, he put Bashútan in temporary charge of the army, saying:

"This Brazen Fortress scorns all feats of arms,
Nor sword nor spear, nor battle-axe, can here
Be wielded to advantage; stratagem
Must be employed, or we shall never gain
Possession of its wide-extended walls,
Placing my confidence in God alone
I go with rich and curious wares for sale,
To take the credulous people by surprise,
Under the semblance of a peaceful merchant."

Isfendiyár then directed a hundred dromedaries to be collected, and when they were brought to him he disposed of them in the following manner. He loaded ten with embroidered cloths, five with rubies and sapphires, and five more with pearls and other precious jewels. Upon each of the remaining eighty he placed two chests, and in each chest a warrior was secreted, making in all one hundred and sixty; and one hundred more were disposed as camel-drivers and servants. Thus the whole force, consisting of a hundred dromedaries and two hundred and sixty warriors, set off towards the Brazen Fortress, Isfendiyár having first intimated to his brother Bashútan to march with his army direct to the gates of the fort, as soon as he saw a column of flame and smoke ascend from the interior. On the way they gave out that they were merchants come with valuable goods from Persia, and hoped for custom. The tidings of travellers having arrived with rubies and gold-embroidered garments for sale, soon reached the ears of Arjásp, the king, who immediately gave them permission to enter the fort. When Isfendiyár, the reputed master of the caravan, had got within the walls, he said that he had brought rich presents for the king, and requested to be introduced to him in person. He was accordingly allowed to take the presents himself, was received with distinguished attention, and having stated his name to be Kherád, was invited to go to the royal palace, whenever, and as often as, he might please. At one of the interviews the king asked him, as he had come from Persia, if he knew whether the report was true or not that Kurugsar had been put to death, and what Gushtásp and Isfendiyár were engaged upon. The hero in disguise replied that it was five months since he left Persia; but he had heard on the road from many persons that Isfendiyár intended proceeding by the way of the Heft-khan with a vast army, towards the Brazen Fortress. At these words Arjásp smiled in derision, and said: "Ah! ah! by that way even the winged tribe are afraid to venture; and if Isfendiyár had a thousand lives, he would lose them all in any attempt to accomplish that journey." After this interview Isfendiyár daily continued to attend to the sale of his merchandise, and soon found that his sisters were employed in the degrading office of drawing and carrying water for the kitchen of Arjásp. When they heard that a caravan had arrived from Irán, they went to Isfendiyár (who recognized them at a distance, but hid his face that they might not know him), to inquire what tidings he had brought about their father and brother. Alarmed at the hazard of discovery, he replied that he knew nothing, and desired them to depart; but they remained, and said: "On thy return to Irán, at least, let it be known that here we are, two daughters of Gushtásp, reduced to the basest servitude, and neither father nor brother takes compassion upon our distresses.

Whilst with bare head, and naked feet, we toil,
They pass their time in peace and happiness,
Regardless of the misery we endure."

Isfendiyár again, in assumed anger, told them to depart, saying: "Talk not to me of Gushtásp and Isfendiyár—what have I to do with them?" At that moment the sound of his voice was recognized by the elder sister, who, in a transport of joy, instantly communicated her discovery to the younger; but they kept the secret till night, and then they returned to commune with their brother. Isfendiyár finding that he was known, acknowledged himself, and informed them that he had undertaken to restore them to liberty, and that he was now engaged in the enterprise, opposing every obstacle in his way; but it was necessary that they should continue their usual labour at the wells, till a fitting opportunity occurred.

For the purpose of accelerating the moment of release, Isfendiyár represented to the king that at a period of great adversity, he had made a vow that he would give a splendid banquet if ever Heaven again smiled upon him, and as he then was in the way to prosperity, and wished to fulfil his vow, he hoped that his majesty would honour him with his presence on the occasion. The king accepted the invitation with satisfaction, and said: "To-morrow I will be thy guest, at thy own house, and with all my warriors and soldiers." But this did not suit the scheme of the pretended merchant, who apologised on account of his house being too small, and proposed that the feast should be held upon the loftiest part of the fortress, where spacious tents and pavilions might be erected for the purpose, and a large fire lighted to give splendour to the scene. The king assented, and every requisite preparation being made, all the royal and warrior guests assembled in the morning, and eagerly partook of the rich viands set before them. They all drank wine with such relish and delight, that they soon became intoxicated, and Kherád seizing the opportunity, ordered the logs of wood which had been collected, to be set on fire, and rapidly the smoke and flame sprung up, and ascended to the sky. Bashútan saw the looked-for sign, and hastened with two thousand horsemen to the gates of the fortress, where he slew every one that he met, calling himself Isfendiyár. Arjásp had enjoyed the banquet exceedingly ; the music gave him infinite pleasure, and the wine had intoxicated him ; but in the midst of his hilarity and merriment, he was told that Isfendiyár had reached the gates, and entered the fort, killing immense numbers of his people. This terrible intelligence roused him and quitting the festive board of Kherád, he ordered his son Kahram, with fifty thousand horsemen, to repel the invader. He also ordered forty thousand horsemen to protect different parts of the walls, and ten thousand to remain as his own personal guard. Kahram accordingly issued forth without delay, and soon engaged in battle with the force under Bashútan.

When night came, Isfendiyár opened the lids of the chests, and let out the hundred and sixty warriors, whom he supplied with swords and spears, and armour, and also the hundred who were disguised as camel-drivers and servants.

> With this bold band he sped,
> Whither Arjásp had fled ;
> And all who fought around,
> To keep untouched that sacred ground ;
> (Resistance weak and vain,)
> By him were quickly slain.

The sisters of Isfendiyár now arrived, and pointed out to him the chamber of Arjásp, to which place he immediately repaired, and roused up the king, who was almost insensible with the fumes of wine. Arjásp, however, sprang upon his feet,

> And grappled stoutly with Isfendiyár,
> And desperate was the conflict: head and loins
> Alternately received deep gaping wounds
> From sword and dagger. Wearied out at length,
> Arjásp shrunk back, when with one mighty blow,
> Isfendiyár, exulting in his power,
> Cleft him asunder.

Two of the wives, two daughters, and one sister of Arjásp fell immediately into the hands of the conqueror, who delivered them into the custody of his son, to be conveyed home. He then quitted the palace, and turning his steps towards the gates of the fortress, slew a great number of the enemy.

Kahram, in the meantime had been fiercely engaged with Bashútan, and was extremely reduced. At the very moment too of his discomfiture, he heard the watchmen call out aloud that Arjásp had been slain by Kheràd. Confounded and alarmed by these tidings, he approached the fort, where he heard the confirmation of his misfortune from every mouth, and also that the garrison had been put to the sword. Leading on the remainder of his troops he now came in contact with Isfendiyár and his two hundred and sixty warriors, and a sharp engagement ensued; but the coming up of Bashútan's force on his rear, placed him in such a predicament on every side, that defeat and destruction were almost inevitable. In short, Kahram was left with only a few of his soldiers near him, when Isfendiyár, observing his situation, challenged him to personal combat, and the challenge was accepted.

> So closely did the eager warriors close,
> They seemed together joined, and but one man.
> At last Isfendiyár seized Kahram's girth,
> And flung him to the ground, and bound his hands;
> And as a leaf is severed from its stalk,
> So he the head cleft from its quivering trunk;
> Thus one blow wins, and takes away a throne.
> In battle heads are trodden under hoofs,
> Crowns under heads.

After the death of Kahram, Isfendiyár issued a proclamation, offering full pardon to all who would unite under his banners. They had no king;

The country had no throne, no crown. Alas!
What is the world without a governor,
What, but a headless trunk? A thing more worthless
Than the vile dust upon the common road.
What could the people do in their despair?
They were obedient, and Isfendiyár
Encouraged them with kind and gentle words,
Fitting a generous and a prudent master.

Having first written to his father an account of the great victory which he had gained, he occupied himself in reducing all the surrounding provinces and their inhabitants to subjection. Those people who continued hostile to him he deemed it necessary to put to death. He took all the women of Arjásp into his own service, and their daughters he presented to his own sons.

Not a warrior of Chín remained;
  The king of Túrán was swept away;
And the realm where in pomp he had reigned,
  Where he basked in prosperity's ray,
Was spoiled by the conqueror's brand,
  Desolation marked every scene,
And a stranger now governed the mountainous land,
  Where the splendour of Poshang had been.
Not a dirhem of treasure was left;
  For nothing eluded the conqueror's grasp;
Of all was the royal pavilion bereft;
  All followed the fate of Arjásp!

When Gushtásp received information of this mighty conquest, he sent orders to Isfendiyár to continue in the government of the new empire; but the prince replied that he had settled the country, and was anxious to see his father. This request being permitted, he was desired to bring away all the immense booty, and return by the road of the Heft-khan. Arriving at the place where he was overtaken by the dreadful winter-storm, he again found all the property he had lost under the drifts of snow; and when he had accomplished his journey, he was received with the warmest welcome and congratulations, on account of his extraordinary successes. A royal feast was prepared, and the king filled his son's goblet with wine so repeatedly, and drank himself so frequently, and with such zest, that both of them at length became intoxicated. Gushtásp then asked Isfendiyár to describe to him the particulars of his expedition by the road of the Heft-khan; for though he had heard the story from others, he wished to have it from his own mouth. But Isfendiyár replied: "We have both drank too much wine, and nothing good can proceed from a drunken man; I will recite my adventures to-morrow, when my head is clear." The next day Gushtásp, seated upon his throne, and Isfendiyár placed before him on a golden chair, again asked for the prince's description of his triumphant progress by the Heft-khan, and according to his wish every incident that merited notice was faithfully detailed to him. The king expressed great pleasure at the conclusion; but envy and suspicion lurked in his breast, and writhing internally like a serpent, he still delayed fulfilling his promise to invest Isfendiyár, upon the overthrow of Arjásp, with the sovereignty of Irán.

The prince could not fail to observe the changed disposition of his father, and privately went to Kitabún, his mother, to whom he related the solemn promise and engagement of Gushtásp, and requested her to go to him, and say: "Thou hast given thy royal word to Isfendiyár, that when he had conquered and slain Arjásp, and restored his own sisters to liberty, thou wouldst place upon his head the crown of Irán; faith and honour are indispensable in princes, they are inculcated by religion, and yet thou hast failed to make good thy word." But the mother had more prudence, and said: "Let me give thee timely counsel, and breathe not a syllable to any one on the subject. God forbid that thou shouldst again be thrown into prison, and confined in chains. Recollect thine is the succession; the army is in thy favour; thy father is old and infirm. Have a little patience, and in the end thou wilt undoubtedly be the King of Persia.

> The gold and jewels, the imperial sway,
> The crown, the throne, the army, all he owns,
> Will presently be thine ; then wait in patience,
> And reign, in time, the monarch of the world."

Isfendiyár, however, was not contented with his mother's counsel, and suspecting that she would communicate to the king what he had said, he one day, as if under the influence of wine, thus addressed his father: "In what way have I failed to accomplish thy wishes? Have I not performed such actions as never were heard of, and never will be performed again, in furtherance of thy glory? I have overthrown thy greatest enemy, and supported thy honour with ceaseless toil and exertion. Is it not then incumbent on thee to fulfil thy promise?" Gushtásp replied: "Do not be impatient—the throne is thine;" but he was deeply irritated at heart on being thus reproached by his own son. When he retired he consulted with Jamásp, and was anxious to know what the stars foretold. The answer was: "He is of exalted fortune, of high destiny; he will overcome all his enemies, and finally obtain the sovereignty of the heft-aklím, or seven climes." This favourable prophecy aggravated the spleen of the father against the son, and he inquired with bitter and unnatural curiosity: "What will be his death? Look to that."

> "A deadly dart from Rustem's bow,
> Will lay the glorious warrior low."

These tidings gladdened the heart of Gushtásp, and he said: "If this miscreant had been slain in his expedition to the Brazen Fortress I should not now have been insulted with his claim to my throne." The king then having resolved upon a scheme of deep dissimulation, ordered a gorgeous banquet, and invited to it all his relations and warriors; and when the guests were assembled he said to Isfendiyár: "The crown and the throne are thine; indeed, who is there so well qualified for imperial sway?" and turning to his warriors, he spoke of him with praise and admiration, and added: "When I was entering upon the war against Arjásp, before I quitted Sístán, I said to Rustem: 'My father Lohurásp is killed, my wife and children made prisoners, wilt thou assist me in punishing the murderer and oppressor?' but he excused himself, and remained at home, and although I have since been involved in numberless perils, he has not once by inquiry shewn himself interested in my behalf; in short, he boasts that Kai-khosráu gave him the principalities of Zábul and Kábul, and Ním-rúz, and that he owes no allegiance to me! It behoves me, therefore, to depute Isfendiyár to go and put him to death, or bring him before me in bonds alive. After that I shall have no enemy to be revenged upon, and I shall retire from the world, and leave to Isfendiyár the crown and the throne of Persia, with confidence and satisfaction." All the nobles and heroes present approved of the measure, and the king, gratified by their approbation, then turned to Isfendiyár, and said: "I have sworn on the Zendavesta, to relinquish my power, and place it in thy hands, as soon as Rustem is subdued. Take whatever force the important occasion may require, for the whole resources of the empire shall be at thy command." But Isfendiyár thus replied: "Remember the first time I defeated Arjásp—what was my reward? Through the machinations of Gurzam I was thrown into prison and chained. And what is my reward now that I have slain both Arjásp and his son in battle? Thy solemn promise to me is forgotten, or disregarded. The prince who forgets one promise will forget another, if it be convenient for his purpose.

Whenever the Heft-khan is brought to mind,
I feel a sense of horror. But why should I
Repeat the story of those great exploits!
God is my witness, how I slew the wolf,
The lion, and the dragon; how I punished
That fell enchantress with her thousand wiles;
And how I suffered, midst the storm of snow,
Which almost froze the blood within my veins;

And how that vast unfathomable deep
We crossed securely. These are deeds which waken
Wonder and praise in others, not in thee!
The treasure which I captured now is thine;
And what is my reward?—the interest, sorrow.
Thus am I cheated of my recompense.
It is the custom for great kings to keep
Religiously their pledged, affianced word;
But thou hast broken thine, despite of honour.

I do remember in thy early youth,
It was in Rúm, thou didst perform a feat
Of gallant daring; for thou didst destroy
A dragon and a wolf, but thou didst bear
Thyself most proudly, thinking human arm
Never before had done a deed so mighty;
Yes, thou wert proud and vain, and seemed exalted
Up to the Heavens; and for that noble act
What did thy father do? The king for that
Gave thee with joyous heart his crown and throne.
Now mark the difference; think what I have done,
What perils I sustained, and for thy sake!
Thy foes I vanquished, clearing from thy mind
The gnawing rust of trouble and affliction.
Monsters I slew, reduced the Brazen Fortress,
And laid Arjásp's whole empire at thy feet,
And what was my reward? Neglect and scorn.
Did I deserve this at a father's hands?"

Gushtásp remained unmoved by this sharp rebuke, though he readily acknowledged its justice. "The crown shall be thine," said he, "but consider my position. Think, too, what services Zál and Rustem performed for Kai-khosráu, and shall I expect less from my own son, gifted as he is with a form of brass, and the most prodigious valour? Forbid it, Heaven! that any rumour of our difference should get abroad in the world, which would redound to the dishonour of both! Nearly half of Irán is in the possession of Rustem." "Give me the crown," said Isfendiyár, "and I will immediately proceed against the Zábul champion." "I have given thee both the crown and the throne, take with thee my whole army, and all my treasure.—What wouldst thou have more? He who has conquered the terrific obstacles of the Heft-khan, and has slain Arjásp and subdued his entire kingdom, can have no cause to fear the prowess of Rustem, or any other chief." Isfendiyár replied that he had no fear of Rustem's prowess; he was now old, and therefore not equal to himself in strength; still he had no wish to oppose him:

For he has been the monitor and friend
Of our Kaiánian ancestors; his care
Enriched their minds, and taught them to be brave;
And he was ever faithful to their cause.
Besides," said he, "thou wert the honoured guest
Of Rustem two long years; and at Sístán
Enjoyed his hospitality and friendship,
His festive, social board; and canst thou now,
Forgetting that delightful intercourse,
Become his bitterest foe?"

Gushtásp replied:

"'Tis true he may have served my ancestors;
But what is that to me? His spirit is proud,
And he refused to yield me needful aid
When danger pressed; that is enough, and thou
Canst not divert me from my settled purpose.

Therefore, if thy aim be still
To rule, thy father's wish fulfil;
Quickly trace the distant road;
Quick invade the chief's abode;
Bind his feet, and bind his hands
In a captive's galling bands;
Bring him here, that all may know
Thou hast quelled the mighty foe."

But Isfendiyár was still reluctant, and implored him to relinquish his design.

"For if resolved, a gloomy cloud
Will quickly all thy glories shroud,
And dim thy brilliant throne;
I would not thus aspire to reign,
But rather, free from crime, remain
Sequestered and alone."

Again Gushtásp spoke, and said: "There is no necessity for any further delay. Thou art appointed my successor, and the crown and the throne are thine; thou hast therefore only to march to the scene of action, and accomplish the object of the war." Hearing this, Isfendiyár sullenly retired to his own house, and Gushtásp, perceiving that he was in an angry mood, requested Jamásp (his minister) to ascertain the state of his mind, and whether he intended to proceed to Sístán or not. Jamásp immediately went, and Isfendiyár asked him, as his friend, what he would advise. "The commands of a father," he replied, "must be obeyed." There was now no remedy, and the king being informed that the prince consented to undertake the expedition, no further discussion took place.

But Kitabún was deeply affected when she heard of these proceedings, and repaired instantly to her son, to represent to him the hopelessness of the enterprise he had engaged to conduct.

> "A mother's counsel is a golden treasure;
> Consider well, and listen not to folly.
> Rustem, the champion of the world, will never
> Suffer himself to be confined in bonds.
> Did he not conquer the White Demon, fill
> The world with blood, in terrible revenge,
> When Saiáwush was by Afrásiyáb
> Cruelly slain? O, curses on the throne,
> And ruin seize the country, which returns
> Evil for good, and spurns its benefactor.
> Restrain thy steps, engage not in this war;
> It cannot do thee honour. Hear my voice!
> Hear the safe counsel of thy anxious mother!
> For Rustem still can conquer all the world."
> Thus spoke Kitabún, shedding ceaseless tears;
> And thus Isfendiyár: "I fear not Rustem;
> I fear not his prodigious power and skill;
> But never can I on so great a hero
> Place ignominious bonds; it must not be.
> Yet, mother dear, my faithful word is pledged;
> My word Jamásp has taken to the king,
> And I must follow where my fortune leads."

The next morning Isfendiyár took leave of the king, and with a vast army, and immense treasure, commenced his march towards Sístán. It happened that one of the camels in advance laid down, and though beaten severely, could not be made to get up on its legs. Isfendiyár, seeing the obstinacy of the animal, ordered it to be killed, and passed on. The people, however, interpreted the accident as a bad omen, and wished him not to proceed; but he could not attend to their suggestions, as he thought the king would look upon it as a mere pretence, and therefore continued his journey.

When he approached Sístán, he sent Bahman, his eldest son, to Rustem, with a flattering message, to induce the champion to honour him with an istakbal, or deputation to receive him. Upon Bahman's arrival, however, he hesitated and delayed, being reluctant to give a direct answer; but Zál interposed, saying: "Why not immediately wait upon the prince?—have we not always been devoted to the Kaiánian dynasty?—Go and bring him hither, that we may tender him our allegiance, and entertain him at our mansion as becomes his illustrious birth." Accordingly Rustem went out to welcome Isfendiyár, and alighting from Rakush, proceeded respectfully on foot to embrace him. He then invited him to his house, but Isfendiyár said: "So strict are my father's commands, that after having seen thee, I am not permitted to delay my departure." Rustem, however, pressed him to remain with him, but all in vain. On the contrary the prince artfully conducted him to his own quarters, where he addressed him thus: "If thou wilt allow me to bind thee, hand and foot, in chains, I will convey thee to the king my father, whose humour it is to see thee once in fetters, and then to release thee!" Rustem was silent. Again Isfendiyár said: "If thou art not disposed to comply with this demand, go thy ways." Rustem replied: "First be my guest, as thy father once was, and after that I will conform to thy will." Again the prince said: "My father visited thee under other circumstances; I have come for a different purpose. If I eat thy bread and salt, and after that thou shouldst refuse thy acquiescence, I must have recourse to force. But if I become thy guest, how can I in honour fight with thee? and if I do not take thee bound into my father's presence, according to his command, what answer shall I give to him?" "For the same reason," said Rustem: "how can I eat thy bread and salt?" Isfendiyár then replied: "Thou needest not eat my bread and salt, but only drink wine.—Bring thy own pure ruby." To this Rustem agreed, and they drank, each his own wine, together.

In a short space Rustem observed that he wished to consult his father Zál; and being allowed to depart, he, on his return home, described in strong terms of admiration the personal appearance and mental qualities of Isfendiyár.

"In wisdom ripe, and with a form
Of brass to meet the battle-storm,
Thou wouldst confess his every boon,
Had been derived from Ferídún."

Bashútan in the meanwhile observed to his brother, with some degree of dissatisfaction, that his enemy had come into his power, on his own feet too, but had been strangely permitted to go away again. To this gentle reproof Isfendiyár confidently replied, "If he does fail to return, I will go and secure him in bonds, even in his own house."—"Ah!" said Bashútan, "that might be done by gentleness, but not by force, for the descendant of Sám, the champion of the world, is not to be subdued so easily." These words had a powerful effect upon the mind of Isfendiyár, and he became apprehensive that Rustem would not return; but whilst he was still murmuring at his own want of vigilance, the champion appeared, and at this second interview repeated his desire that the prince would become his guest. "I am sent here by my father, who relies upon thy accepting his proffered hospitality."—"That may be," said Isfendiyár, "but I am at my utmost limit, I cannot go farther. From this place, therefore, thou hadst better prepare to accompany me to Irán." Here Rustem paused, and at length artfully began to enumerate his various achievements, and to blazon his own name.

"I fettered fast the emperor of Chín,
And broke the enchantment of the Seven Khans;

> I stood the guardian of the Persian kings,
> Their shield in danger. I have cleared the world
> Of all their foes, enduring pain and toil
> Incalculable. Such exploits for thee
> Will I achieve, such sufferings will I bear,
> And hence we offer thee a social welcome.
> But let not dark suspicion cloud thy mind,
> Nor think thyself exalted as the heavens,
> Because I thus invite thee to our home."

Isfendiyár felt so indignant and irritated by this apparent boasting and self-sufficiency of Rustem, that his first impulse was to cast a dagger at him; but he kept down his wrath, and satisfied himself with giving him a scornful glance, and telling him to take a seat on his left hand. But Rustem resented this affront, saying that he never yet had sat down on the left of any king, and placed himself, without permission, on the right hand of Isfendiyár. The unfavourable impression on the prince's mind was increased by this independent conduct, and he was provoked to say to him, "Rustem! I have heard that Zál, thy father, was of demon extraction, and that Sám cast him into the desert because of his disgusting and abominable appearance; that even the hungry Símurgh, on the same account, forebore to feed upon him, but conveyed him to her nest among her own young ones, who pitying his wretched condition, supplied him with part of the carrion they were accustomed to devour. Naked and filthy, he is thus said to have subsisted on garbage, till Sám was induced to commiserate his wretchedness, and take him to Sístán, where, by the indulgence of his family and royal bounty, he was instructed in human manners and human science." This was a reproach and an insult too biting for Rustem to bear with any degree of patience, and frowning with strong indignation, he said, "Thy father knows, and thy grandfather well knew that Zál was the son of Sám, and Sám of Narímán, and that Narímán was descended from Húsheng. Thou and I, therefore, have the same origin. Besides, on my mother's side, I am descended from Zohák, so that by both parents I am of a race of princes. Knowest thou not that the Iránian empire was for some time in my hands, and that I refused to retain it, though urged by the nobles and the army to exercise the functions of royalty? It was my sense of justice, and attachment to the Káís and to thy family, which have enabled thee to possess thy present dignity and command. It is through my fidelity and zeal that thou art now in a situation to reproach me. Thou hast slain one king, Arjásp, how many kings have I slain? Did I not conquer Afrásiyáb, the greatest and bravest king that ever ruled over Túrán? And did I not also subdue the king of Hámáverán, and the Khakán of Chín? Káús, thy own ancestor, I released from the demons of Mázinderán. I slew the White Demon, and the tremendous giant, Akwán Díw. Can thy insignificant exploits be compared with mine? Never!" Rustem's vehemence, and the disdainful tone of his voice, exasperated still more the feelings of Isfendiyár, who however recollected that he was under his roof, otherwise he would have avenged himself instantly on the spot. Restraining his anger, he then said softly to him, "Wherefore dost thou raise thy voice so high? For though thy head be exalted to the skies, thou wert, and still art, but a dependent on the Káís. And was thy Heft-khan equal in terrible danger to mine? Was the capture of Mázinderán equal in valorous exertion to the capture of the Brazen Fortress? And did I not, by the power of my sword, diffuse throughout the world the blessings of my own religion, the faith of the fire-worshipper, which was derived from Heaven itself? Thou hast performed the duties of a warrior and a servant, whilst I have performed the holy functions of a sovereign and a prophet!" Rustem, in reply, said:

"In thy Heft-khan thou hadst twelve thousand men
Completely armed, with ample stores and treasure,
Whilst Rakush and my sword, my conquering sword,
Where all the aid I had, and all I sought,
In that prodigious enterprize of mine.
Two sisters thou released—no arduous task,
Whilst I recovered from the demon's grasp
The mighty Káús, and the monsters slew,
Roaring like thunder in their dismal caves.

This great exploit my single arm achieved;
And when Kai-khosráu gave the regal crown
To Lohurásp, the warriors were incensed,
And deemed Friburz, Káús's valiant son,
Fittest by birth to rule. My sire and I
Espoused the cause of Lohurásp; else he
Had never sat upon the throne, nor thou
Been here to treat with scorn thy benefactor.
And now Gushtásp, with foul ingratitude,
Would bind me hand and foot! But who on earth
Can do that office? I am not accustomed
To hear harsh terms, and cannot brook their sting,
Therefore desist. Once in Káús's court,
When I was moved to anger, I poured out
Upon him words of bitterest scorn and rage,
And though surrounded by a thousand chiefs,
Not one attempted to repress my fury,
Not one, but all stood silent and amazed."

"Smooth that indignant brow," the prince replied
"And measure not my courage nor my strength
With that of Káús; had he nerve like mine?
Thou mightst have kept the timorous king in awe,
But *I* am come myself to fetter *thee!*"
So saying, he the hand of Rustem grasped,
And wrung it so intensely, that the champion
Felt inwardly surprised, but careless said,
"The time is not yet come for us to try
Our power in battle." Then Isfendiyár
Dropped Rustem's hand, and spoke, "To-day let wine
Inspire our hearts, and on the field to-morrow
Be ours the strife, with battle-axe and sword,
And my first aim shall be to bind thee fast,
And shew thee to my troops, Rustem in fetters!"

At this the champion smiled, and thus exclaimed,
"Where hast thou seen the deeds of warriors brave?
Where hast thou heard the clash of mace and sword
Wielded by men of valour? I to-morrow
Will take thee in my arms, and straight convey thee
To Zál, and place thee on the ivory throne,
And on thy head a crown of gold shall glitter.
The treasury I will open, and our troops
Shall fight for thee, and I will gird my loins
As they were girt for thy bold ancestors;
And when thou art the chosen king, and I
Thy warrior-chief, the world will be thy own;
No other sovereign need attempt to reign."

"So much time has been spent in vain-boasting, and extravagant self-praise," rejoined Isfendiyár, "that the day is nearly done, and I am hungry; let us therefore take some refreshment together." Rustem's appetite being equally keen, the board was spread, and every dish that was brought to him he emptied at once, as if at one swallow; then he threw aside the goblets, and called for the large flagon that he might drink his fill without stint. When he had finished several dishes and as many flagons of wine, he paused, and Isfendiyár and the assembled chiefs were astonished at the quantity he had devoured. He now prepared to depart, and the prince said to him, "Go and consult with thy father: if thou art contented to be bound, well; if not, thou wilt have cause to repent, for I will assuredly attend to the commands of Gushtásp."—"Do thou also consult with thy brethren and friends," replied Rustem, "whether thou wilt be our guest to-morrow, or not; if not, come to this place before sunrise, that we may decide our differences in battle." Isfendiyár said, "My most anxious desire, my wish to heaven, is to meet thee, for I shall have no difficulty in binding thee hand and foot. I would indeed willingly convey thee without fetters to my father, but if I did so, he would say that I was unable to put thee in bonds, and that would disgrace my name." Rustem observed that the immense number of men and demons he had contended against was as nothing in the balance of his mind compared with the painful subject of his present thoughts and fears. He was ready to engage, but afraid of meriting a bad name.

"If in the battle thou art slain by me,
Will not my cheek turn pale among the princes
Of the Káiánian race, having cut off
A lovely branch of that illustrious tree?
Will not reproaches hang upon my name
When I am dead, and shall I not be cursed
For perpetrating such a horrid deed?
Thy father, too, is old, and near his end,
And thou upon the eve of being crowned;
But in thy heart thou knowest that I proffered,
And proffer my allegiance and devotion,
And would avoid the conflict. Sure, thy father
Is practising some trick, some foul deception,

To urge thee on to an untimely death,
To rid himself of some unnatural fear,
He stoops to an unnatural, treacherous act,
For I have ever been the firm support
Of crown and throne, and perfectly he knows
No mortal ever conquered me in battle,
None ever from my sword escaped his life."

Then spoke Isfendiyár: "Thou wouldst be generous
And bear a spotless name, and tarnish mine;
But I am not to be deceived by thee:
In fetters thou must go!" Rustem replied:
"Banish that idle fancy from thy brain;
Dream not of things impossible, for death
Is busy with thee; pause, or thou wilt die."
"No more!" exclaimed the prince, "no more of this.
Nor seek to frighten me with threatening words;
Go, and to-morrow bring with thee thy friends,
Thy father and thy brother, to behold
With their own eyes thy downfall, and lament
In sorrow over thy impending fate."
"So let it be," said Rustem, and at once
Mounted his noble horse, and hastened home.

The champion immediately requested his father's permission to go and fight Isfendiyár the following day, but the old man recommended reconciliation and peace. "That cannot be," said Rustem, "for he has reviled thee so severely, and heaped upon me so many indignities, that my patience is exhausted, and the contest unavoidable." In the morning Zál, weeping bitterly, tied on Rustem's armour himself, and in an agony of grief, said: "If thou shouldst kill Isfendiyár, thy name will be rendered infamous throughout the world; and if thou shouldst be killed, Sístán will be prostrate in the dust, and extinguished for ever! My heart shudders at the thoughts of this battle, but there is no remedy." Rustem said to him: "Put thy trust in God, and be not sorrowful, for when I grasp my sword the head of the enemy is lost; but my desire is to take Isfendiyár alive, and not to kill him. I would serve him, and not sever his head from his body." Zál was pleased with this determination, and rejoiced that there was a promise of a happy issue to the engagement.

In the morning Rustem arrayed himself in his war-attire,

helmet and breast-plate, and mounted Rakush, also armed in his bargustuwan. His troops, too, were all assembled, and Zál appointed Zúara to take charge of them, and be careful of his brother on all occasions where assistance might be necessary. The old man then prostrated himself in prayer, and said, "O God, turn from us all affliction, and vouchsafe to us a prosperous day." Rustem being prepared for the struggle, directed Zúara to wait with the troops at a distance, whilst he went alone to meet Isfendiyár. When Bashútan first saw him, he thought he was coming to offer terms of peace, and said to Isfendiyár, "He is coming alone, and it is better that he should go to thy father of his own accord, than in bonds."—"But," replied Isfendiyár, "he is coming completely equipped in mail—quick, bring me my arms."—"Alas!" rejoined Bashútan, "thy brain is wild, and thou art resolved upon fighting. This impetuous spirit will break my heart." But Isfendiyár took no notice of the gentle rebuke. Presently he saw Rustem ascend a high place, and heard his summons to single combat. He then told his brother to keep at a distance with the army, and not to interfere till aid was positively required. Insisting rigidly on these instructions, he mounted his night-black charger, and hastened towards Rustem, who now proposed to him that they should wait awhile, and that in the mean time the two armies might be put in motion against each other. "Though," said he, "my men of Zábul are few, and thou hast a numerous host."

"This is a strange request," replied the prince,
"But thou art all deceit and artifice;
Mark thy position, lofty and commanding,
And mine, beneath thee—in a spreading vale.
Now, Heaven forbid that I, in reckless mood,
Should give my valiant legions to destruction,
And look unpitying on! No, I advance,
Whoever may oppose me; and if thou
Requirest aid, select thy friend, and come,
For I need none, save God, in battle—none."
And Rustem said the same, for he required
No human refuge, no support but Heaven.

The battle rose, and numerous javelins whizzed
Along the air, and helm and mail were bruised;

Spear fractured spear, and then with shining swords
The strife went on, till, trenched with many a wound,
They, too, snapped short. The battle-axe was next
Wielded, in furious wrath; each bending forward
Struck brain-bewildering blows; each tried in vain
To hurl the other from his fiery horse.
Wearied, at length, they stood apart to breathe
Their chargers panting from excessive toil,
Covered with foam and blood, and the strong armour,
Of steed and rider rent. The combatants
Thus paused, in mutual consternation lost.

In the meantime Zúara, impatient at this delay, advanced towards the Iránians, and reproached them for their cowardice so severely, that Núsháwer, the younger son of Isfendiyár, felt ashamed, and immediately challenged the bravest of the enemy to fight. Alwai, one of Rustem's followers, came boldly forward, but his efforts only terminated in his discomfiture and death. After him came Zúara himself:

Who galloped to the charge incensed, and, high
Lifting his iron mace, upon the head
Of bold Núsháwer struck a furious blow,
Which drove him from his steed a lifeless corse.
Seeing their gallant leader thus o'erthrown,
The troops in terror fled, and in their flight
Thousands were slain, among them brave Mehrnús,
Another kinsman of Isfendiyár.

Bahman, observing the defeat and confusion of the Iránians, went immediately to his father, and told him that two of his own family were killed by the warriors of Zábul, who had also attacked him and put his troops to the rout with great slaughter. Isfendiyár was extremely irritated at this intelligence, and called aloud to Rustem: "Is treachery like this becoming in a warrior?" The champion being deeply concerned, shook like a branch, and swore by the head and life of the king, by the sun, and his own conquering sword, that he was ignorant of the event, and innocent of what had been done. To prove what he said, he offered to bind in fetters his brother Zúara, who must have authorized the movement; and also to secure Ferámurz, who slew Mehrnús, and deliver them over to

Gushtásp, the fire-worshipper. "Nay," said he, "I will deliver over to thee my whole family, as well as my brother and son, and thou mayest sacrifice them all as a punishment for having commenced the fight without permission." Isfendiyár replied: "Of what use would it be to sacrifice thy brother and thy son? Would that restore my own to me? No. Instead of them, I will put thee to death, therefore come on!" Accordingly both simultaneously bent their bows, and shot their arrows with the utmost rapidity; but whilst Rustem's made no impression, those of Isfendiyár produced great effect on the champion and his horse. So severely was Rakush wounded, that Rustem, when he perceived how much his favourite horse was exhausted, dismounted, and continued to impel his arrows against the enemy from behind his shield. But Rakush brooked not the dreadful storm, and galloped off unconscious that his master himself was in as bad a plight. When Zúara saw the noble animal, riderless, crossing the plain, he gasped for breath, and in an agony of grief hurried to the fatal spot, where he found Rustem desperately hurt, and the blood flowing copiously from every wound. The champion observed, that though he was himself bleeding so much, not one drop of blood appeared to have issued from the veins of his antagonist. He was very weak, but succeeded in dragging himself up to his former position, when Isfendiyár, smiling to see him thus, exclaimed:

"Is this the valiant Rustem, the renowned,
Quitting the field of battle? Where is now
The raging tiger, the victorious chief?
Was it from thee the Demons shrunk in terror,
And did thy burning sword sear out their hearts?
What has become of all thy valour now?
Where is thy matchless mace, and why art thou,
The roaring lion, turned into a fox,
An animal of slyness, not of courage,
Losing thy noble character and name?"

Zúara, when he came to Rustem, alighted and resigned his horse to his brother; and placing an arrow on his bow-string, wished himself to engage Isfendiyár, who was ready to fight him, but Rustem cried, "No, I have not yet done with thee." Isfendiyár replied: "I know thee well, and all thy dissimulation, but nothing yet is accomplished. Come and consent to be fettered, or I must compel thee." Rustem, however, was not to be overcome, and he said: "If I were really subdued by thee, I might agree to be bound like a vanquished slave; but the day is now closing, to-morrow we will resume the fight!" Isfendiyár acquiesced, and they separated, Rustem going to his own tent, and the prince remaining on the field. There he affectionately embraced the severed heads of his kinsmen, placed them himself on a bier, and sent them to his father, the king, with a letter in which he said, "Thy commands must be obeyed, and such is the result of to-day; Heaven only knows what may befall to-morrow." Then he spoke privately to Bashútan: "This Rustem is not human, he is formed of rock and iron, neither sword nor javelin has done him mortal harm; but the arrows went deep into his body, and it will indeed be wonderful if he lives throughout the night. I know not what to think of to-morrow, or how I shall be able to overcome him."

When Rustem arrived at his quarters, Zál soon discovered that he had received many wounds, which occasioned great affliction in his family, and he said: "Alas! that in my old age such a misfortune should have befallen us, and that with my own eyes I should see these gaping wounds!" He then rubbed Rustem's feet, and applied healing balm to the wounds, and bound them up with the skill and care of a physician. Rustem said to his father: "I never met with a foe, warrior or demon, of such amazing strength and bravery as this! He seems to have a brazen body, for my arrows, which I can drive through an anvil, cannot penetrate his chest. If I had applied the power which I have exerted to a mountain, the mountain would have moved from its base, but he sat firmly upon his saddle and scorned my efforts. I thank God that it is night, and that I have escaped from his grasp. To-morrow I cannot fight, and my secret wish is to retire unseen from the struggle, that no trace of me may be discovered."—"In that case," replied Zál, "the victor will come and take me and all my family into bondage. But let us not despair. Did not the Símurgh promise that whenever I might be overcome by adversity, if I burned one of her feathers, she would instantly appear? Shall we not then solicit assistance in this awful extremity?" So saying, Zál went up to a high place, and burnt the feather in a censer, and in a short time the Símurgh stood before him. After due praise and acknowledgment, he explained his wants. "But," said he, "may the misfortune we endure be far from him who has brought it upon us. My son Rustem is wounded almost unto death, and I am so helpless that I can do him no good." He then brought forward Rakush, pierced by numerous arrows; upon which the wonderful Bird said to him, "Be under no alarm on that account, for I will soon cure him;" and she immediately plucked out the rankling weapons with her beak, and the wounds, on passing a feather over them, were quickly healed.

To Rustem now she turns, and soothes his grief,
And drawing forth the arrows, sucks the blood
From out the wounds, which at her bidding close,
And the illustrious champion is restored
To life and power.

Being thus reinvigorated by the magic influence of the Símurgh, he solicits further aid in the coming strife with Isfendiyár; but the mysterious animal laments that she cannot assist him. "There never appeared in the world," said she, "so brave and so perfect a hero as Isfendiyár. The favour of Heaven is with him, for in his Heft-khan he, by some artifice, succeeded in killing a Símurgh, and the further thou art removed from his invincible arm, the greater will be thy safety." Here Zál interposed and said: "If Rustem retires from the contest, his family will all be enslaved, and I shall equally share their bondage and affliction." The Símurgh, hearing these words, fell into deep thought, and remained some time silent. At length she told Rustem to mount Rakush and follow her. Away she went to a far distance; and crossing a great river, arrived at a place covered with reeds, where the Kazú-tree abounded. The Símurgh then rubbed one of her feathers upon the eyes of Rustem, and directed him to take a branch of the Kazú-tree, and make it straight upon the fire, and form that wand into a forked arrow; after which he was to advance against Isfendiyár, and, placing the arrow on his bow-string, shoot it into the eyes of his enemy. "The arrow will only make him blind," said the Símurgh, "but he who spills the blood of Isfendiyár will never be free from calamity during his whole life. The Kazú-tree has also this peculiar quality: an arrow made of it is sure to accomplish its intended errand—it never misses the aim of the archer." Rustem expressed his boundless gratitude for this information and assistance; and the Símurgh having transported him back to his tent, and affectionately kissed his face, returned to her own habitation. The champion now prepared the arrow according to the instructions he had received; and when morning dawned, mounted his horse, and hastened to the field. He found Isfendiyár still sleeping, and exclaimed aloud: "Warrior, art thou still slumbering? Rise, and see Rustem before thee!" When the prince heard his stern voice, he started up, and in great anxiety hurried on his armour. He said to Bashútan, "I had uncharitably thought he would have died of his wounds in the night, but this clear and bold voice seems to indicate perfect health—go and see whether his wounds are bound up or not, and whether he is mounted on Rakush or on some other horse." Rustem perceived Bashútan approach with an inquisitive look, and conjectured that his object was to ascertain the condition of himself and Rakush. He therefore vociferated to him: "I am now wholly free from wounds, and so is my horse, for I possess an elixir which heals the most cruel lacerations of the flesh the moment it is applied; but no such wounds were inflicted upon me, the arrows of Isfendiyár being only like needles sticking in my body." Bashútan now reported to his brother that Rustem appeared to be more fresh and vigorous than the day before, and, thinking from the spirit and gallantry of his demeanour that he would be victorious in another contest, he strongly recommended a reconciliation.

The Death of ISFENDIYÁR.

Isfendiyár, blind to the march of fate, treated the suggestion of his brother with scorn, and mounting his horse, was soon in the presence of Rustem, whom he thus hastily addressed: "Yesterday thou wert wounded almost to death by my arrows, and to-day there is no trace of them. How is this?

> But thy father Zál is a sorcerer,
> And he by charm and spell
> Has cured all the wounds of the warrior,
> And now he is safe and well.
> For the wounds I gave could never be
> Closed up, excepting by sorcery.
> Yes, the wounds I gave thee in every part,
> Could never be cured but by magic art."

Rustem replied, "If a thousand arrows were shot at me, they would all drop harmless to the ground, and in the end thou wilt fall by my hands. Therefore, if thou seekest thy own welfare, come at once and be my guest, and I swear by the Almighty, by Zerdusht, and the Zendavesta, by the sun and moon, that I will go with thee, but unfettered, to thy father, who may do with me what he lists."—"That is not enough," replied Isfendiyár, "thou must be fettered."—"Then do not bind my arms, and take whatever thou wilt from me."—"And what hast thou to give?"

"A thousand jewels of brilliant hue.
  And of unknown price, shall be thine;
A thousand imperial diadems too,
  And a thousand damsels divine,
Who with angel-voices will sing and play,
And delight thy senses both night and day;
And my family wealth shall be brought thee, all
That was gathered by Narímán, Sám, and Zál."

"This is all in vain," said Isfendiyár. "I may have wandered from the way of Heaven, but I will not disobey the commands of the king. And of what use would thy treasure and property be to me? I must please my father, that he may surrender to me his crown and throne, and I have solemnly sworn to him that I will place thee before him in fetters." Rustem replied, "And in the hopes of a crown and throne thou wouldst sacrifice thyself!"—"Thou shalt see!" said Isfendiyár, and seized his bow to commence the combat. Rustem did the same, and when he had placed the forked arrow in the bow-string, he imploringly turned up his face towards Heaven, and fervently exclaimed, "O God, thou knowest how anxiously I have wished for a reconciliation, how I have suffered, and that I would now give all my treasures and wealth and go with him to Irán, to avoid this conflict; but my offers are disdained, for he is bent upon consigning me to bondage and disgrace. Thou art the redresser of grievances—direct the flight of this arrow into his eyes, but do not let me be punished for the involuntary deed." At this moment Isfendiyár shot an arrow with great force at Rustem, who dexterously eluded its point, and then, in return, instantly lodged the charmed weapon in the eyes of his antagonist.

And darkness overspread his sight,
The world to him was hid in night;
The bow dropped from his slackened hand,
And down he sunk upon the sand.

"Yesterday," said Rustem, "thou discharged at me a hundred and sixty arrows in vain, and now thou art overthrown by one arrow of mine." Bahman, the son of Isfendiyár, seeing his father bleeding on the ground, uttered loud lamentations, and

Bashútan, followed by the Iránian troops, also drew nigh with the deepest sorrow marked on their countenances. The fatal arrow was immediately drawn from the wounded eyes of the prince, and some medicine being first applied to them, they conveyed him mournfully to his own tent.

The conflict having thus terminated, Rustem at the same time returned with his army to where Zál remained in anxious suspense about the result. The old man rejoiced at the issue, but said, "O, my son, thou hast killed thy enemy, but I have learnt from the wise men and astrologers that the slayer of Isfendiyár must soon come to a fatal end. May God protect thee!" Rustem replied, "I am guiltless, his blood is upon his own head." The next day they both proceeded to visit Isfendiyár, and offer to him their sympathy and condolence, when the wounded prince thus spoke to Rustem: "I do not ascribe my misfortune to thee, but to an all-ruling power. Fate would have it so, and thus it is! I now consign to thy care and guardianship my son Bahman: instruct him in the science of government, the customs of kings, and the rules and stratagems of the warrior, for thou art exceedingly wise and experienced, and perfect in all things." Rustem readily complied, and said:

"That duty shall be mine alone,
To seat him firmly on the throne."

Then Isfendiyár murmured to Bashútan, that the anguish of his wound was wearing him away, and that he had but a short time to live.

"The pace of death is fast and fleet,
And nothing my life can save,
I shall want no robe, but my winding sheet,
No mansion but the grave.

And tell my father the wish of his heart
Has not been breathed in vain,
The doom he desired when he made me depart,
Has been sealed, and his son is slain!

And, O! to my mother, in kindliest tone,
The mournful tidings bear,
And soothe her woes for her warrior gone,
For her lost Isfendiyár."

He now groaned heavily, and his last words were:

"I die, pursued by unrelenting fate,
The hapless victim of a father's hate."

Life having departed, his body was placed upon a bier, and conveyed to Irán, amidst the tears and lamentations of the people.

Rustem now took charge of Bahman, according to the dying request of Isfendiyár, and brought him to Sístan. This was, however, repugnant to the wishes of Zúara, who observed to his brother: "Thou hast slain the father of this youth; do not therefore nurture and instruct the son of thy enemy, for, mark me, in the end he will be avenged."—"But did not Isfendiyár, with his last breath, consign him to my guardianship? how can I refuse it now? It must be so written and determined in the dispensations of Heaven."

The arrival of the bier in Persia, at the palace of Gushtásp, produced a melancholy scene of public and domestic affliction. The king took off the covering and wept bitterly, and the mother and sisters exclaimed, "Alas! thy death is not the work of human hands; it is not the work of Rustem, nor of Zál, but of the Símurgh. Thou hast not lived long enough to be ashamed of a grey beard, nor to witness the maturity and attainments of thy children. Alas! thou art snatched away at a moment of the highest promise, even at the commencement of thy glory." In the meanwhile the curses and imprecations of the people were poured upon the devoted head of Gushtásp on account of his cruel and unnatural conduct, so that he was obliged to confine himself to his palace till after the interment of Isfendiyár.

Rustem scrupulously fulfilled his engagement, and instructed Bahman in all manly exercises; in the use of bow and javelin, in the management of sword and buckler, and in all the arts and accomplishments of the warrior. He then wrote to Gushtásp, repeating that he was unblameable in the conflict which terminated in the death of his son Isfendiyár, that he had offered him presents and wealth to a vast extent, and moreover was ready to return with him to Irán, to his father; but every overture was rejected. Relentless fate must have hurried him on to a premature death. "I have now," continued Rustem, "completed the education of Bahman, according to the directions of his father, and await thy further commands." Gushtásp, after reading this letter, referred to Bashútan, who confirmed the declarations of Rustem, and the treacherous king, willing to ascribe the event to an overruling destiny, readily acquitted Rustem of all guilt in killing Isfendiyár. At the same time he sent for Bahman, and on his arrival from Sístan, was so pleased with him that he without hesitation appointed him to succeed to the throne.

"Methinks I see Isfendiyár again,
Thou hast the form, the very look he bore,
And since thy glorious father is no more,
Long as I live thou must with me remain."

The Death of RUSTEM.

Firdausí seems to have derived the account of Shughad, and the melancholy fate of Rustem, from a descendant of Sám and Narímán, who was particularly acquainted with the chronicles of the heroes and the kings of Persia. Shughad, it appears, was the son of Zál, by one of the old warrior's maid-servants, and at his very birth the astrologers predicted that he would be the ruin of the glorious house of Sám and Narimán, and the destruction of their race.

Throughout Sistán the prophecy was heard
With horror and amazement; every town
And city in Irán was full of woe,
And Zál, in deepest agony and grief,
Sent up his prayers to the Almighty Power
That he would purify the infant's heart,
And free it from that quality, foretold
As the destroyer of his ancient house.
But what are prayers, opposed by destiny?

The child, notwithstanding, was brought up with great care and attention, and when arrived at maturity, he was sent to the king of Kábul, whose daughter he espoused.

Rustem was accustomed to go to Kábul every year to receive the tribute due to him; but on the last occasion, it is said that he exacted and took a higher rate than usual, and thus put many of the people to distress. The king was angry, and expressed his dissatisfaction to Shughad, who was not slow in uttering his own discontent, saying, "Though I am his brother, he has no respect for me, but treats me always like an enemy. For this personal hostility I long to punish him with death."—"But how," inquired the king, "couldst thou compass that end?" Shughad replied, "I have well considered the subject, and propose to accomplish my purpose in this manner. I shall feign that I have been insulted and injured by thee, and carry my complaint to Zál and Rustem, who will no doubt come to Kábul to redress my wrongs. Thou must in the meantime prepare for a sporting excursion, and order a number of pits to be dug on the road sufficiently large to hold Rustem and his horse, and in each several swords must be placed with their points and edges upwards. The mouths of the pits must then be slightly covered over, but so carefully that there may be no appearance of the earth underneath having been removed. Everything being thus ready, Rustem, on the pretence of going to the sporting ground, must be conducted by that road, and he will certainly fall into one of the pits, which will become his grave." This stratagem was highly approved by the king, and it was agreed that at a royal banquet, Shughad should revile and irritate the king, whose indignant answer should be before all the assembly: "Thou hast no pretensions to be thought of the stock of Sám and Narímán. Zál pays thee no attention, at least, not such attention as he would pay to a son, and Rustem declares thou art not his brother; indeed, all the family treat thee as a slave." At these words, Shughad affected to be greatly enraged, and, starting up from the banquet, hastened to Rustem to complain of the insult offered him by the king of Kábul. Rustem received him with demonstrations of affection, and hearing his complaint, declared that he would immediately proceed to Kábul, depose the king for his insolence, and place Shughad himself on the throne of that country. In a short time they arrived at the city, and were met by the king, who, with naked feet and in humble guise, solicited forgiveness. Rustem was induced to pardon the offence, and was honoured in return with great apparent respect, and with boundless hospitality. In the meantime, however, the pits were dug, and the work of destruction in progress, and Rustem was now invited to sháre the sports of the forest. The champion was highly gratified by the courtesy which the king displayed, and mounted Rakush, anticipating a day of excellent diversion. Shughad accompanied him, keeping on one side, whilst Rustem, suspecting nothing, rode boldly forward. Suddenly Rakush stopped, and though urged to advance, refused to move a step. At last the champion became angry, and struck the noble animal severely; the blows made him dart forward, and in a moment he unfortunately fell into one of the pits.

It was a place, deep, dark, and perilous,
All bristled o'er with swords, leaving no chance
Of extrication without cruel wounds;
And horse and rider sinking in the midst,
Bore many a grievous stab and many a cut
In limb and body, ghastly to the sight.
Yet from that depth, at one prodigious spring,
Rakush escaped with Rustem on his back;
But what availed that effort? Down again
Into another pit both fell together,
And yet again they rose, again, again;
Seven times down prostrate, seven times bruised and
maimed,

They struggled on, till mounting up the edge
Of the seventh pit, all covered with deep wounds,
Both lay exhausted. When the champion's brain
Grew cool, and he had power to think, he knew
Full well to whom he owed this treachery,
And calling to Shughad, said : "Thou, my brother!
Why hast thou done this wrong? Was it for thee,
My father's son, by wicked plot and fraud
To work this ruin, to destroy my life?"
Shughad thus sternly answered : "'Tis for all
The blood that thou hast shed, God has decreed
This awful vengeance,—now thy time is come!"
Then spoke the king of Kábul, as if pity
Had softened his false heart : "Alas! the day
That thou shouldst perish, so ignobly too,
And in my kingdom; what a wretched fate!
But bring some medicine to relieve his wounds—
Quick, bring the matchless balm for Rustem's cure;
He must not die, the champion must not die!"
But Rustem scorned the offer, and in wrath,
Thus spoke : "How many a mighty king has died,
And left me still triumphant—still in power,
Unconquerable; treacherous thou hast been,
Inhuman, too, but Ferámurz, the brave,
Will be revenged upon thee for this crime."

Rustem now turned towards Shughad, and in an altered and mournful tone, told him that he was at the point of death, and asked him to string his bow and give it to him, that he might seem as a scare-crow, to prevent the wolves and other wild animals from devouring him when dead.

Shughad performed the task, and lingered not,
For he rejoiced at this catastrophe,
And with a smile of fiendish satisfaction,
Placed the strong bow before him—Rustem grasped
The bended horn with such an eager hand,
That wondering at the sight, the caitiff wretch
Shuddered with terror, and behind a tree
Shielded himself, but nothing could avail;
The arrow pierced both tree and him, and they
Were thus transfixed together,—thus the hour
Of death afforded one bright gleam of joy
To Rustem, who, with lifted eyes to Heaven,
Exclaimed : "Thanksgivings to the great Creator,
For granting me the power, with my own hand,
To be revenged upon my murderer!"
So saying, the great champion breathed his last,

And not a knightly follower remained,
Zúara, and the rest, in other pits,
Dug by the traitor-king, and traitor-brother,
Had sunk and perished, all, save one, who fled,
And to the afflicted veteran at Sístán
Told the sad tidings. Zál, in agony,
Tore his white hair, and wildly rent his garments,
And cried: "Why did not I die for him, why
Was I not present, fighting by his side?
But he, alas! is gone! Oh! gone for ever."

Then the old man dispatched Ferámurz with a numerous force to Kábul, to bring away the dead body of Rustem. Upon his approach, the king of Kábul and his army retired to the mountains, and Ferámurz laid waste the country. He found only the skeletons of Rustem and Zúara, the beasts of prey having stripped them of their flesh: he however gathered the bones together and conveyed them home and buried them, amidst the lamentations of the people. After that, he returned to Kábul with his army, and encountered the king, captured the cruel wretch, and carried him to Sístán, where he was put to death.

Gushtásp having become old and infirm, bequeathed his empire to Bahman, and then died. He reigned one hundred and eight years.

BAHMAN.

Bahman, the grandson of Gushtásp, having at the commencement of his sovereignty obtained the approbation of his people, by the clemency of his conduct and the apparent generosity of his disposition, was not long in meditating vindictive measures against the family of Rustem. "Did not Kai-khosráu," said he to his warriors, "revenge himself on Afrásiyáb for the murder of Saiáwush; and have not all my glorious ancestors pursued a similar course? Why, then, should not I be revenged on the father of Rustem for the death of Isfendiyár?" The warriors, as usual, approved of the king's resolution, and in consequence one hundred thousand veteran troops were assembled for the immediate invasion of Sístán. When Bahman had arrived on the borders of the river Behermund, he sent a message to Zál, frankly declaring his purpose, and that he must sacrifice the lives of himself and all his family as an atonement for Rustem's guilt in shedding the blood of Isfendiyár.

Zál heard his menace with astonishment,
Mingled with anguish, and he thus replied:
"Rustem was not in fault; and thou canst tell,
For thou wert present, how he wept, and prayed
That he might not be bound. How frequently
He offered all his wealth, his gold, and gems,
To be excused that ignominious thrall;
And would have followed thy impatient father
To wait upon Gushtásp; but this was scorned;
Nothing but bonds would satisfy his pride;
All this thou know'st. Then did not I and Rustem
Strictly fulfil Isfendiyár's commands,
And most assiduously endow thy mind
With all the skill and virtues of a hero,
That might deserve some kindness in return?
Now take my house, my treasure, my possessions,
Take all; but spare my family and me."

The messenger went back, and told the tale
Of Zál's deep grief with such persuasive grace,
And piteous accent, that the heart of Bahman
Softened at every word, and the old man
Was not to suffer. After that was known,
With gorgeous presents Zál went forth to meet
The monarch in his progress to the city;
And having prostrated himself in low
Humility, retired among the train
Attendant on the king. "Thou must not walk,"
Bahman exclaimed, well skilled in all the arts
Of smooth hypocrisy—"thou art too weak;
Remount thy horse, for thou requirest help."
But Zál declined the honour, and preferred
Doing that homage as illustrious Sám,
His conquering ancestor, had always done,
Barefoot, in presence of the royal race.

Fast moving onwards, Bahman soon approached
Sistán, and entered Zál's superb abode;
Not as a friend, or a forgiving foe,
But with a spirit unappeased, unsoothed;
True, he had spared the old man's life, but there
His mercy stopped; all else was confiscate,
For every room was plundered, all the treasure
Seized and devoted to the tyrant's use.

After remorselessly obtaining this booty, Bahman inquired what had become of Ferámurz, and Zál pretended that, unaware of the king's approach, he had gone a-hunting. But this excuse was easily seen through, and the king was so indignant on the occasion, that he put Zál himself in fetters. Ferámurz had, in fact, secretly retired with the Zábul army to a convenient distance, for the purpose of acting as necessity might require, and when he heard that Zál was placed in confinement, he immediately marched against the invader and oppressor of his country. Both armies met, and closed, and were in desperate conflict three long days and nights. On the fourth day, a tremendous hurricane arose, which blew thick clouds of dust in the face of the Zábul army, and blinding them, impeded their progress, whilst the enemy were driven furiously forward by the strong wind at their backs. The consequence was the defeat of the Zábul troops. Ferámurz, with a few companions, however, kept his ground, though assailed by showers of arrows. He tried repeatedly to get face to face with Bahman, but every effort was fruitless, and he felt convinced that his career was now nearly at an end. He bravely defended himself, and aimed his arrows with great precision; but what is the use of art when Fortune is unfavourable?

When Fate's dark clouds portentous lower,
And quench the light of day,
No effort, none, of human power,
Can chase the gloom away.
Arrows may fly a countless shower,
Amidst the desperate fray;
But not to sword or arrow death is given,
Unless decreed by favouring Heaven.

And it was so decreed that the exertions of Ferámurz should be unsuccessful. His horse fell, he was wounded severely, and whilst, insensible, the enemy secured and conveyed him in fetters to Bahman, who immediately ordered him to be hanged. The king then directed all the people of Sístán to be put to the sword; upon which Bashútan said: "Alas! why should the innocent and unoffending people be thus made to perish? Hast thou no fear of God? Thou hast taken vengeance for thy father, by slaying Ferámurz, the son of Rustem. Is not that enough? Be merciful and beneficent now to the people, and thank Heaven for the great victory thou hast gained." Bahman was thus withdrawn from his wicked purpose, and was also induced to liberate Zál, whose age and infirmities had rendered him perfectly harmless. He not only did this, but restored to him the possession of Sístán; and divesting himself of all further revenge, returned to Persia. There he continued to exercise the functions of royalty, till one day he happened to be bitten by a snake, whose venom was so excruciating, that remedies were of no avail, and he died of the wound, in the eighth year of his reign. Although he had a son named Sassán, he did not appoint him his successor; but gave the crown and the throne to his wife, Húmaí, whom he had married a short time before his death, saying: "If Húmaí should have a son, that son shall be my successor; but if a daughter, Húmaí must continue to reign."

HÚMAÍ AND THE BIRTH OF DÁRÁB.

Wisdom and generosity were said to have marked the government of Húmaí. In justice and beneficence she was unequalled. No misfortune happened in her days, even the poor and the needy became rich. She gave birth to a son, whom she entrusted to a nurse to be brought up secretly, and declared publicly that it had died the same day it was born. At this event the people rejoiced, for they were happy under the administration of Húmaí. Upon the boy attaining his seventh month, however, the queen sent for him, and wrapping him up in rich garments, put him in a box, and when she had fastened down the cover, gave it to two confidential servants, in the middle of the night, to be flung into the Euphrates. "For," thought she, "if he be found in the city, there will be an end to my authority, and the crown will be placed upon his head; wiser, therefore, will it be for me to cast him into the river; and if it please God to preserve him, he may be nurtured, and brought up in another country." Accordingly in the darkness of night, the box was thrown into the Euphrates, and it floated rapidly down the stream for some time without being observed.

Amidst the waters, in that little ark
Was launched the future monarch. But, vain mortal!
How bootless are thy most ingenious schemes,
Thy wisest projects! Such were thine, Húmaí!
Presumptuous as thou wert to think success
Would crown that deed unnatural and unjust.
But human passions, human expectations
Are happily controlled by righteous Heaven.

In the morning the ark was noticed by a washerman; who, curious to know what it contained, drew it to the shore, and opened the lid. Within the box he then saw splendid silk-embroidered scarfs and costly raiment, and upon them a lovely infant asleep. He immediately took up the child, and carried it to his wife, saying: "It was but yesterday that our own infant died, and now the Almighty has sent thee another in its place." The woman looked at the child with affection, and taking it in her arms fed it with her own milk. In the box they also found jewels and rubies, and they congratulated themselves upon being at length blessed by Providence with wealth, and a boy at the same time They called him Dáráb, and the child soon began to speak in the language of his foster-parents. The washerman and his wife, for fear that the boy and the wealth might be discovered, thought it safest to quit their home, and sojourn in another country. When Dáráb grew up, he was more skilful and accomplished, and more expert at wrestling than other boys of a greater age. But whenever the washerman told him to assist in washing clothes, he always ran away, and would not stoop to the drudgery. This untoward behaviour grieved the washerman exceedingly, and he lamented that God had given him so useless a son, not knowing that he was destined to be the sovereign of all the world.

> How little thought he, whilst the task he prest,
> A purer spirit warmed the stripling's breast,
> Whose opening soul, by kingly pride inspired,
> Disdained the toil a menial slave required;
> The royal branch on high its foliage flung,
> And showed the lofty stem from which it sprung.

Dáráb was now sent to school, and he soon excelled his naster, who continually said to the washerman: "Thy son is of wonderful capacity, acute and intelligent beyond his years, of an enlarged understanding, and will be at least the minister of a king." Dáráb requested to have another master, and also a fine horse of Irák, that he might acquire the science and accomplishments of a warrior; but the washerman replied that he was too poor to comply with his wishes, which threw the youth into despair, so that he did not touch a morsel of food for two days together. His foster-mother, deeply affected by his disappointment, and naturally anxious to gratify his desires, gave an article of value to the washerman, that he might sell it, and with the money purchase the horse required. The horse obtained, he was daily instructed in the art of using the bow, the javelin, and the sword, and in every exercise becoming a young gentleman and a warrior. So devouringly did he persevere in his studies, and in his exertions to excel, that he never remained a moment unoccupied at home or abroad. The development of his talents and genius suggested to him an inquiry who he was, and how he came into the house of a washerman; and his foster-mother, in compliance with his entreaties, described to him the manner in which he was found. He had long been miserable at the thoughts of being the son of a washerman, but now he rejoiced, and looked upon himself as the son of some person of consideration. He asked her if she had any thing that was taken out of the box, and she replied: "Two valuable rubies remain." The youth requested them to be brought to him; one he bound round his arm, and the other he sold to pay the expenses of travelling and change of place.

At that time, it is said, the king of Rúm had sent an army into the country of Irán. Upon receiving this information, Húmaí told her general, named Rishnawád, to collect a force corresponding with the emergency; and he issued a proclamation, inviting all young men desirous of military glory to flock to his standard. Dáráb heard this proclamation with delight, and among others hastened to Rishnawád, who presented the young warriors as they arrived successively to Húmaí. The queen steadfastly marked the majestic form and features of Dáráb, and said in her heart: "The youth who bears this dignified and royal aspect, appears to be a Kaiánian by birth;" and as she spoke, the instinctive feeling of a mother seemed to agitate her bosom.

The queen beheld his form and face,
The scion of a princely race;
And natural instinct seemed to move
Her heart, which spoke a mother's love;
She gazed, but like the lightning's ray,
That sudden thrill soon passed away.

The army was now in motion. After the first march, a tremendous wind and heavy rain came on, and all the soldiers were under tents, excepting Dáráb, who had none, and was obliged to take shelter from the inclemency of the weather beneath an archway, where he laid himself down, and fell asleep. Suddenly a supernatural voice was heard, saying:

"Arch stand firm, and from thy wall
Let no ruined fragment fall!
He who sleeps beneath is one
Destined to a royal throne.
Arch! a monarch claims thy care,
The king of Persia slumbers there!"

The voice was heard by every one near, and Rishnawád having also heard it, inquired of his people from whence it came. As he spoke, the voice repeated its caution:

"Arch! stand firm, and from thy wall
Let no ruined fragment fall!
Bahman's son is in thy keeping;
He beneath thy roof is sleeping.
Though the winds are loudly roaring,
And the rain in torrents pouring,
Arch! stand firm, and from thy wall
Let no loosened fragment fall."

Again Rishnawád sent other persons to ascertain from whence the voice proceeded; and they returned, saying, that it was not of the earth, but from Heaven. Again the caution sounded in his ears:

"Arch! stand firm, and from thy wall
Let no loosened fragment fall."

And his amazement increased. He now sent a person under the archway to see if any one was there, when the youth was discovered in deep sleep upon the ground, and the arch above him rent and broken in many parts. Rishnawád being apprised of this circumstance, desired that he might be awakened and brought to him. The moment he was removed, the whole of the arch fell down with a dreadful crash, and this wonderful escape was also communicated to the leader of the army, who by a strict and particular enquiry soon became acquainted with all the occurrences of the stranger's life. Rishnawád also summoned before him the washerman and his wife, and they corroborated the story he had been told. Indeed he himself recognized the ruby on Dáráb's arm, which convinced him that he was the son of Bahman, whom Húmai caused to be thrown into the Euphrates. Thus satisfied of his identity, he treated him with great honour, placed him on his right hand, and appointed him to a high command in the army. Soon afterwards an engagement took place with the Rúmís, and Dáráb in the advanced guard performed prodigies of valour. The battle lasted all day, and in the evening Rishnawád bestowed upon him the praise which he merited. Next day the army was again prepared for battle, when Dáráb proposed that the leader should remain quiet, whilst he with a chosen band of soldiers attacked the whole force of the enemy. The proposal being agreed to, he advanced with fearless impetuosity to the contest.

> With loosened rein he rushed along the field,
> And through opposing numbers hewed his path,
> Then pierced the Kulub-gáh, the centre-host,
> Where many a warrior brave, renowned in arms,
> Fell by his sword. Like sheep before a wolf
> The harassed Rúmís fled; for none had power
> To cope with his strong arm. His wondrous might
> Alone, subdued the legions right and left;
> And when, unwearied, he had fought his way
> To where great Kaisar stood, night came, and darkness,
> Shielding the trembling emperor of Rúm,
> Snatched the expected triumph from his hands.

Rishnawád was so filled with admiration at his splendid prowess, that he now offered him the most magnificent presents; but when they were exposed to his view, a suit of armour was the only thing he would accept.

The Rúmís were entirely disheartened by his valour, and they said: "We understood that the sovereign of Persia was only a woman, and that the conquest of the empire would be no difficult task; but this woman seems to be more fortunate than a warrior-king. Even her general remains inactive with the great body of his army; and a youth, with a small force, is sufficient to subdue the legions of Rúm; we had, therefore, better return to our own country." The principal warriors entertained the same sentiments, and suggested to Kaisar the necessity of retiring from the field; but the king opposed this measure, thinking it cowardly and disgraceful, and said:

"To-morrow we renew the fight,
To-morrow we shall try our might;
To-morrow, with the smiles of Heaven,
To us the victory will be given."

Accordingly on the following day the armies met again, and after a sanguinary struggle, the Persians were again triumphant. Kaísar now despaired of success, sent a messenger to Rishnawád, in which he acknowledged the aggressions he had committed, and offered to pay him whatever tribute he might require. Rishnawád readily settled the terms of the peace; and the emperor was permitted to return to his own dominions.

After this event Rishnawád sent to Húmaí intelligence of the victories he had gained, and of the surprising valour of Dáráb, transmitting to her the ruby as an evidence of his birth. Húmaí was at once convinced that he was her son, for she well remembered the day on which he was enrolled as one of her soldiers, when her heart throbbed with instinctive affection at the sight of him; and though she had unfortunately failed to question him then, she now rejoiced that he was so near being restored to her. She immediately proceeded to the Atish-gadeh, or the Fire-altar, and made an offering on the occasion; and ordering a great fire to be lighted, gave immense sums away in charity to the poor. Having called Dáráb to her presence, she went with a splendid retinue to meet him at the distance of one journey from the city; and as soon as he approached, she pressed him to her bosom, and kissed his head and eyes with the fondest affection of a mother. Upon the first day of happy omen, she relinquished in his favour the crown and the throne, after having herself reigned thirty-two years.

DÁRÁB.

When Dáráb had ascended the throne, he conducted the affairs of the kingdom with humanity, justice, and benevolence; and by these means secured the happiness of his people. He had no sooner commenced his reign, than he sent for the washerman and his wife, and enriched them by his gifts. "But," said he, "I present to you this property on these conditions—you must not give up your occupation—you must go every day, as usual, to the river-side, and wash clothes; for perhaps in process of time you may discover another box floating down the stream, containing another infant!" With these conditions the washerman complied.

Some time afterwards the kingdom was invaded by an Arabian army, consisting of one hundred thousand men, and commanded by Sháíb, a distinguished warrior. Dáráb was engaged with this army three days and three nights, and on the fourth morning the battle terminated, in consequence of Sháíb being slain. The booty was immense, and a vast number of Arabian horses fell into the hands of the victor; which, together with the quantity of treasure captured, strengthened greatly the resources of the state. The success of this campaign enabled Dáráb to extend his military operations; and having put his army in order, he proceeded against Failakús (Philip of Macedon), then king of Rúm, whom he defeated with great loss. Many were put to the sword, and the women and children carried into captivity. Failakús himself took refuge in the fortress of Amúr, from whence he sent an ambassador to Dáráb, saying, that if peace was only granted to him, he would willingly consent to any terms that might be demanded. When the ambassador arrived, Dáráb said to him: "If Failakús will bestow upon me his daughter, Nahíd, peace shall be instantly re-established between us—I require no other terms." Failakús readily agreed, and sent Nahíd with numerous splendid presents to the king of Persia, who espoused her, and took her with him to his own country. It so happened that Nahíd had an offensive breath, which was extremely disagreeable to her husband, and in consequence he directed enquiries to be made everywhere for a remedy. No place was left unexplored; at length an herb of peculiar efficacy and fragrance was discovered, which never failed to remove the imperfection complained of; and it was accordingly administered with confident hopes of success. Nahíd was desired to wash her mouth with the infused herb, and in a few days her breath became balmy and pure. When she found she was likely to become a mother she did not communicate the circumstance, but requested permission to pay a visit to her father. The request was granted; and on her arrival in Rúm she was delivered of a son. Failakús had no male offspring, and was overjoyed at this event, which he at once determined to keep unknown to Dáráb, publishing abroad that a son had been born in his house, and causing it to be understood that the child was his own. When the boy grew up, he was called Sikander; and, like Rustem, became highly accomplished in all the arts of diplomacy and war. Failakús placed him under Aristátalís, a sage of great renown, and he soon equalled his master in learning and science.

Dáráb married another wife, by whom he had another son, named Dárá; and when the youth was twenty years of age, the father died. The period of Dáráb's reign was thirty-four years.

DÁRÁ.

Dárá continued the government of the empire in the same spirit as his father; claiming custom and tribute from the inferior rulers, with similar strictness and decision. After the death of Failakús, Sikander became the king of Rúm; and refusing to pay the demanded tribute to Persia, went to war with Dárá, whom he killed in battle; the particulars of these events will be presently shown. Failakús reigned twenty-four years.

SIKANDER.

Failakús, before his death, placed the crown of sovereignty upon the head of Sikander, and appointed Aristú, who was one of the disciples of the great Aflátún, his vizír. He cautioned him to pursue the path of virtue and rectitude, and to cast from his heart every feeling of vanity and pride; above all he implored him to be just and merciful, and said:

> "Think not that thou art wise, but ignorant,
> And ever listen to advice and counsel;
> We are but dust, and from the dust created;
> And what our lives but helplessness and sorrow!"

Sikander for a time attended faithfully to the instructions of his father, and to the counsel of Aristú, both in public and private affairs.

Upon Sikander's elevation to the throne, Dárá sent an envoy to him to claim the customary tribute, but he received for answer: "The time is past when Rúm acknowledged the superiority of Persia. It is now thy turn to pay tribute to Rúm. If my demand be refused, I will immediately invade thy dominions; and think not that I shall be satisfied with the conquest of Persia alone, the whole world shall be mine; therefore prepare for war." Dárá had no alternative, not even submission, and accordingly assembled his army, for Sikander was already in full march against him. Upon the confines of Persia both armies came in sight of each other, when Sikander, in the assumed character of an envoy, was resolved to ascertain the exact condition of the enemy. With this view he entered the

Persian camp, and Dárá allowing the person whom he supposed an ambassador, to approach, enquired what message the king of Rúm had sent to him. "Hear me!" said the pretended envoy: "Sikander has not invaded thy empire for the exclusive purpose of fighting, but to know its history, its laws, and customs, from personal inspection. His object is to travel through the whole world. Why then should he make war upon thee? Give him but a free passage through thy kingdom, and nothing more is required. However if it be thy wish to proceed to hostilities, he apprehends nothing from the greatness of thy power." Dárá was astonished at the majestic air and dignity of the envoy, never having witnessed his equal, and he anxiously said:

"What is thy name, from whom art thou descended?
For that commanding front, that fearless eye,
Bespeaks illustrious birth. Art thou indeed
Sikander, whom my fancy would believe thee,
So eloquent in speech, in mien so noble?"
"No!" said the envoy, "no such rank is mine,
Sikander holds among his numerous host
Thousands superior to the humble slave
Who stands before thee. It is not for me
To put upon myself the air of kings,
To ape their manners and their lofty state."

Dárá could not help smiling, and ordered refreshments and wine to be brought. He filled a cup and gave it to the envoy, who drank it off, but did not, according to custom, return the empty goblet to the cup-bearer. The cup-bearer demanded the cup, and Dárá asked the envoy why he did not give it back. "It is the custom in my country," said the envoy, "when a cup is once given into an ambassador's hands, never to receive it back again." Dárá was still more amused by this explanation, and presented to him another cup, and successively four, which the envoy did not fail to appropriate severally in the same way. In the evening a feast was held, and Sikander partook of the delicious refreshments that had been prepared for him; but in the midst of the entertainment one of the persons present recognized him, and immediately whispered to Dárá that his enemy was in his power.

Sikander's sharp and cautious eye now marked
The changing scene, and up he sprang, but first
Snatched the four cups, and rushing from the tent,
Vaulted upon his horse, and rode away.
So instantaneous was the act, amazed
The assembly rose, and presently a troop
Was ordered in pursuit—but night, dark night,
Baffled their search, and checked their eager speed.

As soon as he reached his own army, he sent for Aristátalís and his courtiers, and exultingly displayed to them the four golden cups. "These," said he, "have I taken from my enemy, I have taken them from his own table, and before his own eyes. His strength and numbers too I have ascertained, and my success is certain." No time was now lost in arrangements for the battle. The armies engaged, and they fought seven days without a decisive blow being struck. On the eighth, Dárá was compelled to fly, and his legions, defeated and harassed, were pursued by the Rúmís with great slaughter to the banks of the Euphrates. Sikander now returned to take possession of the capital. In the meantime Dárá collected his scattered forces together, and again tried his fortune, but he was again defeated. After his second success, the conqueror devoted himself so zealously to conciliate and win the affections of the people, that they soon ceased to remember their former king with any degree of attachment to his interests. Sikander said to them: "Persia indeed is my inheritance: I am no stranger to you, for I am myself descended from Dáráb; you may therefore safely trust to my justice and paternal care, in everything that concerns your welfare." The result was, that legion after legion united in his cause, and consolidated his power.

When Dárá was informed of the universal disaffection of his army, he said to the remaining friends who were personally devoted to him: "Alas! my subjects have been deluded by the artful dissimulation and skill of Sikander; your next misfortune will be, the captivity of your wives and children. Yes, your wives and children will be made the slaves of the conquerors." A few troops, still faithful to their unfortunate king, offered to make another effort against the enemy, and Dárá was too grateful and too brave to discountenance their enthusiastic fidelity, though with such little chance of success. A fragment of an army was consequently brought into action, and the result was what had been anticipated. Dárá was again a fugitive; and after the defeat, escaped with three hundred men into the neighbouring desert. Sikander captured his wife and family, but magnanimously restored them to the unfortunate monarch, who, destitute of all further hope, now asked for a place of refuge in his own dominions, and for that he offered him all the buried treasure of his ancestors. Sikander, in reply, invited him to his presence; and promised to restore him to his throne, that he might himself be enabled to pursue other conquests; but Dárá refused to go, although advised by his nobles to accept the invitation. "I am willing to put myself to death," said he with emotion, "but I cannot submit to this degradation. I cannot go before him, and thus personally acknowledge his authority over me." Resolved upon this point, he wrote to Faúr,* one of the sovereigns of Ind, to request his assistance, and Faúr recommended that he should pay him a visit for the purpose of concerting what measures should be adopted. This correspondence having come to the knowledge of Sikander, he took care that his enemy should be intercepted in whatever direction he might proceed.

Dárá had two ministers, named Mahiyár and Jamúsipár, who, finding that according to the predictions of the astrologers their master would in a few days fall into the hands of Sikander, consulted together, and thought they had better put him to death themselves, in order that they might get into favour with Sikander. It was night, and the soldiers of the escort were dispersed at various distances, and the vizírs were stationed on each side of the king. As they travelled on, Jamúsipar took

* Faúr is probably Porus. The demand of Sikander and the answer of Faúr correspond exactly with what is said of Alexander and Porus in European history. Firdausí, however, kills him; but the Greeks make him become a friend of Alexander.

an opportunity of plunging his dagger into Dárá's side, and Mahiyár gave another blow, which felled the monarch to the ground. They immediately sent the tidings of this event to Sikander, who hastened to the spot, and the opening daylight presented to his view the wounded king.

> Dismounting quickly, he in sorrow placed
> The head of Dárá on his lap, and wept
> In bitterness of soul, to see that form
> Mangled with ghastly wounds.

Dárá still breathed; and when he lifted up his eyes and beheld Sikander, he groaned deeply. Sikander said, "Rise up, that we may convey thee to a place of safety, and apply the proper remedies to thy wounds."—"Alas!" replied Dárá, "the time for remedies is past. I leave thee to Heaven, and may thy reign give peace and happiness to the empire."—"Never," said Sikander, "never did I desire to see thee thus mangled and fallen—never to witness this sight! If the Almighty should spare thy life, thou shalt again be the monarch of Persia, and I will go from hence. On my mother's word, thou and I are sons of the same father. It is this brotherly affection which now wrings my heart!" Saying this, the tears chased each other down his cheeks in such abundance that they fell upon the face of Dárá. Again, he said, "Thy murderers shall meet with merited vengeance, they shall be punished to the uttermost." Dárá blessed him, and said, "My end is approaching, but thy sweet discourse and consoling kindness have banished all my grief. I shall now die with a mind at rest. Weep no more—

> My course is finished, thine is scarce begun;
> But hear my dying wish, my last request:
> Preserve the honour of my family,
> Preserve it from disgrace. I have a daughter
> Dearer to me than life, her name is Roshung;
> Espouse her, I beseech thee—and if Heaven
> Should bless thee with a boy, O! let his name be
> Isfendiyár, that he may propagate
> With zeal the sacred doctrines of Zerdusht,

The Zendavesta, then my soul will be
Happy in Heaven; and he, at Náu-rúz tide,
Will also hold the festival I love,
And at the altar light the Holy Fire;
Nor will he cease his labour, till the faith
Of Lohurásp be everywhere accepted,
And everywhere believed the true religion."

Sikander promised that he would assuredly fulfil the wishes he had expressed, and then Dárá placed the palm of his brother's hand on his mouth, and shortly afterwards expired. Sikander again wept bitterly, and then the body was placed on a golden couch, and he attended it in sorrow to the grave.

After the burial of Dárá, the two ministers, Jamúsipár and Mahiyár, were brought near the tomb, and executed upon the dar.

Just vengeance falls upon the guilty head,
For they their generous monarch's blood had shed.

Sikander had now no rival to the throne of Persia, and he commenced his government under the most favourable auspices. He continued the same customs and ordinances which were handed down to him, and retained every one in his established rank and occupation. He gladdened the heart by his justice and liberality. Keeping in mind his promise to Dárá, he now wrote to the mother of Roshung, and communicating to her the dying solicitations of the king, requested her to send Roshung to him, that he might fulfil the last wish of his brother. The wife of Dárá immediately complied with the command, and sent her daughter with various presents to Sikander, and she was on her arrival married to the conqueror, according to the customs and laws of the empire. Sikander loved her exceedingly, and on her account remained some time in Persia, but he at length determined to proceed into Ind to conquer that country of enchanters and enchantment.

On approaching Ind he wrote to Kaíd, summoning him to surrender his kingdom, and received from him the following answer: "I will certainly submit to thy authority, but I have four things which no other person in the world possesses, and which I cannot relinquish. I have a daughter, beautiful as an angel of Paradise, a wise minister, a skilful physician, and a goblet of inestimable value!" Upon receiving this extraordinary reply, Sikander again addressed a letter to him, in which he peremptorily required all these things immediately. Kaíd not daring to refuse, or make any attempt at evasion, reluctantly complied with the requisition. Sikander received the minister and the physician with great politeness and attention, and in the evening held a splendid feast, at which he espoused the beautiful daughter of Kaíd, and taking the goblet from her hands, drank off the wine with which it was filled. After that, Kaíd himself waited upon Sikander, and personally acknowledged his authority and dominion.

Sikander then proceeded to claim the allegiance and homage of Faúr, the king of Kanúj, and wrote to him to submit to his power; but Faúr returned a haughty answer, saying:

> "Kaíd Indí is a coward to obey thee,
> But I am Faúr, descended from a race
> Of matchless warriors; and shall I submit,
> And to a Greek!"

Sikander was highly incensed at this bold reply. The force he had now with him amounted to eighty thousand men; that is, thirty thousand Iránians, forty thousand Rúmís, and ten thousand Indís. Faúr had sixty thousand horsemen, and two thousand elephants. The troops of Sikander were greatly terrified at the sight of so many elephants, which gave the enemy such a tremendous superiority. Aristátalis, and some other ingenious counsellors, were requested to consult together to contrive some means of counteracting the power of the war-elephants, and they suggested the construction of an iron horse, and the figure of a rider also of iron, to be placed upon wheels like a carriage, and drawn by a number of horses. A soldier, clothed in iron armour, was to follow the vehicle—his hands and face besmeared with combustible matter, and this soldier, armed with a long staff, was at an appointed signal, to pierce the belly of the horse and also of the rider, previously filled with combustibles, so that when the ignited point came in contact with them, the whole engine would make a tremendous explosion and blaze in the air. Sikander approved of this invention, and collected all the blacksmiths and artizans in the country to construct a thousand machines of this description with the utmost expedition, and as soon as they were completed, he prepared for action. Faúr too pushed forward with his two thousand elephants in advance; but when the Kanújians beheld such a formidable array they were surprised, and Faúr anxiously inquired from his spies what it could be. Upon being told that it was Sikander's artillery, his troops pushed the elephants against the enemy with vigour, at which moment the combustibles were fired by the Rúmís, and the machinery exploding, many elephants were burnt and destroyed, and the remainder, with the troops, fled in confusion. Sikander then encountered Faúr, and after a severe contest, slew him, and became ruler of the kingdom of Kanúj.

After the conquest of Kanúj, Sikander went to Mekka, carrying thither rich presents and offerings. From thence he proceeded to another city, where he was received with great homage by the most illustrious of the nation. He inquired of them if there was anything wonderful or extraordinary in their country, that he might go to see it, and they replied that there were two trees in the kingdom, one a male, the other a female, from which a voice proceeded. The male-tree spoke in the day, and the female-tree in the night, and whoever had a wish, went thither to have his desires accomplished. Sikander immediately repaired to the spot, and approaching it, he hoped in his heart that a considerable part of his life still remained to be enjoyed. When he came under the tree, a terrible sound arose and rung in his ears, and he asked the people present what it meant. The attendant priest said it implied that fourteen years of his life still remained. Sikander, at this interpretation of the prophetic sound, wept, and the burning tears ran down his cheeks. Again he asked, "Shall I return to Rúm, and see my mother and children before I die?" and the answer was, "Thou wilt die at Kashán.*

Nor mother, nor thy family at home
Wilt thou behold again, for thou wilt die,
Closing thy course of glory at Kashán."

Sikander left the place in sorrow, and pursued his way towards Rúm. In his progress he arrived at another city, and the inhabitants gave him the most honourable welcome, representing to him, however, that they were dreadfully afflicted by the presence of two demons or giants; who constantly assailed them in the night, devouring men and goats and whatever came in their way. Sikander asked their names; and they replied, Yájúj and Májúj (Gog and Magog). He immediately ordered a barrier to be erected five hundred yards high, and three hundred yards wide, and when it was finished he went away. The giants, notwithstanding all their efforts, were unable to scale this barrier, and in consequence the inhabitants pursued their occupations without the fear of molestation.

To scenes of noble daring still he turned
His ardent spirit—for he knew not fear.
Still he led on his legions—and now came
To a strange place, where countless numbers met
His wondering view—countless inhabitants
Crowding the city streets, and neighbouring plains;
And in the distance presently he saw
A lofty mountain reaching to the stars.
Onward proceeding, at its foot he found
A guardian-dragon, terrible in form,—
Ready with open jaws to crush his victim;
But unappalled, Sikander him beholding
With steady eye, which scorned to turn aside,
Sprang forward, and at once the monster slew.

Ascending then the mountain, many a ridge,
Oft resting on the way, he reached the summit,
Where the dead corse of an old saint appeared

---

* Kashán is here made to be the death-place of Alexander, whilst, according to the Greek historians, he died suddenly at Babylon, as foretold by the magicians, on the 21st April, B.C. 323, in the 32nd year of his age.

Wrapt in his grave-clothes, and in gems imbedded,
In gold and precious jewels glittering round,
Seeming to show what man is, mortal man!
Wealth, worldly pomp, the baubles of ambition,
All left behind, himself a heap of dust!

None ever went upon that mountain top,
But sought for knowledge; and Sikander hoped
When he had reached its cloudy eminence,
To see the visions of futurity
Arise from that departed, holy man!
And soon he heard a voice: "Thy time is nigh!
Yet may I thy career on earth unfold.
It will be thine to conquer many a realm,
Win many a crown; thou wilt have many friends
And numerous foes, and thy devoted head
Will be uplifted to the very heavens.
Renowned and glorious shalt thou be; thy name
Immortal; but, alas! thy time is nigh!"
At these prophetic words Sikander wept,
And from that ominous mountain hastened down.

After that Sikander journeyed on to the city of Kashán, where he fell sick, and in a few days, according to the oracle and the prophecy, expired. He had scarcely breathed his last, when Aristú, and Bilniyás the physician, and his family, entered Kashán, and found him dead. They beat their faces, and tore their hair, and mourned for him forty days.

The remainder of the Sháh Námeh contains nothing striking either in a poetical or historical point of view, and indeed presents little more than an enumeration of the kings who reigned in Persia from the time of Sikander to that of Yesdjird, embracing among others, the names of Ardshír, Shahpúr, Bahram Gór, Núshervân, and Khosrú Purvíz.

FIRDAUSÍ'S INVOCATION.

THEE I invoke, the Lord of Life and Light!
Beyond imagination pure and bright!
To thee, sufficing praise no tongue can give,
We are thy creatures, and in thee we live!
Thou art the summit, depth, the all in all,
Creator, Guardian of this earthly ball;
Whatever is, thou art—Protector, King,
From thee all goodness, truth, and mercy spring.
O pardon the misdeeds of him who now
Bends in thy presence with a suppliant brow.
Teach him to tread the path thy Prophet trod;
To wash his heart from sin, to know his God;
And gently lead him to that home of rest,
Where filled with holiest rapture dwell the blest.

Saith not that book divine, from Heaven supplied,
"Mustafa is the true, the unerring guide,
The purest, greatest Prophet!" Next him came
Wise Abú Buker, of unblemished name;
Then Omer taught the faith, unknown to guile,
And made the world with vernal freshness smile;
Then Othmán brave th' imperial priesthood graced;
All, led by him, the Prophet's faith embraced.
The fourth was Alí; he, the spouse adored
Of Fatima, then spread the saving word.
Alí, of whom Mahommed spoke elate,
"I am the city of knowledge—he my gate."
Alí the blest. Whoever shall recline
A supplicant at his all-powerful shrine,
Enjoys both this life and the next; in this,
All earthly good, in that, eternal bliss!

From records true my legends I rehearse,

And string the pearls of wisdom in my verse,
That in the glimmering days of life's decline,
Its fruits, in wealth and honour, may be mine.
My verse, a structure pointing to the skies;
Whose solid strength destroying time defies.
All praise the noble work, save only those
Of impious life, or base malignant foes;
All blest with learning read, and read again,
The sovereign smiles, and thus approves my strain:
"Richer by far, Firdausí, than a mine
Of precious gems, is this bright lay of thine."
Centuries may pass away, but still my page
Will be the boast of each succeeding age.

Praise, praise to Máhmúd, who of like renown,
In battle or the banquet, fills the throne;
Lord of the realms of Chín and Hindústan,
Sovereign and Lord of Persia and Túrán,
With his loud voice he rends the flintiest ear;
On land a tiger fierce, untouched by fear,
And on the wave, he seems the crocodile
That prowls amidst the waters of the Nile.
Generous and brave, his equal is unknown;
In deeds of princely worth he stands alone.
The infant in the cradle lisps his name;
The world exults in Máhmúd's spotless fame.
In festive hours Heaven smiles upon his truth;
In combat deadly as the dragon's tooth;
Bounteous in all things, his exhaustless hand
Diffuses blessings through the grateful land;
And, of the noblest thoughts and actions, lord;
The soul of Gabriel breathes in every word.
May Heaven with added glory crown his days;
Praise, praise to mighty Máhmúd—everlasting praise!

FIRDAUSÍ'S SATIRE ON MÁHMÚD.

Know, tyrant as thou art, this earthly state
Is not eternal, but of transient date;
Fear God, then, and afflict not human-kind;
To merit Heaven, be thou to Heaven resigned.
Afflict not even the Ant; though weak and small,
It breathes and lives, and life is sweet to all.
Knowing my temper, firm, and stern, and bold,
Did'st thou not, tyrant, tremble to behold
My sword blood-dropping? Had'st thou not the sense
To shrink from giving man like me offence?
What could impel thee to an act so base?
What, but to earn and prove thy own disgrace?
Why was I sentenced to be trod upon,
And crushed to death by elephants? By one
Whose power I scorn! Could'st thou presume that I
Would be appalled by thee, whom I defy?
I am the lion, I, inured to blood,
And make the impious and the base my food;
And I could grind thy limbs, and spread them far
As Nile's dark waters their rich treasures bear.
Fear thee! I fear not man, but God alone,
I only bow to his Almighty throne.
Inspired by Him my ready numbers flow;
Guarded by Him I dread no earthly foe.
Thus in the pride of song I pass my days,
Offering to Heaven my gratitude and praise.

From every trace of sense and feeling free,
When thou art dead, what will become of thee?
If thou shouldst tear me limb from limb, and cast
My dust and ashes to the angry blast,
Firdausí still would live, since on thy name,
Máhmúd, I did not rest my hopes of fame

In the bright page of my heroic song,
But on the God of Heaven, to whom belong
Boundless thanksgivings, and on Him whose love
Supports the Faithful in the realms above,
The mighty Prophet! none who e'er reposed
On Him, existence without hope has closed.

And thou would'st hurl me underneath the tread
Of the wild elephant, till I were dead!
Dead! by that insult roused, I should become
An elephant in power, and seal thy doom—
Máhmúd! if fear of man hath never awed
Thy heart, at least fear thy Creator, God.
Full many a warrior of illustrious worth,
Full many of humble, of imperial birth:
Túr, Selím, Jemshíd, Minúchihr the brave,
Have died; for nothing had the power to save
These mighty monarchs from the common doom;
They died, but blest in memory still they bloom.
Thus kings too perish—none on earth remain,
Since all things human seek the dust again.

O, had thy father graced a kingly throne,
Thy mother been for royal virtues known,
A different fate the poet then had shared,
Honours and wealth had been his just reward;
But how remote from thee a glorious line!
No high, ennobling ancestry is thine;
From a vile stock thy bold career began,
A Blacksmith was thy sire of Isfahán.
Alas! from vice can goodness ever spring?
Is mercy hoped for in a tyrant king?
Can water wash the Ethiopian white?
Can we remove the darkness from the night?
The tree to which a bitter fruit is given,
Would still be bitter in the bowers of Heaven;

And a bad heart keeps on its vicious course;
Or if it changes, changes for the worse;
Whilst streams of milk, where Eden's flowrets blow,
Acquire more honied sweetness as they flow.
The reckless king who grinds the poor like thee,
Must ever be consigned to infamy!

Now mark Firdausí's strain, his Book of Kings
Will ever soar upon triumphant wings.
All who have listened to its various lore
Rejoice, the wise grow wiser than before;
Heroes of other times, of ancient days,
For ever flourish in my sounding lays;
Have I not sung of Káús, Tús, and Gíw;
Of matchless Rustem, faithful, still, and true.
Of the great Demon-binder, who could throw
His kamund to the Heavens, and seize his foe!
Of Húsheng, Feridún, and Sám Suwár,
Lohurásp, Kai-khosráu, and Isfendiyár;
Gushtásp, Arjásp, and him of mighty name,
Gúdarz, with eighty sons of martial fame!

The toil of thirty years is now complete,
Recórd sublime of many a warlike feat,
Written midst toil and trouble, but the strain
Awakens every heart, and will remain
A lasting stimulus to glorious deeds;
For even the bashful maid, who kindling reads,
Becomes a warrior. Thirty years of care,
Urged on by royal promise, did I bear,
And now, deceived and scorned, the aged bard
Is basely cheated of his pledged reward!

THE STORY OF SOHRÁB.

The following is the translation of the story of Sohráb mentioned in the Preface, and abridged in the body of the work. It forms perhaps one of the most beautiful and interesting episodes in the Sháh Námeh. Had the poet been able to depict the nicer varieties of emotion and passion, the more refined workings of the mind under the influence of disappointment, love, and despair, the poem would have been still more deserving of praise. But, as Dr. Johnson observes of Milton, "he knew human nature only in the gross, and had never studied the shades of character, nor the combinations of concurring, or the perplexity of contending passions;" yet is there much to admire. Sir William Jones had planned a tragedy of Sohráb, and intended to have arranged it with a chorus of the Magi, or Fire-worshippers, but it was found unfinished at the time of his death.

It may be here observed, that the rules of poetical translation are now pretty generally understood. Even in European languages, which are not essentially dissimilar in idiom and imagery, considerable latitude of expression is always allowed. Those who best know the peculiarities of the Persian will acknowledge how requisite it is to adopt a still greater freedom of interpretation in conveying Eastern notions into English verse. I have consequently paid more attention to sentiments than words, to ideas than expressions, avoiding all the repetitions and redundancies which could not be preserved with any degree of success; for it was incumbent upon me to keep in mind that I was writing a poem in English, and that English-Persian will no more do than English-Greek. It was said of Dacier, respecting his translation of Plutarch, that "his book was not found to be French-Greek. He had carefully followed that rule, which no translator ought to lose sight of, the great rule of humouring the genius, and maintaining the structure, of his own language."

SOHRÁB.

O YE, who dwell in Youth's inviting bowers,
Waste not, in useless joy, your fleeting hours,
But rather let the tears of sorrow roll,
And sad reflexion fill the conscious soul.
For many a jocund spring has passed away,
And many a flower has blossomed, to decay;
And human life, still hastening to a close,
Finds in the worthless dust its last repose.
Still the vain world abounds in strife and hate,
And sire and son provoke each other's fate;
And kindred blood by kindred hands is shed,
And vengeance sleeps not—dies not, with the dead.
All nature fades—the garden's treasures fall,
Young bud, and citron ripe—all perish, all.
And now a tale of sorrow must be told,
A tale of tears, derived from Múbid old,
And thus remembered.—
With the dawn of day,
Rustem arose, and wandering took his way,
Armed for the chase, where sloping to the sky,
Túrán's lone wilds in sullen grandeur lie;
There, to dispel his melancholy mood,
He urged his matchless steed through glen and wood.
Flushed with the noble game which met his view,
He starts the wild-ass o'er the glistening dew;
And, oft exulting, sees his quivering dart,
Plunge through the glossy skin, and pierce the heart.—
Tired of the sport, at length, he sought the shade,
Which near a stream embowering trees displayed,
And with his arrow's point, a fire he raised,
And thorns and grass before him quickly blazed.
The severed parts upon a bough he cast,
To catch the flames; and when the rich repast
Was drest; with flesh and marrow, savory food,

He quelled his hunger; and the sparkling flood
That murmured at his feet, his thirst represt;
Then gentle sleep composed his limbs to rest.
Meanwhile his horse, for speed and form renown'd,
Ranged o'er the plain with flowery herbage crown'd,
Encumbering arms no more his sides opprest,
No folding mail confined his ample chest,*
Gallant and free, he left the Champion's side,
And cropp'd the mead, or sought the cooling tide;
When lo! it chanced amid that woodland chase,
A band of horsemen, rambling near the place,
Saw, with surprise, superior game astray,
And rushed at once to seize the noble prey;
But, in the imminent struggle, two beneath
His steel-clad hoofs received the stroke of death;
One proved a sterner fate—for downward borne,
The mangled head was from the shoulders torn.
Still undismayed, again they nimbly sprung,
And round his neck the noose entangling flung:
Now, all in vain, he spurns the smoking ground,
In vain the tumult echoes all around;
They bear him off, and view, with ardent eyes,
His matchless beauty and majestic size;
Then soothe his fury, anxious to obtain,
A bounding steed of his immortal strain.
When Rustem woke, and miss'd his favorite horse,
The loved companion of his glorious course;
Sorrowing he rose, and, hastening thence, began
To shape his dubious way to Samengán;
"Reduced to journey thus, alone!" he said,
"How pierce the gloom which thickens round my head;
"Burthen'd, on foot, a dreary waste in view,
"Where shall I bend my steps, what path pursue?

* The armour called Burgustuwan almost covered the horse, and was usually made of leather and felt-cloth.

"The scoffing Túrks will cry, 'Behold our might!
"'We won the trophy from the Champion-knight!
"'From him who, reckless of his fame and pride,
"'Thus idly slept, and thus ignobly died.'"
Girding his loins he gathered from the field,
His quivered stores, his beamy sword and shield,
Harness and saddle-gear were o'er him slung,
Bridle and mail across his shoulders hung.*
Then looking round, with anxious eye, to meet,
The broad impression of his charger's feet,†
The track he hail'd, and following, onward prest,
While grief and hope alternate filled his breast.
  O'er vale and wild-wood led, he soon descries,
The regal city's shining turrets rise.
And when the Champion's near approach is known,
The usual homage waits him to the throne.
The king, on foot, received his welcome guest
With proffered friendship, and his coming blest:
But Rustem frowned, and with resentment fired,
Spoke of his wrongs, the plundered steed required.
"I've traced his footsteps to your royal town,
"Here must he be, protected by your crown;
"But if retained, if not from fetters freed,
"My vengeance shall o'ertake the felon-deed."

* In this hunting excursion he is completely armed, being supplied with spear, sword, shield, mace, bow and arrows. Like the knight-errants of after times, he seldom even slept unarmed. Single combat and the romantic enterprises of European Chivalry may indeed be traced to the East. Rustem was a most illustrious example of all that is pious, disinterested, and heroic. The adventure now describing is highly characteristic of a chivalrous age. In the Dissertation prefixed to Richardson's Dictionary, mention is made of a famous Arabian Knight-errant called Abu Mahommud Albatal, "who wandered every where in quest of adventures, and redressing grievances. He was killed in the year 738."

† See the Story of the Horse in Zadig, which is doubtless of Oriental origin. In the upper parts of Hindustan, it is said that the people are exceedingly expert in discovering robbers by tracing the marks of their horses' feet. These mounted robbers are called Kussaks. The Russian *Cossack* is probably derived from the same word.

"My honored guest!" the wondering King replied,—
"Shall Rustem's wants or wishes be denied?
"But let not anger, headlong, fierce, and blind,
"O'ercloud the virtues of a generous mind.
"If still within the limits of my reign,
"The well known courser shall be thine again:
"For Rakush never can remain concealed,
"No more than Rustem in the battle-field!
"Then cease to nourish useless rage, and share
"With joyous heart my hospitable fare."
The son of Zál now felt his wrath subdued,
And glad sensations in his soul renewed.
The ready herald by the King's command,
Convened the Chiefs and Warriors of the land; *
And soon the banquet social glee restored,
And China wine-cups glittered on the board;
And cheerful song, and music's magic power,
And sparkling wine, beguiled the festive hour.†
The dulcet draughts o'er Rustem's senses stole,
And melting strains absorbed his softened soul.
But when approached the period of repose,
All, prompt and mindful, from the banquet rose;
A couch was spread well worthy such a guest,
Perfumed with rose and musk; and whilst at rest,
In deep sound sleep, the wearied Champion lay,
Forgot were all the sorrows of the way.
One watch had passed, and still sweet slumber shed
Its magic power around the hero's head—

* Thus Alcinous convenes the chiefs of Phæacia in honour of Ulysses.

† The original gives to the singers black eyes and cheeks like roses. These women are generally known by the term Lúlían, perhaps referring to their beauty, as Lúlú signifies a pearl, a gem, a jewel; though Lúlú is also the name of a people or tribe of Persia.

Thus Hafiz:

"Oh, these wanton damsels, flatterers, and disturbers of the city."

The guests drank "grief-removing wine." The Nepenthe of Homer.—Odyssey, iv. 221.

When forth Tahmíneh came,—a damsel held
An amber taper, which the gloom dispelled,
And near his pillow stood; in beauty bright,
The monarch's daughter struck his wondering sight.
Clear as the moon, in glowing charms arrayed,
Her winning eyes the light of heaven displayed;
Her cypress form entranced the gazer's view,*
Her waving curls, the heart, resistless, drew,
Her eye-brows like the Archer's bended bow;
Her ringlets, snares; her cheek, the rose's glow,†
Mixed with the lily,—from her ear-tips hung
Rings rich and glittering, star-like; and her tongue,
And lips, all sugared sweetness—pearls the while
Sparkled within a mouth formed to beguile.
Her presence dimmed the stars, and breathing round
Fragrance and joy, she scarcely touched the ground,‡
So light her step, so graceful—every part
Perfect, and suited to her spotless heart.
  Rustem, surprised, the gentle maid addressed,
And asked what lovely stranger broke his rest.
"What is thy name," he said,—"what dost thou seek
"Amidst the gloom of night? Fair vision speak!"
  "O thou," she softly sigh'd, "of matchless fame!
"With pity hear, Tahmíneh is my name!

* Theocritus in Idyllium, xviii. 30, compares Helen to the Cypress, but with us, the Cypress is uniformly consecrated to sorrow, amongst the Asiatics to joy and gladness.

† "Ensnaring ringlets." Thus Shakspeare;

Here in her hairs,
The painter plays the Spider—and hath woven
A golden mesh to entrap the hearts of men,
Faster than gnats in cobwebs: But her eyes!
MERCHANT OF VENICE, iii., 2.

‡ Beauty and fragrance are amongst the poets inseparable. The Persians exceed even the Greeks in their love of perfume, though Anacreon thought it so indispensable a part of beauty, that in directing the Rhodian Artist to paint the mistress of his heart, he wishes even her fragrance to be pourtrayed.

"The pangs of love my anxious heart employ,
"And flattering promise long-expected joy;
"No curious eye has yet these features seen,
"My voice unheard, beyond the sacred screen.*
"How often have I listened with amaze,
"To thy great deeds, enamoured of thy praise;
"How oft from every tongue I've heard the strain,
"And thought of thee—and sighed, and sighed again.
"The ravenous eagle, hovering o'er his prey,
"Starts at thy gleaming sword and flies away:
"Thou art the slayer of the Demon brood,
"And the fierce monsters of the echoing wood.
"Where'er thy mace is seen, shrink back the bold,
"Thy javelin's flash all tremble to behold.
"Enchanted with the stories of thy fame,
"My fluttering heart responded to thy name;
"And whilst their magic influence I felt,
"In prayer for thee devotedly I knelt;
"And fervent vowed, thus powerful glory charms,
"No other spouse should bless my longing arms.†

* As a proof of her innocence Tahmíneh declares to Rustem, "No person has ever seen me out of my private chamber, or even heard the sound of my voice." It is but just to remark, that the seclusion in which women of rank continue in Persia, and other parts of the East, is not, by them, considered intolerable, or even a hardship. Custom has not only rendered it familiar, but happy. It has nothing of the unprofitable severity of the cloister. The Zenanas are supplied with every thing that can please and gratify a reasonable wish, and it is well known that the women of the east have influence and power, more flattering and solid, than the free unsecluded beauties of the western world.

† Distinguished valour and achievements in war have always commanded admiration, and there are many instances in which women have, like Tahmíneh, fallen in love with a hero's glory. Josephus has recorded that the king's daughter betrayed the city of Saba, in Ethiopia, into the hands of Moses, having become enamoured of him by seeing from the walls the valour and bravery which he displayed at the head of the Egyptian army. Dido was won by the celebrity of Æneas. Kotzebue has drawn Elvira enamoured of the fame and glory of Pizarro. Her passion is described with great strength and feeling. When at last she discovers the savage, the merciless disposition of the conqueror, she thus addresses him. "Thinkest thou that *my* love will

"Indulgent heaven propitious to my prayer,
"Now brings thee hither to reward my care.
"Túrán's dominions thou hast sought, alone,
"By night, in darkness—thou, the mighty one!
"O claim my hand, and grant my soul's desire;
"Ask me in marriage of my royal sire;
"Perhaps a boy our wedded love may crown,
"Whose strength like thine may gain the world's renown.
"Nay more—for Samengán will keep my word,—
"Rakush to thee again shall be restored."
  The damsel thus her ardent thought expressed,
And Rustem's heart beat joyous in his breast,
Hearing her passion—not a word was lost,
And Rakush safe, by him still valued most;
He called her near; with graceful step she came,
And marked with throbbing pulse his kindled flame.
  And now a Múbid, from the Champion-knight,
Requests the royal sanction to the rite;*
O'erjoyed, the king the honoured suit approves,
O'erjoyed to bless the doting child he loves,
And happier still, in showering smiles around,
To be allied to warrior so renowned.

survive *thy* fame? No! *thy* glory is *my* idol! I *now* find thee a deception, and Elvira is lost to thee for ever!"

The lovely Desdemona affords another instance.

Oth. Her father loved me; oft invited me;
Still questioned me the story of my life,
From year to year; the battles, sieges, fortunes,
That I had passed.
I ran it through even from my boyish days,
Wherein I spoke of most disastrous chances,
Of moving accidents by flood and field.
She wished she had not heard it: yet she wished,
That heaven had made her such a man; she thanked me:
She loved me for the dangers I had passed;
And I loved her that she did pity them. OTHELLO, act i. sc. 3.

* The marriage ceremony was performed conformably to the laws of the country. There was nothing of,

Conjugium vocat: hoc prætexit nomine culpam.
VIRGIL, Æn. iv. 172.

When the delighted father, doubly blest,
Resigned his daughter to his glorious guest,
The people shared the gladness which it gave,
The union of the beauteous and the brave.
To grace their nuptial day—both old and young,
The hymeneal gratulations sung:
"May this young moon bring happiness and joy,
"And every source of enmity destroy."
The marriage-bower received the happy pair,
And love and transport shower'd their blessings there.
Ere from his lofty sphere the morn had thrown
His glittering radiance, and in splendour shone,
The mindful Champion, from his sinewy arm,
His bracelet drew, the soul-ennobling charm;
And, as he held the wondrous gift with pride,
He thus address'd his love-devoted bride!
"Take this," he said, "and if, by gracious heaven,
"A daughter for thy solace should be given,
"Let it among her ringlets be displayed,
"And joy and honour will await the maid;
"But should kind fate increase the nuptial-joy,
"And make thee mother of a blooming boy,
"Around his arm this magic bracelet bind,
"To fire with virtuous deeds his ripening mind;
"The strength of Sám will nerve his manly form,
"In temper mild, in valour like the storm;
"His not the dastard fate to shrink, or turn
"From where the lions of the battle burn;
"To him the soaring eagle from the sky
"Will stoop, the bravest yield to him, or fly;
"Thus shall his bright career imperious claim
"The well-won honours of immortal fame!"
Ardent he said, and kissed her eyes and face,
And lingering held her in a fond embrace.
When the bright sun his radiant brow displayed,
And earth in all its loveliest hues arrayed,

The Champion rose to leave his spouse's side,
The warm affections of his weeping bride.
For her, too soon the winged moments flew,
Too soon, alas! the parting hour she knew;
Clasped in his arms, with many a streaming tear,
She tried, in vain, to win his deafen'd ear;
Still tried, ah fruitless struggle! to impart,
The swelling anguish of her bursting heart.
  The father now with gratulations due
Rustem approaches, and displays to view
The fiery war-horse,—welcome as the light
Of heaven, to one immersed in deepest night;
The Champion, wild with joy, fits on the rein,
And girds the saddle on his back again;
Then mounts, and leaving sire and wife behind,
Onward to Sístán rushes like the wind.
  But when returned to Zábul's friendly shade,
None knew what joys the Warrior had delayed;
Still, fond remembrance, with endearing thought,
Oft to his mind the scene of rapture brought.*
  When nine slow-circling months had roll'd away,
Sweet-smiling pleasure hailed the brightening day—
A wondrous boy Tahmíneh's tears supprest,
And lull'd the sorrows of her heart to rest;
To him, predestined to be great and brave,
The name Sohráb his tender mother gave;
And as he grew, amazed, the gathering throng,
View'd his large limbs, his sinews firm and strong;
His infant years no soft endearment claimed:
Athletic sports his eager soul inflamed;
Broad at the chest and taper round the loins,
Where to the rising hip the body joins;
Hunter and wrestler; and so great his speed,
He could o'ertake, and hold the swiftest steed.

* In the Argonautics of Appollonius Rhodius, the tender parting of Jason and Hypsipyle, is very similar to that of Rustem and Tahmíneh.

His noble aspect, and majestic grace,
Betrayed the offspring of a glorious race.
How, with a mother's ever anxious love,
Still to retain him near her heart she strove!
For when the father's fond inquiry came,
Cautious, she still concealed his birth and name,
And feign'd a daughter born, the evil fraught
With misery to avert—but vain the thought;
Not many years had passed, with downy flight,
Ere he, Tahmíneh's wonder and delight,
With glistening eye, and youthful ardour warm,
Filled her foreboding bosom with alarm.
"O now relieve my heart!" he said, "declare,
"From whom I sprang and breathe the vital air.
"Since, from my childhood I have ever been,
"Amidst my play-mates of superior mien;
"Should friend or foe demand my father's name,
"Let not my silence testify my shame!
"If still concealed, you falter, still delay,
"A mother's blood shall wash the crime away."
"This wrath forego," the mother answering cried,
"And joyful hear to whom thou art allied.
"A glorious line precedes thy destined birth,
"The mightiest heroes of the sons of earth.
"The deeds of Sám remotest realms admire,
"And Zál, and Rustem thy illustrious sire!"
In private, then, she Rustem's letter placed
Before his view, and brought with eager haste
Three sparkling rubies, wedges three of gold,
From Persia sent—"Behold," she said, "behold
"Thy father's gifts, will these thy doubts remove
"The costly pledges of paternal love!
"Behold this bracelet charm, of sovereign power
"To baffle fate in danger's awful hour;
"But thou must still the perilous secret keep,
"Nor ask the harvest of renown to reap;

"For when, by this peculiar signet known,
"Thy glorious father shall demand his son,
"Doomed from her only joy in life to part,
"O think what pangs will rend thy mother's heart!—
"Seek not the fame which only teems with woe;
"Afrásiyáb is Rustem's deadliest foe!
"And if by him discovered, him I dread,
"Revenge will fall upon thy guiltless head."
The youth replied: "In vain thy sighs and tears,
"The secret breathes and mocks thy idle fears.
"No human power can fate's decrees control,
"Or check the kindled ardour of my soul.
"Then why from me the bursting truth conceal?
"My father's foes even now my vengeance feel;
"Even now in wrath my native legions rise,
"And sounds of desolation strike the skies;
"Káús himself, hurled from his ivory throne,
"Shall yield to Rustem the imperial crown,
"And thou, my mother, still in triumph seen,
"Of lovely Persia hailed the honoured queen!
"Then shall Túrán unite beneath my hand,
"And drive this proud oppressor from the land!
"Father and Son, in virtuous league combined,
"No savage despot shall enslave mankind;
"When Sun and Moon o'er heaven refulgent blaze,
"Shall little Stars obtrude their feeble rays?*

* In Percy's Collection, there is an old song which contains a similar idea.

You meaner beauties of the night,
That poorly satisfie our eies,
More by your number, than your light;
You common people of the skies,
What are you when the Moon shall rise?
Sir Henry Wotton.

Thus Lucretius, speaking of Epicurus.

Qui genus humanum ingenio superavit, et omneis
Præstinxit, stellas exortus uti ætherius Sol.
De Rer. Nat. III. 1056.

He paused, and then; "O mother, I must now
"My father seek, and see his lofty brow;
"Be mine a horse, such as a prince demands,
"Fit for the dusty field, a warrior's hands;
"Strong as an elephant his form should be,
"And chested like the stag, in motion free,
"And swift as bird, or fish; it would disgrace
"A warrior bold on foot to show his face."
The mother, seeing how his heart was bent,
His day-star rising in the firmament,
Commands the stables to be searched to find
Among the steeds one suited to his mind;
Pressing their backs he tries their strength and nerve,
Bent double to the ground their bellies curve;
Not one, from neighbouring plain and mountain brought,
Equals the wish with which his soul is fraught;
Fruitless on every side he anxious turns,
Fruitless, his brain with wild impatience burns,
But when at length they bring the destined steed,
From Rakush bred, of lightning's winged speed,
Fleet, as the arrow from the bow-string flies,
Fleet, as the eagle darting through the skies,
Rejoiced he springs, and, with a nimble bound,
Vaults in his seat, and wheels the courser round;
"With such a horse—thus mounted, what remains?
"Káús, the Persian King, no longer reigns!"
High flushed he speaks—with youthful pride elate,
Eager to crush the Monarch's glittering state;
He grasps his javelin with a hero's might,
And pants with ardour for the field of fight.
Soon o'er the realm his fame expanding spread,
And gathering thousands hasten'd to his aid.
His Grand-sire, pleased, beheld the warrior-train
Successive throng and darken all the plain;
And bounteously his treasures he supplied,
Camels, and steeds, and gold.—In martial pride,

Sohráb was seen—a Grecian helmet graced
His brow—and costliest mail his limbs embraced.
Afrásiyáb now hears with ardent joy,
The bold ambition of the warrior-boy,
Of him who, perfumed with the milky breath
Of infancy, was threatening war and death,
And bursting sudden from his mother's side,
Had launched his bark upon the perilous tide.
The insidious King sees well the tempting hour,
Favouring his arms against the Persian power,
And thence, in haste, the enterprise to share,
Twelve thousand veterans selects with care;
To Humán and Bármán the charge consigns,
And thus his force with Samengán combines;
But treacherous first his martial chiefs he prest,
To keep the secret fast within their breast:—
"For this bold youth must not his father know,
"Each must confront the other as his foe,—
"Such is my vengeance! With unhallowed rage,
"Father and Son shall dreadful battle wage!
"Unknown the youth shall Rustem's force withstand,
"And soon o'erwhelm the bulwark of the land.
"Rustem removed, the Persian throne is ours,
"An easy conquest to confederate powers;
"And then, secured by some propitious snare,
"Sohráb himself our galling bonds shall wear.
"Or should the Son by Rustem's falchion bleed,
"The father's horror at that fatal deed,
"Will rend his soul, and 'midst his sacred grief,
"Káús in vain will supplicate relief."
The tutored chiefs advance with speed, and bring
Imperial presents to the future king;*

* Amongst the nations of the East, nothing can be done without presents between the parties, whether the negotiation be of a political, commercial, or of a domestic nature. Homer speaks of presents, but they are only proffered

In stately pomp the embassy proceeds;
Ten loaded camels, ten unrivalled steeds,
A golden crown, and throne, whose jewels bright
Gleam in the sun, and shed a sparkling light.
A letter too the crafty tyrant sends,
And fraudful thus the glorious aim commends.—
"If Persia's spoils invite thee to the field,
"Accept the aid my conquering legions yield;
"Led by two Chiefs of valour and renown,
"Upon thy head to place the kingly crown."
  Elate with promised fame, the youth surveys
The regal vest, the throne's irradiant blaze,
The golden crown, the steeds, the sumptuous load
Of ten strong camels, craftily bestowed;
Salutes the Chiefs, and views on every side,
The lengthening ranks with various arms supplied.
The march begins—the brazen drums resound,*
His moving thousands hide the trembling ground;
For Persia's verdant land he wields the spear,
And blood and havoc mark his groaning rear.†
  To check the Invader's horror-spreading course,
The barrier-fort opposed unequal force;
That fort whose walls, extending wide, contained
The stay of Persia, men to battle trained.

conditionally, as in the Iliad, where Ulysses and Ajax endeavour to conciliate Achilles.

> Ten weighty talents of the purest gold,
> And twice ten vases of refulgent mould;
> Twelve steeds unmatched in fleetness and in force,
> And still victorious in the dusty course,
> All these, to buy his friendship, shall be paid.
>
> POPE, Iliad, ix. 122.

But in the East, the presents *precede* the negotiation.

* Kus is a tymbal, or large brass drum, which is beat in the palaces or camps of Eastern Princes.

† It appears throughout the Sháh Námeh that whenever any army was put in motion, the inhabitants and the country, whether hostile or friendly, were equally given up to plunder and devastation.

"Every thing in their progress was burnt and destroyed.'

Soon as Hujír the dusky crowd descried,
He on his own presumptuous arm relied,
And left the fort; in mail with shield and spear,
Vaunting he spoke,—"What hostile force is here?
"What Chieftain dares our war-like realms invade?"
"And who art thou?" Sohráb indignant said,
Rushing towards him with undaunted look—
"Hast thou, audacious! nerve and soul to brook
"The crocodile in fight, that to the strife
"Singly thou comest, reckless of thy life?"
To this this foe replied—"A Túrk and I
"Have never yet been bound in friendly tie;
"And soon thy head shall, severed by my sword,
"Gladden the sight of Persia's mighty lord,
"While thy torn limbs to vultures shall be given,
"Or bleach beneath the parching blast of heaven."
The youthful hero laughing hears the boast,*
And now by each continual spears are tost,
Mingling together; like a flood of fire
The boaster meets his adversary's ire;
The horse on which he rides, with thundering pace,
Seems like a mountain moving from its base; †
Sternly he seeks the stripling's loins to wound,
But the lance hurtless drops upon the ground;
Sohráb, advancing, hurls his steady spear
Full on the middle of the vain Hujír,
Who staggers in his seat. With proud disdain
The youth now flings him headlong on the plain,

* The circumstances in Sohráb's first encounter somewhat resemble the first engagement of young Ascanius with the boaster Numanus. Virgil, Æn. ix. 592.

† The simile of a moving mountain occurs in the Iliad. Hector with his white plumes, is compared to a moving mountain topt with snow. Book xiii. 754. But Virgil has added considerably to this image. The Trojan hero moves towards Turnus.

Quantus Athos, aut quantus Eryx, aut ipse coruscis
Quum fremit ilicibus, quantus, gaudetque nivali
Vertice se attollens pater Appenninus ad auras. Æn. xii. 701.

And quick dismounting, on his heaving breast
Triumphant stands, his Khunjer firmly prest,
To strike the head off,—but the blow was stayed—
Trembling, for life, the craven boaster prayed.
That mercy granted eased his coward mind,
Though, dire disgrace, in captive bonds confined,
And sent to Húmán, who amazed beheld
How soon Sohráb his daring soul had quelled.
When Gúrd-afríd, a peerless warrior-dame,
Heard of the conflict, and the hero's shame,
Groans heaved her breast, and tears of anger flowed,
Her tulip-cheek with deeper crimson glowed;
Speedful, in arms magnificent arrayed,
A foaming palfrey bore the martial maid;
The burnished mail her tender limbs embraced,
Beneath her helm her clustering locks she placed; *
Poised in her hand an iron javelin gleamed,
And o'er the ground its sparkling lustre streamed;
Accoutred thus in manly guise, no eye
However piercing could her sex descry;
Now, like a lion, from the fort she bends,
And 'midst the foe impetuously descends;
Fearless of soul, demands with haughty tone,
The bravest chief, for war-like valour known,
To try the chance of fight. In shining arms,
Again Sohráb the glow of battle warms;
With scornful smiles, "Another deer!" he cries,
"Come to my victor-toils, another prize!"

* Thus hid in arms, she seemed a goodly knight,
And fit for any warlike exercise;
But when she list lay down her armour bright,
And back resume her peaceful maiden's guise;
The fairest maid she was that ever yet,
Prison'd her locks within a golden net,
Or let them waving hang, with roses fair beset.
Fletcher's Purple Island, Cant. x.

The damsel saw his noose insidious spread,
And soon her arrows whizzed around his head;
With steady skill the twanging bow she drew,
And still her pointed darts unerring flew;
For when in forest sports she touched the string,
Never escaped even bird upon the wing;
Furious he burned, and high his buckler held,
To ward the storm, by growing force impell'd;
And tilted forward with augmented wrath,
But Gúrd-afríd aspires to cross his path;
Now o'er her back the slacken'd bow resounds;
She grasps her lance, her goaded courser bounds,
Driven on the youth with persevering might—
Unconquer'd courage still prolongs the fight;
The stripling Chief shields off the threaten'd blow,
Reins in his steed, then rushes on the foe;
With outstretch'd arm, he bending backwards hung,
And, gathering strength, his pointed javelin flung;
Firm through her girdle belt the weapon went,
And glancing down the polish'd armour rent.
Staggering, and stunned by his superior force,
She almost tumbled from her foaming horse,
Yet unsubdued, she cut the spear in two,
And from her side the quivering fragment drew,
Then gain'd her seat, and onward urged her steed,
But strong and fleet Sohráb arrests her speed:
Strikes off her helm, and sees—a woman's face,
Radiant with blushes and commanding grace!
Thus undeceived, in admiration lost,
He cries, "A woman, from the Persian host!
"If Persian damsels thus in arms engage,
"Who shall repel their warrior's fiercer rage?
Then from his saddle thong—his noose he drew,
And round her waist the twisted loop he threw,—
"Now seek not to escape," he sharply said,
"Such is the fate of war, unthinking maid!

"And, as such beauty seldom swells our pride,
"Vain thy attempt to cast my toils aside."

In this extreme, but one resource remained,
Only one remedy her hope sustained,—
Expert in wiles each siren-art she knew,
And thence exposed her blooming face to view;
Raising her full black orbs, serenely bright,
In all her charms she blazed before his sight;*

* Gúrd-afrid, engaging Sohráb, is exactly the Clorinda of Tasso engaging Tancred, in the third Canto of Gerusalemme Liberata.

Clorinda intanto ad incontrar l'assalto
Va di Tancredi, e pon la lancia in resta.
Ferirsi alle visiere, e i tronchi in alto
Volaro, e parte nuda ella ne resta:
Chè, rotti i lacci all'elmo suo, d'un salto,
(Mirabil colpo) ei le balzò di testa:
E le chiome dorate al vento sparse,
Giovane donna in mezzo al campo apparse,
Lampeggiar gli occhi——
Percosso il Cavalier non ripercote;
Nè sì dal ferro à riguardarsi attende,
Come à guardar i begli occhi, e le gote,
Ond' Amor l'arco inevitabil tende. Stanzas xxi. and xxiv.

Meanwhile, her lance in rest, the warrior-dame,
With eager haste to encounter Tancred came.
Their vizors struck, the spears in shivers flew;
The virgin's face was left exposed to view.
The thongs that held her helmet burst in twain,
Hurled from her head, it bounded on the plain;
Loose in the wind, her golden tresses flowed,
And now a maid confessed to all she stood;
Keen flash her eyes——
Th' enamoured warrior ne'er returns a blow,
But views with eager gaze her charming eyes,
From which the shaft of love unerring flies. HOOLE.

Warrior dames have afforded numerous episodes to the Poets from the earliest times. Penthesilea aided the cause of Priam in the Trojan war. She was killed in battle by Achilles, who was so affected by her beauty, when she was stripped of her armour, that he shed tears. Artemisia, according to Herodotus, assisted Xerxes in his expedition against Greece. Every body is acquainted with the noble description of Camilla in the eleventh Æneid. The Italian Poets, and our own Spenser, have not failed to take advantage of these examples, and hence the beautiful and interesting descriptions of female heroism with which their works abound.

Where is the antique glory now become,
That whylome wont in wemen to appeare?
Where be the brave atchievements doen by some?
Where be the batteilles, where the shield and speare
SPENSER'S FAERIE QUEENE, 3, iv. 1

And thus addressed Sohráb.—" O warrior brave,
" Hear me, and thy imperiled honour save,
" These curling tresses seen by either host,
" A woman conquered, whence the glorious boast ?*
" Thy startled troops will know, with inward grief,
" A woman's arm resists their towering chief,
" Better preserve a warrior's fair renown,
" And let our struggle still remain unknown,
" For who with wanton folly would expose
" A helpless maid, to aggravate her woes ;
" The fort, the treasure, shall thy toils repay,
" The chief, and garrison, thy will obey,
" And thine the honours of this dreadful day."
Raptured he gazed, her smiles resistless move
The wildest transports of ungoverned love.
Her face disclosed a paradise to view,
Eyes like the fawn, and cheeks of rosy hue—
Thus vanquished, lost, unconscious of her aim,
And only struggling with his amorous flame,
He rode behind, as if compelled by fate,
And heedless saw her gain the castle-gate.
Safe with her friends, escaped from brand and spear,
Smiling she stands, as if unknown to fear.
—The father now, with tearful pleasure wild,
Clasps to his heart his fondly-foster'd child ;
The crowding warriors round her eager bend,
And grateful prayers to favouring heaven ascend.

The Warrior-maids, Marpesia, Hippolyte, Lampedo, and Penthesilea, are amongst the first described by the Historians and Poets of the West, and they are all of Asiatic origin. The Amazons are said to have inhabited the country now called Armenia. Marpesia conquered the inhabitants of Caucasus, in consequence of which the mountain was called *Marpesius Mons.* Gúrd-afríd may therefore be considered an indigenous character, and not derived from Western Poetry, although from the circumstance of Longinus having been minister and preceptor to Zenobia, it may be suspected that the works of Homer and Virgil were known in the East.

* Namque, etsi nullum memorabile nomen
Feminea in pœna est, nec habet victoria laudem.—Æneid, ii. 583.

Now from the walls, she, with majestic air,
Exclaims : "Thou warrior of Túran ! forbear,
"Why vex thy soul, and useless strife demand !
"Go, and in peace enjoy thy native land."
Stern he rejoins : "Thou beauteous tyrant ! say,
'Though crown'd with charms, devoted to betray,
"When these proud walls, in dust and ruins laid,
"Yield no defence, and thou a captive maid,
"Will not repentance through thy bosom dart,
"And sorrow soften that disdainful heart ?"
Quick she replied : "O'er Persia's fertile fields
"The savage Túrk in vain his falchion wields ;
"When King Káús this bold invasion hears,
"And mighty Rustem clad in arms appears !
"Destruction wide will glut the slippery plain,
"And not one man of all thy host remain.
"Alas ! that bravery, high as thine, should meet
"Amidst such promise, with a sure defeat,
"But not a gleam of hope remains for thee,
"Thy wondrous valour cannot keep thee free.'
"Avert the fate which o'er thy head impends,
"Return, return, and save thy martial friends !"
Thus to be scorned, defrauded of his prey,
With victory in his grasp—to lose the day !
Shame and revenge alternate filled his mind ;
The suburb-town to pillage he consigned,
And devastation—not a dwelling spared ;
The very owl was from her covert scared ;
Then thus : "Though luckless in my aim to-day,
"To-morrow shall behold a sterner fray ;
"This fort, in ashes, scattered o'er the plain."
He ceased—and turned towards his troops again ;
There, at a distance from the hostile power,
He brooding waits the slaughter-breathing hour.
Meanwhile the sire of Gúrd-afríd, who now
Governed the fort, and feared the warrior's vow ;

Mournful and pale, with gathering woes opprest,
His distant Monarch trembling thus addrest.
But first invoked the heavenly power to shed
Its choicest blessings o'er his royal head.
"Against our realm with numerous foot and horse,
"A stripling warrior holds his ruthless course.
"His lion-breast unequalled strength betrays,
"And o'er his mien the sun's effulgence plays:
"Sohráb his name; like Sám Suwár he shows,
"Or Rustem terrible amidst his foes.
"The bold Hujír lies vanquished on the plain,
"And drags a captive's ignominious chain;
"Myriads of troops besiege our tottering wall,
"And vain the effort to suspend its fall.
"Haste, arm for fight, this Tartar-power withstand,
"Let sweeping Vengeance lift her flickering brand;
"Rustem alone may stem the roaring wave,
"And, prompt as bold, his groaning country save.
"Meanwhile in flight we place our only trust,
"Ere the proud ramparts crumble in the dust."
Swift flies the messenger through secret ways,
And to the King the dreadful tale conveys,
Then passed, unseen, in night's concealing shade,
The mournful heroes and the warrior maid.
Soon as the sun with vivifying ray,
Gleams o'er the landscape, and renews the day;
The flaming troops the lofty walls surround,
With thundering crash the bursting gates resound.
Already are the captives bound, in thought,
And like a herd before the conqueror brought;
Sohráb, terrific o'er the ruin, views
His hopes deceived, but restless still pursues.
An empty fortress mocks his searching eye,
No steel-clad chiefs his burning wrath defy;
No warrior-maid reviving passion warms,
And soothes his soul with fondly-valued charms.

Deep in his breast he feels the amorous smart,
And hugs her image closer to his heart.
"Alas! that Fate should thus invidious shroud
"The moon's soft radiance in a gloomy cloud;
"Should to my eyes such winning grace display,
"Then snatch the enchanter of my soul away!
"A beauteous roe my toils enclosed in vain,
"Now I, her victim, drag the captive's chain;
"Strange the effects that from her charms proceed,
"I gave the wound, and I afflicted bleed!
"Vanquished by her, I mourn the luckless strife;
"Dark, dark, and bitter, frowns my morn of life.
"A fair unknown my tortured bosom rends,
"Withers each joy, and every hope suspends."
Impassioned thus Sohráb in secret sighed,
And sought, in vain, o'er-mastering grief to hide.
Can the heart bleed and throb from day to day,
And yet no trace its inmost pangs betray? *
Love scorns control, and prompts the labouring sigh,
Pales the red lip, and dims the lucid eye;

* Moore has translated the following thought from La Fosse.

In vain the lover tries to veil
The flame which in his bosom lies;
His cheeks' confusion tells the tale,
We read it in his languid eyes:
And though his words the heart betray,
His silence speaks e'en more than they.

Thus Shakspeare:

Fire that is closest kept, burns most of all;
O! they love least, that let men know their love.
GENT. VERONA, i. 2, 30.

Again,

The grief that does not speak,
Whispers the o'erfraught heart, and bids it break.
MACBETH, iv., 3, 210.

And Dryden:

Silent he wept, ashamed to show his tears.

His look alarmed the stern Túránian Chief,
Closely he mark'd his heart-corroding grief; *
And though he knew not that the martial dame,
Had in his bosom lit the tender flame;
Full well he knew such deep repinings prove,
The hapless thraldom of disastrous love.
Full well he knew some idol's musky hair,
Had to his youthful heart become a snare,
But still unnoted was the gushing tear,
Till haply he had gained his private ear:—
"In ancient times, no hero known to fame,
"Not dead to glory e'er indulged the flame;
"Though beauty's smiles might charm a fleeting hour,
"The heart, unsway'd, repelled their lasting power.
"A warrior Chief to trembling love a prey?
"What! weep for woman one inglorious day?
"Canst thou for love's effeminate control,
"Barter the glory of a warrior's soul?
"Although a hundred damsels might be gained,
"The hero's heart shall still be free, unchained.
"Thou art our leader, and thy place the field
"Where soldiers love to fight with spear and shield;
"And what hast thou to do with tears and smiles,
"The silly victim to a woman's wiles?
"Our progress, mark! from far Túrán we came,
"Through seas of blood to gain immortal fame;

* Literally, Húman was not at first aware that Sohráb was wounded in the LIVER. In this organ, Oriental as well as the Greek and Roman poets, place the residence of love. Thus Theocritus, Idyll. xiii. 71, speaking of Hercules lamenting the loss of Hylas, and Anacreon in the beautiful ode of Cupid benighted.

Thus Horace:

Cum tibi flagrans Amor——
Sæviet circa Jecur ulcerosu — I. Od. xxv. 13.

And Shakspeare:

Alas their love may be called appetite,
No motion of the Liver, but the palate.
— Twelfth Night, ii. 4.

"And wilt thou now the tempting conquest shun,
"When our brave arms this Barrier-fort have won?
"Why linger here, and trickling sorrows shed,
"Till mighty Káús thunders o'er thy head!
"Till Tús, and Gíw, and Gúdárz, and Báhrám,
"And Rustem brave, Feramurz, and Rehám,
"Shall aid the war! A great emprise is thine,
"At once, then, every other thought resign;
"For know the task which first inspired thy zeal,
"Transcends in glory all that love can feel.
"Rise, lead the war, prodigious toils require
"Unyielding strength, and unextinguished fire;
"Pursue the triumph with tempestuous rage,
"Against the world in glorious strife engage,
"And when an empire sinks beneath thy sway,
"(O quickly may we hail the prosperous day,)
"The fickle sex will then with blooming charms,
"Adoring throng to bless thy circling arms!"
Húmán's warm speech, the spirit-stirring theme,
Awoke Sohráb from his inglorious dream.
No more the tear his faded cheek bedewed,
Again ambition all his hopes renewed:
Swell'd his bold heart with unforgotten zeal,
The noble wrath which heroes only feel;
Fiercely he vowed at one tremendous stroke,
To bow the world beneath the tyrant's yoke!
"Afrásiyáb," he cried, "shall reign alone,
"The mighty lord of Persia's gorgeous throne!"
Burning, himself, to rule this nether sphere,
These welcome tidings charmed the despot's ear.
Meantime Káús, this dire invasion known,
Had called his chiefs around his ivory throne:
There stood Gurgín, and Báhrám, and Gushwád
And Tús, and Gíw, and Gúdárz, and Ferhád;
To them he read the melancholy tale,
Gust'hem had written of the rising bale;

Besought their aid and prudent choice, to form
Some sure defence against the threatening storm.
With one consent they urge the strong request,
To summon Rustem from his rural rest.—
Instant a warrior-delegate they send,
And thus the King invites his patriot-friend,
"To thee all praise, whose mighty arm alone,
"Preserves the glory of the Persian throne!
"Lo! Tartar hordes our happy realms invade;
"The tottering state requires thy powerful aid;
"A youthful Champion leads the ruthless host,
"His savage country's widely-rumoured boast.
"The Barrier-fortress sinks beneath his sway,
"Hujír is vanquished, ruin tracks his way;
"Strong as a raging elephant in fight,
"No arm but thine can match his furious might.
"Mazinderán thy conquering prowess knew;
"The Demon-king thy trenchant falchion slew,
"The rolling heavens, abash'd with fear, behold
"Thy biting sword, thy mace adorned with gold! *
"Fly to the succour of a King distress'd,
"Proud of thy love, with thy protection blest.
"When o'er the nation dread misfortunes lower,
"Thou art the refuge, thou the saving power.
"The chiefs assembled claim thy patriot vows,
"Give to thy glory all that life allows;
"And while no whisper breathes the direful tale,
"O, let thy Monarch's anxious prayers prevail."

* "Thy mace makes the Sun weep, and thy sword inflames the Stars." (Lit. the planet Venus.) Although this is a strong hyperbole, there are numberless parallel passages, containing equally extravagant personification, in our own Poets. For example: "The Stars are ashamed of thy presence, and turn aside their sparkling eyes." (OSSIAN.)

Swift Severn's flood,
Affrighted with their bloody looks
Ran fearfully among the trembling reeds,
And hid his crisp head in the hollow bank.
HENRY IV Part I, i. 3.

Closing the fragrant page * o'ercome with dread,
The afflicted King to Gíw, the warrior, said :—
"Go, bind the saddle on thy fleetest horse,
"Outstrip the tempest in thy rapid course,
"To Rustem swift his country's woes convey,
"Too true art thou to linger on the way ;
"Speed, day and night—and not one instant wait,
"Whatever hour may bring thee to his gate."
Followed no pause—to Gíw enough was said,
Nor rest, nor taste of food, his speed delayed.
And when arrived, where Zábul bowers exhale
Ambrosial sweets and scent the balmy gale,
The sentinel's loud voice in Rustem's ear,
Announced a messenger from Persia, near ;
The Chief himself amidst his warriors stood,
Dispensing honours to the brave and good,
And soon as Gíw had joined the martial ring,
(The sacred envoy of the Persian King,)
He, with becoming loyalty inspired,
Asked what the monarch, what the state required ;
But Gíw, apart, his secret mission told,—
The written page was speedily unrolled.
Struck with amazement, Rustem—"Now on earth
"A warrior-knight of Sám's excelling worth ?
"Whence comes this hero of the prosperous star ?
"I know no Túrk renowned, like him, in war ;
"He bears the port of Rustem too, 'tis said,
"Like Sám, like Narímán, a warrior bred !
"He cannot be my son, unknown to me ;
"Reason forbids the thought—it cannot be !
"At Samengán, where once affection smiled,
"To me Tahmíneh bore her only child,

* The paper upon which the letters of royal and distinguished personages in the East are written is usually perfumed, and covered with curious devices in gold. This was scented with amber. The degree of embellishment is generally regulated according to the rank of the party.

"That was a daughter?" Pondering thus he spoke,
And then aloud—"Why fear the invader's yoke?
"Why trembling shrink, by coward thoughts dismayed,
"Must we not all in dust, at length, be laid?
"But come, to Nírum's palace, haste with me,
"And there partake the feast—from sorrow free;
"Breathe, but awhile—ere we our toils renew,
"And moisten the parched lip with needful dew.
"Let plans of war another day decide,
"We soon shall quell this youthful hero's pride.
"The force of fire soon flutters and decays
"When ocean, swelled by storms, its wrath displays.
"What danger threatens! whence the dastard fear!
"Rest, and at leisure share a warrior's cheer."
In vain the Envoy prest the Monarch's grief;
The matchless prowess of the stripling chief;
How brave Hujír had felt his furious hand;
What thickening woes beset the shuddering land.
But Rustem, still, delayed the parting day,
And mirth and feasting rolled the hours away;
Morn following morn beheld the banquet bright,
Music and wine prolonged the genial rite;
Rapt by the witchery of the melting strain,
No thought of Káús touch'd his swimming brain.*
The trumpet's clang, on fragrant breezes borne,
Now loud salutes the fifth revolving morn;
The softer tones which charm'd the jocund feast,
And all the noise of revelry, had ceased,
The generous horse, with rich embroidery deckt,
Whose gilded trappings sparkling light reflect,
Bears with majestic port the Champion brave,
And high in air the victor-banners wave.

* Four days were consumed in uninterrupted feasting. This seems to have been an ancient practice previous to the commencement of any important undertaking, or at setting out on a journey.

Prompt at the martial call, Zuára leads
His veteran troops from Zábul's verdant meads,*
Ere Rustem had approached his journey's end,
Tús, Gúdárz, Gushwád, met their champion-friend
With customary honours; pleased to bring
The shield of Persia to the anxious King.
But foaming wrath the senseless monarch swayed;
His friendship scorned, his mandate disobeyed,
Beneath dark brows o'er-shadowing deep, his eye
Red gleaming shone, like lightning through the sky
And when the warriors met his sullen view,
Frowning revenge, still more enraged he grew:—
Loud to the Envoy thus he fiercely cried:—
"Since Rustem has my royal power defied,
"Had I a sword, this instant should his head
"Roll on the ground; but let him now be led
"Hence, and impaled alive." † Astounded Gíw
Shrunk from such treatment of a knight so true;
But this resistance added to the flame,
And both were branded with revolt and shame;
Both were condemned, and Tús, the stern decree
Received, to break them on the felon-tree.
Could daring insult, thus deliberate given,
Escape the rage of one to frenzy driven?
No, from his side the nerveless Chief was flung,
Bent to the ground. Away the Champion sprung;
Mounted his foaming horse, and looking round—
His boiling wrath thus rapid utterance found:—
"Ungrateful King, thy tyrant acts disgrace
"The sacred throne, and more, the human race;

* Zuára, it will be remembered, was the brother of Rustem, and had the immediate superintendence of the Zábul troops.

† The original is, "Seize and inflict upon him the punishment of the dar." According to Burháni-katia, dar is a tree upon which felons are hanged. But the general acceptation of the term is breaking or tearing the body upon a stake.

"Midst clashing swords thy recreant life I saved,
"And am I now by Tús contemptuous braved?*
"On me shall Tús, shall Káús dare to frown?
"On me, the bulwark of the regal crown?
"Wherefore should fear in Rustem's breast have birth,
"Káús, to me, a worthless clod of earth!
"Go, and thyself Sohráb's invasion stay,
"Go, seize the plunderers growling o'er their prey!
"Wherefore to others give the base command?
"Go, break him on the tree with thine own hand.
"Know, thou hast roused a warrior, great and free,
"Who never bends to tyrant Kings like thee!
"Was not this untired arm triumphant seen,
"In Misser, Rúm, Mazinderán, and Chín!
"And must I shrink at thy imperious nod!
"Slave to no Prince, I only bow to God.
"Whatever wrath from thee, proud King! may fall,
"For thee I fought, and I deserve it all.
"The regal sceptre might have graced my hand,
"I kept the laws, and scorned supreme command.
"When Kaí-kobád on Alberz mountain strayed,
"I drew him thence, and gave a warrior's aid;
"Placed on his brows the long-contested crown,
"Worn by his sires, by sacred right his own;
"Strong in the cause, my conquering arms prevailed,
"Wouldst thou have reign'd had Rustem's valour failed
"When the White Demon rag'd in battle-fray,
"Wouldst thou have lived had Rustem lost the day?"
Then to his friends: "Be wise, and shun your fate,
"Fly the wide ruin which o'erwhelms the state;

* In this speech Rustem recounts the services which he had performed for Káús. He speaks of his conquests in Egypt, China, Hamaveran, Rúm, Súksar, and Mazinderán. Thus Achilles boasts of his unrequited achievements in the cause of Greece.

I sacked twelve ample cities on the main,
And twelve lay smoking on the Trojan plain.
POPE.—Iliad ix. 328.

"The conqueror comes—the scourge of great and small,
"And vultures, following fast, will gorge on all.
"Persia no more its injured Chief shall view"—
He said, and sternly from the court withdrew.
The warriors now, with sad forebodings wrung,
Torn from that hope to which they proudly clung,
On Gúdárz rest, to soothe with gentle sway,
The frantic King, and Rustem's wrath allay.
With bitter grief they wail misfortune's shock,
No shepherd now to guard the timorous flock.
Gúdárz at length, with boding cares imprest,
Thus soothed the anger in the royal breast.
"Say, what has Rustem done, that he should be
"Impaled upon the ignominious tree?
"Degrading thought, unworthy to be bred
"Within a royal heart, a royal head.
"Hast thou forgot when near the Caspian-wave,
"Defeat and ruin had appalled the brave,
"When mighty Rustem struck the dreadful blow,
"And nobly freed thee from the savage foe?
"Did Demons huge escape his flaming brand?
"Their reeking limbs bestrew'd the slippery strand.
"Shall he for this resign his vital breath?
"What! shall the hero's recompense be death?
"But who will dare a threatening step advance,
"What earthly power can bear his withering glance?
"Should he to Zábul fired with wrongs return,
"The plunder'd land will long in sorrow mourn!
"This direful presage all our warriors feel,
"For who can now oppose the invader's steel;
"Thus is it wise thy champion to offend,
"To urge to this extreme thy warrior-friend?
"Remember, passion ever scorns control,
"And wisdom's mild decrees should rule a Monarch's soul."*

* Literally, "Kings ought to be endowed with judgment and discretion; no advantage can arise from impetuosity and rage." Gúdárz was one of the

Káús, relenting, heard with anxious ear,
And groundless wrath gave place to shame and fear;
"Go then," he cried, "his generous aid implore,
"And to your King the mighty Chief restore!"
When Gúdárz rose, and seized his courser's rein,
A crowd of heroes followed in his train.
To Rustem, now (respectful homage paid),
The royal prayer he anxious thus conveyed.
"The King, repentant, seeks thy aid again,
"Grieved to the heart that he has given thee pain;
"But though his anger was unjust and strong,
"Thy country still is guiltless of the wrong,
"And, therefore, why abandoned thus by thee?
"Thy help the King himself implores through me."
Rustem rejoined: "Unworthy the pretence,
"And scorn and insult all my recompense?
"Must I be galled by his capricious mood?
"I, who have still his firmest champion stood?
"But all is past, to heaven alone resigned,
"No human cares shall more disturb my mind!"
Then Gúdárz thus (consummate art inspired
His prudent tongue, with all that zeal required);
"When Rustem dreads Sohráb's resistless power,
"Well may inferiors fly the trying hour!
"The dire suspicion now pervades us all,
"Thus, unavenged, shall beauteous Persia fall!

greatest generals of Persia, he conquered Judea, and took Jerusalem under the reign of Lohurasp, of the first dynasty of Persia, and sustained many wars against Afrásiyáb under the Kings of the second dynasty. He was the father of Gíw, who is also celebrated for his valour in the following reigns. The opinion of this venerable and distinguished warrior appears to have had considerable weight and influence with Káús. By the persuasion of his friends he interferes between the King and Rustem, like Nestor,

To calm their passions with the words of age. *Iliad.*

The language is strong, and breathes more of independence than might be supposed in an address to a Persian despot. But Káús was a weak Prince. He is every where called "empty brained"! and treated with very little ceremony.

"Yet, generous still, avert the lasting shame,
"O, still preserve thy country's glorious fame! *
"Or wilt thou, deaf to all our fears excite,
"Forsake thy friends, and shun the pending fight?
"And worse, O grief! in thy declining days,
"Forfeit the honours of thy country's praise?"
This artful censure set his soul on fire,
But patriot firmness calm'd his burning ire;
And thus he said—"Inured to war's alarms,
"Did ever Rustem shun the dim of arms?
"Though frowns from Káús I disdain to bear,
"My threaten'd country claims a warrior's care."
He ceased, and prudent joined the circling throng,
And in the public good forgot the private wrong.
From far the King the generous Champion viewed,
And rising mildly thus his speech pursued:—
"Since various tempers govern all mankind,
"Me, nature fashioned of a froward mind; †
"And what the heavens spontaneously bestow,
"Sown by their bounty must for ever grow.
"The fit of wrath which burst within me, soon
"Shrunk up my heart as thin as the new moon; ‡
"Else had I deemed thee still my army's boast,
"Source of my regal power, beloved the most,

* Ulysses thus addresses Achilles:

But if all this relentless thou disdain,
If honour and if interest plead in vain;
Yet some redress to suppliant Greece afford,
And be, amongst her guardian gods, adored.
If no regard thy suffering country claim,
Hear thy own glory, and the voice of fame

POPE.—Iliad, ix. 300.

† Káús, in acknowledging the violence of his disposition, uses a singular phrase: "When you departed in anger, O Champion! I repented; *ashes fell into my mouth.*" A similar metaphor is used in Hindústaní: If a person falls under the displeasure of his friend, he says, "Ashes have fallen into my meat"; meaning, that his happiness is gone.

‡ This is one of Firdausí's favourite similes.

"My heart became as slender as the new moon.

"Unequalled. Every day, remembering thee,
"I drain the wine cup, thou art all to me;
"I wished thee to perform that lofty part,
"Claimed by thy valour, sanctioned by my heart;
"Hence thy delay my better thoughts supprest,
"And boisterous passions revelled in my breast;
"But when I saw thee from my Court retire
"In wrath, repentance quenched my burning ire.
"O, let me now my keen contrition prove,
"Again enjoy thy fellowship and love:
"And while to thee my gratitude is known,
"Still be the pride and glory of my throne."
Rustem, thus answering said:—"Thou art the King
"Source of command, pure honour's sacred spring;
"And here I stand to follow thy behest,
"Obedient ever—be thy will expressed,
"And services required—Old age shall see
"My loins still bound in fealty to thee."
To this the King:—"Rejoice we then to-day,
"And on the morrow marshal our array."
The monarch quick commands the feast of joy,
And social cares his buoyant mind employ,
Within a bower, beside a crystal spring,*
Where opening flowers, refreshing odours fling,
Cheerful he sits, and forms the banquet scene,
In regal splendour on the crowded green;
And as around he greets his valiant bands,
Showers golden presents from his bounteous hands; †

* The beautiful arbours referred to in the text are often included within the walls of Eastern palaces. They are fancifully fitted up, and supplied with reservoirs, fountains, and flower-trees. These romantic garden-pavilions are called Kiosks in Turkey, and are generally situated upon an eminence near a running stream.

† Milton alludes to the custom in Paradise Lost:

Where the gorgeous east with richest hand
Showers on her Kings barbaric pearl and gold.

In the note on this passage by Warburton, it is said to have been an eastern

Voluptuous damsels trill the sportive lay,
Whose sparkling glances beam celestial day;
Fill'd with delight the heroes closer join,
And quaff till midnight cups of generous wine.
  Soon as the Sun had pierced the veil of night,
And o'er the prospect shed his earliest light,
Káús, impatient, bids the clarions sound,
The sprightly notes from hills and rocks rebound;
His treasure gates are opened :—and to all
A largess given; obedient to the call,
His subjects gathering crowd the mountain's brow,
And following thousands shade the vales below;
With shields, in armour, numerous legends bend;
And troops of horse the threatening lines extend.
Beneath the tread of heroes fierce and strong,
By war's tumultuous fury borne along,
The firm earth shook :* the dust, in eddies driven,†
Whirled high in air, obscured the face of heaven;

ceremony, at the coronation of their Kings, to powder them with *gold-dust* and *seed-pearl*. The expression in Firdausí is, "he showered or scattered gems." It was usual at festivals, and the custom still exists, to throw money amongst the people. In Hafiz, the term used is nisar, which is of the same import. Clarke, in the second volume of his Travels, speaks of the four principal Sultanas of the Seraglio at Constantinople being *powdered with diamonds*. "Long spangled robes, open in front, with pantaloons embroidered in gold and silver, and covered by a profusion of pearls and precious stones, displayed their persons to great advantage. Their hair hung in loose and very thick tresses on each side of their cheeks, falling quite down to the waist, and covering their shoulders behind. Those tresses were quite powdered with diamonds, not displayed according to any studied arrangement, but as if carelessly scattered, by handfuls, among their flowing locks."—Vol. ii. p. 14.

* Ommia cum belli trepido concussa tumultu
Horrida contremuere sub altis ætheris auris.
Lucretius, De Rer. Nat. III. 846.

† Thus Homer:

So wrapt in gathering dust, the Grecian train,
A moving cloud swept on and hid the plain.
Pope.—Iliad, iii. 13.

And Virgil:

Hic subitam nigro glomerari pulvere nubem
Prospiciunt Teucri, ac tenebras insurgere campis. Æneid, ix. 33.

In the Hermosura de Angelica of the famous Lope de Vega, there is a beauti-

Nor earth, nor sky appeared—all, seeming lost,
And swallowed up by that wide-spreading host.
The steely armour glitter'd o'er the fields,*
And lightnings flash'd from gold emblazoned shields;
Thou wouldst have said, the clouds had burst in showers,
Of sparkling amber o'er the martial powers.†
Thus, close embodied, they pursued their way,
And reached the Barrier-fort in terrible array.
  The legions of Túran, with dread surprise,
Saw o'er the plain successive myriads rise;
And showed them to Sohráb; he, mounting high
The fort, surveyed them with a fearless eye;
To Húman, who, with withering terror pale,
Had marked their progress through the distant vale,
He pointed out the sight, and ardent said:—
"Dispel these woe-fraught broodings from thy head,

ful simile, descriptive of the hostile troops of the Moors and Spaniards, which may be well applied to the motley appearance of a Persian army:

Como en le triangular cristal se mira.
De varios y diversos tornasoles,
Campo, cielo, ciudad, o mar; y admira
Ver tan diversos nubes, y arreboles;
Assi la esquadra que entra y se retira,
De Moros Africanos, y Españoles
A la vista, que juntos confundian,
Jardin florida en Mayo parecian:

And in English thus:

As in the prism we pleased survey,
Rich prospects through the crystal play,
The fields, the cities, clouds, and sea,
Appear commingling variously;
Thus moving o'er the battle-plain,
The Moors are mixed with Knights of Spain;
The field, confusedly bright and gay,
Looks like the garden's pride in May.

In the Gúlistan of Sadí there is a similar thought:

"An assembly mixed together like a bed of roses and tulips."

* In his descriptions of battle-array, Firdausí seldom omits "golden slippers," which, however, I have not preserved in this place.

† The original is Sandurūs, sandaraca; for which I have substituted amber. Sandurūs is the Arabic name for Gum Juniper.

"I wage the war, Afrásiyáb! for thee,
"And make this desert seem a rolling sea."
Thus, while amazement every bosom quell'd,
Sohráb, unmoved, the coming storm beheld,
And boldly gazing on the camp around,
Raised high the cup with wine nectareous crowned:
O'er him no dreams of woe insidious stole,
No thought but joy engaged his ardent soul.
  The Persian legions had restrained their course,
Tents and pavilions, countless foot and horse,
Clothed all the spacious plain, and gleaming threw
Terrific splendours on the gazer's view.
But when the Sun had faded in the west,
And night assumed her ebon-coloured vest,
The mighty Chief approached the sacred throne,
And generous thus made danger all his own:
"The rules of war demand a previous task,
"To watch this dreadful foe I boldly ask;
"With wary step the wondrous youth to view,
"And mark the heroes who his path pursue."
The King assents: "The task is justly thine,
"Favourite of heaven, inspired by power divine."
In Túrkish habit, secretly arrayed,
The lurking Champion wandered through the shade,
And, cautious, standing near the palace gate,
Saw how the chiefs were ranged in princely state.
  What time Sohráb his thoughts to battle turned,
And for the first proud fruits of conquest burned,
His mother called a warrior to his aid,
And Zinda-ruzm his sister's call obeyed.
To him Tahmíneh gave her only joy,
And bade him shield the bold adventurous boy:
"But, in the dreadful strife, should danger rise,
"Present my child before his father's eyes!
"By him protected, war may rage in vain,
"Though he may never bless these arms again!"

This guardian prince sat on the stripling's right,
Viewing the imperial banquet with delight·
Húmán and Bármán, near the hero placed,
In joyous pomp the full assembly graced;
A hundred valiant Chiefs begirt the throne,
And, all elate, were chaunting his renown.
Closely concealed, the gay and splendid scene,
Rustem contemplates with astonished mien;
When Zind, retiring, marks the listener nigh,
Watching the festal train with curious eye;
And well he knew, amongst his Tartar host,
Such towering stature not a Chief could boast—
"What spy is here, close shrouded by the night?
"Art thou afraid to face the beams of light?"
But scarcely from his lips these words had past,
Ere, fell'd to earth, he groaning breathed his last;
Unseen he perish'd, fate decreed the blow,
To add fresh keenness to a parent's woe.
  Meantime Sohráb, perceiving the delay
In Zind's return, looked round him with dismay;
The seat still vacant—but the bitter truth,
Full soon was known to the distracted youth;
Full soon he found that Zinda-ruzm was gone,
His day of feasting and of glory done;
Speedful towards the fatal spot he ran,
Where slept in bloody vest the slaughtered man.
  The lighted torches now displayed the dead,
Stiff on the ground his graceful limbs were spread;
Sad sight to him who knew his guardian care,
Now doom'd a kinsman's early loss to bear;
Anguish and rage devour his breast by turns,
He vows revenge, then o'er the warrior mourns:
And thus exclaims to each afflicted Chief:—
"No time, to-night, my friends, for useless grief;
"The ravenous wolf has watched his helpless prey,
"Sprung o'er the fold, and borne its flower away;

" But if the heavens my lifted arm befriend,
" Upon the guilty shall my wrath descend—
" Unsheathed, this sword shall dire revenge pursue,
" And Persian blood the thirsty land bedew."
Frowning he paused, and check'd the spreading woe,
Resumed the feast, and bid the wine-cup flow!
The valiant Gíw was sentinel that night,
And marking dimly by the dubious light,
A warrior form approach, he claps his hands,
With naked sword and lifted shield he stands,
To front the foe; but Rustem now appears,
And Gíw the secret tale astonished hears;
From thence the Champion on the Monarch waits,
The power and splendour of Sohráb relates:
" Circled by Chiefs this glorious youth was seen,
" Of lofty stature and majestic mien; *
" No Tartar region gave the hero birth:
" Some happier portion of the spacious earth;
" Tall, as the graceful cypress he appears;
" Like Sám, the brave, his warrior-front he rears!"
Then having told how, while the banquet shone,
Unhappy Zind had sunk, without a groan;
He forms his conquering bands in close array,
And, cheer'd by wine, awaits the coming day.
When now the Sun his golden buckler raised,
And genial light through heaven diffusive blazed,
Sohráb in mail his nervous limbs attired,
For dreadful wrath his soul to vengeance fired;
With anxious haste he bent the yielding cord,
Ring within ring, more fateful than the sword;

* Girt with many a baron bold,
Sublime their starry fronts they rear,
In the midst a form divine! GRAY.

Beneath a sculptured arch he sits enthroned,
The peers encircling form an awful round.
POPE—Odyssey

Around his brows a regal helm he bound;
His dappled steed impatient stampt the ground.
Thus armed, ascending where the eye could trace
The hostile force, and mark each leader's place,
He called Hujír, the captive Chief addressed,
And anxious thus, his soul's desire expressed:
"A prisoner thou, if freedom's voice can charm,
"And dungeon darkness fill thee with alarm,
"That freedom merit, shun severest woe,
"And truly answer what I ask to know!
"If rigid truth thy ready speech attend,
"Honours and wealth shall dignify my friend."
"Obedient to thy wish," Hujír replied,
"Truth thou shalt hear, whatever chance betide;
"For what on earth to praise has better claim?
"Falsehood but leads to sorrow and to shame!"
"Then say, what heroes lead the adverse host,
"Where they command, what dignities they boast;
"Say, where does Káús hold his kingly state,*
"Where Tús, and Gúdarz, on his bidding wait;

* Similar descriptions of Chiefs and encampments are common amongst the epic poets of the West. In the third book of the Iliad, Helen describes to Priam on the walls of Troy the leaders of the Grecian army. Upon this passage Pope says, "it is justly looked upon as an episode of great beauty, as well as a master-piece of conduct in Homer; who by this means acquaints the readers with the figure and qualifications of each hero in a more lively and agreeable manner." Firdausí is entitled to equal praise for his address in introducing the description of the Persian army. The objection which Scaliger makes in asking, "how it happens that Priam, after nine years' siege, should be yet unacquainted with the faces of the Grecian leaders," does not obtain here. Nothing can be more natural and unforced than the passage as it occurs in the Persian poet. The following is the opening of the parallel passage in Homer:

"But lift thy eyes and say what Greek is he,
"(Far as from hence these aged orbs can see,)
"Around whose brow such martial graces shine,
"So tall, so awful, and almost divine!"
"The King of Kings, Atrides you survey,
"Great in the war, and great in arts of sway.'
This said, once more he viewed the warrior train,
"What's he whose arms lie scatter'd on the plain?"

"Gíw, Gust'hem, and Báhrám—all known to thee,
"And where is mighty Rustem, where is he?
"Look round with care, their names and power display
"Or instant death shall end thy vital day."
"Where yonder splendid tapestries extend,*
"And o'er pavilions bright infolding bend,
"A throne triumphal shines with sapphire rays,
"And golden suns upon the banners blaze;
"Full in the centre of the hosts—and round
"The tent a hundred elephants are bound,

Then Helen thus: "Whom your discerning eyes
"Have singled out, is Ithacus the wise.
"See! bold Idomeneus superior towers
"Amidst yon circle of his Cretan powers,
"Great as a God." POPE.—Iliad, iii. 167.

Chapman's translation of this passage is quaintly expressed:—

Sit then, and name this goodly Greek, so tall and broadly spread;
Who than the rest, that stand by him, is higher than the head;
The bravest man I ever saw and most majesticall;
His only presenee makes me think him king amongst them all!!

Thus also the well-known imitation in the third book of Gerusalemme Liberata:

Erminia il vide, e dimostrollo à dito,
Al Re pagano, e così a dir riprese:
Goffredo è quel, che nel purpureo manto,
Hà di Regio, e d'Augusto in sè cotanto.
Dimmi chi sia colui, c'ha pur vermiglia,
La sopravesta, e seco á par si vede.
E' Baldovin, risponde; e ben si scopre
Nel volto a lui fratel, ma più nell'opre. Stanza 58, 61.

Full on the Chief Erminia cast a look,
Then show'd him to the King, and thus she spoke:—
"There Godfrey stands in purple vesture seen,
"Of regal presenee and exalted mien."
"Say who is he who stands by Godfrey's side,
"His upper garments with vermilion dyed?"
"'Tis Baldwin, brother to the Prince (she cried),
"In feature like, but most in deed allied." HOOLE.

But Sohráb was more peculiarly interested in the description of those warriors amongst whom he expected to meet his father. On this account particularly, as well as with regard to its general fitness, I think that this passage is equal, if not superior, to that in Homer, which has given rise to so many imitations.

* The tents and pavilions of Eastern Princes were exceedingly magnificent; they were often made of silks and velvets, and ornamented with pearls and gold. The tent of Nadir Shah was made of scarlet and broadcloth, and lined with satin, richly figured over with precious stones.

"As if, in pomp, he mocked the power of fate;
"There royal Káús holds his kingly state.
"In yonder tent which numerous guards protect,
"Where front and rear illustrious Chiefs collect;
"Where horsemen wheeling seem prepared for fight,
"Their golden armour glittering in the light;
"Tús lifts his banners, deck'd with royal pride,
"Feared by the brave, the soldier's friend and guide.*
"That crimson tent where spear-men frowning stand,
"And steel-clad veterans form a threatening band,
"Holds mighty Gúdarz, famed for martial fire,
"Of eighty valiant sons the valiant sire;
"Yet strong in arms, he shuns inglorious ease,
"His lion-banners floating in the breeze."
"But mark, that green pavilion; girt around
"By Persian nobles, speaks the Chief renowned;
"Fierce on the standard, worked with curious art,
"A hideous dragon writhing seems to start;
"Throned in his tent the warrior's form is seen,
"Towering above the assembled host between! †
"A generous horse before him snorts and neighs,
"The trembling earth the echoing sound conveys.
"Like him no Champion ever met my eyes,
"No horse like that for majesty and size;
"What Chief illustrious bears a port so high?
"Mark, how his standard flickers through the sky!"
Thus ardent spoke Sohráb. Hujír dismayed,
Paused ere reply the dangerous truth betrayed.
Trembling for Rustem's life the captive groaned;
Basely his country's glorious boast disowned,

* The banners were adorned with the figure of an elephant, to denote his royal descent.

† Thus in Homer:

The king of kings majestically tall,
Towers o'er his armies and outshines them all.

Pope.—Iliad, ii. 483.

And said the Chief from distant China came—
Sohráb abrupt demands the hero's name;
The name unknown, grief wrings his aching heart,
And yearning anguish speeds her venom'd dart;
To him his mother gave the tokens true,
He sees them all, and all but mock his view.
When gloomy fate descends in evil hour,
Can human wisdom bribe her favouring power?
Yet, gathering hope, again with restless mien
He marks the Chiefs who crowd the warlike scene.
"Where numerous heroes, horse and foot, appear,
"And brazen trumpets thrill the listening ear,
"Behold the proud pavilion of the brave!
"With wolves emboss'd the silken banners wave.
"The throne's bright gems with radiant lustre glow,
"Slaves rank'd around with duteous homage bow.
"What mighty Chieftain rules his cohorts there?
"His name and lineage, free from guile, declare!"
"Gíw, son of Gúdarz, long a glorious name,
"Whose prowess even transcends his father's fame.*"
"Mark yonder tent of pure and dazzling white,
"Whose rich brocade reflects a quivering light;
"An ebon seat surmounts the ivory throne;
"There frowns in state a warrior of renown.
"The crowding slaves his awful nod obey,
"And silver moons around his banners play;
"What Chief, or Prince, has grasped the hostile sword?'
"Fraburz, the son of Persia's mighty lord."
Again: "These standards shew one champion more,
"Upon their centre flames the savage boar;†

* The text says that he was also the son-in-law of Rustem.

† The word Guraz signifies a wild boar, but this acceptation is not very accordant to Mussulman notions, and consequently it is not supposed, by the orthodox, to have that meaning in the text. It is curious that the name of the Warrior, Guraz, should correspond with the bearings on the standard. This frequently obtains in the heraldry of Europe. Family bearings seem to

"The saffron-hued pavilion bright ascends,
"Whence many a fold of tasselled fringe depends;
"Who there presides?"
"Guráz, from heroes sprung,
"Whose praise exceeds the power of mortal tongue."
Thus, anxious, he explored the crowded field,
Nor once the secret of his birth revealed;*
Heaven will'd it so. Pressed down by silent grief,
Surrounding objects promised no relief.
This world to mortals still denies repose,
And life is still the scene of many woes.
Again his eye, instinctive turned, descried
The green pavilion, and the warrior's pride.
Again he cries: "O tell his glorious name;
"Yon gallant horse declares the hero's fame!"
But false Hujír the aspiring hope repelled,
Crushed the fond wish, the soothing balm withheld,
"And why should I conceal his name from thee?
"His name and title are unknown to me."
Then thus Sohráb—"In all that thou hast said,
"No sign of Rustem have thy words conveyed;
"Thou sayest he leads the Persian host to arms,
"With him has battle lost its boisterous charms?
"Of him no trace thy guiding hand has shewn;
"Can power supreme remain unmark'd, unknown?"

be used in every country of any degree of civilization. Krusenstern, the Russian circumnavigator, speaking of the Japanese, says, "Every one has his family arms worked into his clothes, in different places, about the size of a half dollar, a practice usual to both sexes; and in this manner any person may be recognized, and the family to which he belongs easily ascertained. A young lady wears her father's arms until after her marriage, when she assumes those of her husband. The greatest mark of honour which a Prince or a Governor can confer upon any one, is to give him a cloak with his arms upon it, the person having such a one wearing his own arms upon his under dress."

* Firdausí considers this to be destiny! It would have been natural in Sohráb to have gloried in the fame of his father, but from an inevitable dispensation, his lips are here sealed on that subject; and he inquires of Rustem as if he only wanted to single him out for the purpose of destroying him. The people of Persia are all fatalists.

"Perhaps returned to Zábul's verdant bowers,
"He undisturbed enjoys his peaceful hours,
"The vernal banquets may constrain his stay,
"And rural sports invite prolonged delay."
"Ah! say not thus; the Champion of the world,
"Shrink from the kindling war with banners furled!*
"It cannot be! Say where his lightnings dart,
"Shew me the warrior, all thou know'st impart;
"Treasures uncounted shall be thy reward,
"Death changed to life, my friendship more than shared.
"Dost thou not know what, in the royal ear,
"The Múbid said—befitting Kings to hear?
"'Untold, a secret is a jewel bright,
"'Yet profitless whilst hidden from the light;
"'But when revealed, in words distinctly given,
"'It shines refulgent as the sun through heaven.'" †
To him, Hujír evasive thus replies:
"Through all the extended earth his glory flies!
"Whenever dangers round the nation close,
"Rustem approaches, and repels its foes;
"And shouldst thou see him mix in mortal strife,
"Thou'dst think 'twere easier to escape with life

* The continued anxiety and persevering filial duty of Sohráb are described with great success. The case is unparalleled. Telemachus at once declares the object of his inquiries.

> My sire, I seek, where'er the voice of fame
> Has told the glories of his noble name;
> The great Ulysses — Pope.

But Sohráb is dark and mysterious, and, as Firdausí says in another place, the unconscious promoter of his own destruction.

† This passage will remind the classical reader of the speech of Themistocles, in Plutarch, addressed to Xerxes. The Persian King had assured him of his protection, and ordered him to declare freely whatever he had to propose concerning Greece. Themistocles replied, "That a man's discourse was like a piece of tapestry which, when spread open, displays its figures; but when it is folded up, they are hidden and lost;" therefore he begged time. The King, delighted with the comparison, bade him take what time he pleased; and he desired a year; in which space he learned the Persian language, so as to be able to converse with the King without an interpreter.

"From tiger fell, or demon—or the fold
"Of the chafed dragon, than his dreadful hold—
"When fiercest battle clothes the fields with fire,
"Before his rage embodied hosts retire!"
"And where didst thou encountering armies see?
"Why Rustem's praise so proudly urge to me?
"Let us but meet and thou shalt trembling know,
"How fierce that wrath which bids my bosom glow:
"If living flames express his boundless ire,
"O'erwhelming waters quench consuming fire!
"And deepest darkness, glooms of ten-fold night,
"Fly from the piercing beams of radiant light."
Hujír shrunk back with undissembled dread,
And thus communing with himself, he said—
"Shall I, regardless of my country, guide
"To Rustem's tent this furious homicide?
"And witness there destruction to our host?
"The bulwark of the land for ever lost!
"What Chief can then the Tartar power restrain!
"Káús dethroned, the mighty Rustem slain!
"Better a thousand deaths should lay me low,
"Than, living, yield such triumph to the foe.
"For in this struggle should my blood be shed,
"No foul dishonour can pursue me, dead;
"No lasting shame my father's age oppress,
"Whom eighty sons of martial courage bless!*
"They for their brother slain, incensed will rise,
"And pour their vengeance on my enemies."
Then thus aloud—"Can idle words avail?
"Why still of Rustem urge the frequent tale?
"Why for the elephant-bodied hero ask?
"Thee, he will find,—no uncongenial task.

* Hujír was the son of Gúdarz. A family of the extent mentioned in the text is not of rare occurrence amongst the Princes of the East. The King of Persia had, in 1809, according to Mr. Morier, "*sixty-five sons!*" As the Persians make no account of females, it is not known how many daughters he had.

"Why seek pretences to destroy my life?
"Strike, for no Rustem views th' unequal strife!"
Sohráb confused, with hopeless anguish mourned,
Back from the lofty walls he quick returned,
And stood amazed.
Now war and vengeance claim,
Collected thought and deeds of mighty name;
The jointed mail his vigorous body clasps,
His sinewy hand the shining javelin grasps;
Like a mad elephant he meets the foe,
His steed a moving mountain—deeply glow
His cheeks with passionate ardour, as he flies
Resistless onwards, and with sparkling eyes,
Full on the centre drives his daring horse—*
The yielding Persians fly his furious course;
As the wild ass impetuous springs away,
When the fierce lion thunders on his prey.†
By every sign of strength and martial power,
They think him Rustem in his direst hour;
On Káús now his proud defiance falls,
Scornful to him the stripling warrior calls:
"And why art thou misnamed of royal strain?
"What work of thine befits the tented plain?
"This thirsty javelin seeks thy coward breast;
"Thou and thy thousands doomed to endless rest.
"True to my oath, which time can never change,
"On thee, proud King! I hurl my just revenge.

* The Kulub-gah is the centre or heart of the army, where the Sovereign or Chief of the troops usually remains.

† Firdausí is generally very brief in his similes, "like a lion," "like a wolf," occur repeatedly. Thus in the fourth book of the Iliad, the Greeks and Trojans are characterized in two words, "like wolves," which Pope has translated:

As o'er their prey rapacious wolves engage.

But in this place the Persian poet is more circumstantial.

"The chiefs fled from him like wild-asses from the claws of a lion.

"The blood of Zind inspires my burning hate,
"And dire resentment hurries on thy fate;
"Whom canst thou send to try the desperate strife?
"What valiant Chief, regardless of his life?
"Where now can Fraburz, Tús, Gíw, Gúdarz, be,
"And the world-conquering Rustem, where is he?"
No prompt reply from Persian lip ensued,—
Then rushing on, with demon-strength endued,
Sohráb elate his javelin waved around,
And hurled the bright pavilion to the ground;
With horror Káús feels destruction nigh,
And cries: "For Rustem's needful succour fly!
"This frantic Túrk, triumphant on the plain,
"Withers the souls of all my warrior train."
That instant Tús the mighty Champion sought,
And told the deeds the Tartar Chief had wrought;
"'Tis ever thus, the brainless Monarch's due!
"Shame and disaster still his steps pursue!"
This saying, from his tent he soon descried,
The wild confusion spreading far and wide;
And saddled Rakush—whilst, in deep dismay,
Girgín incessant cried—"Speed, speed, away."
Rehám bound on the mace, Tús promptly ran,
And buckled on the broad Burgustuwán.
Rustem, meanwhile, the thickening tumult hears
And in his heart, untouched by human fears,
Says: "What is this, that feeling seems to stun!
"This battle must be led by Ahirmun,*
"The awful day of doom must have begun."
In haste he arms, and mounts his bounding steed,
The growing rage demands redoubled speed;
The leopard's skin he o'er his shoulders throws,
The regal girdle round his middle glows.†

* Ahirmun, a demon, the principle of evil.
† This girdle was the gift of the king, as a token of affection and gratitude.

High wave his glorious banners; broad revealed,
The pictured dragons glare along the field
Borne by Zúára. When, surprised, he views
Sohráb, endued with ample breast and thews,
Like Sám Suwár, he beckons him apart;
The youth advances with a gallant heart,
Willing to prove his adversary's might,
By single combat to decide the fight;
And eagerly, "Together brought," he cries,
"Remote from us be foemen, and allies,
"And though at once by either host surveyed,
"Ours be the strife which asks no mortal aid."
Rustem, considerate, view'd him o'er and o'er,
So wondrous graceful was the form he bore,
And frankly said: "Experience flows with age,
"And many a foe has felt my conquering rage;
"Much have I seen, superior strength and art
"Have borne my spear thro' many a demon's heart;*
"Only behold me on the battle plain,
"Wait till thou see'st this hand the war sustain,
"And if on thee should changeful fortune smile,
"Thou needst not fear the monster of the Nile! †

Jonathan gives to David, among other things, his girdle: "Because he loved him as his own soul."—1 Samuel, xviii. 3, 4. Thus Homer:

Œneus a belt of matchless work bestowed,
That rich with Tyrian dye refulgent glowed.
POPE.—Iliad, vi. 219.

And Virgil:

Euryalus phaleras Rhamnetis, et aurea bullis,
Cingula, Tiburti Remulo ditissimus olim,
Quæ mittit dona, hospitio quum jungeret absens,
Cædicus: ille suo moriens dat habera nepoti. Æneid, ix. 359.

* The following boast of Ulysses is less questionable:

Stand forth, ye Champions who the gauntlet wield,
Or ye, the swiftest racers of the field!
Stand forth, ye wrestlers, who these pastimes grace,
I wield the gauntlet, and I run the race!
In such heroic games I yield to none. POPE.—Odyssey, viii. 205.

† A crocodile in war, with Firdausi, is a figure of great power and strength.

"But soft compassion melts my soul to save,
"A youth so blooming with a mind so brave!"
The generous speech Sohráb attentive heard,
His heart expanding glowed at every word:
"One question answer, and in answering shew,
"That truth should ever from a warrior flow;
"Art thou not Rustem, whose exploits sublime,
"Endear his name thro' every distant clime?"
"I boast no station of exalted birth,
"No proud pretensions to distinguished worth;
"To him inferior, no such powers are mine,
"No offspring I of Nírum's glorious line!" *
The prompt denial dampt his filial joy,
All hope at once forsook the Warrior-boy,
His opening day of pleasure, and the bloom
Of cherished life, immersed in shadowy gloom.
Perplexed with what his mother's words implied;—
A narrow space is now prepared, aside,
For single combat. With disdainful glance
Each boldly shakes his death-devoting lance,
And rushes forward to the dubious fight;
Thoughts high and brave their burning souls excite;
Now sword to sword; continuous strokes resound,
Till glittering fragments strew the dusty ground.
Each grasps his massive club with added force,†
The folding mail is rent from either horse;
It seemed as if the fearful day of doom
Had, clothed in all its withering terrors, come.
Their shattered corslets yield defence no more—
At length they breathe, defiled with dust and gore;

* It is difficult to account for this denial of his name, as there appears to be no equivalent cause. But all the famous heroes, described in the Sháh Námeh, are as much distinguished for their address and cunning, as their bravery.

† The original is Umūd, which appears to have been a weapon made of iron. Umūd also signifies a column, a beam.

Their gasping throats with parching thirst are dry,
Gloomy and fierce they roll the lowering eye,
And frown defiance. Son and Father driven
To mortal strife! are these the ways of Heaven?
The various swarms which boundless ocean breeds,
The countless tribes which crop the flowery meads,
All know their kind, but hapless man alone
Has no instinctive feeling for his own!
Compell'd to pause, by every eye surveyed,
Rustem, with shame, his wearied strength betrayed;
Foil'd by a youth in battle's mid career,
His groaning spirit almost sunk with fear;
Recovering strength, again they fiercely meet;
Again they struggle with redoubled heat;
With bended bows they furious now contend;
And feather'd shafts in rattling showers descend;
Thick as autumnal leaves they strew the plain,*
Harmless their points, and all their fury vain.
And now they seize each other's girdle-band;
Rustem, who, if he moved his iron hand,
Could shake a mountain, and to whom a rock
Seemed soft as wax, tried, with one mighty stroke,
To hurl him thundering from his fiery steed,
But Fate forbids the gallant youth should bleed;
Finding his wonted nerves relaxed, amazed
That hand he drops which never had been raised
Uncrowned with victory, even when demons fought,
And pauses, wildered with despairing thought.
Sohráb again springs with terrific grace,
And lifts, from saddle-bow, his ponderous mace;
With gather'd strength the quick-descending blow
Wounds in its fall, and stuns the unwary foe;

* Thick as autumnal leaves that strew the brooks
In Vallombrosa, where the Etrurian shades,
High over-arched, imbower. MILTON.—Par. Lost, i. 303.

Then thus contemptuous: "All thy power is gone;
"Thy charger's strength exhausted as thy own;
"Thy bleeding wounds with pity I behold;
"O seek no more the combat of the bold!"
Rustem to this reproach made no reply,
But stood confused—meanwhile, tumultuously
The legions closed; with soul-appalling force,
Troop rushed on troop, o'erwhelming man and horse;
Sohráb, incensed, the Persian host engaged,
Furious along the scattered lines he raged;
Fierce as a wolf he rode on every side,
The thirsty earth with streaming gore was dyed.
Midst the Turanians, then, the Champion sped,
And like a tiger heaped the fields with dead.
But when the Monarch's danger struck his thought,
Returning swift, the stripling youth he sought;
Grieved to the soul, the mighty Champion view'd
His hands and mail with Persian blood imbrued;
And thus exclaimed with lion-voice—"O say,
"Why with the Persians dost thou war to-day?
"Why not with me alone decide the fight,
"Thou'rt like a wolf that seek'st the fold by night."
To this Sohráb his proud assent expressed—
And Rustem, answering, thus the youth addressed.
"Night-shadows now are thickening o'er the plain,
"The morrow's sun must see our strife again;
"In wrestling let us then exert our might!"
He said, and eve's last glimmer sunk in night.*
Thus as the skies a deeper gloom displayed,
The stripling's life was hastening into shade!
The gallant heroes to their tents retired,
The sweets of rest their wearied limbs required:

* Thus the single combat between Hector and Ajax is ended by the approach of night.

But now the night extends her awful shade,
The goddess parts you: be the night obey'd!

Pope.—Iliad, vii. 282

Sohráb, delighted with his brave career,
Describes the fight in Húmán's anxious ear:
Tells how he forced unnumbered Chiefs to yield,
And stood himself the victor of the field!
"But let the morrow's dawn," he cried, "arrive,
"And not one Persian shall the day survive;
"Meanwhile let wine its strengthening balm impart,
"And add new zeal to every drooping heart."
The valiant Gíw with Rustem pondering stood,
And, sad, recalled the scene of death and blood;
Grief and amazement heaved the frequent sigh,
And almost froze the crimson current dry.
Rustem, oppressed by Gíw's desponding thought,
Amidst his Chiefs the mournful Monarch sought;
To him he told Sohráb's tremendous sway,
The dire misfortunes of this luckless day;
Told with what grasping force he tried, in vain,
To hurl the wondrous stripling to the plain:
"The whispering zephyr might as well aspire
"To shake a mountain—such his strength and fire.
"But night came on—and, by agreement, we
"Must meet again to-morrow—who shall be
"Victorious, Heaven knows only:—for by Heaven,
"Victory or death to man is ever given."
This said, the King, o'erwhelmed in deep despair,
Passed the dread night in agony and prayer.
The Champion, silent, joined his bands at rest,
And spurned at length despondence from his breast;
Removed from all, he cheered Zúára's heart,
And nerved his soul to bear a trying part:—
"Ere early morning gilds the etherial plain,
"In martial order range my warrior-train;
"And when I meet in all his glorious pride,
"This valiant Túrk whom late my rage defied,
"Should fortune's smiles my arduous task requite,
"Bring them to share the triumph of my might;

"But should success the stripling's arm attend,
"And dire defeat and death my glories end,
"To their loved homes my brave associates guide;
"Let bowery Zábul all their sorrows hide—
"Comfort my venerable father's heart;
"In gentlest words my heavy fate impart.
"The dreadful tidings to my mother bear,*
"And soothe her anguish with the tenderest care;
"Say, that the will of righteous Heaven decreed,
"That thus in arms her mighty son should bleed.
"Enough of fame my various toils acquired,
"When warring demons, bathed in blood, expired.
"Were life prolonged a thousand lingering years,
"Death comes at last and ends our mortal fears;
"Kirshásp, and Sám, and Naríman, the best
"And bravest heroes, who have ever blest
"This fleeting world, were not endued with power,
"To stay the march of fate one single hour;
"The world for them possessed no fixed abode,
"The path to death's cold regions must be trod;
"Then, why lament the doom ordained for all?
"Thus Jemshíd fell, and thus must Rustem fall."
When the bright dawn proclaimed the rising day,
The warriors armed, impatient of delay;
But first Sohráb, his proud confederate nigh,
Thus wistful spoke, as swelled the boding sigh—
"Now, mark my great antagonist in arms!
"His noble form my filial bosom warms;
"My mother's tokens shine conspicuous here,
"And all the proofs my heart demands, appear;
"Sure this is Rustem, whom my eyes engage!
"Shall I, O grief! provoke my Father's rage?

* In the East, peculiarly strong attachment to the mother is universal. Nothing can be more affecting than the filial tenderness of Rustem, or more rational and just than his observations on human glory.

"Offended Nature then would curse my name,
"And shuddering nations echo with my shame."
He ceased, then Húmán: "Vain, fantastic thought,
"Oft have I been where Persia's Champion fought;
"And thou hast heard, what wonders he performed,
"When, in his prime, Mazinderán was stormed;
"That horse resembles Rustem's, it is true,
"But not so strong, nor beautiful to view."
Sohráb now buckles on his war-attire,
His heart all softness, and his brain all fire;
Around his lips such smiles benignant played,
He seemed to greet a friend, as thus he said:—
"Here let us sit together on the plain,
"Here, social sit, and from the fight refrain;
"Ask we from heaven forgiveness of the past,
"And bind our souls in friendship that may last;
"Ours be the feast—let us be warm and free,
"For powerful instinct draws me still to thee;
"Fain would my heart in bland affection join,
"Then let thy generous ardour equal mine;
"And kindly say, with whom I now contend—
"What name distinguished boasts my warrior-friend!
"Thy name unfit for champion brave to hide,
"Thy name so long, long sought, and still denied;
"Say, art thou Rustem, whom I burn to know?
"Ingenuous say, and cease to be my foe!"
Sternly the mighty Champion cried, "Away,—
"Hence with thy wiles—now practised to delay;
"The promised struggle, resolute, I claim,
"Then cease to move me to an act of shame."
Sohráb rejoined—"Old man! thou wilt not hear
"The words of prudence uttered in thine ear;
"Then, Heaven! look on."
Preparing for the shock,
Each binds his charger to a neighbouring rock;

And girds his loins, and rubs his wrists, and tries
Their suppleness and force, with angry eyes;
And now they meet—now rise, and now descend,
And strong and fierce their sinewy arms extend;
Wrestling with all their strength they grasp and strain,
And blood and sweat flow copious on the plain;
Like raging elephants they furious close;
Commutual wounds are given, and wrenching blows.
Sohráb nows claps his hands, and forward springs
Impatiently, and round the Champion clings;
Seizes his girdle belt, with power to tear
The very earth asunder; in despair
Rustem, defeated, feels his nerves give way,
And thundering falls. Sohráb bestrides his prey:
Grim as the lion, prowling through the wood,
Upon a wild ass springs, and pants for blood.
His lifted sword had lopt the gory head,
But Rustem, quick, with crafty ardour said:—
"One moment, hold! what, are our laws unknown?
"A Chief may fight till he is twice o'erthrown;
"The second fall, his recreant blood is spilt,
"These are our laws, avoid the menaced guilt."
  Proud of his strength, and easily deceived,
The wondering youth the artful tale believed;
Released his prey, and, wild as wind or wave,
Neglecting all the prudence of the brave,
Turned from the place, nor once the strife renewed,
But bounded o'er the plain and other cares pursued,
As if all memory of the war had died,
All thoughts of him with whom his strength was tried.
  Húmán, confounded at the stripling's stay,
Went forth, and heard the fortune of the day;
Amazed to find the mighty Rustem freed,
With deepest grief he wailed the luckless deed.
"What! loose a raging lion from the snare,
"And let him growling hasten to his lair?

"Bethink thee well; in war, from this unwise,
"This thoughtless act what countless woes may rise;
"Never again suspend the final blow,
"Nor trust the seeming weakness of a foe!" *
"Hence with complaint," the dauntless youth replied,
"To-morrow's contest shall his fate decide."
When Rustem was released, in altered mood
He sought the coolness of the murmuring flood;
There quenched his thirst; and bathed his limbs, and prayed,
Beseeching Heaven to yield its strengthening aid.
His pious prayer indulgent Heaven approved,
And growing strength through all his sinews moved; †
Such as erewhile his towering structure knew,
When his bold arm unconquered demons slew.
Yet in his mien no confidence appeared,
No ardent hope his wounded spirits cheered.
Again they met. A glow of youthful grace,
Diffused its radiance o'er the stripling's face,
And when he saw in renovated guise,
The foe so lately mastered; with surprise,
He cried—"What! rescued from my power, again
"Dost thou confront me on the battle plain?
"Or, dost thou, wearied, draw thy vital breath,
"And seek, from warrior bold, the shaft of death?
"Truth has no charms for thee, old man; even now,
"Some further cheat may lurk upon thy brow;
"Twice have I shewn thee mercy, twice thy age
"Hath been thy safety—twice it soothed my rage."
Then mild the Champion: "Youth is proud and vain!
"The idle boast a warrior would disdain;

* Thus also Sádí, "Knowest thou what Zál said to Rustem the Champion? Never calculate upon the weakness or insignificance of an enemy."

† Rustem is as much distinguished for piety as bravery. Every success is attributed by him to the favour of Heaven. In the achievement of his labours in the Heft-Khan, his devotion is constant, and he everywhere justly acknowledges that power and victory are derived from God alone.

"This aged arm perhaps may yet control,
"The wanton fury that inflames thy soul!"
Again, dismounting, each the other viewed
With sullen glance, and swift the fight renewed;
Clenched front to front, again they tug and bend,
Twist their broad limbs as every nerve would rend;
With rage convulsive Rustem grasps him round;*
Bends his strong back, and hurls him to the ground;
Him, who had deemed the triumph all his own;
But dubious of his power to keep him down,
Like lightning quick he gives the deadly thrust,
And spurns the Stripling weltering in the dust.
—Thus as his blood that shining steel imbrues,
Thine too shall flow, when Destiny pursues;†
For when she marks the victim of her power,
A thousand daggers speed the dying hour.
Writhing with pain Sohráb in murmurs sighed—
And thus to Rustem—"Vaunt not, in thy pride;
"Upon myself this sorrow have I brought,
"Thou but the instrument of fate—which wrought
"My downfall; thou art guiltless—guiltless quite;
"O! had I seen my father in the fight,

* Thus Entellus renews the combat with increased vigour.

Acrior ad pugnam redit, ac vim suscitat ira.
Tum pudor incendit vires, et conscia virtus— *Æneid*, v. 454.

† The expression in the original is remarkable. "Assuredly, as thou hast thirsted for blood, Destiny will also thirst for thine, *and the very hairs upon thy body will become daggers to destroy thee.*" This passage is quoted in the preface to the Sháh Námeh, collated by order of Bayisunghur Khan, as the production of the poet Unsarí. Unsarí was one of the seven poets whom Mahmúd appointed to give specimens of their powers in versifying the History of the Kings of Persia. The story of Rustem and Sohráb fell to Unsarí, and his arrangement of it contained the above verses, which so delighted the Sultán that he directed the poet to undertake the whole work. This occurred before Firdausí was introduced at Court and eclipsed every competitor. In compliment to Mahmúd, perhaps he ingrafted them on his own poem, or more probably they have been interpolated since.

"My glorious father! Life will soon be o'er,
"And his great deeds enchant my soul no more!
"Of him my mother gave the mark and sign,
"For him I sought, and what an end is mine!
"My only wish on earth, my constant sigh,
"Him to behold, and with that wish I die.
"But hope not to elude his piercing sight,
"In vain for thee the deepest glooms of night;
"Couldst thou through Ocean's depths for refuge fly,
"Or midst the star-beams track the upper sky! *
"Rustem, with vengeance armed, will reach thee there,
"His soul the prey of anguish and despair."
An icy horror chills the Champion's heart,
His brain whirls round with agonizing smart;
O'er his wan cheek no gushing sorrows flow,
Senseless he sinks beneath the weight of woe;
Relieved at length, with frenzied look, he cries:
"Prove thou art mine, confirm my doubting eyes!
"For I am Rustem!" Piercing was the groan,
Which from burst his torn heart—as wild and lone,
He gazed upon him. Dire amazement shook
The dying youth, and mournful thus he spoke:
"If thou art Rustem, cruel is thy part,
"No warmth paternal seems to fill thy heart;
"Else hadst thou known me when, with strong desire,
"I fondly claimed thee for my valiant sire;
"Now from my body strip the shining mail,
"Untie these bands, ere life and feeling fail;
"And on my arm the direful proof behold!
"Thy sacred bracelet of refulgent gold!
"When the loud brazen drums were heard afar,
"And, echoing round, proclaimed the pending war,

* Literally, "Wert thou a fish in the sea, or a star in the heavens." Thus also Æneas to Turnus:

Verte omnes tete in facies; et contrahe, quidquid
Sive animis sive arte vales: opta ardua pennis
Astra sequi, clausumque cava te condere terra. *Æneid*, xii. 891.

"Whilst parting tears my mother's eyes o'erflowed,
"This mystic gift her bursting heart bestowed:
"'Take this,' she said, 'thy father's token wear,
"'And promised glory will reward thy care.'
"The hour is come, but fraught with bitterest woe,
"We meet in blood to wail the fatal blow."
The loosened mail unfolds the bracelet bright,
Unhappy gift! to Rustem's wildered sight;
Prostrate he falls—"By my unnatural hand,
"My son, my son is slain—and from the land
"Uprooted."—Frantic, in the dust his hair
He rends in agony and deep despair;
The western sun had disappeared in gloom,
And still, the Champion wept his cruel doom;
His wondering legions marked the long delay,
And, seeing Rakush riderless astray,
The rumour quick to Persia's Monarch spread,
And there described the mighty Rustem dead.
Káús, alarmed, the fatal tidings hears;
His bosom quivers with increasing fears.
"Speed, speed, and see what has befallen to-day
"To cause these groans and tears—what fatal fray!
"If he be lost, if breathless on the ground,
"And this young warrior, with the conquest crowned—
"Then must I, humbled, from my kingdom torn,
"Wander like Jemshíd, through the world forlorn."*
The army roused, rushed o'er the dusty plain,
Urged by the Monarch to revenge the slain;
Wild consternation saddened every face,
Tús winged with horror sought the fatal place,
And there beheld the agonizing sight,—
The murderous end of that unnatural fight.
Sohráb, still breathing, hears the shrill alarms,
His gentle speech suspends the clang of arms:

* Jemshíd's glory and misfortunes, as said before, are the constant theme of admiration and reflection amongst the poets of Persia.

"My light of life now fluttering sinks in shade,
"Let vengeance sleep, and peaceful vows be made.
"Beseech the King to spare this Tartar host,
"For they are guiltless, all to them is lost;
"I led them on, their souls with glory fired,
"While mad ambition all my thoughts inspired.
"In search of thee, the world before my eyes,
"War was my choice, and thou the sacred prize;
"With thee, my sire! in virtuous league combined,
"No tyrant King should persecute mankind.
"That hope is past—the storm has ceased to rave—
"My ripening honours wither in the grave;
"Then let no vengeance on my comrades fall,
"Mine was the guilt, and mine the sorrow, all;
"How often have I sought thee—oft my mind
"Figured thee to my sight——o'erjoyed to find
"My mother's token; disappointment came,
"When thou deniedst thy lineage and thy name;
"Oh! still o'er thee my soul impassioned hung,
"Still to my Father fond affection clung!
"But fate, remorseless, all my hopes withstood,
"And stained thy reeking hands in kindred blood."
His faltering breath protracted speech denied:
Still from his eye-lids flowed a gushing tide;
Through Rustem's soul redoubled horror ran,
Heart-rending thoughts subdued the mighty man.
And now, at last, with joy-illumined eye,
The Zábul bands their glorious Chief descry;
But when they saw his pale and haggard look,
Knew from what mournful cause he gazed and shook,
With downcast mien they moaned and wept aloud;
While Rustem thus addressed the weeping crowd:
"Here ends the war! let gentle peace succeed,
"Enough of death, I—I have done the deed!"
Then to his brother, groaning deep, he said—
"O what a curse upon a parent's head!

"But go—and to the Tartar say—no more,
"Let war between us steep the earth with gore."
Zúára flew and wildly spoke his grief,
To crafty Húmán, the Turanian Chief,
Who, with dissembled sorrow, heard him tell
The dismal tidings which he knew too well;
"And who," he said, "has caused these tears to flow?
"Who, but Hujír? He might have stayed the blow,
"But when Sohráb his Father's banners sought;
"He still denied that here the Champion fought;
"He spread the ruin, he the secret knew,
"Hence should his crime receive the vengeance due!"
Zúára, frantic, breathed in Rustem's ear,
The treachery of the captive Chief, Hujír;
Whose headless trunk had weltered on the strand,
But prayers and force withheld the lifted hand.
Then to his dying son the Champion turned,
Remorse more deep within his bosom burned;
A burst of frenzy fired his throbbing brain;
He clenched his sword, but found his fury vain;
The Persian Chiefs the desperate act represt,
And tried to calm the tumult in his breast:*
Thus Gúdarz spoke—"Alas! wert thou to give
"Thyself a thousand wounds, and cease to live;
"What would it be to him thou sorrowest o'er?
"It would not save one pang—then weep no more;
"For if removed by death, O say, to whom
"Has ever been vouchsafed a different doom?
"All are the prey of death—the crowned, the low,
"And man, through life, the victim still of woe."
Then Rustem: "Fly! and to the King relate,
"The pressing horrors which involve my fate;

* Antilochus thus restrains the fury of Achilles on being told of the fate of Patroclus: He

Hangs on his arms, amidst his frantic woe,
And oft prevents the meditated blow. POPE.—Iliad, xviii. 34.

"And if the memory of my deeds e'er swayed
"His mind, O supplicate his generous aid;
"A sovereign balm he has whose wondrous power,
"All wounds can heal, and fleeting life restore;*
"Swift from his tent the potent medicine bring."
—But mark the malice of the brainless King!
Hard as the flinty rock, he stern denies
The healthful draught, and gloomy thus replies:
"Can I forgive his foul and slanderous tongue?
"The sharp disdain on me contemptuous flung?
"Scorned 'midst my army by a shameless boy,
"Who sought my throne, my sceptre to destroy!
"Nothing but mischief from his heart can flow,
"Is it, then, wise to cherish such a foe?
"The fool who warms his enemy to life,
"Only prepares for scenes of future strife."
Gúdarz, returning, told the hopeless tale—
And thinking Rustem's presence might prevail;
The Champion rose, but ere he reached the throne,
Sohráb had breathed the last expiring groan.
Now keener anguish rack'd the father's mind,
Reft of his son, a murderer of his kind;
His guilty sword distained with filial gore,
He beat his burning breast, his hair he tore;
The breathless corse before his shuddering view,
A shower of ashes o'er his head he threw;†

* These medicated draughts are often mentioned in Romances. The reader will recollect the banter upon them in Don Quixote, where the Knight of La Mancha enumerates to Sancho the cures which had been performed upon many valorous champions, covered with wounds. The Hindús, in their books on medicine, talk of drugs for the recovery of the dead!

† Scattering ashes over the head is a very ancient mode of expressing grief. Thus 2 Samuel, iii. 31: "And David said to Joab, and to all the people that were with him, Rend your clothes, and gird you with sackcloth, and mourn before Abner." Also, xiii. 19: "And Tamar put ashes on her head, and rent her garment." And thus Homer:

A sudden horror shot through all the Chief,
And wrapt his senses in the cloud of grief,
Cast on the ground, with furious hands he spread
The scorching ashes o'er his graceful head. POPE.—Iliad, xviii. 22.

"In my old age," he cried, "what have I done?
"Why have I slain my son, my innocent son!
"Why o'er his splendid dawning did I roll
"The clouds of death,—and plunge my burthened soul
"In agony? My son! from heroes sprung;
"Better these hands were from my body wrung;
"And solitude and darkness, deep and drear,
"Fold me from sight than hated linger here.
"But when his mother hears, with horror wild,
"That I have shed the life-blood of her child,
"So nobly brave, so dearly loved, in vain,
"How can her heart that rending shock sustain?"
Now on a bier the Persian warriors place
The breathless Youth, and shade his pallid face;
And turning from that fatal field away,
Move towards the Champion's home in long array.
Then Rustem, sick of martial pomp and show,
Himself the spring of all this scene of woe,
Doomed to the flames the pageantry he loved,*
Shield, spear, and mace, so oft in battle proved;
Now lost to all, encompassed by despair;
His bright pavilion crackling blazed in air;
The sparkling throne the ascending column fed;
In smoking fragments fell the golden bed;
The raging fire red glimmering died away,
And all the Warrior's pride in dust and ashes lay.
Káús, the King, now joins the mournful Chief,
And tries to soothe his deep and settled grief;

* There is something in Virgil similar to this paroxysm of wrath against inanimate things, where Dido bids her sister erect a pile to burn the arms and presents of Æneas.

Tu secreta pyram tecto interiore sub auras,
Erige, et arma viri, thalamo quæ fixa reliquit,
Impius, exuviasque omnes, lectumque jugalem,
Quo perii, superimponas. *Æneid*, iv. 494.

But there is more of grandeur in the despairing anguish of Rustem. I know nothing of the kind in any of our Epic or Dramatic poets superior to this fine burst of agonized feeling and remorse.

For soon or late we yield our vital breath,
And all our worldly troubles end in death!
"When first I saw him, graceful in his might,
"He looked far other than a Tartar knight;
"Wondering I gazed—now Destiny has thrown
"Him on thy sword—he fought, and he is gone;
"And should even Heaven against the earth be hurled,
"Or fire inwrap in crackling flames the world,
"That which is past—we never can restore,
"His soul has travelled to some happier shore.
"Alas! no good from sorrow canst thou reap,
"Then wherefore thus in gloom and misery weep?"
But Rustem's mighty woes disdained his aid,
His heart was drowned in grief, and thus he said:
"Yes, he is gone! to me for ever lost!
"O then protect his brave unguided host;
"From war removed and this detested place,
"Let them, unharmed, their mountain-wilds retrace;
"Bid them secure my brother's will obey,
"The careful guardian of their weary way,*
"To where the Jihún's distant waters stray."
To this the King: "My soul is sad to see
"Thy hopeless grief—but, since approved by thee,
"The war shall cease—though the Túránian brand
"Has spread dismay and terror through the land."
The King, appeased, no more with vengeance burned,
The Tartar legions to their homes returned;
The Persian warriors, gathering round the dead,
Grovelled in dust, and tears of sorrow shed;
Then back to loved Irán their steps the monarch led.
But Rustem, midst his native bands, remained,
And further rites of sacrifice maintained;
A thousand horses bled at his command,
And the torn drums were scattered o'er the sand;

* Zúára conducted the troops of Afrasiyáb across the Jihún. Rustem remained on the field of battle till his return.

And now through Zábul's deep and bowery groves,
In mournful pomp the sad procession moves.
The mighty Chief on foot precedes the bier;
His Warrior-friends, in grief assembled near:
The dismal cadence rose upon the gale,
And Zál astonished heard the piercing wail;
He and his kindred joined the solemn train;
Hung round the bier and wondering viewed the slain.
"There gaze, and weep!" the sorrowing Father said,
"For there, behold my glorious offspring dead!"
The hoary Sire shrunk backward with surprise,
And tears of blood o'erflowed his aged eyes;
And now the Champion's rural palace gate
Receives the funeral group in gloomy state;
Rúdábeh loud bemoaned the Stripling's doom;
Sweet flower, all drooping in the hour of bloom,
His tender youth in distant bowers had past,
Sheltered at home he felt no withering blast;
In the soft prison of his mother's arms,
Secure from danger and the world's alarms.
O ruthless Fortune! flushed with generous pride,
He sought his sire, and thus unhappy, died.
Rustem again the sacred bier unclosed;
Again Sohráb to public view exposed;
Husbands, and wives, and warriors, old and young,
Struck with amaze, around the body hung,
With garments rent and loosely flowing hair;
Their shrieks and clamours filled the echoing air;
Frequent they cried: "Thus Sám the Champion slept!
"Thus sleeps Sohráb!" Again they groaned, and wept.
Now o'er the corpse a yellow robe is spread,
The aloes bier is closed upon the dead;
And, to preserve the hapless hero's name,
Fragrant and fresh, that his unblemished fame
Might live and bloom through all succeeding days,
A mound sepulchral on the spot they raise,
Formed like a charger's hoof.

In every ear
The story has been told—and many a tear,
Shed at the sad recital. Through Túrán,
Afrásiyáb's wide realm, and Samengán,
Deep sunk the tidings;—nuptial bower, and bed,
And all that promised happiness, had fled!
But when Tahmíneh heard this tale of woe,
Think how a mother bore the mortal blow!*
Distracted, wild, she sprang from place to place;
With frenzied hands deformed her beauteous face;
The musky locks her polished temples crowned.
Furious she tore, and flung upon the ground;
Starting, in agony of grief, she gazed,—
Her swimming eyes to Heaven imploring raised;
And groaning cried: "Sole comfort of my life!
"Doomed the sad victim of unnatural strife,
"Where art thou now with dust and blood defiled?
"Thou darling boy, my lost, my murdered child!
"When thou wert gone—how, night and lingering day,
"Did thy fond mother watch the time away;
"For hope still pictured all I wished to see,
"Thy father found, and thou returned to me,
"Yes—thou, exulting in thy father's fame!
"And yet, nor sire nor son, nor tidings, came:
"How could I dream of this? ye met—but how?
"That noble aspect—that ingenuous brow,
"Moved not a nerve in him—ye met—to part,
"Alas! the life-blood issuing from the heart.
"Short was the day which gave to me delight,
"Soon, soon, succeeds a long and dismal night;

* The death of Euryalus, in the Æneid (ix. 473), exhibits an exquisite display of natural maternal feeling, but less complicated and agonizing than the death of Sohráb. Euryalus was killed in the bloom of youth by the enemy: Sohráb by his Father. It would appear that Húmán, on his return, sent to Tahmíneh the war-horse, armour, and every thing belonging to her unfortunate son.

"On whom shall now devolve my tender care?
"Who, loved like thee, my bosom-sorrows share?
"Whom shall I take to fill thy vacant place,
"To whom extend a mother's soft embrace?
"Sad fate! for one so young, so fair, so brave,
"Seeking thy father thus to find a grave.
"These arms no more shall fold thee to my breast,
"No more with thee my soul be doubly blest;
"No, drowned in blood thy lifeless body lies,
"For ever torn from these desiring eyes;
"Friendless, alone, beneath a foreign sky,
"Thy mail thy death-clothes—and thy father, by;
"Why did not I conduct thee on the way,*
"And point where Rustem's bright pavilion lay?
"Thou hadst the tokens—why didst thou withhold
"Those dear remembrances—that pledge of gold?
"Hadst thou the bracelet to his view restored,
"Thy precious blood had never stained his sword."
The strong emotion chóked her panting breath,
Her veins seemed withered by the cold of death:
The trembling matrons hastening round her mourned,
With piercing cries, till fluttering life returned;
Then gazing up, distraught, she wept again,
And frantic, seeing 'midst her pitying train,
The favourite steed—now more than ever dear,
The hoofs she kissed, and bathed with many a tear;
Clasping the mail Sohráb in battle wore,
With burning lips she kissed it o'er and o'er;
His martial robes she in her arms comprest,
And like an infant strained them to her breast;
The reins, and trappings, club, and spear, were brought,
The sword, and shield, with which the Stripling fought,

* There is a similar thought in Douglas:

My murdered child! had thy fond mother feared
The loss of thee, she had loud fame defied,
And wandered with thee through the scorning world.

HOME'S DOUGLAS.

These she embraced with melancholy joy,
In sad remembrance of her darling boy.
And still she beat her face, and o'er them hung,
As in a trance—or to them wildly clung—
Day after day she thus indulged her grief,
Night after night, disdaining all relief;
At length worn out—from earthly anguish riven,
The mother's spirit joined her child in Heaven.

THE END.